THE CONSTITUTION OF ENGLAND
FROM QUEEN VICTORIA TO GEORGE VI

THE
CONSTITUTION OF ENGLAND
FROM QUEEN VICTORIA
TO GEORGE VI

BY

ARTHUR BERRIEDALE KEITH

D.C.L., D.LITT., LL.D., F.B.A.

OF THE INNER TEMPLE, BARRISTER-AT-LAW; ADVOCATE OF THE SCOTTISH
BAR; REGIUS PROFESSOR OF SANSKRIT AND COMPARATIVE PHILOLOGY,
AND LECTURER ON THE CONSTITUTION OF THE BRITISH EMPIRE, AT THE
UNIVERSITY OF EDINBURGH; FORMERLY ASSISTANT SECRETARY TO THE
IMPERIAL CONFERENCE

VOL. II

MACMILLAN AND CO., LIMITED
ST. MARTIN'S STREET, LONDON
1940

COPYRIGHT

PRINTED IN GREAT BRITAIN
BY R. & R. CLARK, LIMITED, EDINBURGH

CONTENTS

PART V—*continued*

PARTIES AND POLITICAL OPINION

CHAPTER XII

PART VI

THE EXECUTIVE DEPARTMENTS AND THEIR FUNCTIONS

CHAPTER XIII

CHAPTER XIV

CHAPTER XVIII

CHAPTER XIX

CHAPTER XX

PART VII

THE JUDICIARY AND ITS FUNCTIONS

CHAPTER XXI

CHAPTER XXII

THE FUNCTIONS OF THE JUDICIARY AND THE CHARACTERISTICS OF
ENGLISH JUDICIAL PROCEDURE 307

PART VIII

THE STATE AND THE PEOPLE

CHAPTER XXIII

ALLEGIANCE AND THE STATUS OF SUBJECTS AND ALIENS . . 341

CHAPTER XXIV

THE SECURITY OF THE STATE AND CLAIMS BY AND AGAINST THE CROWN 355

CHAPTER XII

PUBLIC OPINION AND GOVERNMENT

1. *The Pressure of Public Opinion on the Government and Parliament*

THE growth of the influence of public opinion on Government was strongly promoted by the removal of the repressive measures imposed on the press under the influence of the conservative reaction evoked by the French revolution. Of the six Acts of 1819 one struck at the pamphlets and papers which were freely in circulation and encouraging resistance to the autocratic attitude of the ministry, and it was not until 1836 that the stamp duty on newspapers was reduced from fourpence to a penny and not until 1855 was it abolished. There remained as an obstacle to the wide circulation of newspapers the paper duty, and Mr. Gladstone removed that incubus in 1861. Free libraries, the cheapening of newspapers, the multiplication of books, have all tended to increase largely, in conjunction with the spread of higher education, the number of persons who are capable of forming intelligent opinions on political issues, and more recently the adoption of the policy of educating the public by broadcast lectures and debates has presented the public with amazing facilities for mastering the essentials of important problems.

Further, the knowledge of Parliamentary proceedings has been extended widely since the advent of the Queen to the throne. The labours of Cobbett resulted in the establishment of reports of Parliament, which even the House of Commons formally recognised in 1845, and since then a long series of improvements has resulted in the existence of full reports of proceedings both in the house and in its Committees, while the supply of Parliamentary papers has steadily grown. The use of royal commissions and all kinds of departmental committees has rendered available great masses of material which render intelligent study of the questions brought before Parliament and of issues which should be considered by Parliament far more simple.

In like manner, even as early as 1852 we find Mr. Disraeli insisting on the benefits to be derived from permitting the public to study important Bills after their introduction before they proceeded to second reading, and it is now an established practice for departments such as the Ministry of Labour, that of Health, the Mining Department, the Board of Education, the Ministry of Agriculture and Fisheries, to discuss issues to be dealt with in communication with representative bodies of all sorts. Merchant shipping legislation is discussed with representatives of the great shipowners, the organisation of officers of the mercantile marine, and the spokesmen of the sailors. Copyright is discussed with the societies concerned therein, and publishers and printers. All issues that concern local government are discussed with local government associations and with the organisations which represent the interests of officers employed in local government. Health is dealt with in consultation with medical societies, sanitary experts, surveyors, architects, and so forth. The efforts of the Government since 1931 to aid agriculture have necessitated constant co-operation with farmers, with middlemen and users of farm products, in order to achieve some measure of satisfaction as in the

creation of marketing boards and allied institutions. The
press and public as well as associations were invited to
criticise the Highway Code.

The principle of publicity in the case of regulations was
fully recognised by the Rules Publication Act, 1893,
which enjoined prior or subsequent publication for those
classes of rules of most general importance, and the system
has been extended since. The presentation of draft rules,
even if immediately operative, allows of detailed criticism.
In some cases the power to make rules is expressly conferred subject to consultation with specified bodies expert
in the subject matter to be dealt with.

The effect of public opinion on the actions of ministries
is in part direct, in part through its operation on the minds
of individual members of Parliament or on groups of
members such as those which spontaneously form themselves in Parliament to take up study of a special subject,
and invite experts to give them instruction thereon.
Thus the Government of India Bill resulted in intense
study of the situation by members of the Conservative
party who were doubtful of the wisdom of the changes
suggested. The day is long past when ministers refused
to look beyond the members of the Commons for evidence
of the wishes of the people. Sir R. Peel [1] might exalt the
authority of members, but, when Mr. Asquith voiced
similar sentiments [2] on the Parliament Bill, his views must
be read as meant especially with regard to that special
position, which was a constitutional issue, and not as a
general proposition regarding questions in general. On
many of the social and economic or financial issues of the
day ministries look readily elsewhere than the Commons.

Methods of bringing public opinion to bear on ministers
and members have remained constant, though with varying

[1] 58 *Hansard*, 3 s. 817 (1841).   [2] 21 *H.C. Deb.* 5 s. 1748.

importance. The formal *petition* has an honourable and ancient origin ; in 1680 [1] the Commons resolved that it has ever been the undoubted right of the subjects of England to petition the King for the calling and sitting of Parliaments and the redressing of grievances, and the Bill of Rights gave statutory authority. The petitions against slavery presented in 1814 and 1833 were signed by about a million and a million and a half people respectively, and petitions were poured in on all hands, when reform was at stake. The use of monster petitions, however, declined after the failure of 1848 of the great Chartist petition, and, though petitions became more and more numerous up to the 'seventies, thereafter they declined, though they are still presented in no small numbers and on occasion are very numerously signed. The decline in importance is now accompanied by the reduction in the number of petitions which the Select Committee on Petitions reports as suitable to be printed, and by the rule that, save in case of urgency, no debate is allowed on petitions when presented. Moreover, by long-standing usage petitions for grants of money are not received.[2] There are more easy methods of stirring public opinion than mere petitions, and, where petitions are still in use, they may be directed to ministers rather than to Parliament, taking the form of representations promoted by deputations which ministers must receive unless they are willing to cause annoyance to their constituents. The deputation, headed by the Duke of Cambridge and the Archbishops, which in 1863 waited on Mr. Gladstone to persuade him not to remove the exemption of charitable corporations from payment of income tax, succeeded in attaining their aim, despite the Chancellor's personal dislike of the proposal, and deputations have the great advantage under modern

---

[1] *Parl. Hist.* iv. 1174. On their value see Disraeli : 101 *Hansard*, 3 s. 673.
[2] Standing Order No. 63.

conditions that they are allowed to argue their case, and are often asked questions and aided in making clear the issues which they press. Nor is there any doubt that a well-managed deputation is much more likely to achieve results than a mere petition which no authority is specially concerned to deal with. That is not to say that petitions [1] serve no purpose. The collection of signatures helps to focus public attention on the issues involved, and is a useful mode of propaganda, while the announcement that a petition with an imposing number of signatures has been presented has some propaganda value.

The use of *public meetings* to insist on reforms is of early date, but their intensive development was first seen in 1779 and 1780. It was defended by Fox but disliked by the ministry and legislation was passed in 1795, 1817, and 1819 to discourage meetings for political purposes. But they served a useful purpose in furthering the passage of the Reform Bill, and in 1832 and 1833 like technique was employed in Lancashire and Yorkshire in order to promote the chances of passage of the Ten Hours Bill promoted by Lord Ashley. In 1866 a monster public meeting in Hyde Park in the case of reform aroused anxiety, but Mr. Disraeli was sensible enough to admit that they were the recognised and indispensable organs of a free constitution and useful as safety-valves.[2] Another monster meeting was arranged for May 6, 1867. The Home Secretary under Cabinet pressure agreed to issue warnings that it was not legal thus to use the park, but the Reform League and the Liberals contested the claim, and in fact the meeting was held. Mr. Walpole resigned office despite Lord Derby's advice to the contrary, and the issue was settled only in 1872 when the

---

[1] Letters to members from constituents are often organised, and have some effect.

[2] Walpole, *Hist.* ii. 173, 197 ; 35 & 36 Vict. c. 15.

Office of Works was authorised by statute to regulate meetings by rules subject to control by Parliament. The question was again raised in 1888 in respect of a great meeting
in Trafalgar Square [1] which led to a judicial ruling that no
right of meeting existed in a public thoroughfare, but on
the other hand it has been laid down that the fact that
public meetings are held on a highway does not *ipso facto*
make them illegal.[2]

Political associations became prominent in 1779–80 also.
But they were disliked by the Government and accused of
revolutionary tendencies, and the London Corresponding
Society, which was created in 1792 to promote Parliamentary reform and adult suffrage, was suppressed by an Act
of 1799. In 1817 [3] repression was carried to the extent of
declaring any society electing delegates to meet with other
societies or delegates to be unlawful. In 1825 the right to
create an association assuming to represent the people, and
in that capacity to bring about a reform in Church and
State, was declared by Mr. Plunket to be denied by the
constitution in the debate on the Bill for the suppression
of unlawful societies in Ireland, which was aimed at the
Catholic Association founded by Mr. O'Connell to secure
Catholic emancipation.[4] It is characteristic that it was the
Anti-Slavery Association, which had no party affiliations,
which first was welcomed by ministers when a convention
of delegates met in London in 1833. Its success was due
to the steps taken to spread its literature and to canvass
support widely. The Anti-Corn Law League's activities
between 1838 and 1846 were regarded by protectionists
with hostility and its suppression was urged in Parliament.

---

[1] *R.* v. *Graham and Burns* (1888), 16 Cox C.C. 420.
[2] *Burden* v. *Rigler*, [1911] 1 K.B. 335.
[3] 57 Geo. III. c. 19, s. 25. Cf. *Luby* v. *Warwickshire Miners Assocn.*,
[1912] 2 Ch. 371.
[4] 12 *Hansard*, 2 s., 315 f., 471.

But its efforts were successful ; in 1842–3 it distributed five million tracts to voters and four million to non-electors, while it successfully fought selected constituencies. The Political Unions of 1831–2 by their meetings helped to secure reform, though they were declared illegal and unconstitutional by a proclamation in November 1831, which was not seriously enforced. The obstacles to effective central organisations, enacted especially in 1799,[1] hampered any combined movement, and it was not until 1840 that it was found possible for the Chartists, who took up the agitation when the Reform Act proved to have done nothing for the workers, to form a National Charter Association to aid in the centralisation of the movement, which hitherto had had nothing more effective than a convention of delegates, which met in 1832, but excited suspicion by its apparent hostility to Parliament. The Chartist movement's failure in 1848 was largely due to its inability to secure any real support by representatives in Parliament, to its confinement to one political class, to the division of opinion among its leaders, and their indiscretion, and to the legal restrictions on combined action, which drove members to form secret leagues, which rendered them liable to prosecution for high treason.

Reform was still agitated for by the National Reform League, a body representing the working classes, but its action was supported by the National Reform Union, which was a middle-class organisation headed by Radicals who had representation in the Commons and could enforce their views by votes. After the Reform Act of 1832 the way was open for political agitation of all kinds, and many different interests have thus been promoted. Among these of special importance was the struggle for female suffrage by the Women's Social and Political

[1] 39 Geo. III. c. 79, s. 2.

Union ; steady but so far very fruitless effort has marked the work of the Proportional Representation Society, whereas the Free Trade Union long served as a powerful safeguard against the efforts of supporters of protection in the Tariff Reform League and other bodies. The taxation of land values evoked enthusiastic efforts, now represented by the United Committee for the Taxation of Land Values. The National Union of Teachers has brought strong pressure on many occasions to bear on ministers, the National Federation of Property Owners has endeavoured to assert the sacred rights of property against Socialistic schemes, and the Protestant Alliance and the Protestant Truth Society represent influences in favour of the maintenance unimpaired of the Protestant character of the Church of England against the dangers of Anglo-Catholic views, which in their turn are effectively organised.

The most important, however, of all political forces is the Trades Union Congress, whose connection with the Labour party has been elsewhere noted. The first Congress, resting on the activities of local trades councils, dates from 1868, and the unions performed important functions in promoting individually candidatures of Labour representatives until the Labour party was created in 1900. There is necessarily now some duplication of authority between the Congress, which meets annually, and its General Council and the Labour party proper, but the possibility of friction is lessened by their co-operation in the National Council of Labour, which is made up of representatives of the Congress, the party executive, and the Labour party in Parliament. It was from this body in December 1938 that there was issued a declaration refusing Labour consent to any form of compulsory service, but affirming willingness to co-operate in a voluntary and democratically controlled scheme for national civilian defence. The Congress, despite much pressure during 1938, refused to take up the line that industrial action in the form of refusing co-operation in production of munitions,[1] unless certain assurances as to the foreign policy of ministers in regard especially to Spain were given, would be justified. It insisted that political action of this kind lay outside the scope of its functions, and would constitute a challenge to the principles of democratic government.

This attitude is an important development, as compared with the position adopted in 1920 [2] when the Congress and the Labour party threatened to resort to any and every form of withdrawal of labour which circumstances might require in the event of any form of military and naval intervention against the Soviet Government. It does not appear that such intervention was really under contemplation, and so the threat had not to be made good. But in 1926 the threat of a general strike materialised, and was only defeated by the effective measures taken by the ministry to maintain communications and the food supply, and the resolute determination of the people to refuse to allow their freedom to be destroyed by any sectional influences.[3] Since then it has been made clear that the strike was not approved by a very considerable section of Labour opinion, and that its more violent aspects, such as the efforts to wreck trains, had no authorisation whatever from any responsible quarters. The legislation evoked by the strike is discussed elsewhere.

---

[1] The Amalgamated Engineering Union on Apr. 4, 1938, refused to speed-up production unless assured as to use of armaments.

[2] Cf. Clynes, *Memoirs*, i. 322 f., with Spender, *Great Britain*, pp. 606 f.

[3] Cf. Spender, *op. cit.* pp. 672-6, who exaggerates the good temper of the strikers ; Clynes, *Memoirs*, ii. 80 ff. There is no reason to doubt the illegality of the strike ; it would be a grave blot on English law were it otherwise ; *National Seamen's and Firemen's Union* v. *Reed*, [1926] Ch. 536 ; Keith, *Letters on Imperial Relations, 1916–35*, pp. 264 f.

2. *The Consultation of the Electorate and the Mandate*

The consultation of the electorate may be traced in rudimentary form from 1680, and sometimes the issues were fairly directly posed, as in Bishop Atterbury's *English Advice to the Freeholders of England,* circulated at the election following the death of Queen Anne. There was some attempt to make the passing of the Septennial Act an issue at the next election in 1722 ; petitions were organised widely in 1701 asking the King to dissolve Parliament in the hope of thus securing a strong movement against France, and in 1710 the resentment felt at the trial of Dr. Sacheverell led to petitions from Tories for a new election. The Wilkes controversy evoked in 1768–1771 petitions for a dissolution, but the royal replies showed deep resentment of such action as disrespectful, injurious, and irreconcilable with the principles of the constitution.[1] Nor in this case as in the former was any step taken to dissolve, though Lord Chatham made, as a result of their presentation, two motions in favour of dissolution in the Lords in 1770. Lord North was inclined to regard petitions of this type as unconstitutional, but that was plainly an untenable view.[2] In 1774 and 1784 alike we find some appearance of desire to discover the popular will, but there was little reality in such consultation, and still less can we ascribe to the dissolutions of Lord Grenville in 1806 and of the Duke of Portland in 1807 any real anxiety as to the popular will. The state of Parliamentary representation denied any reality to such apparent appeals.

On the other hand, the electorate was definitely given the duty of deciding on reform. This was in striking contrast with the action of the Duke of Wellington and Sir R. Peel in 1829 in passing Catholic emancipation without any

---

[1] *Parl. Hist.* xvi. 894.   [2] *Ibid.* 578 ; Lecky, *Hist.* iii. 346.

consultation of the electorate and in clear disregard of
previous pledges, though they could justify their *volte-face*
by the results of the Clare election, which had a clear warning for any statesmen.[1] Sir R. Peel's apologia involved an
insistence that the result of county and large city constituencies by-elections indicated the readiness of the people
for the change. It is, however, clear that reform was not a
real issue at the election of 1830 consequent on the demise
of the Crown. But the July revolution in Paris lent force
to an agitation which was widespread in the country among
local Political Unions, and Lord Grey had full justification
for placing himself at the head of the movement even without a mandate. But that was forthcoming at the election
of 1831, which led to an appeal from Lord Grey for a mandate not merely for his continued tenure of power but also
for the passing of a reform Act. Moreover not only in this
respect did the appeal differ from that of Mr. Pitt in 1784,
but, as the Duke of Wellington stressed,[2] it was an appeal
for a mandate to pass reform in a definite shape, a course
which he naturally regarded as unconstitutional. The
passing of the Act was, therefore, the result of a clear answer
of the people to a definite inquiry, and it established the
principle that it was not enough to return a ministry to
power but that the ministry should receive endorsement
of a definite policy, which its return to office would give it
the power to make effective.

The lesson was not lost on Sir R. Peel, when he took
office on Lord Melbourne's resignation without any chance
of expounding in the Commons his programme by which
he must seek to obtain votes to control the Commons. He
prepared a manifesto for his electors at Tamworth, but not
only obtained for it Cabinet assent, but communicated

---

[1] *Memoirs*, i. 274 ff., 343 ff. ; May, *Const. Hist.* ii. 232 ff.
[2] 7 *Hansard*, 3 s. 1193.

it to the London press, thereby establishing a precedent, which he vainly later regretted.[1] In 1841 the Royal Speech prior to the dissolution made it clear that the people were asked for a verdict on matters gravely affecting their welfare. On the other hand, in 1846 Sir R. Peel proceeded to propose the abolition of the corn laws in the Commons, with the natural result of being censured by Mr. Disraeli [2] for his failure in duty in proposing a measure diametrically opposed to his attitude at the election of 1841. His own reasons for his failure to dissolve before taking up the new policy were that he did not desire to inflame public feeling by laying before the electorate an issue touching their essential food. In 1847, however, he issued a manifesto once more, and Lord John Russell and Lord George Bentinck were equally ready to impress their proposals on the voters.

With Sir R. Peel's reluctance to appeal to the people may be paralleled that of Lord Russell in 1866 when he insisted on resignation rather than dissolve, despite Mr. Gladstone's contention [3] that the principles of the constitution demanded dissolution, even if that involved a second election in a brief space of time and might cause a loss of votes. But Mr. Disraeli was equally anxious not to dissolve, and, although he had defeated the ministry on the score that its reform Bill was too democratic, he proceeded to carry a Bill of very much more advanced type, thus certainly evading any regard for the earlier views he had professed.[4] Mr. Gladstone, however, showed equally little anxiety in 1868 to take the decision of the electors, although he had no mandate for the policy of disestablishment of the Irish Church on which he had defeated Mr. Disraeli, and he

[1] *Memoirs*, ii. 58 ff. Cf. Grenville, *Journal*, iii. 178.
[2] Monypenny and Buckle, i. 725 ff.
[3] *Later Corr. of Lord J. Russell*, ii. 351.
[4] Monypenny and Buckle, i. 218 ff.

argued that it was the constitutional duty of his rival to resign, not to dissolve, a view supported only by Sir R. Peel's action in 1846.[1] Earl Grey [2] tried to support the Gladstonian thesis on the score that Parliament should not be reduced to the condition of a set of delegates, but Lord Cairns pressed the great constitutional importance of the question and the propriety of consulting the electorate upon it. The dissolution by Mr. Disraeli had the great advantage for all concerned of giving an unequivocal support to the idea of disestablishment, and no doubt it was this factor which secured royal assistance in converting the project into law. The idea of consulting the people was revived with energy by Lord Salisbury in 1872 [3] when he opposed the Ballot Bill on the score of the absence of a popular mandate, and when in 1884 [4] he urged that consultation of the people on the franchise and redistribution should have preceded the Bill of 1884.

The issue of the mandate became especially important in the election of 1885, as Mr. Gladstone's programme was in vague terms, dealing only with " the grant to portions of the country of enlarged powers " for dealing with their own affairs, and other issues were at stake, Mr. J. Chamberlain's radical proposals, Mr. Jesse Collings' " three acres and a cow " against the Tory democracy of Lord R. Churchill. Mr. Gladstone's definite conversion to Home Rule precluded Lord Hartington joining his ministry, and when the proposals were laid before the Commons he enunciated in the firmest manner the doctrine of mandate.[5] Mr. Gladstone defended himself by reference to the bringing forward of reform by Lord Grey in 1830, but this was rather ancient history, and, after defeat on his Bill, he dissolved in order

---

[1] 191 *Hansard*, 3 s. 1710 ff.
[2] *Ibid.* 1688 f.   [3] 211 *ibid.* 1494 f.
[4] 290 *ibid.* 468 f.   [5] 304 *ibid.* 1241 ff.

to obtain a direct verdict from the people,[1] though this proved to be unfavourable.

The doctrine of the extent of the mandate became marked when in 1900 the ministry appealed for the support of the electors to conclude the war in South Africa, and then undertook drastic reforms of education, calculated to win the gratitude of the Church of England, and in licensing, certain to make the liquor interests warm allies of the Conservative party. But, though Sir H. Campbell-Bannerman denied the right of the ministry to act in this manner, Mr. Balfour [2] rejected the suggestion and Mr. Morley dissociated himself from it altogether; it was later [3] pointed out by him that the Liberal ministry of 1868 had a perfectly definite and limited mandate, but that it had dealt with the abolition of army purchase, the law of Irish land tenure, the reform of the Civil Service, and so forth. It must, however, be noted that the doctrine of mandate was then only slowly developing and that it was Lord Salisbury who had popularised it. At any rate, when Mr. Chamberlain developed his tariff proposals, he was emphatic that a mandate must be asked for, and Mr. Balfour was glad to shelter himself from the necessity of action by accepting the impossibility of raising the issue in a Parliament during the elections for which it had not been discussed. Later on,[4] he advanced to a further position : there must be a dissolution to authorise the discussion of the issue with the colonies whose co-operation would be essential ; then, if that resulted in a scheme, there must be a second general election to obtain approval

[1] 304 *Hansard*, 3 s. 1547.

[2] 132 *ibid.* 4 s. 1014 ; 141 *ibid.* 160 ff. ; 8 *H.L. Deb.* 5 s. 783 f. ; Spender, *Campbell-Bannerman,* ii. 147 ff.

[3] 4 *H.L. Deb.* 5 s. 1142.

[4] Spender, ii. 168 ff. ; cf. Balfour, 131 *Hansard*, 4 s. 678. f. See also 141 *ibid.* 121 f., 190, 338.

of the scheme. The agreement by both parties on a Chapter
mandate was complete, but the ministry held that it was XII.
not necessary to hurry on the taking of that mandate,
and the decisive moment for action was only fixed by
Mr. Chamberlain, when he demanded at the close of 1905
that the issue should be solved by a dissolution, though
Mr. Balfour preferred to resign and to leave the question
for others to deal with. The mandate by the electorate
was overwhelming in support of free trade.

The issue revived on the question of the relations of
the two houses forced upon the Liberal ministry by the
rejection of its Education and Plural Voting Bills. The
demand of Sir H. Campbell-Bannerman, in June 1907,
that the supremacy of the Commons should be established
so that its final decision should prevail within the limits
of a single Parliament, raised the point whether a general
election conferred on the Commons an unlimited mandate,
which forbade the Lords from rejecting measures on the
plea that they had not received the approval of the people.
The claim made for the Government by Sir H. Campbell-
Bannerman denied the existence of any binding system of
mandate, and, in the absence of mandate or referendum or
plebiscite, gave full authority to the elected members of
Parliament. In this he represented, as did Mr. Morley,
the older school of Liberal thought. But Sir W. Anson
insisted on the danger of so wide a claim.[1] In 1909 the
question once more was debated. Could the ministry claim
that the Lords must accept the Finance Bill which it was
urged introduced principles of a non-financial character ?
The right of the Lords to insist on reference of the principle
to the people was contended for by the Lords, and by
their friends in the Commons ; Lord Curzon insisted that
the Lords could compel reference of a principle not

[1] 176 *Hansard*, 4 s. 911, 918 ff., 1002.

previously submitted ; Lord Courtney admitted the right to reject Bills of such a kind as did not compel dissolution, but negatived the right to force a dissolution ; while Lord Morley retained his opposition to the whole doctrine of mandate and asserted the right of a ministry to bring forward any measure it deemed necessary in the interest of the country, just as in 1880 Mr. Gladstone did not ask for any mandate for coercion in Ireland, but readily applied it when circumstances arose to make it necessary.[1]

In regard to the Parliament Bill itself, the issue was strongly fought. The Liberals had secured in January 1910 a mandate for the Finance Bill which the Lords had obeyed. In December they asked for a mandate for the Parliament Bill, whose terms were disclosed before the election. The party, therefore, was united in claiming that it had a mandate for the measure, not merely for the principle ; in 1893 the Duke of Devonshire [2] had insisted that there was no mandate for Home Rule, because the form of the measure had not been submitted at the election, but that objection no longer had validity. The Conservative replies to Mr. Asquith, and Lords Loreburn and Haldane, were various ; Mr. Balfour's view was that the election turned on various considerations, and could be quoted only as showing a desire for reform, not for the Parliament Bill. Lord Curzon and Sir W. Anson stressed instead the fact that the Conservative party had not been given sufficient time to criticise the proposals, and that the people had not had opportunity for mature consideration, especially as the issues before them were far from plain.[3] Needless to say there was even more controversy over the Government of Ireland Bill. The ministry con-

[1] 4 *H.L. Deb.* 5 s. 731 ff., 1139, 1260, 1266, 1345.
[2] 17 *Hansard*, 4 s. 30 f.
[3] 26 *H.C. Deb.* 5 s. 1055 f., 1089, 1111; 25 *ibid.* 1693, 1701 f.; 8 *H.L. Deb.* 5 s. 678, 762 ; 9 *ibid.* 442, 573, 820, 1005.

tended that the passing of the Parliament Bill had been carried out, as every one knew, expressly to secure a mandate on the issue of Home Rule for Ireland, and that the attempt to deny this was worthless. They declined to consider another election at which it was certain there would be no chance of obtaining a mandate on the essential issue, for the election would no doubt have turned on such issues as the Insurance Act, the alleged Marconi share scandals, etc.[1]

In the Parliament Act, 1911, the power of a ministry to secure legislation is left unaffected by the issue of a mandate. The one safeguard on this score implicit in the measure is the fact that it takes full two years to pass a Bill without assent of the peers, and, the duration of Parliament being reduced to five years, it is clear that the ministry could not thus pass measures of importance which would not in all probability have been before the people in some form at the last election. The possibility of the Lords having the right to insist on delaying measures on the score of lack of a mandate was envisaged in the proposals of the Bryce Committee on the second chamber,[2] but that report was never adopted by any Government, and its value as a statement of opinion is now problematic. If any general opinion exists, it is that the ministry should not take action on matters of high importance without prior reference to the people if that be possible. Yet the difficulty of laying down any definite rule was shown conclusively by the royal abdication in 1936. Never was there an occasion when it was less desirable to have the people consulted, for the delay and confusion therein involved would gravely have endangered the stability of the realm. Fortunately the

---

[1] Asquith's memo. in Spender, ii. 32 ff. : contrast Dugdale, *Balfour*, ii. 100 ff.

[2] *Parl. Pap.* Cd. 9038.

　　　　　　　　　　　　　　　　　　　　　C

King declined to consider any such idea, and made it clear that the matter must be disposed of between himself and the ministry.

The issue arose again in a rather acute form after 1935 in view of the mandate obtained by the ministry for a policy based on the League of Nations Covenant and aiming at collective security. The policy of the abandonment of sanctions in 1936 presented the ministry in the light of violating its mandate absolutely, and further violations were noted in the agreement of April 16, 1938, with Italy, and above all in the surrender of Czechoslovakian integrity and independence by the Munich agreement of September 29, 1938. Yet it can hardly be said that the demand for an election to secure a decision of the people was very earnestly pressed by the Labour or Liberal Opposition. They no doubt felt that the ministry would appeal on the ground that they were aiming at peace and would insist on the ghastly effects of air warfare and the difficulty of resistance, as stressed in December 1938 by Lord Maugham as justifying the surrender to Germany. In such circumstances it seemed better to leave the initiative for a dissolution to the ministry in the hope that, when it came, the actions of the Government would have been so discredited by their fruits that defeat would be assured.

It follows from this attitude that the parties regard the people as by no means very well fitted to come to correct decisions on the issues put before them. There is early authority for the doctrine adopted by E. Burke from Montesquieu that the power of the people lies in passing judgment on ministries and on the mode in which they have conducted the affairs of the country, as contrasted with their power to judge a policy submitted for their consideration. This power demands, it is said, a capacity denied to them of combining with expert political intelligence a natural imagination.[1] Sir R. Peel, when the Reform Bill was in the balance, was ready to urge that the desires of the people should not be gratified, for they were poor judges of what in the long run would conduce to their benefit, and Prince Albert complacently adopted the maxim of James Harrington that the people can feel but they cannot see. Mr. Gladstone in a more expansive mood [2] declared the electors to be excellent judges of policy, but there is probably more truth in Mr. Bryce's more modest hope [3] that they are tending to attain to a sound perception of the main and broad issues of national and international policy, especially in their moral aspects, in sufficient degree to enable them to keep the nation's action upon sound lines. It is in fact impossible to deny to the electors the duty of trying to judge not merely what ministers have done but what they propose to do, and it may be that on sufficiently broad issues they are well adapted to decide. In 1935 their preference for a policy of adherence to League tenets and to co-operative security was no doubt fully deliberate. They had been well instructed in the questions involved by the propaganda for and against the Peace Ballot, and there was little excuse for them not to have an elementary idea of what was at stake. To place complicated questions before them is no doubt a blunder, and for this the evidence of trade union practice [4] has value ; to hold a referendum on complex issues has shown itself unwise, but to vote on emergent problems of a straightforward character is well within their capacity. It remains, however, a source of difficulty that the franchise is so very widely distributed that it includes, and must always include, a vast mass of electors who are not even willing to understand politics.

[1] A. F. Pollard, *Evolution of Parliament* (2nd ed.), pp. 346 ff.
[2] *Speeches*, ix. 133 f. [3] *Studies in History*, ii. 31.
[4] S. and B. Webb, *Industrial Democracy* (1920), pp. 36, 60 ; Emden, *The People and the Constitution*, pp. 308 ff.

3. *The Submission of Issues*

In the history of the submission of issues it may be noted that verdicts on past conduct were not early in appearance. But we find in 1831 the Duke of Wellington [1] contrasting the question referred in 1784 to the electors as a judgment on ministers as opposed to the proposal of reforms to be carried out in 1831. In 1846, again, when he was discussing with Sir R. Peel on what issues an appeal should be made to the people, he recommended that the only question should be whether Sir R. Peel should remain in power or not, as opposed to the latter's proposed slogan of " free trade and the destruction of protection ".[2] We have in 1865 a very complete instance of an appeal really personal in essence ; no doubt Mr. Disraeli's challenge [3] that Lord Palmerston should stand by the issue of the Chinese war and no further reform was accepted, but it was not on anything except whether Lord Palmerston should be Prime Minister that the votes were cast. The matter was put quite frankly by Lord Derby in 1859 ; [4] in agreement with Mr. Disraeli his appeal to the electors was on their personal position, not on reform. Though Lord Palmerston [5] denounced this attitude and insisted reform must be the matter for decision, he had no hesitation himself in making his appeal in 1865 turn on his personal retention of power. In like manner Lord R. Churchill [6] denounced, without historical accuracy, the appeal of Mr. Gladstone in 1886 as " a most perilous innovation in constitutional practices, a pure unadulterated personal plebiscite, a political expedient borrowed from the last and worst days of the second Empire ".

Apart from this aspect of issues, there is often great

[1] 7 *Hansard*, 3 s. 1192.
[2] *Memoirs*, ii. 295.
[3] Morley, i. 564.
[4] 153 *Hansard*, 3 s. 1289 ff., 1307.
[5] 154 *ibid*. 182.
[6] W. Churchill, ii. 495.

difficulty in deciding what were the issues on which judg-   Chapter
XII.
ment has been passed by the electorate, for, as is natural,
both sides submit their views, and on what special point
the votes are cast must remain speculative. In 1837 the
Liberals stressed their exploits as responsible for the
Reform Act, the Tories presaged danger from the grant
to them of a further tenure of office. In 1841 the Liberals,
having no great achievement to vaunt, predicted dire
things from the protectionist designs of their opponents,
while the latter published a list of the sins of the ministry
and asked the voters to pass judgment effectively thereon.
Mr. Disraeli [1] in 1874 pursued like tactics ; he denounced
the blunders of his predecessor and he confined himself to
general sentiments regarding his own proposals, but Mr.
Gladstone stressed instead the abolition of the income tax
and the reform of local taxation as likely to win him
votes. In 1880 Mr. Gladstone took his turn in attack on
the imperialism and ruinous foreign policy of his rival,[2]
who endeavoured to turn the tide by predicting that his
opponent would press forward the destructive doctrine of
Home Rule, " a danger in its ultimate results scarcely
less disastrous than pestilence and famine ". Mr. Gladstone [3] energetically combated this effort to make the
election turn not on the past record of the ministry or on
its own future plans, but on the dangers of a policy imputed
without warrant to the Opposition. In 1880, of course,
Home Rule was very far from standing in the programme
of the Liberals. But in 1892 Mr. Gladstone put Home
Rule in the forefront of his policy, while the Government
quite fairly exalted their own past deeds and assaulted the
Opposition proposals.

[1] Monypenny and Buckle, ii. 615.
[2] *Ibid.* ii. 427 f.
[3] *Speeches in Scotland*, i. 57 f. ; ii. 21 f.

The making of lavish promises to the electors is a feature foreseen by Sir R. Peel in 1831, but becoming most frequent only after the increase in the number of the electorate in 1867, and especially in 1918 and 1928. The Liberal reforms from 1906 were naturally represented as bribes to the electorate rather than as proper measures for spreading more equally the advantages to be derived from wealth, to which all sections of the people contributed. Lord Rosebery [1] even questioned the value of the mandates given by the electors in 1910, on the score that old-age pensions had been promised as a bribe to the voters. In the post-war elections promises of boons were freely made by all parties in 1922 and in 1923, though in the latter case hostility to tariff reform was stressed also by Liberals and Labour, both having their own panaceas to offer. Labour had a capital levy to suggest, Liberals a scheme of national development. In 1929 the Conservative programme was not exciting ; further Imperial preference and safeguarding of industry were coupled with the demand for votes for Mr. Baldwin as the advocate of " safety first ". Liberals and Labour were rivals in positive policies, and it fell to Labour to endeavour to give proof in office of its possession of a panacea for the mass of unemployment, a task which proved beyond its powers. It is impossible to deny that the making of promises of rash character was prominent in 1929 and again in 1935, and the recent conversion of Labour to the theory that it can provide old-age pensions sufficient to maintain the workers is doubtless made with some lack of consideration for the seriousness of such an undertaking. On the other hand, in 1931 the mandate asked for by the National Government was indefinite in content.

It is obvious that it is far more incumbent on a ministry

[1] 9 *H.L. Deb.* 5 s. 1005.

which dissolves to put forward detailed statements of intention than on an Opposition which has not the means to mature policy as fully as the Government; but this disability may be exaggerated, as it was by Mr. Disraeli when in 1873[1] he refused to take office, partly on this score. For a ministry to rely, as in 1880, on the supposed plans of the Opposition is undesirable, and unlikely to be successful, nor is there any obligation on the Opposition to play into the hands of its rivals by revealing its policy further than it desires : the Liberals in 1905 refused to gratify Mr. Balfour by saying what they would do on licensing, education, Chinese labour, and so forth. They had the excellent excuse that their critic had made no clear statement on the tariff policy which he advocated.

It rests, of course, with the party leaders to decide what issues shall be chosen as those upon which they will stand or fall, but it remains to be considered what influences can be brought to bear on them in the decision. On the whole, the efforts of the federations of Liberal and Conservative associations alike to influence their leaders in this regard have fallen short of achieving any great results. The Conservatives indeed have shown no inclination to obey mandates attempted thus to be given, and the National Union has treated its activities as sub-servient to the views of ministers. The Liberal federation, on the other hand, was planned to be a Parliament of Liberalism, to be used by Mr. J. Chamberlain for the laudable purpose of stirring Liberal leaders to action in the sense desired by the rank and file, but after the New-castle programme of 1891, which proved itself a heavy burden on the weak ministry of 1892–5, the influence of the Union or its latest successor, the Assembly, has declined. Naturally this point must not be exaggerated.

[1] 214 *Hansard*, 3 s. 1931 ff.

Chapter
XII.

The views of earnest workers [1] cannot be treated with disrespect, and the leaders must bear the resolutions sent up in mind when they themselves take decisions on the matters to be put forward. In the case of the Labour party, the annual Conference has much higher authority ; it decides what specific proposals of legislative, financial, or administrative reform shall be included in the party programme. The National Executive Committee and the Executive Committee of the Parliamentary Labour party decide what items shall be actually included in the manifesto for a general election. But it is difficult to avoid the impression that in such a decision the actual leaders of the party have great weight, as best qualified, from experience in Parliament, to know how far measures can best be pressed.

Efforts on the part of public associations to induce ministers to adopt lines of policy are not rare, and in earlier days were often of high importance. The Anti-Slavery Society, active from 1823, won distinction by its success in bringing the issue so strongly before the Whigs in 1832 that next year saw the great measure for the ending of slavery accepted. The Reform Act of 1832 was largely the result of efforts by political unions throughout the country, and more especially the National Political Union formed by Francis Place in London for the definite purpose of supplying the driving power necessary to carry reform. The Chartists stood by a People's Charter promulgated in 1838 by the London Working Men's Association, to which various local bodies adhered, sending representatives to a People's Parliament next year in London. The growth of the movement was weakened by internal dissensions and, after the cancellation of its

[1] In Feb. 1939 the Labour Executive stressed this aspect in attacking Sir S. Cripps.

projected great procession from Kennington Common to Parliament to present a petition for its points, it died away. The Anti-Corn Law League, on the other hand, while no occasion arose on which its principles could be presented as issues to Parliament, unquestionably was largely responsible for the growth of feeling which rendered the action of Sir R. Peel intelligible. Its success led to the dissolution of the Union, whose purpose had been fulfilled. The existence of bodies which are eager to induce parties to take up their principles is still common. The Liberation Society once strove actively to have disestablishment put on the Liberal programme : the Free Church Federation was active in the years following the imposition on the country of the educational reforms of 1902. The National Trade Defence Association arose to protect the liquor trade, and efforts were made repeatedly after the war by representatives of that interest to secure the adoption by the Conservative party of the reduction in the duties on whisky in special as a popular election cry. The Tariff Reform League fought a long war for changes in the tariff policy of Britain, but success tarried until it was brought about, first by the policy of the war period in favour of aiding Allied powers, and finally by the necessity of altering the balance of British trade after the *débâcle* of 1931. The Home Rule cause was once urgently pressed by the United Irish League of Great Britain, and the Cobden Club stood out for free trade.

The position of distinguished members of a party in regard to issues may be of importance, and historically cases of this have occurred. Mr. Bright in 1865, despite the apathy of Lord Palmerston did something to keep alive the cause of electoral reform. Mr. J. Chamberlain embarrassed his leader no less than the Queen by his

democratic tendencies, and his programme at the election of
1885 was, if not inconsistent with the general Liberal outlook, distinctly in advance of what was advocated by more
restrained leaders. On the other hand, Lord R. Churchill,
in his Dartford programme of 1886,[1] insisted on such topics
as land reform, allotments, and local taxation reform in
such a manner as to cause some misgivings that he was
assuming the rôle of the Premier. Mr. Jesse Collings for
his part had the pleasure of bringing about the fall of Lord
Salisbury's ministry by his amendment to the address in
reply to the Speech from the Throne in favour of an agricultural policy aiming at the provision of allotments. That
the issue of tariff reform bulked large in the Unionist programme of 1906 was due to Mr. J. Chamberlain, though out
of the ministry since 1903, and it was Mr. Lloyd George's
insistence which in 1929 compelled all parties to stress unemployment as the essential matter with which they were
determined to deal if they received authority from the
electors.

Cases where division of opinion among leaders prevent
any clear lead being given are rare. In 1852 Lord Derby [2]
did not care to put forward protection, but left individual
members full discretion to act, with the result that it was
soon clear that the plan had no attractions for the mass of
the electors. In 1895 Lord Rosebery wanted to fight on the
issue of the House of Lords, Mr. Morley on Home Rule, Sir
W. Harcourt on local option, while other members insisted
that they stood by the Newcastle programme of 1891 as
the authorised faith of Liberals.

The mode of formulation of issues shows a definite progress. The earliest form in use was that of the Royal Speech

---

[1] Spender, *Great Britain*, p. 9. It is amusing to read the declamations of
Lord Hartington against Mr. Chamberlain ; Holland, ii. 72 ff. ; Chamberlain,
Politics from Inside, p. 338.

[2] Monypenny and Buckle, i. 1184 ff.

before the dissolution, for by 1841 the speech had come to be recognised as definitely the work of ministers, as asserted by Swift, Wilkes, and others, though the Duke of Wellington was unwilling to admit the claim.[1] But it was only in 1831 that we find any really definite issue formulated. Thereafter appears the election manifesto popularised by the initiative of Sir R. Peel in 1841, and the use of the dissolution speech becomes rare, though the issue of Home Rule was posed in 1886 and that of protection in 1923.

The address to the electors of one's own constituency, intended for general circulation, was difficult in the case of a peer, but Lord Beaconsfield solved it by sending it in 1880 to the Duke of Marlborough, then Viceroy in Ireland, and it was duly published.[2] In 1857[3] Mr. Gladstone inaugurated his practice of appealing in public speeches widely to the electorate as a whole, and this plan reached complete expression in his Midlothian campaign of 1879, a policy followed in 1886 when Mr. Gladstone was in power, much to the annoyance of Queen Victoria, whose favourite, Lord Beaconsfield, had eschewed appeals outside his own constituency except on some very special ground. On the other hand, Mr. Gladstone cited in support of his action the practice of two such sound Conservatives as Lords Salisbury and Iddesleigh, and in no wise altered his plans.[4] Lord Salisbury was again an innovator in 1892, for he then adopted the simple and common-sense plan of issuing a manifesto to the electors of the United Kingdom urging on them the danger to the Irish of permitting the terrible experiment of Home Rule. A joint manifesto was issued by Mr. Lloyd George and Mr. Bonar Law in 1918, and in 1929 Mr. Baldwin, who had clung to the older plan of an

[1] 59 *Hansard*, 3 s. 77, 81 ; Emden, *The People and the Constitution*, pp. 282 f.

[2] Monypenny and Buckle, ii. 1386 ff.

[3] Argyll, *Autobiography*, ii. 75.   [4] Morley, iii. 344.

address to his constituents, came into line by publishing a *Message to Britain*, which he varied in 1931 by publishing an election manifesto to the members of the Conservative and Unionist party, a precedent followed in 1935. By a novel development it is permitted to the party leaders at a general election to add to their written appeals the potency of the spoken voice broadcasted. This has the invaluable result of commanding from the leaders more explicit and precise declarations than those merely published, but it cannot be said that so far the leaders have been distinguished by any special force of the spoken appeal.

It is clear that any submission to the electorate cannot affect more than the principles of the measures proposed. To ask for a general approval is one thing, to compel the electors to pronounce an opinion on details another. It was this fact which invalidated the attempt of the Duke of Devonshire [1] in 1893 to hold that the only valid mandate for Home Rule must be one based on the making known of the details of the Bill, and there is no answer to the arguments of Lords Courtney [2] and Morley that the demand for the submission of a budget to the electorate was unsustainable. In fact the majority obtained for the budget included the Irish party, which bitterly disliked the whisky duties, but which accepted it simply because it was the only means of keeping in accord with the Liberal party and enabling the latter to proceed with Home Rule.

An interesting controversy broke out between Mr. Asquith and Mr. Balfour on the Parliament Bill. It was contended by the former that, as the Bill had been published before the dissolution, the affirmative verdict of the electorate must be deemed to apply to the whole of the measure. Mr. Balfour disputed this proposition, and, though he went too far in minimising the effect of the

[1] 17 *Hansard*, 4 s. 30 f.   [2] 4 *H.L. Deb.* 5 s. 1143.

mandate after the Bill had been made public, the true view was rather that of Lord Haldane,[1] who insisted that the electorate gave a general approval but left the details to be worked out by the members of Parliament and the Government. Of the essential truth of that doctrine no doubt is possible.

4. *The Referendum*

The difficulty of ascertaining the existence and the extent of the mandate from the electorate is the basis of the strength of the desire of certain politicians to see the establishment in Britain of the doctrine of the referendum. Historically the question came into serious political consideration only in the struggle over the Parliament Bill, when it was taken up by certain Conservatives as offering a reasonable solution of the problem of making a fair offer to the Liberals in lieu of the Parliament Bill. Lord Lansdowne's proposed alternative provided that, while Bills on which there was a difference of opinion between the houses should normally go to a joint sitting, " if the difference relates to a matter which is of great gravity, and has not been adequately submitted for the judgment of the people, it shall not be referred to the joint sitting, but shall be submitted for decision to the electors by referendum ".[2] The obvious difficulty which arose was that the Lords themselves would decide what Bills must be so referred, and that referendum would be confined to cases where the Liberals were in power in the lower chamber. This obvious defect was so severely criticised that, at the Albert Hall on November 29, 1910, Mr. Balfour[3] committed himself to acceptance of a referendum on tariff reform, a declaration believed to have saved his party a

---

[1] 8 *H.L. Deb.* 5 s. 678, 762.   [2] May, *Const. Hist.* iii. 370 ff.
[3] For A. Chamberlain's protest see *Politics from Inside*, pp. 303 ff.

few seats in Lancashire, but viewed with disgust by orthodox tariff reform advocates.   The proposal, of course, involved the admission that all seriously controversial Bills
should go to a referendum, even if there were no dispute
between the houses, and suggested ultimately that the
House of Lords might be unnecessary.   In the ensuing
Parliament Lord Balfour of Burleigh put forward a Bill
for a Referendum which provided for it being held, not
merely in cases of difference of opinion between the houses,
but also on the demand of two hundred members of the
Commons, though he made it clear that he did not stress
this figure, which indeed was unduly high.   The Bill
secured a second reading, but naturally, in view of the progress of the Parliament Bill, it was not further proceeded
with, once it was obvious that it had no chance of being
regarded by the Liberals as an adequate substitute for the
Parliament Bill.

The essential point of the referendum is that it isolates
some issue, and thus can be used wholly regardless of any
question of disputes between the houses.   If, however, it
is used for that purpose there is the gain that there is no
question of a penal dissolution, and the utter confusion
connected with a general election is avoided ; no one will
dispute that a general election, whether good or bad, is
never a decision on a single issue,[1] though no doubt in 1831
and 1868 the issues of reform and the Irish Church overshadowed all other considerations.   It is, however, true
that at times one issue does overshadow others ; in 1910
the first election turned on the right of the Lords to reject
a Finance Bill, but it was bound up in less measure with
the merits of the exact proposals in the budget and on the
rival policy of changes in the fiscal system.   In 1931 it
might be said that the grant of a blank cheque to the

---

[1] Balfour, 21 *H.C. Deb.* 5 s. 1752 ; Lord Salisbury, 8 *H.L. Deb.* 5 s. 783 f.

ministry for the restoration of financial stability was the main issue, but certainly it was not that only, nor was the question in 1935 merely the necessity of maintenance of the principles of the League of Nations. In 1906 three things co-operated to render the government victorious, Chinese labour, tariff reform, and the education policy of the late ministry. Even in 1900 the post-war settlement was not quite alone in the public mind, and it was certainly not in 1918, when the hope of the making of a " world fit for heroes to live in " was a strong factor in the minds of many electors.

Chapter XII.

There are many difficulties in the theory of the referendum. It may be taken as admitted that it would not be any real use to submit any really complex issue to the people, because they would find it impossible to pass an intelligent verdict upon such issues. The question would have, as in the case of trade-union referenda, to be simplified and put in its plainest terms. This contention, however, rules out merely matters essentially complex ; it is not relevant in cases where the issue can be simplified. A more serious contention is that it would prove impossible to isolate the issue so that the electorate would vote without being swayed by other considerations. The ministry, it would be felt, would lose prestige if the matter were not decided in accordance with its preference and this so far as it goes is supported by constitutional referenda in Australia. No ministry emerges without some loss from the rejection of its schemes. Similarly, when in 1929 it was proposed in the Commonwealth to treat the general election of 1929 as a referendum on the merits of the governmental proposal to withdraw from the exercise of arbitral power over industry so far as the Commonwealth was concerned, leaving the issues to the States, in practice other important issues served to affect the electors, so that their defeat of the Government was not really a clear-cut decision on the issue in question. It appears also that in Switzerland [1] it is not always found easy by the electors to isolate the issues, though there is now a long tradition of familiarity with the operation of the system in that State. The Labour opposition to the referendum has been in part based on that doctrine.

On the other hand, some weight must be allowed to the fact that a referendum could avoid the utter mixing of issues which is often the case at an election. Thus in 1892 it is clear that the vote for the Liberal Government rested in various areas on very different considerations. The miners wished an eight-hours Bill, the town workers an Employers' Liability measure, the agricultural labourers parish councils for local purposes, the London electors municipal reform, the Welsh the Disestablishment of the Welsh Church, and so on. Clearly it would have been impossible to say that any of these demands really had the support of the majority of electors, and, in case of real desire to ascertain that will, the referendum might be used. The answer, of course, to this point of view is that consideration that the essence of the duty of electors is to vote for a grand pattern of political construction, and that they cannot be expected to choose out individual points and to give a verdict on them.

It is further urged that the holding of referenda would come to overshadow the general elections, and the latter would come to be regarded as verdicts on issues of personal and retrospective character.

Again, it is held that the system would reduce the importance of Parliament and diminish the sense of responsibility of members. The Conference on the Reform

[1] R. MacDonald, 21 *H.C. Deb.* 5 s. 1770. For a denial of the possibility of segregating an issue, see Asquith, 15 *H.C. Deb.* 5 s. 1174 f.

of the Second Chamber of 1918 [1] hinted that it might tend to lower the authority and dignity of Parliament, and Mr. Asquith [2] thought that it would reduce a general election to a sham parade and degrade the House of Commons to the level of a talking club.   But Lord Curzon [3] insisted with good authority from Swiss precedent [4] that the existence of the referendum rather enhanced the responsibility of members, since they knew that at any time they might be called to account by a popular referendum. The whole argument is highly hypothetical, and unfortunately the differences between the Swiss and the British systems of government and mode of thought is such as to render the experience of Switzerland of minor relevance. In the Dominions [5] referenda on specific issues such as liquor licensing, religious education in schools, and other matters, have been conducted without special objection of any kind, but there is no such general experience of referenda as to afford any real guidance for British conditions.

[1] *Parl. Pap.* Cd. 9038.   [2] 21 *H.C. Deb.* 5 s. 1751.
[3] 6 *H.L. Deb.* 5 s. 946.
[4] F. Bonjour, *Real Democracy in Operation*, p. 84.   See Finer, *Mod. Govt.* ii. 925-41 ; Emden, *The People and the Constitution*, pp. 294 ff.
[5] Keith, *The Dominions as Sovereign States*, pp. 250 f.

PART VI

THE EXECUTIVE DEPARTMENTS AND THEIR FUNCTIONS

CHAPTER XIII

THE MINISTERS OF THE CROWN AND THEIR POWERS

1. *The Ministers of the Crown*

(i) The Cabinet

AN important summary of the ministries of the Crown is provided for the first time statutorily by the Ministers of the Crown Act, 1937. The measure was an interesting one, for it was introduced and carried without any mandate whatever from the electorate. It is indeed noteworthy that in the Dominions, as in the United Kingdom, it has seemed the wiser course to avoid definitely announcing at a preceding general election the purpose of increasing the emoluments of ministers or members. In this case the decision to augment salaries of ministers was manifestly accepted by the Commons on the understanding that the members thereof should participate in the demands made on the public exchequer. The only rather unfortunate aspect of the transaction was that the addition to the public expenses came at a time when rearmament was imposing grave burdens, and legislators and ministers might have been expected to show their sense of the situation by refusing to take additional emoluments. Apart from this, the measure might have passed without comment.

The principle of the Act is to signal out a class of ministers given salaries of £5000 a year, who therefore will normally be in the Cabinet. The equalisation of salaries puts an end to an undesirable anomaly, under which a minister might have to sacrifice work in which he was specially interested in order to obtain an adequate emolument, or have to stint himself of money, which he might need for family or other reasons. The only advantage to be set off against the loss through the unequal pay was the fact that a minister by change of office might become a more valuable member of the ministry through the possession of all-round knowledge.

The ministers so provided for are the Chancellor of the Exchequer, the Secretaries of State, First Lord of the Admiralty, President of the Board of Trade, Minister of Agriculture and Fisheries, President of the Board of Education, and the Ministers of Health, Labour, and Transport and for the Co-ordination of Defence. But only eight Secretaries of State may receive payment, though there are nine ; this rule is due to the fact that the India and Burma Offices fall to be held by the same minister in view of their essential relations. There is also the possibility of the same ministers combining the Dominions and the Colonial Offices, as was originally done from 1925 to 1930 and at times later as in 1938–9, but that union of offices is in theory objectionable, though hardly in practice. The other Secretaries of State are those for Home and for Foreign Affairs, for War and for Air, and for Scotland. The Prime Minister himself, who is First Lord of the Treasury, the two offices being intended to be held together, receives £10,000 and may draw a pension of £2000 a year.

Of the members of the Cabinet other than the Prime Minister only fifteen may sit in the Commons at any one time, so that two ministers at least, in addition to the Lord Chancellor, are secured for the Lords, though the number is normally greater.

There is a second category of ministers who receive £3000 salary, but £5000 if members of the Cabinet, which here appears formally recognised by statute. These ministers are the Lord President of the Council, Lord Privy Seal, Postmaster-General, and First Commissioner of Works. The number of these ministers who can sit in the Commons may not exceed three, so that, when all are in the Cabinet, one at least must be in the Lords. The Chancellor of the Duchy of Lancaster, if placed in the Cabinet, receives £5000 in lieu of his normal pay of £2000 from the funds of the Duchy, the extra amount being made up by Parliament.

The unfortunate Minister of Pensions receives only £2000, and there is no supplementary salary for him if in the Cabinet, a fact which clearly shows that his office is deemed too unimportant to deserve Cabinet status. The holder, therefore, would be given some other post if it were desired to find a place for him in the Cabinet.

Other ministers are ranked by the Act under the style of Parliamentary Under-Secretaries, though that name originally was confined to those ministers who were Under-Secretaries of State. The list now includes the Parliamentary Secretary to the Treasury (salary £3000), the Financial Secretary (£2000), the Secretary for Mines (£2000), the Secretary of the Department of Overseas Trade (£2000), the Parliamentary Under-Secretaries of State, the Foreign Office having two, one especially for League of Nations Affairs, the Parliamentary and Financial Secretary to the Admiralty, and the Civil Lord, the Financial Secretary to the War Office, the Parliamentary Secretaries to the Boards of Education and Trade, and to the Ministries of Agriculture and Fisheries, Health, Labour, and Transport, and the Assistant Postmaster-General whose modest pay is £1200, while the others, except as indicated above, receive £1500 a year. Of these only twenty may sit in the Commons.

There is provided also a salary of £1000 for five junior Lords of the Treasury. All the salaries are as usual votable annually ; exceptional provision is made for a salary to the leader of the party in the Commons in opposition to His Majesty's Government, at the rate of £2000 a year, charged on the Consolidated Fund, as is also the pension of the Prime Minister ; in case of doubt as to what party in opposition has the greatest numerical strength or who is its leader, the decision of the Speaker is decisive. The provision, which follows Dominion precedent is significant in its admission of the fundamental principle of responsible government,[1] which demands that there shall be a responsible Opposition prepared to accept the task of governing if the Commons withdraws its confidence from the ministry.

(ii) The Sinecure Ministries

The office of Lord Privy Seal had ceased to involve any personal action by its holder other than purely formal long before the use of the privy seal was abolished wholly by a statute of 1884, which negatived its employment as a necessary preliminary to the affixing of the great seal. But the office, having no substantive duties, had long been used to provide for a minister whose advice was deemed desirable, but who did not feel able to take an ordinary portfolio. It was thus that, when Lord Salisbury resigned the Foreign Office in 1900, he remained as head of the ministry as Lord Privy Seal until he resigned in 1902. In 1924–9 the party leader in the Lords occupied the office. In 1929 it was for a time held by Mr. J. H. Thomas, who was deputed to seek a solution of the unemployment impasse for the Labour ministry. In 1932 it was held for a time by Mr. Eden when deputed to deal

---

[1] Cf. Disraeli's insistence on Her Majesty's opposition as serving to secure her comfort and welfare ; Nov. 23, 1868 (Monypenny and Buckle, ii. 438).

with League of Nations business for the Foreign Office, but in his case it was not held as a Cabinet post. In 1938, when the demand for more effective dealing with air-raid precautions was vocal, the office was given to a former Civil Servant and Indian provincial governor with a view to his specialising in that regard.

The Chancellorship of the Duchy of Lancaster is equally a sinecure office, for the management of the royal estates in the Duchy, which extend beyond the limits of the County Palatine, is undertaken by subordinate officials and the Chancellor's only independent work is probably the appointment of the county court judges and their removal, should that become necessary for the County Palatine, which does not agree in extent with the Duchy, a matter of no constitutional importance. The minister thus has spare time for other work for the Government, and indeed it would not be worth while filling the post if it were not desired to give the Cabinet his aid. Earl Winterton in 1938 was given the office with a seat in the Cabinet, to answer in the Commons for the Air Ministry, whose head was then in the Lords. Later, on his replacement by Sir Kingsley Wood, Lord Winterton gave some assistance to the Home Office, but in January 1939 surrendered his office and Cabinet seat to Mr. Morrison, receiving in lieu the unpaid office of Paymaster-General, and continuing to preside over the Inter-Governmental Committee, which continues the work of the Evian Conference on Refugees.

(iii) The Parliamentary Under-Secretaries

These ministers perform numerous and useful rôles, which normally are a valuable preparation for later advancement to Cabinet office. Failure in a minor office, on the other hand, normally means relegation to the ranks whenever a convenient opportunity arises.

Of these posts the highest in importance is indicated by its special salary, the Parliamentary Secretary to the Treasury. The First Lord is leader of the house, and must secure the maximum amount of sound legislation to fulfil promises, to enhance the reputation of the ministry, or to advance the public well-being. For these ends he must make the fullest use of Parliamentary time, and in the Parliamentary Secretary who is Chief Whip he should find his trusted adviser as to the temper of his followers, who can tell him what measures can best be taken up and how changes in programme should be made, if need be, to secure the maximum result from the time available.

The Financial Secretary to the Treasury relieves the Chancellor of much of the detail work of passing the estimates through the Commons. Moreover, he serves as his agent in disposing of any departmental issues of considerable importance but not of sufficient weight to demand his personal attention. The experience is very useful and often ensures its holder a Cabinet seat at the next opportunity.

The position of the Under-Secretaries of State [1] varies ; the general rule requires them to be in their departments assistants to the Secretary of State in dealing with such lines of business as he can delegate, and in aiding him with other business which he does not desire to reserve to himself only. Their importance depends largely on whether they sit in the Commons or the Lords, the rule being that, if possible, every important department shall have a representative in both houses,[2] though there are not seldom

[1] Mr. Lowther, when at the Foreign Office, hardly had any contact with Lord Salisbury, who would not even see Ambassadors : Ullswater, *A Speaker's Commentaries*, i. 329.

[2] Thus Mr. Morrison was given the duty to represent the Minister for the Co-ordination of Defence in the Commons (Mr. Chamberlain, House of Commons, Feb. 13, 1939).

cases where both ministers are in the Commons. In the case of the Foreign Office, when the Secretary of State is in the Lords, the work of the Under-Secretary becomes very important, and it can hardly be satisfactorily dealt with by him only. Hence in 1938–9, when Lord Halifax was Foreign Secretary, the Prime Minister who had virtually asserted control of foreign policy, undertook to deal with issues of importance in the Commons, answering questions thereon, and correcting indiscretions of the Under-Secretary regarding reinforcements which had passed to Spain from Italy despite the non-intervention agreement.

Much depends on the character of the Under-Secretary regarding the work he does, and in the case of busy offices such as the Home Office there is due possibility of delegation of duty ; there are many deputations to be interviewed and the Under-Secretary may deputise. In the case of Scotland the Under-Secretary may be present there on occasions when his chief may not be able to leave Whitehall. In the Admiralty and War Office the Financial Secretaries have definite spheres of utility open to them within which they can relieve their chiefs of all but theoretic responsibility ; that the minister must always accept, for he cannot repudiate anything his office does, though patently it is easy for a junior minister to resign if he finds that he has erred. The Secretary of the Department of Overseas Trade and the Secretary for Mines are in positions of wide responsibility in these special spheres, though both owe allegiance to the President of the Board of Trade, and the former to the Foreign Secretary also. This more independent position may have been reflected in the fact that, when the Under-Secretaries at the War and Colonial Offices made their peace in 1939 with Mr. Chamberlain over their attacks on the conduct of preparations against attack, the Secretary of the Overseas Trade

Department was not reported to have shared in the recantation of their views.

2. *Prerogative and Statutory Executive Powers*

It is sufficient, as the matters have already been touched upon incidentally, to note that the chief functions of the executive, whether based on prerogative or as now constantly on statute, reinforcing or superseding prerogative, are the conduct of the international relations with other States, and the League of Nations ; the making of treaties ; the declaration of war and the conclusion of peace, in case of attack ; and the maintenance of neutrality in foreign conflicts which involve no essential British interest ; the conduct of relations with the self-governing Dominions which are on a footing of equality with the United Kingdom, and the control of dependencies, including the Indian Empire, pending its attainment of Dominion status. The executive is bound to secure the country from aggression, and therefore to provide defence preparations on a scale demanding a great share of the resources in men and money of the country. It secures the convening and the dissolution of the legislature, and it takes the initiative in all the vital legislation passed by it ; it obtains from Parliament authority for expenditure and the grant of funds whence that expenditure can be derived. It administers the law of the land through the departments of state, preserving internal order as the first condition of progress, and it studies to expand the trade and to improve in every way the social and economic conditions of the realm. It secures the appointment of the judiciary, and, while holding aloof from interference in its judicial action, it provides it with means to ensure that judicial decisions shall be given effect, and it exercises that power to mitigate the severity of the exact execution of the law which the variety of circumstances renders necessary.

The forms taken by these powers are various. Prerogative is the basis of authority in foreign affairs, reinforced in certain cases by statute. Thus the dubious right of the Crown to extradite has been given force and effect by the Extradition Acts, and its authority to preserve neutrality has been strengthened by the Foreign Enlistment Act, 1870, and certain treaties require legislative authority. In regard to control of the colonies, the prerogative is largely unaffected by statute, which has been necessary mainly to remodel colonial constitutions after prerogative power to legislate had been surrendered in respect of conquered or ceded colonies, by the establishment therein of representative legislatures.[1] In domestic matters there has been far greater reinforcement of prerogative by legislation. The ancient rights of the Crown to raise military forces and maintain a navy have long needed statutory support, and in the sphere of maintenance of order the modern police is a creation of statute. For social advancement of all kinds and the furtherance of trade, statute has been inevitable and regular since the days of the Tudors.

The exercise of the great powers given to the executive is subject to control by the legislature, as has been already noted, and the system of judicial control will be discussed below.

The executive can take advantage of various important privileges of the Crown. As will be shown later, the exemption of the Crown from suit in contract prevents any action being brought against the officers who carry through the contract. Again, the maxim *Nullum tempus*

---

[1] *Campbell* v. *Hall* (1774), 1 Cowp. 204; *Sammut* v. *Strickland*, [1938] A.C. 678; *Bishop of Natal, In re* (1865), 3 Moo. P.C. 115, 152.

occurrit regi is available for proceedings in the name of the
Crown,[1] but in informations for the purpose of testing
usurpation of corporate office or franchises the limit set
is six years, and in claims for the recovery of land the
Crown is barred under the Nullum Tempus Act, 1769, by
delay of sixty years. The rule that statutes do not bind
the Crown, except by express mention or necessary implication, will be noted elsewhere. It serves to exempt,
unless otherwise provided by statute, servants of the
Crown from necessity to observe speed limits [2] or to obey
the rules regarding weights and measures with regard to
scales.[3] Lands of the Crown may not be made to contribute to the cost of street paving, and rates are imposed
on Government property only under special authority.
Property of the Crown can claim exemption from dock
dues, except where this is specially provided against.

The Crown's property rights are numerous. Escheat
per defectum sanguinis was not abolished until the Administration of Estates Act, 1925, and instead the property
still goes to the Crown as *bona vacantia* together with the
other estate of a person dying intestate without kin entitled to share, or the property of a corporation which has
been dissolved without disposing of its property.[4] Until
the Forfeiture Act, 1870, the personal estate of felons went
to the Crown, but that penalty then disappeared. The
Crown is entitled to gold and silver, and, what in England
is more important, has been given by statute ownership of
petroleum and natural gas, which may yet be discovered

---

[1] *Public Works Commrs.* v. *Pontypridd Masonic Hall*, [1920] 2 K.B. 233.

[2] *Cooper* v. *Hawkins*, [1904] 2 K.B. 164. It is not clear that this immunity
now applies in view of s. 121 of the Road Traffic Act, 1930. Cf. also *Chare* v.
Hart (1919), 88 L.J.K.B. 833. For the general principle of Crown immunity,
see *Att.-Gen.* v. *Donaldson* (1842), 10 M. & W. 117.

[3] *R.* v. *Kent Justices* (1890), 24 Q.B.D. 181.

[4] *Wells, In re*; *Swinburne-Hanham* v. *Howard* (1932), 101 L.J.Ch. 346;
Companies Act, 1928, s. 71; 1929, s. 296.

to exist in substantial quantities in England.[1] The value of the right to gold and silver was, of course, of high importance in Australia especially. The Crown still has rights in wreck, not claimed within a year, treasure trove, waifs (stolen goods thrown away by a thief in flight), estrays (wandering animals whose owner cannot be found), swans swimming in open and common rivers and unmarked, and whales and sturgeon caught within territorial waters. The foreshore is vested in the Crown except in the Duchy of Cornwall, where it appertains to the Duke, and in cases where it had been granted out to the lords of manors, and land formed by alluvion or left bare by diluvion falls to the Crown, a matter of minor importance to Britain but not without value in India. Legislation as regards both bankruptcy and the winding-up of companies has diminished, but not wholly ended, the royal priority in the matter of payment of debts.[2]

The rights of the Crown as *parens patriae* are now virtually all exercised judicially. Jurisdiction for the protection of infants rests with the Chancery Division of the High Court ;[3] charities are by statute looked after by the Charity Commissioners, and jurisdiction appertains to the Chancery division. Custody and care of the property of lunatics and idiots are by statute entrusted to the Board of Control and the judge in lunacy and the master,[4] though the Lord Chancellor still is given by sign-manual warrant administration.

The doctrine that the Crown can do no wrong has the effect of compelling those who act illegally, though in good faith, to accept responsibility in tort and even criminally ;

---

[1] Petroleum (Production) Act, 1934 (24 & 25 Geo. V. c. 36).
[2] *Food Controller* v. *Cork,* [1923] A.C. 647.
[3] 15 & 16 Geo. V. c. 49, s. 56 (1).
[4] Lunacy Acts, 1890–1922 ; Mental Deficiency Acts, 1913–38 ; Mental Treatment Act, 1930.

but in the latter case the Crown can always stay proceedings by entering a *nolle prosequi*, and in any case not
one of personal wrongdoing, it would normally do so,
except of course where the crime alleged was one of
murder or manslaughter or serious bodily injury.

CHAPTER XIV

INTERNAL AFFAIRS

1. *Home Affairs*

(i) The Home Office

AT Queen Victoria's accession there were still only three Secretaries of State, for Home Affairs, for Foreign Affairs, for War and the Colonies, the first two representing the formal division of older commingling of functions by Mr. Fox in 1782, while the third Secretaryship of State was created in 1801 under the stress of the Napoleonic War. The Crimean War saw the creation by declaration in Council of a fourth office in 1854 ; India demanded a fifth in 1858 ; the Great War produced a Secretaryship for Air in 1918 ; the Dominions Secretaryship was formally created in 1925, that for Scotland in 1926, and that for Burma, held by the Secretary for India, in 1937. All Secretaries of State can in theory act for one another, unless the power is specifically given to one, but the Home Secretary pre-eminently maintains the position of having entrusted to him any work which does not obviously belong to any special department of State.

The Home Secretary is the channel of communication between the subject and the King in all matters not otherwise specially provided for, and thus receives and by royal instructions replies to all manner of addresses ; he receives petitions [1] and secures their reference to the suitable

---

[1] The right to petition the King is statutory under the Bill of Rights (1 Will. & Mar. sess. 2, c. 2).

department ; failing this, he causes a suitable reply to be sent, again on royal authority. It is to his department that there appertains the right to advise the Crown to grant or refuse a fiat to a petition of right asking that the High Court be permitted to entertain a claim on contract or other like matters.[1] By him are submitted to the King sign-manual warrants for many purposes, including the preparation of letters patent for the creation of peerages, though it is the Prime Minister who decides on the appointment. He is the channel of communication with the Convocations, and the Lieutenant-Governors in the Channel Islands and the Isle of Man and the Governor of Northern Ireland are in communication with him for the signification of the royal pleasure in regard to matters falling within the authority of the Imperial Government.

The Home Secretary has also important functions regarding the internal safety of the realm. He controls the naturalisation of aliens,[2] having absolute discretion to grant naturalisation or withhold it, and he has considerable range of discretion as to cancelling naturalisation under certain conditions. He also is concerned with the application of the legislation regarding aliens, and determines whether or not to deport undesirable aliens who are recommended for deportation, as well as questions of the admission of aliens.[3] He enforces the Foreign Enlistment Act, 1870, though in 1936 this duty was rather markedly neglected.[4] He also secures the due recognition of the privileges given to diplomatic agents under common law and by statute.

[1] As no remedy lies in law for refusal of a fiat it should not lightly be declined : *Irwin* v. *Grey* (1862), 3 F. & F. 635 ; *Ryves* v. *Duke of Wellington* (1846), 9 Beav. 579, 600 ; *Nathan, In re* (1884), 12 Q.B.D. at p. 479.

[2] British Nationality and Status of Aliens Acts, 1914–33.

[3] Aliens Restriction (Amendment) Act, 1919 (9 & 10 Geo. V. c. 92), and Aliens Orders in Council, 1920–31.

[4] Keith, *The King, the Constitution, the Empire, and Foreign Affairs, 1936–7*, pp. 162 ff.

The right to authorise the opening of letters in the post was exercised in 1844 by Sir James Graham [1] in circumstances which elicited much public feeling and resulted in investigation by a committee of the Commons whose report showed the necessity of such a power. It was again freely used in connection with Irish activities in 1882,[2] and on a very wide scale it was employed in the Great War, while in 1934 it was found useful in countering the clever devices used to enable non-patriotic Englishmen to take chances in the Irish sweepstakes, which involved a very considerable loss to Britain.[3] The control applies to telegraphic or telephonic communications, and he has powers to control the use of the telegraphs in case of emergency.[4]

Where he has reason to anticipate disorder, even if no tumult, riot, or felony has taken place, he may approve or put into operation arrangements for the appointment of special police. He can call on the Air Ministry, War Office, or Admiralty to supply forces to maintain order ; moreover whenever possible his approval should be obtained for the moving of forces at local requisition to meet disorder. The great powers of the Crown under the Emergency Powers Act, 1920, are essentially to be used on his recommendation. To him necessarily falls the work of maintaining secret service agents in case of any dangerous espionage or incitement of unrest. How serious these issues may be is shown by the increase of what in the Victorian era was a negligible sum to £180,000 in 1934–5, and £450,000 in 1938–9. One curious survival of formerly important powers which are often alluded to in eighteenth-century history is the right of the Secretary of State to commit suspected persons for treason or other offences

---

[1] Parker, *Graham*, i. chap. xiv. [2] 267 *Hansard*, 3 s. 294.
[3] Betting and Lotteries Act, 1934, s. 21.
[4] 26 & 27 Vict. c. 112, s. 52 ; 29 & 30 Vict. c. 3.

against the State.   All Privy Councillors now are placed in the commission of the peace for every county, but the Secretary of State enjoys this as an older power.

He supervises the execution of the Extradition Acts, 1870–1935. The principle which the Act of 1870 adopted is that it is contrary to the interests of Britain and foreign countries alike that criminals should escape justice by finding refuge in another country. On the other hand, certain doctrines had to be borne in mind, and to them effect is duly given. The right of political asylum was accepted as essentially worth preserving, so that in treaties with foreign States extradition for such crimes is banned ; [1] the Secretary of State, therefore, will not send instructions to a police magistrate or a justice to secure persons demanded for extradition by a foreign State if he holds that the crime is a political one, and if a person should be committed by a magistrate or justice for extradition, he will not be extradited ; moreover the Secretary of State has an unfettered discretion to refuse extradition. In any case the accused must always be given at least fifteen days within which he may secure by *habeas corpus* a judicial investigation of the regularity of the process. Should a criminal's extradition be obtained for one crime and he be tried for another, the British Government will remonstrate with the foreign power. The surrender of subjects is regulated by treaty ; it may be excluded, or be rendered purely facultative. In any case no criminal who has committed an offence punishable in England can be surrendered until he has been duly dealt with under English law.

He is concerned also with inter-Imperial extradition, provided for in the Fugitive Offenders Act, 1881, and it falls to him to authorise proceedings against aliens under the Territorial Waters Jurisdiction Act, 1878, and to

[1] *Castioni, In re*, [1891] 1 Q.B. 149 ; *Meunier, In re*, [1894] 2 Q.B. 415.

declare the limits of British jurisdiction in such areas
as the Bristol Channel, where the matter is not ruled by
statute.

He is responsible for the general control of the Metropolitan Police, whose district extends far beyond the
immediate London area, but from whose activities the City
is excepted. He recommends to the Crown the officers
of highest rank, Commissioner, Assistant Commissioners,
and the Receiver for the Metropolitan Police District. All
that appertains to their conditions of service must finally
be decided by him subject to the principles laid down by
statute which give powers of representation on many subjects to organisations representing the police.[1] He approves the appointment of the Commissioner of the City
Police and sanctions the regulations for that force. He
approves the appointment of the chief constables in the
counties and has wide powers of making regulations for
police forces in counties and boroughs alike, while by his
control of grants he can secure compliance with his views
on matters which he is not empowered directly to regulate
or which he deems it wiser to deal with indirectly.

The Home Secretary decides whether boroughs may
have separate commissions of the peace, and be given
separate Quarter Sessions ; in the latter case he appoints
the recorder, who presides ; he appoints also the assistant
judge of the London Sessions, and stipendiary magistrates
in boroughs, as well as the Metropolitan Police magistrates.
over whom his control is wide. He confirms appointments
of clerks to the justices.

Over prisons for the detention of prisoners pending trial
and on conviction the powers of the Home Secretary were
steadily developed by a series of statutes beginning in
1835 ; the first stage gave rights of inspection ; from **1865**

[1] The Police Act, 1919 (9 & 10 Geo. V. c. 46).

he could regulate, and from 1877 [1] he was placed in complete control of everything connected with prisons, all powers possessed by existing prison authorities, justices in session at common law, by statute or by charter, being transferred to him. Over convict prisons, which were provided for those sentenced to long periods of detention in lieu of the old punishment of transportation, he was from the first given full authority to regulate conditions, and licences to be at liberty were granted by the Crown on his advice; on revocation he was empowered to secure recapture by the issue of a warrant by a metropolitan magistrate, which was made executable anywhere in the United Kingdom and the Channel Islands. His power over prisoners, found insane on arraignment, or against whom a verdict of guilty but insane is returned, or who become insane in prison, is complete, and he appoints a council for the management of the State asylums at Broadmoor and Parkhurst.

The prerogative of pardon, discussed above, is exercised on the advice of the Home Secretary, whose responsibility in this field is by convention absolute. His knowledge of all matters affecting the detention of prisoners explains the very far-reaching character of the reforms in criminal law submitted in 1938–9 to Parliament, involving the abolition of the time-honoured distinction between penal servitude and imprisonment with or without hard labour, and the wider use of sentences of detention for remedial purposes, together with the abolition, contrary to the opinion of many judges, of the use of flogging except as a punishment for violent attacks made by prisoners, a curious exception.

The Home Secretary is also charged with control of approved schools. These under legislation beginning in

[1] 40 & 41 Vict. c. 21.

1908 [1] have superseded the old reformatory schools, which under legislation of 1866 were set up for the detention of young offenders under age sixteen, found guilty of offences normally punishable with penal servitude or imprisonment, and the industrial schools set up under legislation of 1857 for the care of children over age five, neglected or not under proper control, or vagrant, or in criminal associations. He safeguards the sending of children abroad for participation in theatrical and other performances.

To the Home Secretary still appertains the great subject of the Factory Acts and precautions regarding such dangerous substances as petroleum and explosive substances. Control of liquor licensing falls under the Home Office, which has limited powers regarding control of betting. Burials, cremation, and vivisection fall under its care, while it has powers regarding safety in theatres and cinematograph displays. Dangerous drugs, and the care of inebriates, prevention of cruelty to animals, and inspection of fire brigades are minor functions, while the duty of air-raid precautions is a recent development of the most remarkable magnitude.

Electoral registration and control of elections so far as exercised by the former Local Government Board, and then by the Ministry of Health, were given in 1921 to the Home Secretary.

The Secretary and Under-Secretary are on the Council for the State Management Districts for the few areas in Great Britain where control by the State of liquor sale was taken over during the war and is still retained. The great work of dealing with prisons is entrusted to a Prison Commission, while a Poison Board advises as to dangerous drugs.

[1] Children and Young Persons Act, 1933 ; Approved Schools Rules, July 28, 1933.

The events of 1938–9 caused special efforts to organise against the danger from air raids which had already been dealt with in a rather inadequate manner, as was admitted after public attention had been called to the matter by the crisis of September. Earl Winterton was for a time attached to the Home Office, and later the Lord Privy Seal was given the duty of supervising this branch of protection, which involves the grant of advice and assistance to local authorities in arranging both personnel and material to serve in event of attacks. Special stress was first laid on the provision of gas masks, then on fire-brigade services, then on the provision at a cost of £20,000,000 of shelters against aerial bombing, although experts claimed that deep trenches and large underground shelters alone could serve as useful protection. Wide powers are given to the Minister by the Civil Defence Act, 1939.

(ii) The Scottish Office

For Scotland the services of the Home Office were available from 1746 to 1885, although the burden was lightened by the aid given by the Lord Advocate, who in addition to services similar to those of the Attorney-General in England, acted as a Parliamentary Under-Secretary for Scottish business. The creation of a Secretary for Scotland was allowed in 1885,[1] but his elevation to the rank of a Secretary of State was delayed until 1926.[2] Originally appointed by sign-manual warrant, though made the keeper of the great seal of Scotland, he was appointed from 1892 by the delivery of the seal. In 1928 [3] he was given direct control of the departments of Health, Agriculture, and Prisons, formerly under Boards with some

[1] 48 & 49 Vict. c. 61.
[2] 16 & 17 Geo. V. c. 18, s. 1 ; Order in Council, July 26, 1926.
[3] 18 & 19 Geo. V. c. 34.

measure of independence, while in 1939 further reorganisa- tion gave him the position of controlling directly as an ordinary department Education, with regard to which he had acted as Vice-President of an imaginary committee of the Privy Council. Moreover, by degrees a complete measure of decentralisation of staff has taken place, under which the main departments have their headquarters in Edinburgh ; their heads have direct access to the minister in London, who, however, has an Under-Secretary there with some sort of advisory functions, whose evolution is uncertain.

There remain excepted from the authority of the Scottish Office certain matters including extradition, naturalisation, aliens, dangerous drugs, air-raid precautions, workmen's compensation, and certain powers as to factories, explosives, cruelty to animals, etc. These issues are excluded mainly on grounds of convenience, as is also the control of the Ministry of Agriculture with regard to diseases among animals. In this case it is clearly arguable that the risk of the spread of foot-and-mouth disease is such that it would be extremely unwise to risk delay in joint action ; still less is it desirable to create the possibility of different policies being adopted in the two countries regarding the treatment of the diseased animals.

The decentralisation of control, of course, has been effected solely as the result of constant pressure from Scottish opinion on the ground of the serious delay and inefficiency caused by the necessity of reference to London or visits of deputations thither, and as a means of countering the arguments derived thence by supporters of Home Rule for Scotland. No doubt the administrative improvements which have already resulted have proved completely justified.

(iii) The Irish Office

In the case of Ireland the completeness of union of administration, which existed in the case of Scotland prior to 1885, was never attained.[1] The Lord-Lieutenant remained at the head of the formal administration, acting under the control of the Home Secretary, while a Chief Secretary sitting in the Commons dealt with minor points which might be raised. But, with the growing activity of Government in social matters, the position of the Chief Secretary grew in importance, and as early as 1881 Sir W. Harcourt could explain[2] that, though the Home Secretary was the channel of communication between the Crown and the Lord-Lieutenant, he had no responsibility for details of Irish business, for which the Chief Secretary answered. For this purpose it became normal that he should be in the Cabinet as Irish affairs grew more and more important, though on occasion the Lord-Lieutenant instead had a place therein.[3] The settlement of 1920, which gave a limited local self-government to Northern Ireland, returned to the Home Secretary control of relations with that territory, while relations with the Irish Free State as a Dominion fell to the Dominions Secretary.

2. *The Ministries for Trade and Production*

(i) The Board of Trade

The commencement of Queen Victoria's reign saw the activities of Government mainly confined to the more

---

[1] The Privy Council of Scotland was abolished on Union; that of Ireland maintained, and is now continued in a degree in the Privy Council of Northern Ireland.

[2] 262 *Hansard*, 3 s. 22; Gardiner, *Harcourt*, i. 422 f.

[3] Sir H. Campbell-Bannerman was not in the Cabinet in 1885, and was not a member of the Committee of Cabinet which drafted the Home Rule Bill of 1886.

obvious duties of the conduct of foreign relations and the provision of internal order. The control of trade, so far as it was exercised at all, was in the hands of a Committee of the Council, constituted by an Order in Council of August 23, 1786, which included the great officers of State, the Archbishop of Canterbury, and the Speaker of the House of Commons. This reflected the earlier history of the Committee which, better known as the Board of Trade,[1] had been concerned in the main with the government of the colonies and to some extent with foreign trade. The Committee seldom met, but a President was declared in Council, and also until 1867 a Vice-President, and individuals were added on occasion for special purposes. Until 1840 its work was mainly consultative, as had been that of the old Board ; it collected statistics regarding trade, and was ready to advise the Foreign Office regarding commercial treaties and to report, when required, on colonial affairs to the Colonial Secretary. Lord Grey thus used it to report on constitutions for Australia and South Africa.[2] Moreover, as a relic of the activities of the old Board, it reported on colonial legislation prior to the decision being taken to allow it to stand or to disallow. In 1840 it began its work as an executive body, being called upon to settle and approve the by-laws of railway companies. In this capacity it came to exercise an administrative control over railways, harbours, shipping, and company organisation, and various other matters given to it by statute without any attempt at co-ordination. In 1862 the style of Board of Trade was formally accorded ;[3] in 1867 the Vice-President gave way to a Parliamentary Secretary. On the other hand its consultative functions waned. In

[1] Keith, *Const. Hist. of First British Empire*, pp. 273-7.

[2] 106 *Hansard*, 3 s. 1120.

[3] 24 & 25 Vict. c. 47, s. 65 ; Interpretation Act, 1889 (52 & 53 Vict. c. 63), s. 12.

Palmerston's [1] time it was consulted on trade negotiations, but Mr. Cardwell [2] thought it should advise only on matters arising out of those questions entrusted to it for executive purposes ; in the 'sixties the Treasury did not trouble to ask its advice on tariff changes ; in 1865 the Foreign Office established a special department to carry on correspondence on commercial matters with the representatives of foreign powers in London as well as with the Board of Trade, and in 1872 its consultative branch was discontinued, so little business was referred to it.

On the other hand, the Board superseded in 1851 an abortive Railway Commission ; the Merchant Shipping Act, 1854, conferred on it very numerous duties ; in 1866 the control of fisheries was made over to it by the Office of Works ; in 1872 it became responsible in lieu of the Emigration Commissioners for the administration of the Acts regulating the welfare of passengers. In 1883 the administrative business of bankruptcy proceedings was separated from the judicial and transferred to the Board, and in the same year the arrangements for the grant of patents for invention and manufactures were transferred from the Patents Commissioners,[3] who in 1852 were set up to deal with matters which obviously should be made the subjects of a procedure quite different from that of the issue of patents for other governmental purposes ; in 1852 applications still passed through nine different stages at seven offices in different parts of London, fees being exacted on each transaction. In 1886 the Commons accepted a proposal by Mr. Bradlaugh that there should be publication of statistics, collection of which had long been organised by the Board ; even for agriculture a voluntary system to ascertain acreage, crops, and livestock was

---

[1] *Parl. Pap.* 1864, vii. Q. 2450.   [2] *Ibid.* Q. 2581.
[3] L. Smith, *Board of Trade*, pp. 173, 195 ; 15 & 16 Vict. c. 83.

instituted, and the *Board of Trade Journal* began to publish commercial information and the tariffs of foreign States, of which records were duly kept.

The determination of the National Government in 1932 to adopt a system of protection added considerably to the functions of the Board, which, so long as free trade was in force, had been drastically limited and had only been increased when the Great War resulted in the commencement of safeguarding of industries under a carefully limited procedure. Among the specific powers granted to the Board is that of securing the imposition of discriminating duties against imports from countries which treat differentially British exports ; in 1934 this was effective in terminating discrimination practised by France. The Board is specially concerned in seeking advantages for British manufactures in trade agreements, both by facilitating exports and limiting imports likely to injure established industries, and has thus been deeply concerned in the Ottawa agreements with the Dominions and India, and the trade negotiations with Foreign countries, of which that with the United States in 1938 ranked as the most important.

The work of the Board has been extended by the necessity of close control and reorganisation of the mining industry, the decision having been made effective in 1938 to acquire for the State the ownership of mining rights, and to carry further the reorganisation of the coal-mining industry so as to allow of more economic production, the payment of larger profits and wages, and the provision of coal for consumption in industry and for domestic use at reasonable rates. The Board therefore has a Parliamentary Secretary for Mines, and is connected with a number of committees. Overseas trade is controlled by a Parliamentary Secretary, who is appointed by the Board and Foreign

Office jointly ; there is a special branch for the guarantee of exports credits, the sum for this purpose having been increased in 1939 to £75,000,000. Patents and industrial property, including merchandise marks, are under a Comptroller-General ; the department for Industries and Manufactures is associated with a Director of Gas Administration and a Controller of Standards, weights and measures being placed under the Board. There are departments for commercial relations and treaties ; statistics ; mercantile marine ; companies, with the winding up of which the Board is also charged ; bankruptcy ; finance ; establishment ; and general ; while the solicitor's department gives legal advice on all issues referred to it. The Board has an advisory committee and there are numerous committees for census of production, cinematograph films, the cotton-spinning industry, dyestuffs, merchandise marks, pilotage, prohibition of import of plumage, merchant shipping, miners' welfare, safety in mines, research, etc.

To the Coal Commission under the Act of 1938 [1] is given the duty of dealing with the compensation of £66,450,000 granted to owners of coal and coal rights, authority to borrow £76,450,000 being granted for that purpose. From July 1, 1942, as owners of the coal they must act in such manner as they think best for promoting the interests, efficiency, and better organisation of the coal-mining industry. The valuation of holdings is to be carried out by Central and Regional Valuation Boards appointed by the Board of Trade, while the amalgamation of colliery undertakings will fall to the functions of the Coal Commission. But compulsory amalgamations if opposed fall to be decided on by Select Committees of Parliament, and local authorities and other interests are assured the right to be heard in opposition.

[1] 1 & 2 Geo. V. c. 52.

(ii) The Ministry of Transport

Part of the functions of the Board of Trade passed in 1919 to a newly created Ministry of Transport.[1] The minister is of Cabinet rank under the Ministers of the Crown Act, 1937, and has a Parliamentary Secretary. The subjects transferred to him include railways, light railways, canals, waterways, and inland navigation ; tramways ; roads, bridges, and ferries ; vehicles and traffic ; harbours, docks, and piers. Roads formed the subject of the Road Traffic Act, 1930,[2] under which were established a set of twelve regional commissioners empowered to regulate traffic competition subject to appeal to the ministry, while in 1933 a further Act[3] established authorities to deal with the licensing of vehicles ; the minister appoints the members of the appeal tribunal which deals with appeals from their decisions. The ministry has also wide powers of making regulations under the Road and Rail Traffic Act, 1933, and the Road Traffic Act, 1934. The railways, which had been run by a committee of general managers under the Board of Trade during the war, were provided for by an Act of 1921 which set up an Amalgamation Tribunal under which they were consolidated into four great companies for Great Britain. The passenger traffic in the London area by rail and road fell to be governed under the London Passenger Traffic Act, 1933, by a new board ; regulations under the Act for various purposes may be made by the ministry. The main-line railways in the area do not fall under the Board, but co-ordination is supplied in some measure by the Standing Joint Committee on London transport, while the London and Home Counties Advisory Committee advises on the general problems of

---

[1] 9 & 10 Geo. V. c. 50.   [2] 20 & 21 Geo. V. c. 43.

[3] 23 & 24 Geo. V. c. 53.

transport in that area. There are also advisory committees on railways, rates, tramways, and roads. The
Trunk Roads Act, 1936, places on the ministry responsibility
for 4,500 miles of main roads, and it has powers under the
Restriction of Ribbon Development Act, 1935.

In 1919 five Electricity Commissioners,[1] appointed since
1920 by the Minister of Transport, were established to
co-ordinate the electrical industry, and in 1927 was set
up a Central Electricity Board [2] of a chairman and seven
members of financial and business experience, appointed by
the minister after consultation with local authorities, electricity companies, industry, transport, agriculture, and
labour. They were authorised to prepare a scheme which
might be confirmed by the Commission after hearing parties
interested with or without alteration. The Board supplies
electricity in bulk to electricity undertakers and railways.
The minister exercises through the Commission certain
powers of control over joint electricity authorities and
undertakers. He has an Advisory Committee.

The ministry is interested in the Railway Rates
Tribunal and the Road and Railway Appeal Tribunal, but
controls neither.

(iii) The Ministry of Agriculture and Fisheries

Like the Board of Trade, the Board of Agriculture
acquired powers from various sources. In 1868–9 the Privy
Council Office had a department for cattle plague, and
in 1877 powers were given to the Council in respect of
destructive insects, in especial the Colorado beetle, and
further Acts included the prevention of contagious diseases
in animals in the scope of the Committee, the Agricultural
Department, which was set up in 1883. In 1889 [3] a Board

---

[1] Electricity (Supply) Act, 1919, ss. 1, 39.
[2] *Ibid.* 1926.   [3] 52 & 53 Vict. c. 30.

nominally composed of high officers of State, with a President who could sit in Parliament, was established. In 1909 a Parliamentary Secretary was added.[1] The Board also took over the powers and duties of the Land Commissioners, who were charged with functions regarding the commutation of tithes, the enfranchisement of copyhold land, and the enclosure of commons, matters originally entrusted to distinct bodies of commissioners. The Land Commissioners also had power in respect of the authorisation of limited owners of land to secure advances thereon for drainage and other improvements, or to employ thus monies raised by sale of such land under the Settled Land Acts.

In 1889 the chief new power created was that concerned with the control of dogs, which was necessary to prevent the spread of rabies, and the injury done to livestock by straying animals. In 1903[2] the Board of Trade handed over the care of fisheries to the ministry which provided the loaves, and power was given to transfer to it from any other department duties in respect of agriculture, forests, or fisheries. In 1919 the Board, which was never a reality, disappeared, a ministry being created in lieu, but the Forestry Act, 1919,[3] provided for the development of forests, in view of their wholesale destruction in the war, which has impressed on the Government the necessity of regeneration of timber supplies, by a Forestry Commission, whose eight members are incorporated by letters patent and appointed by sign-manual warrant, and are subject only to a limited amount of Treasury control, being in the main free at discretion to employ the funds placed at their disposal to encourage reafforestation. The care of Crown

---

[1] 9 Edw. VII. c. 15.
[2] 3 Edw. VII. c. 31 ; 124 *Hansard*, 4 s. 222.
[3] Charter, S. R. & O. 1920 (No. 646), i. 748.

F

woods passed to them from the Commissioners of Crown
Lands under an Act of 1923.[1]

During the war a Food Production Department had
been established to stimulate, with the aid of advisory
committees throughout the country, the extension of the
production of all kinds of foodstuffs. In 1931 the ministry
commenced to plan for agriculture a definite organisation
and assistance, which was in harmony with the contemporary determination to regulate imports. The Act of
1931 [2] aimed at the creation of machinery for the organisation and distribution of any given commodity by a
majority of those producing it, despite the objections of
a minority. A further Act of 1933 [3] provided for the
co-operation of the Board of Trade with the ministry. The
Board may impose restriction of agricultural imports if it,
in conjunction with the ministry, is satisfied that only thus
can a marketing scheme for such products be made effective,
and the ministry is empowered to appoint certain members
to marketing boards for the organisation of trade in special
products. Schemes are prepared either by producers or
the Agricultural Marketing Reorganisation Commission,
and registered producers vote for their acceptance or otherwise ; when accepted, they bind minorities. Such Marketing Boards have been set up for bacon, for which there is
also a Development Board, hops, milk, pigs, and potatoes.
Loans may be made to a Board on the advice of the
Agricultural Marketing Facilities Committee. Provision is
made for the minister to establish if necessary a Consumers'
Committee to watch interests of consumers, and, to investigate complaints not dealt with by it, a Committee of
Investigation. For herring a Herring Industry Board
exists ; it does not quite agree in constitution with the

---

[1] 13 & 14 Geo. V. c. 21, s. 1.   [2] 21 & 22 Geo. V. c. 42.
[3] 23 & 24 Geo. V. c. 31.

ordinary Marketing Board.[1] For wheat growers, who are specially favoured by arrangements for a levy on imports whence payments are made, a Wheat Commission controls the fund ; extension of aid to growers of oats and barley and in respect of cattle and sheep has already been necessary.

The ministry controls the somewhat limited powers of local authorities as to agriculture, and must approve their schemes for the composition of the agricultural committees they are intended to appoint. It controls also the special authorities locally charged with dealing with land drainage and fisheries. The Ordnance Survey is under it, as well as the Royal Botanic Gardens at Kew.

The ministry has abundant advisory assistance, an Agricultural Advisory Council, Councils of Agriculture for England and Wales, a Livestock Advisory Committee, a Fertilisers and Feeding Stuffs Committee, a Land Fertility Committee, a White Fish Commission, a Committee on Grants to Unemployed Persons, etc. An Agricultural Wages Board determines minimum wages for agriculturists through local committees.

(iv) The Ministry of Labour

Labour in general is cared for by the Ministry of Labour constituted under the New Ministers and Secretaries Act, 1916. It had been found necessary in the war to pass the Munitions of War Act, 1915, and drastically to limit the rights of labour as regards place of employment, control of wages, and the right to strike, while corresponding control was placed on profits and the right to lock-out taken away. In August 1917 the Ministry of National Service was created to secure a due appropriation of men as between military and civil requirements. The powers of

---

[1] Herring Industry Act, 1938 (1 & 2 Geo. VI. c. 42) ; *Parl. Pap.* Cmd. 5762.

the Ministry of Labour are in part taken from the Board of Trade, in part new powers, the outcome of experience of war conditions. The minister controls Labour Exchanges, the promotion of conciliation and arbitration in industrial matters under the Industrial Courts Act, 1919, and, since 1917, the working of the Trade Boards [1] system under which wages are fixed for employees in industries with low wage rates ; already the Coal Mines (Minimum Wage) Act, 1912, had made provision for the fixing of minimum wages in that industry, and in 1924 the system was extended under the Ministry of Agriculture to agricultural workers. The London Passenger Transport Wages Board is concerned with the wages of employees on that great system. It falls to the minister to decide whether to set up enquiries into industrial disputes with a view to assisting their settlement by bringing to bear on them the weight of public opinion ; compulsory arbitration has not yet been provided by law, but in various industries, including the railway industry, systems of conciliation have been highly elaborated.

Unemployment is provided for in two ways. There is Unemployment Insurance, with regard to which the minister is advised by the Unemployment Insurance Statutory Committee under the Unemployment Insurance Act, 1935. It is chiefly concerned with the solvency of the Insurance Fund and its obligations to the insured persons and the State, and it advises on draft orders and regulations submitted by the ministry. The minister appoints also the umpire and the deputy umpires, who give decisions under the Act on claims to benefit, and is concerned with the appointment of the courts of referees under the Act, from whom appeal lies to the umpire. The ministry is concerned also with the administration of schemes for the

[1] Trade Boards Acts, 1909 and 1918.

training of unemployed workers, advice to juvenile workers, their transfer to areas where employment can be found, and their training, and the sums voted to aid employment schemes (£3,520,000 in 1938–9). For other persons provision is made by the Unemployment Assistance Board under the Act of 1934, which is not under the control of the minister, but whose regulations require approval by Parliament. The minister is the authority for the grant of permits to foreigners to undertake work in the United Kingdom, publishes statistics collected by his direction on labour matters of many kinds, and with other departments is responsible for British governmental action in connection with the International Labour Organisation under the treaties of peace.

3. *The Ministries for Social Welfare*

(i) The Board of Education

Education was in 1833 encouraged to the meagre extent of £20,000 a year, voted by Parliament for disbursement by the Treasury in aid of voluntary contributions in support of public elementary education. In 1839 the sum was raised to £30,000 and entrusted to a Committee of the Privy Council. In 1856 by statute the creation of a Vice-President of the Committee with power to sit in Parliament was permitted.[1] In 1899 [2] the position was altered ; there was constituted a Board on the analogy of the Board of Agriculture, with a President and a Parliamentary Secretary, thus giving a minister for both houses if desired ; the Lord President of the Council, who until 1899 could act for the Committee, may represent the Board in the Lords if both ministers happen to be in the Commons. The Act of 1899 gave power, by Order in Council, to transfer

[1] 19 & 20 Vict. c. 116.   [2] 62 & 63 Vict. c. 33.

to the Board the authority of the Charity Commissioners regarding educational charities, and it now lies with the Board to adapt from time to time such charities to meet emergent needs, while the Commissioners retain the right to decide what charities are in whole or part educational.[1]

The evolution of the Board was hampered by the limited character of its functions as dispensing money ; objection to the abolition of the Committee of Council was opposed by Mr. Lowe on the score that it was not desirable that a minister unaided should deal with considerable sums by way of grant. But it became desirable to adopt a more effective system when, from 1888, there arose an over-lapping between the work done by the school boards created by the Education Act, 1870,[2] to supply elementary education, under the control of the Committee, and that done by the county councils, created in 1888, in the way of technical education under the Science and Art Department. The Bryce Commission recommended the placing of the whole subject under one head, and thus the Board was evolved.

Under the legislation of 1870–76 [3] elementary education became compulsory and was further regulated in 1902–3, 1918, and 1921,[4] while higher education has been placed largely within the reach of all qualified to profit by it ; the raising of the school age to fifteen gives the opportunity for a great improvement in the scientific organisation of instruction so that scientific and technical studies can secure just consideration on a footing of equality with secondary education of the grammar-school type. The control of the Board depends essentially on its powers to make grants,

[1] Orders in Council, Aug. 7, 1900 ; July 24, 1901 ; Aug. 11, 1902.
[2] 33 & 34 Vict. c. 75.   [3] 39 & 40 Vict. c. 79.
[4] 2 Edw. VII. c. 42 ; 3 Edw. VII. c. 24 ; 8 & 9 Geo. V. c. 39 ; 11 & 12 Geo. V. c. 51 ; 26 Geo. V. & 1 Edw. VIII. c. 41 ; L. A. S. Bigge, *The Board of Education.*

which are rendered conditional on the local authorities
(since 1902, the county councils, county borough councils,
and in certain cases urban district councils) complying
with the rules laid down in the code of the Board regarding
the subjects to be taught, the staffing of schools, the qualifications of teachers, and the size and sanitary condition
of the buildings. To voluntary schools brought into the
State system aid from the rates was extended under the
Act of 1902, leaving on their managers only a limited
obligation regarding fabric and maintenance, and even
towards these ends governmental aid has been given. The
Board has powers to decide issues between local authorities
and the managers of voluntary, non-provided schools,
and to determine what numbers of schools shall be maintained. Higher educational establishments are in part controlled through the system of offering grants. For teachers
a registration council was set up in 1907 and reconstituted
in 1926 ; by the grant regulations the training and tenure
of office of teachers are widely affected, and a contributory
superannuation scheme provides for pensions. The functions of the Board demand a very large inspectorate for
elementary schools, secondary schools, technical and continuation schools, training colleges, domestic subjects, art,
special schools which are provided for blind, deaf, and
dumb, epileptic and defective children, and physical exercises. Appropriately the National Fitness Council for
England and Wales is attached to the Board. The Royal
College of Art, the Victoria and Albert Museum, and the
Bethnal Green Museum are under its authority, and it
is connected with the Imperial War Museum. Over the
Universities it has no control, for the grants made thereto
are determined by the Treasury on the advice of a University Grants Committee.

The Act of 1899 provided for a Consultative Committee

which, as constituted by an Order in Council of July 22, 1920, was continued in being by the Act of 1921. This body has powerfully influenced the Board in its educational policy both as regards secondary and elementary education.

In order to meet Welsh demands for distinct consideration of the conditions of that bilingual land, there is a separate inspectorate for Wales and a Permanent Secretary of the Welsh Department.[1]

Medical inspection of school children is provided for by arrangement between the Minister of Health and the Board. The chief medical officer holds that position in the Ministry of Health, thus eliminating friction.

Control over approved schools which replace the former industrial schools is still vested in the Home Office. These schools are for the reception and care of children found destitute or begging, or in bad surroundings, or convicted of offences, or persistent in truancy from school and beyond parental control.

(ii) The Ministry of Health

The beginnings of governmental assistance to public health and the poor law were modest. In 1834 the scandals of poor relief administration compelled the setting up of three Poor Law Commissioners who were not responsible to Parliament, and who, when assailed, were unable themselves to reply. This led to their supersession by a Poor Law Board with a Parliamentary head, which in effect meant that the work fell to Civil servants. The connection between poverty and ill-health was revealed by the reports of the Poor Law Commission, and in 1848 Mr. Chadwick secured the creation of a Board of Health for five years, with the head of the Office of Woods and Forests, an unpaid

---

[1] For Mr. Lloyd George's rash suggestion of a minister for Wales, resented by the King, see Lee, ii. 455 f.

member, and two paid members. In 1854 this body, whose activities had annoyed many susceptibilities, was reconstituted under a President and *ex officio* members, but in 1858 it was dissolved as a result of friction between its members, and its health functions went to the Privy Council, and its local government work to the Home Office. The Royal Sanitary Commission of 1871 pointed out that the unity of control of poor law and public health was imperative in view of their interaction, and the ministry created the Local Government Board to consist of the Lord President, the Secretaries of State, the Chancellor of the Exchequer, and a President and a Secretary who might sit in Parliament.[1] To it was given the work in public health of the Council, in local government of the Home Office, in poor relief of the Poor Law Board; the poor-law aspect of the work of the department for long worked the more efficiently.

Legislation, however, provided for extensive activities on the part of progressive local authorities, in the shape of Public Health Acts, Isolation Hospital Acts, Artisans' Dwellings Acts, and Acts as to the sale of food and drugs. In 1911 there was created a vast system of public health insurance under separate Commissions for England, Wales, Scotland, and Ireland. The Poor Law Commission in 1909 urged wise extensions of activity regarding public health, mental deficiency, poor law, unemployment insurance, and old-age pensions. In 1913 the Board of Control, which took the place of the Lunacy Commissioners, stressed the importance of public health. The Midwives Act, 1902, gave to the Privy Council the approval of rules of the Central Midwives Board regarding the conduct and qualifications of midwives, while the Children Act, 1908, gave to the Home Office responsibility in respect of infant life protection.

[1] 34 & 35 Vict. c. 70.

Chapter
XIV.
———

The Haldane Committee in 1918 stressed the necessity of creating a Ministry of Health with wider outlook, and this step was taken in 1919,[1] a Minister of Health and a Parliamentary Secretary being assigned to the new department, which took over the work of the Local Government Board and the Insurance Commissions ; the control of the machinery of elections was transferred more suitably to the Home Office in 1921. The importance of its functions was increased by the reorganisation of local government by the Local Government Act, 1929, which abolished the Boards of Guardians who had administered the poor law locally, assigning the functions to the county and county borough councils, and at the same time made a momentous change in the system of central grants and rating. The necessities of agriculture had led already to derating, and now the necessities of export trade, which was hampered also by the heavy burden of rates in depressed areas, led to the decision to derate agricultural land entirely and by three-fourths industrial hereditaments and freight transport. To make up to the local authorities the loss from rates and from the discontinuance of certain specific grants-in-aid, amounting to £40,000,000 in all, there was accorded a general Exchequer contribution of £45,000,000 to be distributed according to a formula which was devised to take account of the special needs of each area. At the same time the ministry was given wider powers to vary the grant to any authority which failed to develop properly its health services or spent money unwisely, a system held to be superior to that in which specific grants alone were provided for.

The ministry is concerned with the administration of the Widows', Orphans', and Old Age Contributory Pensions Scheme, and with appeals under the non-contributory Old Age Pensions Scheme. In its concern with health insur-

[1] 9 & 10 Geo. V. c. 21 ; Sir A. Newsholme, *The Ministry of Health.*

ance it has the advice of the National Health Insurance Joint Committee, which includes the ministers responsible in England, Scotland, and Northern Ireland. There is also a Therapeutic Substances Joint Committee. An important aspect of its work is connected with housing and town planning, the destruction of slums, and the prevention of overcrowding ; there is a Town and Country Advisory Committee and a Central Housing Advisory Committee. The ministry also supervises the audit of local authorities' accounts, though boroughs may retain for expenditures not out of Government grants their own audit.

Certain functions are delegated to the Welsh Board of Health. The General Register Office, which registers births, marriages, and deaths, and the Board of Control, which deals with lunatics and mental deficients, are subordinate to the minister, who controls also the Pathological Laboratory and the Government Lymph Establishment. The minister has powers in respect of water supply over public utility companies as well as local authorities, and in respect of housing over such companies. He is connected with the Central Midwives Board and the registration of nurses.

(iii) The Ministry of Pensions

The Ministry of Pensions owes its origin to the necessity of establishing a system for dealing with those injured in the Great War and for making provision for the maintenance of their dependants. Much of this work has been directed towards the rehabilitation, as far as possible, of those who suffered in body or mind during the war, while efforts have been made to employ to the best advantage the sums allocated for the benefit of children. The ministry was established by the Ministry of Pensions Act, 1916, and an Act of 1917 provided for a Special Grants Committee, while there is a Central Advisory Committee and local

Pensions Committees, in order as far as possible to de-
centralise the work. There are Ministry Appeal Tribunals
and Pensions Appeal Tribunals, the latter independent of
the ministry.

4. *The Commissioners of Works and Public Buildings*

In 1832 [1] the control of His Majesty's works and public
buildings was taken out of the hands of the Surveyor-
General, who had in 1814 [2] been appointed to deal with
these works, whether the cost was defrayed from the civil
list or from Parliamentary funds. Their control was given
to the Commissioners, who were charged with the care
of the woods, forests, and land revenues of the Crown.
Naturally enough, the Commissioners applied the revenues
which accrued towards the provision of buildings and the
maintenance of royal parks, without troubling to obtain
Parliamentary sanction for this treatment of the revenues.
In 1851 [3] there was a change made. The expenses of the
Commissioners of Woods and Forests were to be defrayed
by Parliament, while the revenues they collected were to
be paid to the Exchequer, and a new Board of Works
and Public Buildings was set up with a First Commissioner
who may sit in the Commons, while the Secretaries of
State and the President of the Board of Trade were also
made members; this body, of course, must apply to
Parliament for funds. The First Commissioner is appointed by sign-manual warrant; the Board never meets,
though it could do so in emergency if the office of First
Commissioner were vacant.

The minister is responsible for royal palaces and parks,
for all governmental buildings, unless special provision
otherwise is made, and for oversea legations. He controls

[1] 2 & 3 Will. IV. c. 1.   [2] 54 Geo. III. c. 157.   [3] 14 & 15 Vict. c. 42.

the Crown interests in Epping Forest,[1] can erect or repair statues in the Metropolitan Police district,[2] and has the supervision of ancient monuments,[3] and the Royal Botanic Garden, Edinburgh. His former control of the geological survey is exercised [4] by the Department of Scientific and Industrial Research.

5. *Minor Non-political Departments*

There are a considerable number of departments of considerable importance in many ways, but of essentially non-political character. For many of them the Treasury is responsible in so far as it presents estimates for them, and therefore controls their expenditure and must answer in Parliament if any serious issue arose concerning them. But normally they raise no political issues.

They include the British Museum, which has a very distinguished Board of Trustees ; the Meteorological Office, which is under the administrative control of the Air Ministry ; the Royal Mint ; the Civil Service Commission, whose functions in respect of the Civil Service are mentioned elsewhere ; the London Gazette Office ; the National Gallery and National Portrait Gallery ; the Wallace Collection ; the Record Office, with its amazing collection of records under the control of the Master of the Rolls ; the Stationery Office, whose Controller is under letters patent the King's Printer of Acts of Parliament, and who superintends the supply of books, etc., to public offices and secures the carrying out of the great amount of printing demanded ; the Central Registry Office for Friendly Societies ; the Government Actuary, etc.

[1] 29 & 30 Vict. c. 62, s. 6. [2] 17 & 18 Vict. c. 33.
[3] 3 & 4 Geo. V. c. 32 ; 21 & 22 Geo. V. c. 16.
[4] Since Nov. 1, 1919.

The Exchequer and Audit Department is under Treasury control as regards salaries, etc., of the staff exclusive of the Comptroller and Auditor-General. The Central Valuation Committee is constituted under the Rating and Valuation Act, 1925, to secure some uniformity on valuation of property for rating purposes ; its members are appointed by the Minister of Health, and the associations representing the county councils, the municipal corporations, the urban district councils, and the rural district councils. The Development Commissioners were established under Acts of 1909 and 1910, and make grants from funds placed at their disposal by Parliament for the development of agriculture and rural industries, the drainage and reclamation of land, harbours, and fisheries ; their grants are subject to Treasury control. The Forestry Commission is noticed elsewhere.

The National Debt Office was first constituted in 1786 for the purpose of dealing with the sinking funds for the National Debt ; since then it has been entrusted under statute with the investment and financial management of many public funds, including those of the savings banks, local loans fund, national health and unemployment insurance funds, Irish land fund, etc. The Commissioners include the Governor and Deputy Governor of the Bank of England, while the office is under the charge of a Comptroller-General ; while not technically under the Treasury, the fact that the Chancellor of the Exchequer is a Commissioner ensures due control and there is liaison with the Bank of England. The Public Works Loan Board was created in 1817 to make advances to municipal authorities for local works ; of recent years it has advanced very considerable sums, especially for housing. The National Savings Committee dates from the organisation of war savings under Treasury authority, and the Trustee Savings Banks Inspection Committee was established under the Savings Banks Act, 1891, to investigate the accounts of Trustee Savings Banks.

The Treasury has as subordinate departments those of H.M. Procurator-General and Solicitor to the Treasury, of King's and Lord Treasurer's Remembrancer, Edinburgh, and the Parliamentary Counsel, now numbering five with assistant counsel. It controls also the King's Proctor, who deals with divorce questions demanding governmental intervention.

The Land Registry was established in 1862 and increased in importance by the Land Transfer Act, 1897, under which registration of land on sale was made compulsory in the administrative county of London ; it has been extended to Middlesex, Eastbourne, and Hastings, and the procedure is consolidated in the Land Registration Act, 1925. The office is controlled by the Lord Chancellor, who is also in authority over the office of the Public Trustee established in 1908 to undertake work similar to that of a private trustee.

The office of the Director of Public Prosecutions is subject to the control of the Attorney-General.

Trinity House is under charter and statute the authority for the administration of the lighthouse and sea-marks service of England and Wales, with certain statutory jurisdiction regarding Scotland, Ireland, the Channel Islands, and Gibraltar ; it is also the chief pilotage authority in the United Kingdom, while, as a charitable corporation, it administers certain trusts for the benefit of aged and distressed mariners and their dependants. The cost of administration of lighthouses is defrayed from a fund raised by dues on ships using the ports of the United Kingdom. The Elder Brethren are in part men of high distinction in the State, in part active mariners, who sit as assessors in the Probate, Divorce, and Admiralty Division of the High Court in marine causes.

Of many minor offices may be noted those of the Duchy of Cornwall, which appertain to the King when there is no male heir-apparent ; there is a council, a solicitor, and a sheriff. The Duchy of Lancaster appertains to the King ; Edward VII insisted on his right to the style against the views of Lord James of Hereford.[1] The Chancellor is a minor minister, drawing £2000 from the Duchy funds if not in the Cabinet. There is an Attorney-General and Solicitor, a Receiver-General, and Auditor. The net revenue in 1937 allowed of £85,000 being paid to the Crown. For the County Palatinate of Durham there are an Attorney-General and a Solicitor-General, and a Chancellor of the Court, while in Lancaster the office is filled by a Vice-Chancellor, these two courts having been left untouched when the courts of pleas were merged in the jurisdiction of the High Court.

Three survivals of ancient pageantry exist in the College of Arms, of which the head is the Duke of Norfolk ; [2] there are three kings of arms, six heralds, and four pursuivants. The power of the College on the grant and use of armorial bearings can no longer be made effective by the jurisdiction of the constable and marshal,[3] and, therefore, is not coercive. It is otherwise with the Court of the Lord Lyon in Scotland, whose authority is still valid in law and can be enforced by his court ; there are three heralds and three pursuivants, who serve to render ornamental formal proclamations in Edinburgh, while the fees exacted on the grant of arms help to make good the salary which is provided

---

[1] Lee, *Edward VII*, ii. 298, n. 1.

[2] He was specially allowed, though a Roman Catholic, to exercise his functions by 5 Geo. IV. c. 109.

[3] *Chambers* v. *Jennings* (1702), 7 Mod. 125. The last case recorded is *Sir H. Blount's Case* (1737), 1 Atk. 296.

from public funds ; happily the Court of Session has negatived any right of the court to determine the headship of
clans, thus preventing heroic legal battles over an issue
of no public value whatever. There is still an Ulster King
of Arms at the Castle, Dublin, and two heralds.

The Charity Commissioners were created as the outcome
of long consideration in 1853.[1] A Parliamentary Commission had investigated the condition of charities from
1818 to 1837, and a Select Committee of the Commons in
1835 examined its report, while in 1849 a Royal Commission was set up to consider the final report of the Commission of 1818. The essential difficulty was that for any
change in the treatment of the capital of a trust or in the
use of the income thereof, reference had to be made to
the slow process of Chancery, while there was unavoidable
difficulty in securing the due maintenance of bodies of
trustees ready to fulfil the purposes of the trust. In 1853,
therefore, the Crown was authorised by sign-manual
warrant to appoint four commissioners, three to hold during
good behaviour and one during pleasure and without pay,
so as to be eligible to speak for the commissioners in the
Commons. In 1874 [2] the work of the Endowed Schools
Commission was handed over, two more commissioners
being appointed, and in 1883 two more were added under
the City Parochial Charities Act.[3] War charities were
brought under their scope in 1916,[4] and in 1920 [5] their
powers under that Act were applied to charities for the
blind. In 1860 [6] they were given the power to frame new
schemes for effecting the intention of founders when circumstances change ; in such cases an appeal lies to the

[1] 16 & 17 Vict. c. 137 ; 18 & 19 Vict. c. 124.
[2] 37 & 38 Vict. c. 87. See for powers transferred, 32 & 33 Vict. c. 56 ;
36 & 37 Vict. c. 87. [3] 46 & 47 Vict. c. 36.
[4] 6 & 7 Geo. V. c. 43. [5] 10 & 11 Geo. V. c. 49.
[6] 23 & 24 Vict. c. 136 ; 32 & 33 Vict. c. 110.

Chancery Division.[1] In 1899 educational charities were made transferable by Order in Council to the Board of Education, from which an appeal lies to the Privy Council in case of dispute.[2] There are now two paid commissioners and a Parliamentary commissioner, unpaid.

An interesting modern development is the Racecourse Betting Control Board, established under the Racecourse Betting Act, 1928, to set up and control the operation of totalisators in England and Scotland. The profits thence are devoted for the improvement of the breeds of horses, the sport of horse-racing, and the promotion of veterinary science and education. The Home Secretary approves the use made, and appoints a member of the Board, while other members are appointed by other departments and by the Jockey Club and other institutions concerned with racing.

Research at governmental cost is provided by a number of organisations, of which the most important is the Department of Scientific and Industrial Research. A Committee of the Privy Council was created by Order in Council of July 28, 1915, since amended on February 6, 1928, to direct the application of any sums of money provided by Parliament for the organisation and development of scientific and industrial research. By a charter of November 23, 1916, amended by a further charter of April 27, 1928, the members of the Committee were incorporated as " The Imperial Trust for the Encouragement of Scientific and Industrial Research," and on December 15, 1916, a separate department with its own vote was created for the service of the Committee. The Order in Council of 1915 established an Advisory Committee to whom all proposals for researches stand referred. The Lord President of the

---

[1] *Campden Charities, In re* (1881), 18 Ch. D. 310.
[2] *St. Leonard, Shoreditch, Parochial Schools, In re* (1885), 10 App. Cas. 304.

Council is also President of the Committee. In 1918 the National Physical Laboratory was taken over from the Royal Society and its work widely expanded. The department provides for building research, chemical research, food investigation, forest products research, fuel, radio, road, and water pollution research, and the Geological Survey and Museum of Practical Geology are under the department. Under the National Health Insurance Act there was established in 1913 a Medical Research Committee,[1] which by royal charter, on April 1, 1920, became the Medical Research Council, which is under the administrative direction of a Committee of Council consisting of the Lord President, the Minister of Health, and the Secretaries of State for Home Affairs, Dominion Affairs, the Colonies, and Scotland. The members of the Council are mainly experts, and the Council secures that money obtained from Parliament or private sources is effectively devoted to research.[2]

6. *The Legal Departments*

The Lord Chancellor remains one exception to the general rule that all offices of the ministry are open to persons of any religion. It seems probable that he may not be a Roman Catholic, perhaps that he may not be a Jew. He is also an exception to the rule that executive office should not be combined with judicial functions. He is normally selected because of legal capacity, combined with important political services usually in legal office as a member of the Commons, as in the case of Lords Halsbury, Loreburn, Haldane, Cave, Birkenhead, and Hailsham.

[1] 1 & 2 Geo. V. c. 55, s. 16 (2); 9 & 10 Geo. V. c. 21, s. 3; Order in Council, March 11, 1920 (S. R. & O. 1919, ii. 8).

[2] Cf. Dugdale, *Balfour*, ii. 371 f.

The case of Lord Sankey in 1929 and of Lord Maugham in 1938 were unusual, but in the latter instance its occupant in office showed himself an energetic supporter of ministerial foreign policy. The objections to the holding of executive and judicial office are lessened by the fact that the Lord Chancellor does not preside at criminal trials in issues affecting the ministry, but he does preside at discussions in the Privy Council of actions ordered by the ministry, and his position in that regard is open to serious criticism.[1] The propriety of setting up a Ministry of Justice to deal with all non-judicial business now performed by the Lord Chancellor can hardly be denied. The burden of both functions must disable the minister for the full study of the numerous problems which would properly fall to be dealt with by such a minister.

In addition to his judicial functions in the House of Lords and the Privy Council, described elsewhere, the Chancellor recommends the appointment of puisne judges and may be consulted by the Prime Minister in regard to other judicial appointments. He appoints the Justices of the Peace and can remove them ; he obtains the advice of Lord-Lieutenants, who, again, are aided by committees in recommending suitable persons with a view to representation impartially of the community, but he need not take the advice tendered. He is also responsible for the appointment and removal of county court judges ; in this and in the appointment to benefices valued at not above £20 a year *temp.* Henry VIII he acts without actual reference to the King, to whom normally appointments[2] to Crown offices are formally submitted by the responsible minister.

He is served by the Crown Office in Chancery, whose

[1] Cf. *Marais (D. F.), Ex parte,* [1902] A. C. 109 ; *Sammut* v. *Strickland,* [1938] A.C. 678.

[2] The Prime Minister has the other patronage : Spender, *Lord Oxford,* ii. 379.

Clerk is appointed by sign-manual warrant and claims to be first Clerk of England. He sees to the issue of writs for elections, receives and lists the returns, attends in the House of Lords to read the lists of Acts to be assented to, when the Clerk of the Parliaments pronounces the words of formal assent ; he attends in the court when the sheriffs are chosen and notes those selected ; he appends his signature to documents bearing the great seal as proof that there has been due warrant. Full powers to sign treaties and ratification thereof are, however, excepted from his activities.

The Lord Chancellor is in charge of the County Courts department which deals with the administrative work of the county courts, but the judges control much of the work of the Central Office of the Supreme Court. He is a member of the Rule Committee of the Supreme Court, and he confirms the rules made by the Rule Committee of the county courts.

The Land Registry and the Public Trustee's Office are subject to his authority, and he appoints, or shares in the appointment of, members of various tribunals with semi-judicial powers and of certain arbitrators, as under the Electricity (Supply) Act, 1926. He has the power to remove coroners.

His functions as Speaker of the House of Lords, in respect of which he receives £4000 salary in addition to £6000 judicial salary, are dealt with elsewhere.

As it is no longer customary to appoint a Keeper of the Great Seal, the office has only theoretic importance. If the Chancellor is out of England, it is customary to appoint commissioners in whose charge the great seal remains until he returns to exercise his duty as custodian.

The Law officers, the Attorney-General, and the Solicitor-General, are now essentially political officers who must

sit in the Commons to aid the Government. They advise
the Cabinet or individual departments when they are asked
to do so ; they defend the legality of governmental actions
in Parliament. Moreover, they act for the Crown in regard
to the prosecution of offenders in important cases of public
interest ; [1] the office of the Director of Public Prosecutions
is subject to the control of the Attorney-General.

In a large number of cases the authority of the Attorney-
General is requisite as a condition of proceedings being
taken, as under the Official Secrets Acts, 1911 and 1920,
the Prevention of Corruption Act, 1906, the Public Order
Act, 1936, the Summary Procedure (Domestic Proceedings) Act, 1937, the Coinage Offences Act, 1936, the Explosive Substances Act, 1883, the Foreign Marriage Act, 1892,
the Geneva Convention Acts, 1911 and 1937, the Punishment of Incest Act, 1908, and the Solicitors Act, 1932. He
is empowered, under the Trade Disputes and Trade Unions
Act, 1927, to secure that funds of unions may not be
employed in furthering illegal strikes, and his permission
is necessary for the determination by the House of Lords
of a criminal appeal dealt with by the Court of Criminal
Appeal. The Solicitor-General is usually authorised to
exercise the powers of his senior, when the latter is unable
or finds it inconvenient to act. Both law officers are put in
the Commission of the Peace for each county.

It is not unusual to place the Attorney-General in the
Privy Council, and in 1913 both law officers enjoyed that
distinction. Occasionally, as in 1912 when Sir R. Isaacs
was placed in the Cabinet, and when in 1924 Sir D. Hogg
was given that rank, the Attorney-General is admitted to
the full position of a member of the body which directs

[1] They can also stop any prosecution by intimating a *nolle prosequi* :
R. v. *Allen* (1862), 1 B. & S. 850 ; even after verdict : *R.* v. *Leatham* (1861),
7 Jur. (N.S.) 674. Before a petition of right is allowed to proceed, the
Attorney-General advises under the Petitions of Right Act, 1860.

general policy. But that is not normally the case, and there is a rather strong view that the law officers should not be in the Cabinet ; no doubt it is preferable to obtain legal advice which cannot be deemed to be affected directly by knowledge of its implications.[1]

In Scotland the law officers are the Lord Advocate and the Solicitor-General, of whom the former must, the latter may, be in the House of Commons. They have functions analogous to those of the English law officers, but it must be remembered that in Scotland all criminal prosecutions are conducted by officers of the Crown.

---

[1] Birkenhead, *Birkenhead,* ii. 112. During the war the Attorney-General had been for convenience in the Cabinet, but not in 1919. The salaries are now £4500 and £4000 *plus* fees.

CHAPTER XV

THE TREASURY AND THE NATIONAL REVENUE AND EXPENDITURE

1. *The Treasury*

SINCE 1714 the office of Lord High Treasurer has been in commission, the Crown by letters patent appointing from time to time Commissioners who are the First Lord of the Treasury, the Chancellor of the Exchequer, and a number of junior lords, now normally five. The Board originally met for discussion of matters brought before it, but in the nineteenth century, owing to pressure of business, this became impossible and the meetings of the Board became formal. In 1827 the First Lord and the Chancellor ceased to attend, and in 1856 the junior Lords gave up what had long been an idle form. Their duties became essentially those of Whips as defined by Mr. Canning, " to make a house, keep a house, and cheer the minister ", though two Lords sign a certain number of documents.

The appointment of the junior Lords was made on the nomination of the First Lord from 1711, and the First Lord from the time of Sir R. Walpole normally was also Prime Minister. Exceptions to that combination of offices appeared only in exceptional cases — Lord Salisbury in 1885, 1887, and 1895 preferred to hold the Foreign Secretaryship, as did Mr. MacDonald in 1924, but the excessive burden of such a position was so clearly marked in his case that in 1929 he did not repeat the experiment, though he exercised a wide control over foreign affairs, as did Mr Chamberlain from 1937. Mr. Gladstone in 1873–4, when Parliament was not in session, held the Chancellorship of the Exchequer, and again in 1880–82, but the short tenure of the office of First Lord by Lord Iddesleigh in 1885, when neither Prime Minister nor in the Commons, was a rare anomaly due to quite exceptional circumstances. The Ministers of the Crown Act, 1937, secures that the office of First Lord shall be combined with that of Prime Minister. But the only essential signs of his connection with the Treasury are his considerable patronage and his function of acting either alone or as head of the Cabinet in the difficult business of adjusting disagreements between the Chancellor of the Exchequer and other ministers as to estimates.

The Chancellor, on the other hand, who is appointed by separate patents to that office and that of Under-Treasurer, has undertaken the duty of control of finance, presenting the annual budget of expenditure and revenue and proposing to Parliament the means of securing a balance, whether by new taxation if necessary or by a loan or both. The measure of Treasury control has varied greatly with the personality of the Chancellors as compared with that of their colleagues, but still more with the tendency of national policy. The place taken as the watchdog of economy was vitally weakened when the coming into office in 1905 of the Liberal Government was followed by the adoption of a policy which involved the readiness to spend large sums on ameliorating the position of the people. Formerly the aim of ministries had on the whole been directed to providing for the minimum necessary to maintain national defence, law and order, and such activities as those of the Board of Trade, but now the positive policy demanded large outlays on old-age pensions, Labour

Exchanges, national insurance, and so forth. The new policy altered the attitude of the Treasury, which now could no longer regard any expenditure with suspicion, but must consider chiefly how best to use the possible resources of the country to further social welfare. Thus simpler methods had to yield to complex calculations involving the decision of the Cabinet as to how far they dare risk higher taxation in order to provide for popular expenditure. The financing of the war added enormously to the difficulties of finance, and the following period was complicated by the decision to afford a certain measure of protection to selected industries in danger from foreign imports. The moderate principle of safeguarding industries was followed by the determination in 1932 to adopt a policy of protection modified by Imperial preference, and a burden which might have been intolerable was placed upon the Treasury. The creation, however, of an Import Duties Advisory Committee in 1932 as part of the new policy relieved the Treasury of a most difficult task. Moreover, by the development of the Committee of Imperial Defence and the Defence Requirements and Policy Committee of the Cabinet, the burden of dealing with defence estimates is greatly lessened, and there is scant prospect of incidents like the resignation [1] of Lord R. Churchill in 1886 and Mr. Gladstone [2] in 1894 on defeat in the Cabinet regarding reductions in what they regarded as unduly large estimates.

The functions of the Treasury were authoritatively described by the Haldane Committee on the Machinery of Government in 1918. They include the duty of securing through Parliament the imposition and the regulation of taxation and of supervising the collection of the revenue through the instrumentality of the Boards of Inland

[1] Spender, *Great Britain*, pp. 9 ff.   [2] *Ibid.* pp. 68 f. ; *Lord Oxford*, i. 89 f.

Revenue, the Board of Customs and Excise, and the Post Office ; the last-named department, however, has now been placed in a special position because the Treasury now is allocated only a fixed revenue from this source. The Treasury arranges for the provision of the funds required from day to day to meet the necessities of the public service, and for this purpose it is regularly given by the Acts passed to authorise expenditure very large powers of borrowing. It has the control of the public debt and is responsible for arrangements for payment of interest and sinking fund. In like manner it is concerned with currency and with banking. The Bank of England is not under its control in the ordinary sense of the term, but under modern conditions of finance and exchange control the co-operation of the Bank of England and the Treasury is indispensable for the maintenance of solvency and the prevention of excessive drain of capital. Hence it has become the regular practice for the Treasury and the Bank to determine when and on what conditions the raising of loans for foreign Governments or other authorities can be permitted, and these regulations may be relaxed, as they were in February 1938, or made more stringent, as they were in December 1938, in accord with the need of strengthening British reserves. It was in close communication with the Bank that the decision in 1931 to abandon the gold standard, restored in 1925, perhaps prematurely, after its abrogation in the war period, was taken. The proposal of the Labour party to subject the Bank of England and other banks to complete governmental control is justified by the party on the ground that the relations of the Bank and the Government are so close that there is no longer any justification for the separation, while there is danger lest the interest of the Bank in capitalism may induce it to give unsatisfactory counsel.

The Treasury has also the duty of prescribing the form of the national accounts, and of controlling public expenditure in a variety of ways so as to give effect to the policy of Parliament, which itself is dedicated by the Cabinet working through the Treasury.

2. *Departments concerned with Collection of Revenue*

The Crown Lands of England were surrendered to the public account in 1760 by George III, at a time when their net value was no more than £11,000 ; in 1820 those of Ireland were added to the surrender, and those of Scotland were handed to the Commissioners in 1833. On the other hand, those appertaining to the area of the Irish Free State were taken over by that Government from April 1, 1923. The net revenue surrendered to the Exchequer, after deduction of expenses of all kinds, in 1937–8 amounted to £1,330,000.

The Commissioners include *ex officio* the Minister of Agriculture and Fisheries, who can represent the Commission in Parliament, and a paid Commissioner and an Assistant Commissioner, appointed by sign-manual warrant. The details of their work is not supervised, but the Treasury determines matters of principle.

The Board of Customs dates back to the commissioners appointed in 1671, and with it in 1909 was amalgamated the Excise Department which had hitherto been under the Department of Inland Revenue. The Board is constituted by letters patent, while the chairman is marked out by appointment to that post by sign-manual warrant.

The Board of Inland Revenue has a like constitution ; under its activities fall the collection of taxes, death duties, and stamp duties. Part of the staff makes up the Special Commissioners of Income Tax, and there is a Death Duties

Office and a Valuation Office, while the Controller of Stamps is registrar of companies, business names, newspaper and bank returns. Both Boards have large inspectorates.

The Post Office was long regarded as an ordinary revenue department but it now occupies a special position, and for that and other reasons its representation in Parliament is essential. Prior to 1837,[1] the office, which had been made statutory in 1710,[2] though usually given to a peer who could speak in Parliament for it, was not, strictly speaking, political; thenceforward the holder changed with the ministry, and in 1866[3] the common-sense step of providing for his eligibility to the Commons was enacted. An Assistant Postmaster-General to sit in Parliament was provided in 1909.[4]

In 1837 a new consolidating Act simplified the legal position of the Post Office, conferring a monopoly of conveyance of letters and newspapers, and in 1908 another consolidation was carried out. The powers of the Post Office, however, were for a prolonged period very strictly regulated by the necessity of constant reference to the Treasury for authority for the making of contracts for inland and external conveyance of mails, for the fixing of rates, and for approval of the many international arrangements as to mails, telegraphs, and telephone or wireless communications. In 1933 a fairer position was achieved; the Treasury was given a payment of £10,750,000, while the Post Office was permitted to apply any surplus over that amount on certain conditions to the improvement of the services rendered by that department,[5] which, it must be remembered, is compelled to be a good employer by

---

[1] 7 Will. IV. & 1 Vict. cc. 32, 33.　　　[2] 9 Anne c. 12.

[3] 29 & 30 Vict. c. 55 ; see 182 *Hansard*, 3 s. 1077, 1082.

[4] 9 Edw. VII. c. 14.

[5] *Parl. Pap.* Cmd. 4149 (1932). In 1939 increased pay prevented the arrangement working and it is to be revised.

the pressure of Parliamentary opinion and the jurisdiction of the Industrial Court.

The department is also given many functions additional to its postal duties ; thus it receives various duties on account of the Inland Revenue Department, licence fees for the Customs and Excise Department and the county councils, and for National Insurance, both in respect of health and unemployment. The office pays also widows', orphans', and old-age pensions, and naval, military, and air-force pensions and allowances. The post was enormously extended in 1840 when the penny post was introduced ; book post dates from 1855, the Post Office savings bank from 1861 ; telegraphs in 1870 ; postal orders in 1881 ; parcel post in 1883, and the telephone service in 1892. A certain control is exercised over the British Broadcasting Corporation, whose Governors are chosen by the Prime Minister, and which receives payments for licences collected by the Post Office.

By a recent reorganisation a Post Office Board under the chairmanship of the Postmaster-General determines, with the assent of the minister, the general policy of the office. In January 1933 the Postmaster-General constituted an Advisory Council to act as a connecting link with the public, and to serve in a general consultative capacity. It has three panels, air mail, postal and miscellaneous, and telecommunications, which contain members of Parliament and people of distinction of various kinds.

3. *The Control and Audit of Estimates*

Just before the beginning of Queen Victoria's reign, the system of the issue of public funds and audit of public accounts had been essentially reformed. In 1834 the old Exchequer offices were abolished, and with their disappearance, which involved the abolition of numerous sinecure offices and great waste of public funds, was introduced what is largely the present system. Of the earlier chaos it suffices to note that not until 1787 was there created the Consolidated Fund into which was to flow every stream of the public revenue, and from which was to issue the supply for every public service, replacing an utterly confused system under which particular charges were imposed on specific items of revenue. It was only in 1822 that balanced accounts of revenue and expenditure were presented to Parliament, and in 1832 the navy accounts were presented for the first time to show the appropriation of the sums provided by Parliament, a system obviously essential for any control of the expenditure of departments of State.

From 1834 the revenue of the country was to be paid into the Bank of England and the Bank of Ireland respectively, and a Paymaster of the Civil Services was set up to make the payments which had hitherto been made at the Exchequer itself, as distinct from those made by the paymasters of the army, navy, and ordnance. The work of control and partially of audit, hitherto most ineffectively performed, was given to a new officer, the Comptroller-General, who was made incapable of sitting in Parliament and was to hold office during good conduct, but subject to removal by the Crown on addresses from both houses. His authority became necessary for the issue by either bank of sums from the Exchequer account, and every credit which he granted thereon in favour of any public department was recorded in his office, to form the basis of the public accounts. In 1836 a single Paymaster-General undertook payments for the army, navy, and Civil services.

In establishing the office of Comptroller-General instructions were given to him to keep an account of payments into the Exchequer, of credits granted and moneys drawn for the year ending April 5, while from 1832 the supplies asked for were for a year ending March 31, and the Treasury year ended January 5 ; in 1854 all the years were to end March 31. In 1866 the office of Comptroller-General was abolished and new arrangements substituted by the Exchequer and Audit Departments Act, 1866, which, as amended in 1921, forms the basis of present practice.

Under the statute receipts collected by the Commissioners of Customs and Excise and of Inland Revenue and the Post Office are paid into the Consolidated Fund ; the net balance of the Department of Crown Lands only is paid in. Where other departments earn monies in any form, they are treated as appropriations-in-aid, and are paid into the cash account of the Paymaster-General. Payments-out are divided into two classes, according as they fall to be charged under permanent legislation against the Consolidated Fund, or are to be met from annual grants which are initiated in Committee of Supply in Parliament and are so-called supply services.

In the former case procedure is simple. The Treasury makes a requisition on the Comptroller and Auditor-General, whose office was created by the Act, and who enjoys a similar status to that of the Comptroller-General. He satisfies himself that the Treasury demand is duly authorised by statute, and then grants a credit to the Treasury at the Bank of England. The Treasury then authorises the Bank to transfer the sums credited to the account of a principal accountant, usually the Paymaster-General, and to send the authority to the Comptroller and Auditor-General, who thus keeps an account of issues from the Exchequer. The Consolidated Fund charges are of great magnitude, for they include interest and cost of management of the National Debt, payments to Northern Ireland, the sum due to the Post Office fund, and a large number of less important payments, including the salaries of the judges, of the Comptroller and Auditor-General, of the leader of the Opposition, the Speaker, and other persons of distinction.

The supply services are voted under a procedure described elsewhere. The estimates for the departments are invited by the Treasury in October and are supplied by December. Those for the defence departments, as has been already mentioned, depend now largely upon decisions taken by the Cabinet on reports from the Committee of Imperial Defence, which has the advice of the Chiefs of Staff Committee, a body which has been criticised on the score that its members agree to support one another's claims rather than cut down estimates. The estimates of the civil departments and the revenue departments are subject to a more careful Treasury scrutiny. But the Treasury is usually consulted in advance of the submission of estimates on anything which is likely to need special approval. There are rules which bind departments and from which any departure, therefore, needs Treasury approval, for instance regarding contracts, expenditure on works, and so forth. Above all, proposals involving changes in the number of staff, or their classification, or their conditions of service, have to be specially sanctioned, and the financial staff of the departments is ready to co-operate with the Treasury officials in securing the maximum result for the money to be spent. Thus the actual estimates are often fully covered in essentials by authority already existing.

The estimates are presented in the case of those for defence by the minister in the Commons, the others by the Financial Secretary to the Treasury. Over them there is

some difference in Treasury control, for the resources of
the Treasury are more adapted to criticism of details of the
civil and revenue than of the defence estimates.   But the
Treasury may adopt towards all the estimates the attitude
that the sums desired exceed what can properly be raised
by taxation or borrowed, and in that case the Cabinet may
agree and all estimates will have to be revised within limits.
Such a *modus operandi* is preferable to efforts of the
Treasury to cut down items, for the experts in the departments, if they know that there must be economies, will
probably succeed in making the maximum reduction with
minimum injury to the services affected.   There is the
authority of Mr. Gladstone, Lord R. Churchill,[1] and Sir M.
Hicks Beach [2] in favour of this mode of control as the more
effective.   There remains the difficulty that departmental
estimates are sometimes unduly inflated, in anticipation
of reductions being asked by the Treasury ; [3] but there
is reason to believe that this practice is now obsolescent.
The extent of control is naturally much diminished, when
increases are automatic in the sense that they are governed
by legislation, under which the cost grows with numbers
affected, and for long periods there are inevitable increments, as in the case of health and unemployment insurance, old-age pensions contributory and non-contributory.
The expenses which then are under some form of control
are those involved in administration.   Again, where Parliament provides for grants in aid of services such as housing,
police, education, air raid precautions, and so on, the power
of the Treasury practically vanishes.

In case of war Treasury control is inevitably reduced,
and that of Parliament disappears, because a vote of credit

---

[1] Lord G. Hamilton, *Parl. Rem.* i. 303 f.
[2] Lady V. Hicks Beach, *Hicks Beach*, ii. 151.
[3] Hamilton, *op. cit.* i. 304.

is moved and passed without detail. In 1914–18, however, the departments gave estimates of a sort to the Treasury though not to Parliament, and, as the vote is normally given to the Treasury, it can exercise a measure of control. It must, however, be remembered that policy is a matter for the Cabinet, and that the desire to husband British resources, which must guide the Treasury outlook from force of tradition, has to give way to considerations of higher order. The disputes in the Liberal ministry of 1906–14 over the question of the allocation of funds as between social schemes and defence were at times severe, but the important decision of 1913 to construct eight Dreadnoughts was the result of prolonged Cabinet consideration,[1] in which Mr. Asquith, by skill and persuasive power, succeeded in obtaining the assent of the Cabinet for the whole number desired by Mr. Churchill and the experts of the Admiralty. The Cabinet, again, has to have regard to electoral prospects. The decision to review the whole situation as regards agriculture announced on December 22, 1938, involving, as it must, large expenditure, was patently produced by the widespread indignation of the farming community which resulted at Ipswich, in Lincolnshire, in the refusal of a hearing to the Minister of Agriculture.

The Treasury is also entitled to question estimates of revenue sent up by the revenue departments, to enquire into allowances for sums which cannot, it is held, be collected, to suggest that appropriations-in-aid are underestimated, or that larger returns might be expected from the Crown lands. Questions as to the attitude of the British representatives on the Suez Canal Board towards a reduction of the profits from dues on traffic through the Canal would obviously fall to be dealt with by the Treasury

[1] Churchill, *World Crisis*, i. 172, 178.

from the point of view of revenue, even if the Foreign Office on international grounds favoured sacrifices for the sake of appeasement towards Italy. Over appropriations-in-aid, it must be noted, the Treasury alone has control, for it has been ruled by the Speaker that it is not open for members of Parliament, when dealing with estimates, to reduce items in those presented, though obviously in this way such control as Parliament might exercise is very seriously reduced.

The estimates agreed upon, they are duly approved by the Commons by votes in Committee of Supply, reported to and adopted by the house, followed up by grants made by resolutions in Committee of Ways and Means likewise approved. The next step is a Consolidated Fund Act which gives the authority of Parliament for the expenditure of public money, while the session is in progress. Such an Act must be passed before April 1, so that there may be funds available to carry on until the house has discussed the estimates and the Appropriation Act is passed. It is usual, therefore, for the Government to secure in a Consolidated Fund Act some votes (men, pay, works) for the army, air force, and navy respectively, and a vote on account for the various branches of the civil and revenue estimates. This distinction is due to the fact that in the case of the defence services money granted under any vote may be applied temporarily to purposes specified under other votes, one account for each service being kept, while for the civil and revenue estimates a distinct account is opened for each vote at the Pay Office.

The Appropriation Act passed at the close of the session embodies the Consolidated Fund Act or Acts, details the votes sanctioned in the Committee of Supply, and appropriates to them specifically the necessary amounts from the Consolidated Fund.

If the sums granted by Parliament are found to be inadequate, supplementary estimates may fall to be presented with Treasury authority and to be passed. They must be dealt with in the same way as original estimates, included in a Consolidated Fund Act before March 31, and then final appropriation is given in the following Appropriation Act.

Further, if after the accounts of the year have been closed, it appears that an excess has been spent which cannot be met in ways authorised by statute or practice, the matter must be brought before the Public Accounts Committee of the Commons. An excess vote then is recommended and is duly passed by the Commons, and the item is included in the Appropriation Act. Thus the Appropriation Act of 1939 covers not only the estimates for 1938-9, but supplementary estimates for 1937–8 and excess votes for 1936–7.

The sums voted are made available for actual issue by the process above referred to ; a royal order under the sign-manual countersigned by two Lords of the Treasury desires the Treasury to authorise the Bank to make payments from time to time in accordance with the grant. The Treasury then obtains credits from the Comptroller and Auditor-General for the sums desired on the Exchequer account at the Bank, and thereafter directs the Bank from time to time to transfer the sums specified in the royal order to the supply or Exchequer credit account of the Paymaster-General, such transfers being communicated by the latter to the Comptroller and Auditor-General. The departments are duly informed of the placing of sums to their account, and they become then responsible for their employment in accordance with the votes, and this responsibility is enforced by the efforts of the Treasury and the final control of the Comptroller and Auditor-General, backed by the Public Accounts Committee of the Commons.

The Appropriation Act does not set out the details of the votes which it disposes of. The votes themselves, as presented in the estimates, are divided into sub-heads, and these contain items, but neither the sub-heads or items are finally set out in the Act. So far, therefore, as Parliament is concerned, the only thing that would be illegal would be the exceeding of the votes, while the sub-heads might be ignored. But it is clear that it would be unfair to Parliament to allow free transfers by the authority of the department interested between sub-heads, for thus the purposes of the Commons might easily be defeated. Even between items in sub-heads transfers require watching. Hence the Treasury [1] is active in both regards. It does not claim so much authority as regards items, but even in their case it claims to be consulted as to any increase of establishment, or of salary, or of cost of a service, or additional works or new services which Parliament has not specifically provided for. These rules, laid down as early as 1868, are patently necessary if the control of the Treasury over Civil Service conditions is not to be frittered away. As regards transfer between sub-heads, the Treasury does not deny that it may be desirable to sanction a new service, or an extension of an existing service, which has not been provided for by Parliament, subject to the rule that the vote is not exceeded. But the Treasury demands that its sanction must first be obtained, and not asked for *ex post facto*, when asking is a mere formality, and it will not give such sanction unless it is satisfied that there is no real need to give the Commons the decision. The Public Accounts Committee may even be consulted, and

[1] *Epitome of the Reports from the Committee of Public Accounts, 1857 to 1937*, pp. 10 ff., 16 ff., 91, 224 ff., 252, 328, 487 f., 620, 622, 744 (transfer between votes); 77 f., 213, 248, 252 ff., 347, 349 ff., 621, 640, 643, 732 between sub-heads).

in any case the action of the Treasury is open later to
comments by the Comptroller and Auditor-General and
the Committee.

In the case of the defence services, the Treasury has a
definite statutory power to allow transfer between the
several votes which are presented for these estimates. This
is given annually by the Appropriation Act, and, so long as
the total sums voted for any service are not exceeded, any
surplus arising on any vote may be applied with Treasury
sanction either to make up a deficiency in appropriations-
in-aid, or to defray expenditure in the same service, which
has not been provided for, and which it may be detrimental
to the public service to postpone until provision can be
made by Parliament in due course. The permission is
purely temporary ; each case of its employment has to be
reported to Parliament and final approval has to be given
in the Appropriation Act. This procedure, though approval
is patently inevitable, does at least secure that the facts
shall be known to, and the action taken can be criticised
by, Parliament. This is a remarkable power, but with
historical explanation. The navy was accustomed up to
1832 to transfer without notice of any kind ; thereafter, by
direction of Sir James Graham, an appropriation audit was
presented to Parliament showing what surpluses had been
transferred. In 1846 the army departments were required
to provide appropriation audits also, but retained the
power to transfer unquestioned, and, when the War Office
took over the ordnance and commissariat in 1856–7, the
power was restricted within each main grant, but extended
in 1858 to allow unlimited transfer. This raised some
comment, and after discussion the plan was adopted of
permitting transfers but not without subsequent authority
of Parliament. The decision was influenced by the consideration that the recent Russian War, the Indian Mutiny,

and hostilities in China precluded the possibility of presenting precise estimates.

The system is open to question, but its dangers are
lessened by certain principles, and by the fact that it is
partly excused by the difficulty of obtaining information as
to expenditure incurred, as is so much of the service expenditure, from time to time abroad.   It is also clearly necessary
in time of war if votes of credit are not used.   But it is
required by the Treasury that it shall be consulted in
advance if the excess can be foreseen, and the matter must
be reported if it arises from automatic causes, moreover
urgency in some degree must exist.   The Comptroller and
Auditor-General reports on such transfers, and the Public
Accounts Committee can call for fuller explanations, if it
thinks fit, from the department and the Treasury.

The system of formal audit is complete for all practical
purposes.   The Comptroller and Auditor-General is fur-
nished daily by the banks with an account of receipts by
and issues from the Consolidated Fund, while the revenue
departments report their payments in both to him and to
the Treasury.   Test audits as to receipts are carried out by
him from time to time.   Expenditure in the large departments is audited concurrently by members of his staff,
while in the case of the smaller departments a monthly
audit suffices.   As it is impossible to audit completely, he is
authorised by the Exchequer and Audit Departments Act,
1921, to take sections of expenditure for test purposes in
regard to civil as well as defence votes.   In preventing
illegal or irregular expenditure he has the help of the
accounting officer, selected by the Treasury in each great
department who is normally its head.   He is pecuniarily
responsible for any irregular expenditure, unless he shows
that he had protested in writing and been overruled by the
minister, and even then he may report to the Treasury and

the Comptroller and Auditor-General. It must be admitted however, that very curious errors are made ; thus in 1921 the Air Council had to be admonished for spending £15,000 without sanction on the Cape-Cairo route. In 1934 the mode of authorising transfer, virement, in the technical jargon, was reconsidered, and with the sanction of the Public Accounts Committee simplified. In March only a general view of the surpluses and deficits is given to Parliament, leaving full adjustments until December.

The accounts presented to Parliament are of two kinds, finance and appropriation. The former are laid by June 30, and are prepared by the Treasury to give a detailed statement of receipts and of issues for both supply and Consolidated Fund services, but they merely state the purpose of issues. The appropriation accounts, on the other hand, are prepared by the departments, and the Comptroller and Auditor-General audits them to see whether the items of charge are duly vouched for ; whether the items charged are placed under the proper heads ; and whether there is legal authority for the expenditure. He considers if any special provisions of statutes, Orders in Council, royal warrants, or other binding authority have been observed, and whether new posts have been created or rates of salary altered without the due sanction of the Treasury. He co-operates with the Treasury to ensure that its control is not evaded. While the appropriation accounts are formally confined to supply services, he examines also and reports on the Consolidated Fund services. Under the Act of 1921 he was formally authorised to report on trading and commercial accounts, and instructions have been given to departments to present such accounts with due regard to commercial practice. The expenditure of Secret Service money is exempt from detailed investigation, but the minister concerned must certify that the sum has been expended, and it has been laid down that incidental appropriations-in-aid must be surrendered to the Exchequer and not employed for the purpose of increasing the sums available to be expended on such services. On the other hand, the Government Hospitality Fund,[1] obviously open to abuse, which was started in 1908 to facilitate the entertainment of foreign and other persons on suitable occasions, was duly regulated by rules in detail, and the Comptroller and Auditor-General was asked to report on any irregularities to Parliament. Since 1934 many new funds — Wheat, Agricultural Marketing, Post Office, Cattle, Special Areas, Unemployment Assistance, etc. — have come within his scope of interest.

The reports of the departments do not necessarily come into the hands of the Comptroller and Auditor-General before December 31, but in February his report is normally presented, dealing separately with each department. The Committee of Public Accounts,[2] of fifteen members, then considers the report and investigates any points it deems of interest ; it is often presided over by a member of the Opposition with experience of finance, for example an ex-Financial Secretary of the Treasury. It is entitled to call for explanations from the departments and the Comptroller-General. The report of the Committee is considered by the Treasury, which adopts so much of it as it thinks fit and requires the departments to act thereon ; in this way the Treasury unquestionably acquires a substantial support as against any department which is resentful of Treasury supervision. On the other hand, the Treasury may disagree,[3] and in that case it will endeavour to induce the Committee to alter its views, in which case the matter

---

[1] *Epitome,* p. 631.
[2] *Ibid.* pp. 5, 7, 745 ff. ; Standing Orders, No. 74, as extended in 1935.
[3] *Ibid.* pp. 130, 159 f., 169.

will be discussed on the next report of the Committee. The report is of course laid before the Commons, but while it is possible that some serious blunder might give the Opposition a handle for attack on the Government, it seems very dubious. The attitude of the Commons towards extravagance and waste of public funds is one of almost remarkable levity,[1] despite the fact that notwithstanding all the checks existing many instances occur in which there is needless loss of public money through dishonesty, and still more through adoption of unbusinesslike methods. Moreover, there remains the fundamental difficulty that the whole scheme serves in the main a formal purpose. It is not designed to secure that the funds of the State shall be wisely dealt with in the sense that the most for the public welfare will be made out of their employment.

One fund is of a very unusual character and of modern origin, the Exchange Equalisation Account, created in 1932 in order to enable the Treasury to even out variations in the foreign exchanges so as to prevent undue fluctuations therein, which unquestionably are a serious hindrance to trade and which benefit mainly speculators. The fund has been successively increased to £575,000,000 and there is no full account given of its proceedings, though the Comptroller and Auditor-General is authorised to conduct a formal audit ; the policy of the fund and the mode of its exercise do not fall within his province.

Payments also made under the powers granted by Parliament in respect of export credits, which are allowed to British exporters in order to stimulate foreign trade, are not controlled as regards their expediency by the Comptroller and Auditor-General. Under the Export

---

[1] Some pressure appeared in 1938–9 to prevent profiteering by aeroplane firms and promise of improved control methods was given.

Guarantees Act, 1937, the Board of Trade is given discretion, which it exercises through an Export Credits Guarantee Department which is guided by an executive committee, while its general policy is laid down by an advisory committee. In 1939 a rather wider freedom of action was given, as the sum to be risked was raised to £75,000,000, and up to £60,000,000 was allowed to be advanced in cases where, on ordinary commercial grounds, the risk might not be acceptable. The intention was to help British competition with Germany in eastern Europe by allowing longer term credits than business principles would regard as safe.

From the general principle of payments of all revenue receipts to the Paymaster-General and that payments are made through him, there are certain exceptions. The departments are permitted to obtain advances from the Treasury to sub-accountants at distant stations. This is done from the Treasury Chest Fund,[1] a statutory fund with a capital of from £700,000 to £1,000,000. The Treasury reclaims the sums advanced from the departments to which moneys are voted, and at the close of the financial year an account is rendered to the Comptroller and Auditor-General. In 1914 the Committee on Public Accounts raised a question on the propriety of delay in repayment of advances made thence to the Government of Persia, and a pledge was given in Parliament that the rule would be followed that repayment in such cases should be provided for in the estimates not later than the year following the advance. The Committee stressed also its view that the fund should be confined to the purpose of a banking fund, *i.e.* laying down money abroad for the purpose of carrying on the public service generally. An effort was

[1] *Epitome*, pp. 6 f., 13 f., 451-3, 538, 547, 554; 40 & 41 Vict. c. 45; 56 & 57 Vict. c. 18.

made in 1913 to obtain from the Treasury an assurance that the fund would not be employed under any circumstances to supplement the Civil Contingencies Fund, but, while the principle was admitted by the Treasury, it felt unable to bind itself never under an emergency, however grave, to avail itself of a resource legally open when the alternative was to dislocate the public service. No charges fall to be finally defrayed from the fund, and if in any year there is a surplus over the amount allowed, then it must be paid to the Exchequer, while any deficit must be voted by Parliament. The annual account of the fund is audited by the Comptroller and Auditor-General, who can question any employment thereof outwith the very wide terms of the statutes which regulate its use.

The Treasury has also control over the Civil Contingencies Fund.[1] When the rules for the use of this fund to meet expenditure in excess of votes or for new services were laid down in 1862, it was contemplated that the amounts thus expended would be provided for in the estimates of the following year if not in the estimates in the current year ; but the practice changed, so that in 1925 the Treasury view was that such payments should be included in the supplementary estimates for the current year, and only as a rare exception should postponement to next year be allowed. A rather keen discussion on this head arose in 1934. The *Codex Sinaiticus* was for reasons presumably political purchased from the Soviet Government for £100,000, and of this £93,000 was paid from the Civil Contingencies Fund in December 1933, but no estimate was presented until July 1934 when £41,440 was provided, the balance being met by private contributions. The purchase being a controversial one, the Committee not unnaturally questioned the wisdom of the delay, but

[1] *Epitome*, pp. 5, 6, 7, 8, 538 f., 547, 634, 642, 723, 725, 753.

the Treasury contended that this procedure limited the amount which the Government had finally to pay, and induced a wider number of subscriptions. It gave, however, a pledge that it would normally see that the sums paid from the fund were included in the estimates of the current year. The total, fixed at £120,000, was in 1913 increased to £300,000, and after a temporary increase to £120,000,000, under war conditions, stabilised by the Finance Act, 1921, at £1,200,000. The Comptroller-General audits it as usual.

Revenue collectors are authorised to meet from the revenue thus collected the expenses of their establishments and to advance cash to the local agencies of other departments, *e.g.* of the army department. All these amounts, however, are ultimately recovered and paid to the Exchequer account in due course.

The general principle is that the accounts are cash accounts, so that expenditure is charged against the year in which it is actually paid out and revenue credited to the year in which it is actually paid. In case of payments the date of charge is that of the order to pay, which must not be ante-dated, provided it is issued to the payee, but this applies only if the payment is claimed within the period allowed for the closing of the account. For the purpose of stating at any moment the position of the national accounts, on the other hand, issues from the Consolidated Fund to the departments are regarded as expenditure, though not for the purpose of the appropriation accounts and audit thereof.

In the system of keeping the public accounts important changes were recommended by the Committee on National Expenditure of 1918,[1] which held that for the existing system of cash accounts there should be substituted

[1] *Epitome*, pp. 692 ff.

income and expenditure accounts such as are usual in non-governmental business. This was applied to the War Office as an experiment, but it was abandoned on the recommendation of the Public Accounts Committee of 1925, on the score that it involved for successful working a measure of decentralisation which could not be accepted by the Army Council. The trading accounts, however, of public departments are kept on such a basis, and special financial studies have been conducted in respect of the work of other departments which make up in some degree for the absence of such accounts.

The tendency of Treasury control of recent years has been in favour of better co-operation with the departments. The Haldane Committee of 1918 [1] stressed the fact that departments tended to be extravagant and that the Treasury was held to be parsimonious and hostile to expenditure without sufficient concern for its merits. It suggested that, correlative with the obligation of departments to put forward full reasons for increases in expenditure, there should be an obligation on the Treasury to avoid a merely negative attitude. It also advocated more frequent enquiries by the Treasury into the general administration of departments, and the creation in the Treasury of an Establishments Branch to deal with questions of staffing, while in each department there should be such an officer. In 1919 the last recommendation was acted upon, and the result appears to have been satisfactory. Prior to the innovation the Treasury learned only of proposed increases of establishment in departments when its sanction was necessary ; decreases and reorganisation it learned of only at the pleasure of the departments. The new system ensures that the question of staffing is under continuous investigation by officers who are experts

[1] *Parl. Pap.* Cd. 9230 (1918).

in the work, and who are anxious to secure the maximum
efficiency, and the Treasury has readily encouraged
investigation and employment when suitable of modern
means of transaction of business.

4. *Revenue and Taxation*

In 1837 the navigation system still retained a strong
hold on British taxation policy. The Governments of
earlier years had afforded by the Corn Law of 1815 effective
protection to British agriculture, there were important
preferential duties for West Indian sugar and other produce, the East India Company's monopoly had only been
relaxed in 1833, raw materials were heavily, manufactured
goods almost prohibitively, taxed on import. The ex-
ploitation of new industrial processes gave every motive
for manufacturers to aim at the liberation of trade from
its bonds, and Sir R. Peel soon took up the work, as a
business expert, of reducing the complication of tariffs by
cutting down the number of imports on which duties were
raised and of freeing as many raw materials as possible
from taxation ; in 1845 he abolished duties on 450 out
of some 2000 items under charge. In 1846 the principle
of free trade won a great triumph in the decision to sweep
away protection for corn, in 1849 the navigation Acts were
withdrawn, and an impetus given to foreign trade by this
cessation of the British monopoly of inter-Imperial trade.
The agricultural industry suffered in some degree, but for a
long time the loss was made good by the general prosperity
and growth of population as a result of the new industrial
policy. The revival of ideals of protective trade was in
part due to the adoption in the colonies of the desire for
the restoration of the preferences between the colonies and
Britain, which had been an essential part of the navigation

system and had fallen with it.[1] The imposition of a small duty on corn as a fiscal expediency during the South African War led to the proposal of Mr. J. Chamberlain [2] to maintain the impost against foreign corn while waiving it in respect of colonial supplies, and the failure of this project through the abolition of the duty by a Chancellor of the Exchequer who was convinced of the merits of free trade, led ultimately to Mr. Chamberlain's conversion to preference and a form of protection allied therewith. The times were not ripe for the general acceptance of his thesis, which seemed to be contradicted by the prevalence of prosperity under free trade, and the victory of the Liberals in 1906 was in no small degree contributed to by the votes of free-trade Unionists.

The Great War saw the introduction by Mr. McKenna of a number of productive duties on luxury imports, and the acceptance of the general principle that preference was due to Imperial and Allied trade as against that with enemy countries. But the very limited preferences continued after the war period fall far short of protection, and Mr. Baldwin's effort in 1923 to obtain a mandate for protection failed entirely. There was a limited safeguarding of key industries under a careful procedure, with the result that in 1927 only one out of two hundred British workers was employed in a safeguarded industry, and not more than 3 per cent of imports were liable to safeguarding or other protective duties. But the situation changed vitally. In 1925 the Government decided to return to the gold standard, as the Act forbidding free exportation of gold was about to expire and its renewal would have destroyed British credit throughout the world. The result, however, was that the British pound came to be overvalued by

---

[1] Keith, *Responsible Government in the Dominions*, Part V, Chap. VI.
[2] Holland, *Devonshire*, ii. 287 ff.; Spender, *Campbell-Bannerman*, ii. 93 ff.

I

some 10 per cent, and British trade in 1925–9 suffered
from this overvaluation. Both the Balfour and the Macmillan Committees, however, in 1929 and 1931 were anxious
to secure the retention of the standard, though in 1929
there was considerable depression in important industries
at a time when other countries were fairly prosperous.
External conditions, however, brought about grave inability on the part of foreign countries to purchase from
Britain ; in 1913 rough guesses put the total excess receipts
of Britain as £330,000,000, £200,000,000 from investments
and the balance from shipping, commissions, and miscellaneous services. It was thus possible to purchase some
60 per cent of the food supply from abroad, and to lend
£180,000,000 overseas. In the war period the losses were
high, and in 1926 there was hardly any balance, but in
1929 it was estimated at £139,000,000, though it is well
to note that all these figures are purely conjectural. In
1931 there was an adverse balance of £104,000,000, and
it became imperative to act. The temporary legislation
against abnormal importations in 1931 and the abandonment in September of the gold standard showed the
response of Britain to the financial situation created by
the widespread panic regarding British financial stability.
That was in considerable measure based on the policy of
uncontrolled borrowing to deal with unemployment which,
begun by the Conservative régime, had been continued by
the Labour Government. It was helped by the drastic
character of the recommendations for the curtailment of
expenditure made by the report of a Committee under
Sir George May [1] which the ministry had been induced
by Liberal pressure to set up ; these suggested to foreign
opinion that the country was in a grave condition, whereas
it was, compared to any other great State, perfectly sound.

[1] *Parl. Pap.* Cmd. 3920, 3952.

The failure of the Austrian Credit-Anstalt in June resulted in a desperate effort by the creditors of Germany to withdraw their monies ; this President Hoover sought to counter by a moratorium of reparation and war-debt payments, which Britain and France accepted.[1] It was, however, impossible to secure commercial debts due from Germany, and large sums advanced by the Bank of England could not be realised when demands by foreign lenders became urgent. No return to the gold standard has seemed ever possible, and the Import Duties Act, 1932, showed that the Commons had accepted protection as inevitable.

To restrict reckless grants of protection, the new measure adopted a wise principle. A general duty of 10 per cent *ad valorem* was enacted, with certain exceptions, where no duty or higher duties may be levied. An Import Duties Advisory Committee [2] receives applications for the imposition or the removal of duties, and the Treasury may act on its recommendations. The Board of Trade with Treasury consent may also impose additional duties on countries which discriminate against British trade. This power was used successfully against France in 1934, and a special Act [3] gave authority to the Treasury to impose extra duties on imports from the Irish Free State to make good the failure of the latter to implement her obligations under the treaty of 1921 and the financial agreement of 1926. The control of Parliament was secured by giving the Commons the duty of approving affirmatively any duty imposed, while it might annul any other order

---

[1] *Parl. Pap.* Cmd. 3947.

[2] Three members are held sufficient ; they are appointed by the Treasury. Subsequent Finance Acts add to their duties of recommendation.

[3] Irish Free State (Special Duties) Act, 1932 (22 & 23 Geo. V. c. 30). The dispute was settled in 1938 ; Eire (Confirmation of Agreements) Act, 1938 (1 & 2 Geo. VI. c. 25).

made. The wisdom of the establishment of the Committee procedure has not been questioned ; it can investigate fully all reasons for and against duties, though inevitably there is difficulty in securing a full representation of the views of the public in general.

The adoption of free trade involved the establishment of excise duties on competitive home products so as to avoid protection, and, though this could not always be avoided, in the main the result was achieved. After the adoption of protection excise duties continued to be levied on goods for the advantage of the revenue. But under the head " Excise " there are classed the various licence duties imposed by statute ; there are those on the selling of commodities or to carry on a trade, such as dealing in beer or spirits, pawnbroking, distilling, selling tobacco, or acting as a house-agent ; these are the former assessed taxes, now styled establishment licences. In the same way licences were formerly required to keep male servants, and are still necessary to keep dogs, or carriages, or to shoot game, or to use armorial bearings, and until 1940 a contribution to the revenue is made from patent medicines, though this must have suffered from the sale of many preparations with disclaimer of special rights.

Entertainment duty is levied on tickets of admission in accordance with their price, exemption now being accorded on seats not costing more than sixpence ; there is differentiation in favour of those entertainments where the artistes actually appear. The administration of licences is in part given to county councils, which collect armorial bearings, dog and gun and game licences, as well as those in respect of horse-drawn carriages and a vast mass of mechanically propelled vehicles. Motors must be registered with, and licences to drive obtained on prescribed conditions from, the clerks of county councils.

Duties on estates were levied as probate duties until the Finance Act, 1894, introduced a new system, which has since been extended. Bitterly denounced as an intolerable impost, it has become accepted as an essential part of the financial system and as just and fair. The estate duty falls on real and personal property in the United Kingdom passing on death, and on other personal property where the person who is dead was domiciled in the United Kingdom. Legacy duty, on a graduated scale as in the case of estate duty, falls on personal property passing to legatees or on intestacy, and includes personal property anywhere if the deceased was domiciled in the United Kingdom. Where legacy duty is not payable, succession duty was established in 1853 and modified later, especially in 1910 : it falls on realty in the United Kingdom ; personalty, including leaseholds of a predecessor domiciled in the United Kingdom at the time of creation of the succession ; but, where the predecessor was domiciled abroad, duty is leviable on foreign personalty only in so far as it is property subject to a British trust or recoverable only in a British court. The duty is payable by the successor as a rule.

By the famous Finance Act passed in 1910 duties were imposed on (1) the increment value on grants of land or leases or interests passing on death ; (2) reversions of leases ; (3) undeveloped land, and (4) mineral rights. But the amendments accepted to the measure were such as to delay considerably its coming into operation, and the entry of Mr. Lloyd George into a coalition with the Conservatives resulted in the abandonment of the measure by Acts of 1920 and 1921. The principle of course was easily defended ; the gain by unearned increment to landowners is patent and undeniable, and the grievance in the case of leaseholders so manifest that it has been mitigated by subsequent legislation protecting leaseholders from exorbitant exactions on the expiry of leases. In 1931 the Labour Government contemplated a revival of the legislation which had been abandoned, but the need for economy in 1932 secured the dropping of the suggestion to renew valuation of properties as a basis for later taxation.

Stamps are used to show payments of death and other duties, but their specific employment is in respect of commercial and legal transactions, and the sanction for failure to stamp is in part that unstamped documents may not be available in legal proceedings either at all or unless stamped, which may involve a considerable penalty. The transactions so charged vary from simple receipts for sums of or over £2, which now cost 2d., to sums payable on leases, bills of exchange and promissory notes, contracts for sale of stock, conveyances, bonds, leases, mortgages, admission to the bar or as a solicitor, bills of sale, hire-purchase agreements, etc.

Land tax, fixed at 4s. in the £ in 1798, later reduced to a maximum of 1s., is liable to redemption ; the quota payable by each area is now raised by an equal assessment, less the amount redeemed. The inhabited-house duty, which was abandoned in 1834 but reimposed in 1851, when the window tax was dropped, was itself abolished by the Finance Act, 1924.

At the beginning of the Queen's reign income tax was in abeyance, having been treated as a war tax and so dropped in 1815. It was revived by Sir R. Peel at the rate of 7d. in the £, and since then, though Mr. Gladstone came out with a personal policy of its abolition in 1874 without securing the popular support he desired, it has remained the essential basis of much of the economy of the State. Its value as a war-time tax was manifested in the Great War, when at one time it rose to 6s. a £, and so remained until 1921–2. In quasi-war conditions it rose in 1938–9 to 5s. 6d. Since 1920 earlier exemptions and abatements have been standardised and increased ; a reduction of 20 per cent but not exceeding £300 is allowed of the total of earned income, while no income under £100 is taxed ; there are personal allowances, allowances for children, dependent relatives, housekeepers, etc., and the first £135 of any taxable income, after allowing deductions, is charged at one-third the ordinary rate.

Super-tax was imposed in 1910, and replaced by sur-tax, which was first made payable on January 1, 1930, in the form of a deferred additional tax on the income for 1928–9. It is levied on incomes over £2000 in amount. It is payable in a single instalment, while ordinary income falls to be paid on January 1 and July 1.

Income tax is levied under five schedules : rents and profits of ownership of land ; profits from the use or occupation of land ; income on investments in loans of the British, other Empire Governments, and foreign Governments ; profits of trades, professions, and other occupations ; and employment by the State, corporations, companies, and certain other bodies. The collection involves the services of assessors of taxes, of surveyors, and of general [1] and special commissioners who exercise a quasi-judicial position ; from their holdings, on demand by the Surveyor or the person claimed against, there is appeal to the High Court, thence to the Court of Appeal, and the Lords.[2] It is not unusual, where a point of law requires elucidation, for the Inland Revenue to agree to pay the costs incurred by the subject. The latter has a remedy in suitable cases by *mandamus* or petition of right,

[1] General Commissioners are appointed the by Land Tax Commissioners; the Special Commissioners are Civil servants, but independent in the exercise of their functions.

[2] 8 & 9 Geo. V. c. 40, s. 149.

and a claim for a declaration [1] has been successfully made in the analogous case of the now extinct land-value duties. Sums due can be enforced by penalties, distraint in priority to the landlord's right to rent, and sale, and the general commissioners can commit to prison in default of bail or security for payment. In practice they exercise a considerable discretion in enforcement of payment in cases of large amounts due by companies and others, and, though the legality of this discretion has been questioned *obiter*, it has not been denied. [2]

The National Defence contribution was intended by Mr. N. Chamberlain as a tax on the extra profits, which would be raised from businesses which would profit from the rearmament schemes of the Government, but opposition by interested parties rendered it expedient to drop this very desirable principle and to place the burden even on companies and businesses which are losers by the rearmament movement. It is a charge on the profits made in each year from April 1, 1937, to March 31, 1942, from any trade or business carried on in the United Kingdom or carried on personally or through an agent by persons ordinarily residing in the United Kingdom. The rate is 5 per cent in respect of a body-corporate, 4 per cent in other cases. But no tax is charged where there are only profits of £2000 or less, and an abatement is allowed where profits are less than £12,000 in any year of charge.

The Road Fund was originally, under the Finance Acts of 1926 and 1934, in an anomalous position, as after certain sums were taken from the receipts for motor-licence duties, the remainder of these revenues went to the fund, whence under the control of the Minister of Transport grants were made for roads, etc., to local authorities. The grants in

[1] *Dyson* v. *Att.-Gen.*, [1912] 1 Ch. 158.   [2] 8 & 9 Geo. V. c. 40, s. 222.

1936–7 amounted to £20,579,030, so that it was clearly wise to end, from April 1, 1937, this system and to restore the usual control of Parliament. From the same date the Minister of Transport was given direct concern with some 4500 miles of roads, known as trunk roads. The sum provided in 1939–40 was £24,000,000.

The Post Office, as above mentioned, makes a fixed contribution to revenue, but its total cost is included in the estimates, being in 1939–40 fixed at £79,634,000.

5. *Expenditure*

The growth in national expenditure from the Victorian epoch has been phenomenal. With its restricted estimate of the functions of the State in the 'thirties of the nineteenth century a total of £50,000,000 a year seemed sufficient; in the 'nineties it had risen to £90,000,000, and in 1913–14 it had reached nearly £200,000,000 as a result of increased defence expenditure, partly due to the decision to build the terribly costly Dreadnoughts, and of health insurance and old-age pensions, together with Labour Exchanges and other social amenities. In 1932–3, as a result of the great changes brought about by war, the total was about £859,000,000. The burden for debt charges has become greater than the largest pre-war budget, and the argument that, if money could be found for war, it could also be found for social advance, had proved so strong that, despite retrenchments of all kinds after the 1931 crisis, the total of social expenditure was shortly to rise rapidly. Even in 1937–9, when the imposition of crushing defence costs was necessary, the ministry was prompt to insist that it would not retrench on social services, but would maintain and expand, an attitude which has the merits of securing the ministry against

wholesale loss of votes at the general election. How far
this mode of action is consonant with the essential welfare
of the country is open to controversy ; the argument of
most obvious weight is that a ministry which desires to
secure ready co-operation in defence measures may not
risk the cry of the Opposition that it is starving mothers
and children to provide munitions.

Hence, despite the enormous increase in the amounts
to be spent on defence in 1939–40, the civil estimates,
together with those for the revenue departments, totalled
£534,596,081, an increase of £2,177,705 over those for the
previous year. The chief items were, in addition to the
provision for the revenue departments, which included
Post Office, £79,634,000, Ministry of Labour, £24,264,000,
and £43,930,000 for the Unemployment Assistance Board ;
of the Ministry's expenditure £22,701,600 is for unemployment insurance. The Board of Education was given
£52,242,026 ; the Ministry of Health, £23,235,789 ; old-
age pensions, £48,717,000 ; the Ministry of Pensions,
£38,377,000 ; and the Exchequer contribution to local
revenues totalled for England and Wales, £47,202,000.
The police for England and Wales cost £12,922,065, and
roads £24,000,000. The beet sugar subsidy claimed
£3,000,000, the livestock industry and cattle fund,
£4,402,000. For aid-raid precautions, £5,190,707 was given,
and was to be augmented by sums from loan funds ; the
same remark applies to the £3,500,000 allocated to the
Essential Commodities Reserves Fund, on which over
£8,500,000 had been spent the year before.

6. *The National Debt*

The National Debt attained grave dimensions through
the reckless finance of the Napoleonic wars, but in 1829

efforts to reduce it from surplus revenue were begun. This gave the old sinking fund. In 1875 there was introduced by Sir S. Northcote a new sinking fund, namely, any saving on the annual charge voted for meeting debt charges. By 1899 the debt was reduced to £635,040,695, but the South African War destroyed the work of many laborious years. In 1914 it fell to £708,000,000, but the Great War created a staggering burden, for all possibility of prudent finance disappeared when it became obvious that only by reckless expenditure on aiding the Allies could the war be won. Moreover, after the entry of the United States into the war, that power proved unwilling to finance the Allied needs, and Britain, which provided the finance, could do so only at the cost of enormous indebtedness to the United States. The debt, therefore, on March 31, 1938, stood at £8,026,143,422, classed as funded debt, terminable annuities, and unfunded debt, which includes Treasury bills, savings certificates, and a number of mainly short-term loans. This total includes a portion of the total of £800,000,000 to be borrowed in five years from April 1, 1937, and to be paid off in thirty equal instalments from 1942 ; until then 3 per cent is payable from the defence votes ; the amount to be borrowed falls to be reduced by any surplus of revenue over expenditure.

In addition to any saving on the annual debt charge, which goes under the Finance Acts, 1928 and 1937, to reduce the debt, there are sinking funds for the Victory Bonds issue, and for the 3 and 4 per cent Funding Loans ; and payments for death duties under the War Loan Act, 1919, mainly in securities, are held for debt reduction. The large sums owed by British Dominions and foreign countries as war debts cannot be deemed effective assets, while the debt includes roughly £900,000,000 due to the United States, which will presumably never be paid in full.

The management of the debt is under the control of the National Debt Commissioners, whose primary business is the application of the sinking funds to the reduction of the debt, but who also perform other duties. The office is under a Comptroller-General.

7. *The Control of Currency*

It has always been the deliberate policy of the country to leave as far as possible the regulation of currency questions to the operation of business considerations as viewed by the Bank of England, representing the best available judgments on banking questions. The task, carried out effectively in pre-war days, was enormously complicated by the war finance which was followed by the issue of reparations and war debts, the former of which were financed by very large borrowings by Germany, in particular from the United States and Britain ; then an orgy of high protective policies destroyed any normality in trade and financial conditions. The Bank's function thus became one of ever-increasing difficulty. The restoration of the gold standard in 1925 [1] appeared to offer reasonable prospects of return to the principles of earlier times, but in 1931 the necessity of immediate suspension of gold issues, which was carried out at the bidding of the ministry and at once indemnified by Act of Parliament,[2] opened up for the Bank a very difficult duty in the maintenance, as far as possible, of a reasonable stability in currency relations with other countries, especially the United States. In 1933 a World Economic Conference [3] was duly summoned, but all possibility of it serving any useful purpose

---

[1] The Gold Standard Act, 1925 (15 & 16 Geo. V. c. 29).
[2] The Gold Standard (Amendment) Act, 1931 (21 & 22 Geo. V. c. 46).
[3] *Parl. Pap.* Cmd. 4357, 4403.

was destroyed when, just as it set to work, the President of the United States made it clear that currency stabilisation was not in his view a helpful objective. The Conference then dissolved without the slightest profit. The Finance Act, 1932, had recognised the necessity of affording aid to the Bank in its firm efforts to prevent speculative attacks on currency levels by creating an Exchange Equalisation Account of £150,000,000, which was increased first to £375,000,000 and in 1938 to £575,000,000. This meant that the Bank could receive close co-operation from the Chancellor of the Exchequer in his effort to maintain a reasonable level of exchange. In pursuance of this policy in December 1938 the ban on foreign lending, which had been relaxed in February, was reimposed, and in January 1939 a transfer of £200,000,000 from the fund to the Bank [1] marked a further effort by speculators to injure the currency position, which France, the United States, and the United Kingdom seek to maintain stable, if at all possible.

The power of the Bank is obviously enormous, and it is this consideration which has determined the Labour party to seek at the outset of any Government in which it has real power to obtain control of the Bank and to compel it to adopt a policy in accord with socialism. The implications of such action do not appear to have been fully thought out by the party in conjunction with banking experts, and the project undoubtedly excites considerable doubt as to its wisdom, while the risk of such action is admitted by advocates of the policy, who, however, hold that it is so vital that risks must be run.[2]

---

[1] This was followed by revaluation of the gold reserve.
[2] Cf. Laski, *Parl. Govt.* pp. 195 ff.

CHAPTER XVI

FOREIGN AFFAIRS

1. *The Conduct of Foreign Policy*

REFERENCE has already been made to the special position
of the Secretary of State for Foreign Affairs, in that the
sovereign [1] and the Prime Minister alike, by custom and
for reasons both obvious and cogent, are more deeply concerned in these issues than they are in the work of most
of the other departments. The Cabinet also takes continuous note of foreign questions, though no doubt in the
pre-war period the vital importance of the work of the
ministry was insufficiently appreciated by ministers deeply
immersed in social reforms, and in the political struggle
with the House of Lords.

In the post-war period the burden of the work so increased that relief was found for the Secretary of State
by giving him a second Parliamentary Under-Secretary of
State to specialise in work affecting the League of Nations,[2]
while Mr. Eden was created in 1934 Lord Privy Seal in
order to aid the minister in matters of this type. But in
the following year, on Sir S. Hoare's resignation, Mr. Eden
was given his office, and on his resignation in February
1938 Lord Halifax was appointed, in neither case further

[1] See Chap. III, § 12 (ii). For Mr. Balfour's cynical view, see Dugdale,
ii. 271-3.

[2] On Lord Plymouth's resignation in May 1939 on grounds of health, he
was not forthwith replaced, and it was suggested that the appointment of a
second Parliamentary Under-Secretary might not be permanent.

ministerial assistance being deemed necessary in view of
the great share in foreign affairs assumed by the Prime
Minister, who thus revived the tradition of Mr. Lloyd
George, and naturally overshadowed the Foreign Secretary.
A further anomaly was produced by the creation of the
office of Chief Diplomatic Adviser, who thus seems to
duplicate the work of the Permanent Under-Secretary ;
neither officer was taken by the Prime Minister to Munich,
scarcely a very flattering position in which to put two
such highly paid servants of the Crown.

The Foreign Secretary together with the Board of Trade
appoints the Parliamentary Secretary of the Overseas
Trade Department, who acts in some degree as a third
Parliamentary Under-Secretary of State.

The control of foreign policy applies to the whole of the
Empire except the Dominions, which in this matter have
been recognised, as the result of recommendations of the
Imperial Conferences, 1917–37, as fully autonomous. It rests
with their Governments to act independently, appointing
their own diplomatic representatives and making their own
treaties, directly advising the King, or to make use of the
machinery of the Foreign Office and British representatives
overseas, or they may adopt both methods of operation.
Canada, the Union of South Africa, and Eire maintain
diplomatic representatives at several courts ; the two latter
make treaties, advising the King direct, while Canada uses
the machinery of the Dominions Office ; Australia and New
Zealand employ the British agencies.[1] It rests with each
unit to decide whether or not to recognise a foreign State ;
thus Eire first recognised the conquest *de jure* of Ethiopia
and the King of Italy as Emperor thereof ; then Britain,

[1] Keith, *The Dominions as Sovereign States*, and Chap. XVII, *post*.
Mr. Menzies, on becoming Prime Minister, indicated the intention to establish
legations in the United States, Japan, and later China.

Chapter
XVI.

Australia, and the Union followed; then Canada. So Eire first recognised General Franco *de jure*, Britain only on February 26, 1939.

The right to make war and peace and to declare neutrality is vested in the Crown as part of the prerogative, and such a declaration would be effective for the whole of the Empire except the Dominions. In their case it is not yet decided whether foreign States would recognise the right to remain internationally in a state of neutrality, but constitutionally their sole right to decide if and to what extent they would afford aid to Britain is established beyond question. The assent of the Commons to the making of war is demanded by constitutional usage; its support was awaited in 1914, though steps had been taken in preparation to have naval and military forces ready for defence. In like manner in 1938 the mobilisation of the fleet was ordered in the crisis before it was known whether war could be avoided. It is, however, noteworthy that in that case a guarantee to Czechoslovakia [1] of her remaining territories was offered by the Prime Minister before consulting the House of Commons,[2] which was compelled to homologate it or to repudiate his leadership. In the case of the Locarno Pact, on the other hand, the guarantee was definitely brought before the Commons and approved by the House.

It lies with the executive Government to make binding

---

[1] *Parl. Pap.* Cmd. 5847, p. 9; 5848, p. 4. The utter worthlessness of this offer was patent to impartial observers, and on March 14, 1939, the dismemberment of Czechoslovakia was completed without any effort of Britain and France to honour their obligations. The Prime Minister in the Commons denied that the German action involved the unprovoked aggression which called the guarantee into being.

[2] So the recognition of General Franco was accorded before the Commons was informed on Feb. 27, and accepted by 344 to 137 votes, and guarantees to Poland and to Rumania and Greece were given before the Commons was informed on March 31 and April 13.

pronouncements on certain issues. Thus the courts will accept declarations as to the status of a foreign Government[1] and as to recognition or non-recognition of a Government or of state of belligerency. They accept also any declaration as to whether any person is entitled to recognition as a diplomatic agent or a foreign sovereign, immune from British jurisdiction.[2] The extent of the foreign jurisdiction of the Crown is by statute placed wholly within the control of the Crown, through the Foreign or Colonial Secretary.[3] The extent of British territory proper is declared by the Crown through the Home Secretary.[4] The existence and determination of a war are likewise so declared,[5] though in the absence of any declaration on this or on the other points mentioned, the court might have to act on its own judgment.

But the court will not deal with an alien, who might, if the Crown thought fit, be deprived of its protection on the ground of hostile action, on the assumption that such protection has been withdrawn.[6] It expects, moreover, as clear guidance as possible on such issues from the executive, but this was rather ineffectively accorded in some of the cases regarding both Spain and Ethiopia.

In June 1939 a Foreign Publicity Department was created, whose head would become Director-General of the Ministry of Information to be created in the event of war. It controls foreign broadcasts and is in touch with the British Council whose function is to disseminate a knowledge of British culture.

[1] *Duff Development Co.* v. *Govt. of Kelantan*, [1924] A.C. 797 ; *The Gagara*, [1919] P. 95 ; *The Annette*, *ibid.* 105.

[2] *Engelke* v. *Musmann*, [1928] A.C. 433 ; *The Amazone* (1939), 55 T.L.R. 787.

[3] See Foreign Jurisdiction Act, 1890, s. 4 ; *Ratshekedi Khama* v. *Ratshosa*, [1931] A.C. 784 ; Keith, *Journ. Comp. Leg.* xix. 118 f.

[4] *The Fagernes*, [1927] P. 311.

[5] *Janson* v. *Driefontein Consol. Mines*, [1902] A.C. 404.

[6] *Johnstone* v. *Pedlar*, [1921] 2 A.C. 262.

2. *Diplomats and their Immunities*

To the Foreign Secretary appertains the duty of advising the sovereign as to the appointing of British ambassadors and ministers, and the acceptance of proposed appointments of foreign agents. Ambassadors and envoys extraordinary are accredited by foreign States to the King personally,[1] and he sends letters of credence to foreign sovereigns ; ministers resident and chargés d'affaires to the Secretary of State, and *vice versa*. Ambassadors have the special character of being fully representative of the sovereign, and they may ask for a royal audience. Hence Queen Victoria was unwilling to extend their number, though she agreed in the case of Italy and the United States. The war resulted in certain extensions of the acceptance of ambassadors in honour of the friendship of the Argentine and Brazil, while by an innovation, under the alliances with Iraq and Egypt, the ambassadors accredited to these powers by the Crown have precedence over the other members of the Diplomatic Corps. The Foreign Secretary controls the Diplomatic service in its various branches both by appointment and transfer, and by standing regulations and correspondence and personal discussion.

The question of the privileges of diplomatic agents in Britain is regulated in part by international law recognised by the British courts, in part by a statute of 7 Anne c. 12, passed to make reparation to the Czar of Russia for the arrest on a private debt of his representative ; it accords full immunity from suit on any account to diplomatic representatives.[2] The privilege, however, may be waived

[1] The King at Ottawa on May 19, 1939, received the credentials of the United States Minister.

[2] *Taylor* v. *Best* (1854), 14 C.B. 487 ; *Engelke* v. *Musmann*, [1928] A.C. 433 ; Dicey and Keith, *Conflict of Laws*, pp. 197 f. ; *Viveash* v. *Becker* (1814), 3 M. & S. 284 ; *Macartney* v. *Garbutt* (1890), 24 Q.B.D. 368 (even if the envoy is a British subject).

by the sovereign of the diplomat,[1] and, if he brings an
action, he subjects himself to the jurisdiction of the court
so far as is necessary to secure that justice shall be done
between the parties in respect of the suit. But it does not
seem that execution can ever be granted against the
property of the minister. The principle is extended to
the house of the minister, which is free from the territorial
jurisdiction, so far as is necessary to allow him fully to
effect his functions. But misuse of the official dwelling
to detain therein a subject of the Chinese Emperor resulted
in effective representations to secure release in the case of
the Chinese patriot Sun Yat Sen.[2] Serious breach of law
by a diplomat would mean, of course, an intimation to
his Government that his continued presence would be undesirable. Diplomats and their property are exempt from
taxation and under statute from rates,[3] and free entry of
imported goods is normally given.

The privileges ascribed to diplomats are extended
to their servants, except in so far as they engage in
trade, under the statute. The question of recognition of
diplomats is entirely one for the Crown. In *Engelke* v.
Musmann[4] the House of Lords determined that the
matter was not one in which the courts were entitled to
seek evidence other than the formal assertion of the
Secretary of State, in whose office is kept a list of all
persons entitled to diplomatic immunity.

The immunity of diplomats extends also to sovereigns
if present in England and to their property. The sovereign
however, is entitled only so long as he is recognised as
such by the Crown. When on November 16, 1938, the

---

[1] *Suarez, In re*; *Suarez* v. *Suarez*, [1918] 1 Ch. 176; *Dickinson* v. *Del
Solar*, [1930] 1 K.B. 376.

[2] Wheaton, *Int. Law* (ed. Keith), i. 456.

[3] *Parkinson* v. *Potter* (1886), 16 Q.B.D. 152.

[4] [1928] A.C. 433; *The Amazone* (1939), 55 T.L.R. 787.

Crown, in breach of the covenant of the League of Nations, recognised the King of Italy as Emperor of Ethiopia, it withdrew its recognition of Haile Selassie as Emperor of Ethiopia, and he ceased to be entitled to any immunity.[1] The immunity is not confined to sovereigns who are independent of British control. It has been extended to the princes of Indian States and the rulers of the Malay States.[2]

The exemption of the property of States has caused serious difficulties in recent years with the development of the trading activities of foreign States. In one instance, that of Soviet Russia, the fact that the State undertook foreign trade as a governmental business led to the agreement of February 16, 1934, under which diplomatic immunity for the ambassador and his property is definitely restricted. But, apart from that, the issue was treated by the courts as settled in favour of the view that property of a foreign State was exempt, whether that property was in the case of ships engaged in trade or not. The issue was first raised in the case of the *Parlement Belge*,[3] a Belgian mail-ship, which was denied immunity by Sir R. Phillimore as being merely engaged in trading, but was given it by the Court of Appeal, on the score that the vessel was engaged in governmental service proper. This was extended in the *Porto Alexandre*[4] to a vessel wholly engaged in trade, and in subsequent cases. In the *Cristina*,[5] however, when the matter came before the

[1] *Haile Selassie* v. *Cable and Wireless Ltd.* (No. 2), (1938), 55 T.L.R. 209 ; a very unfortunate decision.

[2] *Mighell* v. *Sultan of Johore*, [1894] 1 Q.B. 149 ; *Statham* v. *Statham*, [1912] P. 92 ; *Duff Development Co.* v. *Govt. of Kelantan*, [1924] A.C. 797.

[3] (1880), 5 P.D. 197.

[4] [1920] P. 30 ; *The Gagara*, [1919] P. 95 ; *The Jupiter*, [1924] P. 236 ; (No. 2) [1925] P. 69.

[5] *Vascongada* (*Compania Naviera*) v. *S.S. Cristina*, [1938] A.C. 485. Recognition of one government *de jure* does not exclude recognition of another

House of Lords, it was pointed out that, where a vessel was simply used in trade, there was lacking such international usage as to compel the grant of immunity, so that the question may yet be decided in the opposite sense. The proposal to provide by international agreement for the non-immunity of trading ships has so far not been carried into effect, though such an agreement was reached. The *Cristina* judgment clears up one difficult point ; the exemption from jurisdiction of property refers to cases where the property is effectively in the possession of a foreign sovereign. It does not mean that, where there is no possession, a sovereign can by mere assertion obtain it. Nor would the fact that a foreign sovereign held some shares in a company prevent it being sued.

Chapter XVI.

3. *The Treaty Power*

Difficult issues have arisen regarding the power of the Crown to conclude treaties so as to affect the subject's rights. The sole right to make treaties is vested in the Crown in its executive aspect. The most formal method is by negotiations carried on by plenipotentiaries under full powers issued by the King under the great seal, on the authority of a sign-manual warrant countersigned by the Foreign Secretary, and ratified by the King on like advice. Less formal agreements are made in the names of the Governments or States and usually, not always, require some form of ratification, but may be expressed not to need this form.[1] Ratification is always optional, though

de facto in part of the area : *Bank of Ethiopia* v. *National Bank of Egypt and Liguori*, [1937] Ch. 513 ; *The Arantzazu Mendi* (1938), 55 T.L.R. 74, 454 (H.L.).

[1] The Munich agreement, Sept. 29, 1938, is signed by the Prime Minister without any reference to royal authority, and is unique. The guarantee of Czechoslovakia equally rested on his promise, repeated in the Lords by Lord Halifax on several occasions, and explained by Sir T. Inskip, Oct. 1938.

obviously it is contrary to effective international co-operation if it is refused without good cause ; in the United
States, where the ratification requires a two-thirds majority
in the Senate, ratification may easily be withheld ; but the
executive in Britain has normally the certainty that it will
be accorded. In the case of agreements with the Dominions
it is normal to couch agreements in the form of governmental accords, so as not to emphasise the position of the
existence of separate sovereigns in the Commonwealth.

A treaty ratified is internationally binding, but that
does not involve, as in the United States, the corollary
that it becomes part of the municipal law of the United
Kingdom. To do this it must be adopted by judicial
decision or by legislation.[1] The courts will accept the
power of the Crown to conclude certain kinds of treaty
and thereby to alter international law as previously existing, and they will give effect to these alterations if the
matters come before them ; thus the Crown has effectively
concluded conventions regarding the abolition of privateer-
ing, the rules as to days of grace, the definition of contra-
band, the duties of neutrality, and other topics. Parts
of the Declaration of London were put in operation during
the Great War without any Parliamentary authority at
all. Indeed so far as the House of Lords was concerned,
in 1909 it had refused to agree to a Bill promoted in order
to allow effect to be given to the proposal that an appeal
should be allowed from the highest British tribunal in
prize to the proposed International Prize Court.[2] On the
other hand, the Crown has been denied the right to alter
international law by the prerogative alone so as to compel

---

[1] *R.* v. *Keyn* (1876), 2 Ex.D. 63 ; *West Rand Central Gold Mining Co.* v. *R.*,
[1905] 2 K.B. 391 ; *Niboyet* v. *Niboyet* (1879), 4 P.D. 1, 20 *per* Brett, L.J. ;
Mortensen v. *Peters* (1906), 8 F. (J.C.), 93, 101 *per* Lord Dunedin ; *Ferdinand,
Ex-Tsar of Bulgaria, In re,* [1921] 1 Ch. 107.

[2] Halévy, *Hist. 1905–15*, pp. 391 f.

British prize courts which administer international law to give effect to its orders.[1]

4. *The Recognition of States*

The Crown has unfettered power to recognise *de facto* or *de jure* foreign sovereigns, and the courts accept important results as being thence derived. If a State is recognised *de facto*, then the acts of sovereignty which it exercises in its territory, such as the confiscation of property,[2] must be accepted by the courts. Further, in the case of Ethiopia it was held by the courts that it was possible for one sovereign to be recognised *de facto* and one *de jure* simultaneously, with the result that the latter could sue an English corporation for sums due in respect of a contract existing before the conquest of his country, but that his right to sue expired on the recognition *de jure* of the conquest.[3] In the case of Spain the result of this doctrine was curious ; it appeared that the courts would not exercise jurisdiction over either Government, so that ships in the possession of the insurgents and ships in the possession of the recognised Government were equally immune from jurisdiction.[4]

It appears also in strict law that a surrender of British territory by the prerogative would deprive those British subjects who remained in the ceded area of their nationality, so that in this way the King could of his own motion destroy the allegiance of subjects.[5] But, as mentioned

---

[1] *The Zamora*, [1916] 2 A.C. 77. The courts give effect to statute provisions violating treaty obligations : *Californian Fig Syrup Co.'s Trademark, In re* (1884), 40 Ch.D. 620 ; *Croft* v. *Dunphy*, [1933] A.C. 156 ; *The Bathori*, [1934] A.C. 91, 98.

[2] *Aksionairnoye Obschestvo A. M. Luther* v. *Sagor & Co.*, [1921] 3 K.B. 532.

[3] *Haile Selassie* v. *Cable and Wireless Ltd.* (No. 2), (1938), 55 T.L.R. 209.

[4] See cases cited, p. 132, *ante*.

[5] *Doe d. Thomas* v. *Acklam* (1824), 2 B. & C. 779 ; Keith, *State Succession*, pp. 42 ff.

elsewhere, since 1890 this doctrine is not acted on, and Parliamentary intervention is now regular.

The general issue as to the power of the Crown, when not ceding territory, to modify the rights of subjects without the aid of Parliament was touched upon in *Walker* v. *Baird*,[1] where the issue indirectly touched on was whether the Crown by a *modus vivendi* with France over the Newfoundland fishery question could interfere with the rights of fishermen. But the question was not decided, as the point finally disposed of was merely whether it was an answer to claims to allege Act of State, and it was held by the Privy Council that such an answer was inadequate. As compensation was duly paid by the Crown, and as further action was taken only under statutory enactments, it may be assumed that the Crown abandoned any right by treaty to invade private rights. Nor has it ever been contended that it could thus introduce a tariff, or reduce a tariff if fixed, or impose upon the Exchequer the duty of paying a sum to a foreign power. In all such cases the aid of Parliament must be invoked.

Grave difficulties have arisen regarding the duties of Britain in the case of insurgency. The right to recognise belligerency is undoubted, and it was duly exercised in the conflict in the United States. There, however, the issue had been clarified by the decision of the United States to declare a blockade of part of the coast, which could only mean that belligerency existed in the fullest measure.[2] Even so the action taken was resented by the United States. On the other hand, no recognition was accorded to the belligerent status of the Cuban rebels.

---

[1] [1892] A.C. 491. The right to cede in India is discussed in *Damodhar Gordhan* v. *Deoram Kanji* (1876), 2 App. Cas. 332; *Lachmi Narayan* v. *Raja Pratab Singh* (1878), Ind. L.R. 2 All. 1.

[2] Wheaton, *Int. Law* (ed. Keith), i. 53 f. Contrast the British objections to Gen. Franco's blockade in March 1939.

Against the grant of aid to them by British subjects a warning was duly given in accordance with the terms of the Foreign Enlistment Act, 1819, then in force, and steps were taken to enforce it.[1] The issue arose again under the Foreign Enlistment Act, 1870, when the Spanish revolt broke out in 1936. It was clear under the Act that it was illegal for British subjects to leave the United Kingdom to afford aid to either side, but the Government took no steps to prevent the sailing from England of members of an Irish brigade enlisted in Ireland for the service of the rebels, and warnings of the placing in operation of the Act were only forthcoming when it was found that some volunteers were going to Spain to succour the recognised Government.[2] The British Government, however, declined in 1937–8 to accord belligerent rights, despite the rebel demand for recognition. It was admittedly the case that the successes of the rebels had resulted in a condition in which rights might readily have been given; but there was the objection that these successes had been due to intervention by Italy and Germany in open violation of the undertakings of these powers in the Non-intervention Agreement,[3] and that it would be unfair of Britain herself to refuse to intervene in favour of the Government, but to recognise what had been brought about by the intervention of other powers in breach of agreement. At the same time the British Government refused to protect British shipping engaged in trade with the Spanish Government when in Spanish territorial waters, endeavoured without complete success

---

[1] *R.* v. *Carlin* ; *The Salvador* (1870), 6 Moo. P.C. (N.S.) 509.

[2] Keith, *The King, the Constitution, the Empire, and Foreign Affairs, 1936–7*, pp. 162 ff.

[3] *Parl. Pap.* Cmd. 5521, 5570 (1937) ; 5793 (1938). For Germany's admission of intervention see *The Times*, May 31, June 7, 1939 ; for Italy's, *ibid.*, June 9, 12.

to protect such shipping when attacked on the high seas by bombing aircraft, presumably Italian, and contented itself with protests when General Franco's forces seized ships *en route* for Britain with cargoes purchased by the British Government.[1] Moreover, strong steps were taken to render effective the British share in the non-intervention policy ; the Merchant Shipping (Carriage of Munitions to Spain) Act, 1936, was passed to forbid the normal right to supply munitions to a friendly Government by shipping them from ports where they were legally available, and in 1937 the Merchant Shipping (Spanish Frontiers Observation) Act was part of a plan for preventing the shipping to Spain of volunteers or munitions. Italy, on the other hand, kept the insurgents fully supplied with men and munitions, leaving it inexplicable how the British Government could in November 1938 bring into force the agreement of April 16, 1938, with Italy, whose operation had been stated explicitly to be dependent on a settlement in Spain.[2]

5. *The League of Nations*

The creation of the League of Nations by the Treaty of Versailles, 1919, introduced a new element into the conduct of British foreign policy by placing Britain under definite obligations with regard to the maintenance of the sovereignty and territorial integrity of the other members

---

[1] Curiously Britain after recognising the Franco government on Feb. 26, 1939, still raised difficulties regarding the blockade proclaimed by it, and insisted on the release of the S.S. *Stangate* captured on the open sea. For the Nyon anti-piracy accord, see Cmd. 5568, 5569 (1937).

[2] The visit of the Prime Minister to Rome in Jan. 1939 to toast the King as Emperor of Ethiopia was a natural preliminary to recognition of General Franco, in the hope of detaching him from his Italian and German connections, see Mr. Chamberlain, House of Commons, Feb. 27, 28, 1939. The uselessness of the efforts appears from Spanish denunciation of Britain's hold on Gibraltar and policy of encirclement : Don Suñer reported in *The Times*, June 16, p. 16 ; June 17, p. 12.

of the League. The Covenant was endorsed by Parlia- Chapter
XVI.
ment, and in the Italo-Ethiopian War advantage was
taken of the authority to execute the treaty by Order in
Council to issue such Orders imposing,[1] and later taking
off, sanctions. Parliament also approved the other treaties
of peace. On the other hand, it was not found necessary
to secure legislative confirmation of the further treaties
in support of the peace settlement, the Locarno Pact of
1925, the Paris Pact of 1928, for the renunciation of war
as an instrument of policy, the acceptance of compulsory
jurisdiction under the Statute of the Permanent Court of
International Justice, and that of the General Act of
1928 for the Pacific Settlement of International Disputes.[2]
But the House of Commons approved these instruments
with cordiality. On the same principle the termination of
the régime of sanctions against Italy was approved by the
Commons preparatory to it being advocated by the British
Government at Geneva in July 1936, and the final renunciation of obligation to Ethiopia was preceded by a vote in
the Commons, which likewise approved the surrender of
Czechoslovakia, *ex post facto*, a course followed in the
recognition of General Franco.

The attitude of the Government and Parliament as
regards Ethiopia and Czechoslovakia marks a complete
repudiation of the binding nature of the League Covenant,
and the matter is made clear by the Prime Minister's
declaration[3] on October 6, 1938 : "We had no treaty
obligations and no legal obligations to Czechoslovakia ",

[1] Treaty of Peace Act, 1919 (9 & 10 Geo. V. c. 33); Orders in Council,
Oct. 25, Nov. 9, 19, Dec. 20, 1935, revoked July 10, 1936 ; Keith, *Current
Imperial and International Problems, 1935–6*, pp. 145 ff.

[2] Keith, *Speeches and Documents on the British Dominions, 1918–1931*,
pp. 252 ff. On the other hand, the agreements on naval limitation in 1922,
1930, and 1936 were followed by legislation, 12 & 13 Geo. V. c. 21 ; 20 & 21
Geo. V. c. 48 ; 1 Edw. VIII. & 1 Geo. VI. c. 65.

[3] 339 *H.C. Deb.* 5 s. 546.

and his repeated denial of treaty obligations on March 15 when dealing with the subjection of Bohemia and Moravia and their conversion into German dependencies. It is clear that the Prime Minister thus repudiates the legal force of Article 10 of the League Covenant binding Britain to maintain the sovereignty and territorial integrity of Czechoslovakia, and of Article 20 imposing on Britain a solemn undertaking not to enter into any engagement inconsistent with the terms of the covenant. In precisely the same way Lord Maugham on November 3,[1] in defending the decision to recognise the King of Italy as Emperor of Ethiopia, deliberately ignored the covenant, and relied on international law apart from the covenant, which, of course, was framed as the essential basis of a new international law for the signatory powers. By their votes in support of the ministry in both houses on these occasions, Parliament must be taken to have homologated and accepted responsibility for actions which seem wholly incompatible with national honour, respect for solemn treaties, and morality, and which undermine the whole basis of the assertion that Germany acted dishonourably in violating the treaty of 1839 regarding Belgian neutrality.

The worthless character of the guarantee to Czechoslovakia given by Mr. Chamberlain at Munich, and formally defined as morally binding by Sir T. Inskip on October 4, 1938, was displayed on the occupation of Prague and the addition of Bohemia and Moravia to Germany's territory. Mr. Chamberlain explained that the declaration of Slovakian independence deprived the guarantee of any obligatory force. It was clear from the first that it could never be kept, once the Czechs handed over their fortifications, and it must be deeply regretted that

---

[1] 110 *H.L. Deb.* 5 s. 1678 f. Lord Cecil was in the minority of 6 to 55.

it was ever used as a means to induce Czech acceptance of the Munich terms.

At Godesberg during the then abortive negotiations, Mr. Chamberlain had pointed out that acceptance of Herr Hitler's terms regarding the immediate occupation of the Sudeten areas must ruin Czechoslovakia, and in these circumstances his persistence in a guarantee which he knew he could not keep was indefensible.

Logical as was the fate of Czechoslovakia,[1] it was further foreshadowed by the British and French failure to take any steps to secure the operation of the terms intended to safeguard the Czecho-Slovaks, and Herr Hitler was doubtless justified in his obvious view that the Munich agreement was intended as a disguised surrender of the territory to him. Mr. Chamberlain at first seems to have shared this view, for in the Commons on March 15 he declined to make charges of breach of faith. But on March 17, presumably as the result of expressions of public disapproval of the result, which had come as a shock to those who had not followed the Munich agreement and its sequel, he altered his attitude, and announced a policy of resistance to aggression as the result of the failure of appeasement at the expense of the liberty of other peoples. This was followed on March 31 in the Commons by an announcement of pledges given by Britain and France to Poland of aid in the event of a menace to her independence, and of the intention of creating collective security, with the support if possible of Russia, against aggression : on April 6 it was announced that Poland would enter into a permanent arrangement on a basis of reciprocity. The reply of the axis powers was rapid : Italy with German support speedily overran Albania and forced its acceptance

---

[1] It was pointed out categorically on Sept. 30, 1938 ; Keith, *The Scotsman,* Oct. 1, 1938. For the French betrayal see A. Werth, *France and Munich.*

Chapter
XVI.

of the King of Italy as sovereign, with complete indifference to the obligations assumed by Italy under the Anglo-Italian agreement of 1938. On April 13, the houses having been specially recalled from adjournment, it was explained that, in order to meet the threat to the position of Britain in the Mediterranean, unilateral guarantees had been given to Greece and Rumania against aggression, but that the Anglo-Italian agreement would not be denounced, apparently in the hope that Italy would thus be induced to withdraw her forces [1] from Spain, though obviously this would not mean any diminution in Italian assurance of Spanish aid in demands on France. It seems that Mr. Chamberlain still hoped to be able to induce Signor Mussolini to betray Herr Hitler. President Roosevelt intervened by an appeal for Germany to give assurances of pacific intentions, preparatory to a conference to settle causes of unrest, but Herr Hitler, in a very able speech on April 28, sought to prove that the axis powers were only seeking justice against the efforts at encirclement by Britain and France. On May 11, Turkey agreed to conclude an accord against aggression with Britain, to be followed by accord with France on the surrender of The Hatay to Turkish sovereignty. The essential alliance with Russia still hung fire, the proposals being manifestly unfair and one-sided, as shown by M. Molotoff on May 31 when he laid down the essentially just conditions that any pact should be exclusively defensive, should guarantee all the neighbours of Russia, and give concrete undertakings for

---

[1] But not her aircraft, despite categorical promise in the agreement. But from admissions extracted from Mr. Chamberlain on June 7 and 14 it appears that he was aware in March 1938 that Italy intended to hand over war material to Spain, so that he could not protest. This grave concealment of facts from the Commons, when asked to approve the Anglo-Italian agreement, strikes at the root of democracy, and is a precedent of the greatest danger, for it renders it impossible to expect foreign powers to put any faith in British assertions.

mutual help if one of the signatories was attacked. It is clear that the British projects involved serious risk that Russia would fail to receive just aid from Britain and France in event of her being attacked in retaliation for her entering into accord with these powers : the repudiation of categorical obligations by Britain and France to Ethiopia and Czechoslovakia, as well as their treatment of China and Spain, has naturally given Russia, which has scrupulously fulfilled her obligations since entering the League, just ground for suspicion.

It is a minor matter that, despite clear assurances given at Munich to Mr. Chamberlain regarding Memel, that area should have been taken from Lithuania under threat of immediate war. In all these moves since March Mr. Chamberlain has been assured of Opposition support, save as regards his reluctance, asserted in some quarters to be due to his inner circle of advisers on foreign affairs in the Cabinet, to deal fairly with Russia as an equal.

In all these matters the rôle of the League of Nations has been formal. It did nothing to aid Czechoslovakia in September 1938 or in March 1939, and Norway, Sweden, Denmark, Finland, Holland, the Balkan Entente, and other powers have made it clear that Article 16 regarding sanctions has no longer any binding force. Equally, nothing was done for Albania, and the Anglo-Italian agreement of 1938 expressly binds Britain and Egypt to keep open the Suez Canal to Italian transit even in case of war with these powers. The promise would no doubt be violated in practice, but it clearly negatives the use of the closing of the canal as a sanction. That course was plainly due during the war on Ethiopia, but it was negatived by France owing to the secret accord of M. Laval to abandon Ethiopia, and the refusal of Britain to impose any sanction not acquiesced in by Italy.[1] It is claimed that the new agreements are all in accord with the spirit of the League Covenant, but the value of that instrument is patently negligible, apart from the fact that Germany and Italy have concluded on May 22 an effective military alliance, and that they expect those powers which adhere to the axis, such as Hungary and Spain, to have nothing to do with the League.

International law indeed must now be regarded as having been reduced to unreality by the action of all the Great Powers except Russia, and it is significant that as early as February 1939 Britain notified the League that, in case of war, it would not regard itself as bound by its acceptance of the General Act of 1928 for the Pacific Settlement of International Disputes. It is clear also that the basis of the whole mandatory system is gone, and that the German claim for the return of her former possessions can no longer be met by reference to treaties which Britain and France have violated as fully as their rivals. It is plainly impossible to accept the view that British policy in Palestine must depend on the views of the Council of the League. As the British Government was compelled to admit in the debates in the Commons on Palestine on May 22 and 23, the promises [2] made to the Arabs preclude the perpetuation of the policy of promoting Jewish immigration to such an extent that the Arabs will be reduced to a helpless minority under the domination of a Jewish State. It should be remembered that on June 21, 1922, the House of Lords, despite the appeal of Lord Balfour, who had fallen under the spell of Dr. Weizmann's Zionism,[3]

[1] Keith, *Letters on Current Imperial and International Problems, 1935–1936*, pp. 154, 156, 163, 184.

[2] The effort of Lord Maugham to show that Palestine was excluded from Sir H. McMahon's promise is wholly unconvincing.

[3] Cf. Dugdale, *Arthur James Balfour*, ii. 222 ff.

determined by 60 votes to 29 that the terms of the mandate were not compatible with the pledges given to the Arabs in 1915 and 1918, and that four Lords of Appeal were included in the majority against the Government. The strength of Jewish political influence is shown by the fact that, despite an urgent whip, the ministry was only able to carry approval of its policy by 89 votes, and that Mr. Belisha and Mr. Elliot, Cabinet ministers, did not vote. Yet these proposals include an immigration of 75,000 Jews in five years, and only thereafter will the Arabs be allowed to determine the amount of immigration, while the prospect of self-government for the Arabs is dependent on the devising of a constitution which will secure the Jewish National Home. Meanwhile unauthorised immigration probably exceeds authorised, and *The Times* [1] correspondent in Jerusalem admits that the failure to stop this influx endangers the retention by the Arabs of any of the land. It is difficult to avoid the conclusion that the policy of Jewish immigration to the destruction of Arab liberty, though favoured by the Liberal and Labour parties and a large body of Conservative opinion, is a grave breach of elementary principles of morality, while it has certainly exposed Britain to a most damaging fire of criticism in the Arab States and in India.[2]

It seems probable that British recognition *de jure* of the conquest of Albania [3] will not be delayed, and that that of Czechoslovakia, as dissolved into the German protectorates of Bohemia and Moravia and of Slovakia,

[1] *The Times*, May 31, 1939. By June 2 some 3000 had entered since the announcement of the new policy.

[2] Keith, *Letters on Current Imperial and International Problems, 1935–1936*, pp. 110-18 ; *The King, the Constitution, the Empire and Foreign Affairs, 1936–1937*, pp. 182 ff. ; *The Scotsman*, Oct. 21, 1938.

[3] The new British Ambassador was not required to have credentials to the King of Albania.

will follow. It has been indicated [1] in the failure of the British Government to use its influence to secure that the Bank for International Settlements should not transfer to German control the Czecho-Slovak funds in its hand. Not even Conservative members were satisfied at the explanations of Sir John Simon of the position, and it may be doubted if the bank has not outlived its utility. Incidentally reference was made to the fact that the representatives of the Bank of England on the B.I.S. did not keep in touch with the Chancellor in consideration of questions of policy. It certainly appears that the independence of the Bank of England is likely to become dangerous to national interests, and that there is accumulating strong reason to secure that its management shall be brought into closer accord with the interests of the public as opposed to those of financiers. Few incidents have evoked more evidence of the waning of confidence [2] in the bank direction.

6. *The Consuls and Consular Jurisdiction*

The consular service is under the control of the Foreign Office and of the Overseas Trade Department, whose Secretary is appointed by the Foreign Secretary and the Board of Trade. The ranks in the service include agents and consuls-general, consuls, vice-consuls, consular agents and pro-consuls, and recent practice aims at the reservation as far as possible of even minor consular offices to British subjects. They are commissioned by the Crown through the Foreign Secretary, and their duties include the preparation of statistics and other information on the trade of the places where they act with special regard to

[1] House of Commons, May 24 and 26. Slovakia had already been recognised, *de facto*.
[2] *The Times*, June 1, 1939, p. 19.

openings for British trade ; the grant of advice and assistance to British subjects ; the administration so far as local law allows of estates of such subjects dying within their jurisdiction ; arbitration in cases of disputes referred to them, various duties as to merchant shipping and aircraft ; the legalisation of documents by affixing the consular seal ; the granting of a visa to passports and the issuing in certain cases of passports ; the performance of marriages under the Foreign Marriage Act, 1892 ; and so forth. In case of injustice to British subjects, they use good offices and report ; in all matters where diplomatic action is needed, they deal with the British representative, for they have no diplomatic status. They do not enjoy therefore the immunities of diplomats,[1] but respect should be paid to their papers, though in civil and criminal matters alike they are subject to local jurisdiction. These principles [2] apply to consular officers appointed from foreign countries to Britain, who must be approved by the Crown before they can enter on the performance of their functions. In the case of British officers those of the rank of consul or of higher rank are appointed by royal commission, and request for their recognition is made through the diplomatic representative of the Crown and is usually accorded by an *exequatur* ; vice-consuls if appointed by commission receive like treatment, but others, consular agents and pro-consuls, are recognised less formally, and are appointed by letter from higher consular officers.

Consular officers must obey instructions from the diplomatic representative of the Crown, though, if these

---

[1] Cf. for English law, *Barbuit's Case* (1737), Cas. *temp.* Talb. 281 ; *Viveash v. Becker* (1814), 3 M. & S. 284.

[2] Serious allegations of complicity of the German Consulate at Liverpool in the sale of information by a British subject, who was sentenced to 10 years imprisonment, were made in May 1939. In such a case the *exequatur* can be withdrawn.

contradict the standing consular instructions, they may refer back for confirmation. They are subject to the Official Secrets Acts, 1911 and 1920, as well as to dismissal for breach of duty.

The former system, by which the Crown was accorded jurisdiction over British subjects and British protected persons in certain foreign countries by consent of the sovereign, has been in steady decline of recent years. It was under Queen Victoria that it was made effective in operation by legislation,[1] and for a time it was steadily extended from Turkey and Turkish dependencies to China, Siam, Persia, Zanzibar, Ethiopia, etc. But the Treaty of Lausanne of 1923 terminated the system in Turkey, the Persian Government by unilateral action in 1928 [2] obtained release from the system, and the last remains of it disappeared as regards Siam in 1938.[3] In the case of Egypt the system was reduced to minor aspects, subject to a time limit, at an international conference in 1937.[4] In French Morocco, British jurisdiction was surrendered in the same year.[5] In Japan it had been abandoned by a treaty of 1894. The acceptance of the conquest of Ethiopia *de jure* in 1938 ended any possibility of its maintenance there ; it had already been allowed to lapse in Tunis under the French Protectorate. In the territories detached from Turkey and placed under British and French mandates, including at first Iraq, the system had lapsed in favour of steps taken by the mandatory powers to secure effective administration of justice, and this is provided for in the arrangements with Iraq. In China proposals to abandon jurisdiction were favourably considered until the aggression

---

[1] 6 & 7 Vict. c. 94 ; see now 53 & 54 Vict. c. 37 extended by 19 & 20 Geo. V. c. 23, s. 106 ; 22 & 23 Geo. V. c. 9, ss. 36 (2), 39 (1), 64 (2), 67 (1), (3) ; 24 & 25 Geo. V. c. 49, s. 13.

[2] Order in Council, May 7, 1928.

[3] *Parl. Pap.* Cmd. 5921.

[4] *Ibid.* 5491.

[5] *Ibid.* 5538.

of Japan on China rendered further action for the time being impossible. There remains thus jurisdiction in respect of China, Kashgar, Bahrein, Kuwait, and Maskat, relations with these three last territories being controlled by the Government of India in view of the special concern of India with the Persian Gulf. In Egypt there survives full jurisdiction under Order in Council, October 2, 1937, over the British forces maintained therein and the British military mission, and in matters of status over British subjects, except nationals of the Union of South Africa and of Eire, whose Governments preferred to assert their complete independence by declining to permit the jurisdiction of a court created and controlled by the British Government. Over the Anglo-Egyptian Sudan, which is a condominium with Egypt, the British control rests ultimately in the Foreign Office, but the Governor-General is accorded a wide autonomy. Ultimate British cession of sovereignty may be foreshadowed by the omission of the territory in the list of territories connected with the Crown in the Official Coronation Souvenir Programme.[1]

[1] Keith, *The King, the Constitution, the Empire, and Foreign Affairs, 1936–1937*, pp. 135 ff.

CHAPTER XVII

IMPERIAL AFFAIRS

1. *The Dominions Office*

REFERENCE has been already made to the creation of a distinct Secretaryship of State for War as the outcome of the Crimean War, and the resulting restriction of the activities of the Secretary of State for War and the Colonies to colonial affairs. The development of the constitutional status of the self-governing colonies rendered the control of relations with them and the direction of the administration of the colonies rather incongruous duties for a single Secretary of State to perform, and an impression was diffused in the colonies which were developing into States that their affairs were misunderstood by the staff of the Colonial Office, because they were accustomed to controlling colonies which had no capacity for self-government. In 1911 [1] the Imperial Conference decided not to press for division of the work and the handing over of matters affecting Dominion relations to the care of the Prime Minister, aided by a minister in the Lords, nor even to accept the suggestion of duplicating the Under-Secretaryship of State so as to maintain a distinction between the staff dealing with the colonies and that concerned with Dominion affairs. In fact, however, a Dominions Department had already been created, though there was one Permanent Under-Secretary only. The arrangement continued until 1925

---

[1] Keith, *Responsible Government in the Dominions* (2nd ed.), ii. 1186 f.

without serious dissatisfaction in the Dominions, but in that year, rather unnecessarily, Mr. Amery secured the creation of a new Secretaryship of State for Dominion Affairs, but the office was in fact held together with that of the Colonies and the distinction was purely formal, but separate appointment was made of a Parliamentary Under-Secretary for Dominion Affairs. Separate offices were decided upon in 1930,[1] but the Secretaryships were again combined for a time in 1938–9 after the death of Lord Stanley. The offices were separated once more in 1939 when Sir T. Inskip was transferred to the Dominions Office, no doubt as a result of the difficulties experienced by the ministry in meeting the persistent attacks made upon him by members of the rank and file on the Government side for failure to make any improvement in the measures for co-ordination of defence and for alleged lack of constructive activity in securing better measures of defence against air attack.

The division of work now in force assigns to the Dominions Secretary the duty of dealing with the Empire in alliance as opposed to the Empire in subordination. He conducts British relations with Canada, the Commonwealth of Australia, the Union of South Africa, and Eire. Though Newfoundland since 1934 [2] has surrendered temporarily her self-government as a result of financial stress and the necessity of restoring equilibrium between revenue and expenditure and ameliorating the economic position of the people, control rests with the Dominions Secretary. The administration is conducted by a Commission with executive and legislative powers, while the necessary funds for the purpose of maintaining the public services

[1] Mr. Thomas was given the Dominions Office after the complete failure of his efforts as Lord Privy Seal to solve unemployment; Somervell, *George V.*, pp. 412-14.

[2] Keith, *The Dominions as Sovereign States*, pp. 93-8.

and restoring economic prosperity have been given or lent by the British Government. The Dominions Secretary is also entrusted with relations with Southern Rhodesia, a colony which in internal affairs is almost wholly autonomous, and he controls the Native Territories of Basutoland, which is a colony, and the Bechuanaland Protectorate and Swaziland, in view of the intimate relations of these areas with the Union of South Africa, which seeks to secure their transfer to Union control, while this is opposed by the native populations. To the Dominions Secretary falls also the control of the question of overseas settlement, opportunities for which are, of course, mainly confined to the Dominions. He is also a member of the Imperial Conference, and his department is the normal channel of communications connected therewith. The Prime Minister, however, is the final authority in matters affecting the Conference, and the Cabinet Secretariat provides part of the British Secretariat for the Conference, each Dominion also contributing members.

The development of Dominion status does not fall here to be discussed.[1] The present position is that the Dominions may be regarded as in effect sovereign States linked together, and to the United Kingdom by the possession of a common sovereign, though in the case of Eire that sovereign is denied any internal sovereignty and serves only in a restricted field of external relations. Nationals of Eire are regarded in Eire as not possessing British nationality, but are accepted by Britain as British subjects [2] at least when outside Eire. In issues of external affairs affecting Eire and the Union of South Africa they

---

[1] Keith, *op. cit.* (1938).

[2] Hence they are admitted of right to the United Kingdom. Eire also gives free admission, having placed British subjects of all kinds in a favoured position. See Minister of Labour, House of Commons, Feb. 16, 1939; Keith, *The Scotsman*, April 22, May 2, 1939.

act as far as possible through their own diplomatic representation in foreign countries ; otherwise, in accordance
with the agreement of the Imperial Conference of 1930,
they use British diplomatic representatives. Canada has
diplomatic representation in Washington, Paris, and Tokyo,
but in the rest of the world is normally content to act
through British agencies. In the making of treaties and
diplomatic and consular appointments, Eire and the Union
employ their own seals, and the King acts on the advice
of these Governments without British mediation ; Canada
still uses the British seals for treaties, and Australia and
New Zealand employ British agencies for the conclusion
of formal treaties, as opposed to agreements of less importance, which the Governments conclude direct with consular
representatives of foreign States.

In internal affairs since the Statute of Westminster,
1931, Canada, Eire, and the Union are freed from the
supremacy of British legislative power ; Eire has cut off
all appeal to the Privy Council,[1] and Canada [2] and the
Union are free thus to act. The Commonwealth and New
Zealand as well as Newfoundland are not yet under the
Statute, as in their case it applies only if so declared by their
legislatures, but the two former are for all practical purposes
as free of British control as Eire, the Union, or Canada.

The Parliamentary Under-Secretary of State is chairman of the Oversea Settlement Committee, which is
concerned with the carrying-out of the policy declared in
the Empire Settlement Act, 1922, and of the Oversea
Settlement Board, whose function it is to advise on specific
schemes of migration suggested and on any other issues
referred to it.

[1] See *Moore* v. *Att.-Gen. of Irish Free State*, [1935] A.C. 484.
[2] Canada has abolished criminal appeals : *British Coal Corpn.* v. *R.*,
[1935] A.C. 500.

In a number of important matters there is inter-Imperial co-operation and consultation. The Imperial Economic Committee was established in 1925 ; its functions were extended by decisions of the Imperial Conferences of 1926 and 1930, and under a report of an Imperial Committee on Economic Consultation and Co-operation, 1933. There is an executive council of the Imperial Agricultural Bureaux set up in 1929, which supervises the administration and finances of the Imperial Institute of Entomology established in 1913, and the Imperial Mycological Institute founded in 1920. The Imperial Shipping Committee was set up in 1920, and its activities have been markedly useful. The Imperial Communications Advisory Committee dates from 1929, as a result of the Imperial Wireless and Cable Conference of 1928, and has certain responsibilities in matters of policy affecting the operations of Cable and Wireless Ltd., the corporation created to co-ordinate the telegraphic services connecting the various parts of the Empire. The Empire Forestry Conference meets at intervals to discuss forestry policy in general, and there is a Standing Committee on Empire Forestry.

The British Government is now represented in each Dominion, including since 1939 New Zealand, but excepting Eire, by a High Commissioner with political and economic functions, while the Dominions are similarly represented in London, and the Australian States send Agents-General. One Canadian province has an Agent-General, but, under the Canadian constitution, the High Commissioner is as regards relations with the British Government the accredited spokesman for Canada.

2. *The Colonial Office*

The Colonial Secretary is responsible for the final control over all colonies, over protectorates, and over territories placed under the mandate of the British Government. In the case of the colonies this control varies in proportion to the amount of local autonomy which is conceded. Ceylon has been given a constitution allowing a considerable amount of autonomy, and a measure of responsible government. In the case of the Bahamas, Bermuda, and Barbados, the bicameral legislatures, a survival from the old colonial régime, are not subject to the control of the Colonial Secretary, though he has authority over the executive. In the great majority of the colonies the Colonial Secretary is in a position to control the legislature as well as the executive government ; in many cases the legislature, as against elected and nominated members, has a majority of official members ; in others British Guiana, Jamaica, Mauritius, and the new (1939) constitution of Malta, the official and nominated members, with the support of the Governor, can outvote the elected members, and in addition the Governor has power to pass enactments over the head of opposition if he deems fit. In others there are only official and nominated members, and in a few the Governor alone legislates.

Of protectorates there are two kinds. The one comprises territories which are assimilated in effect to colonies in respect of government ; such are Nyasaland and Uganda which have legislatures, partly official, partly nominated. For Nigeria and Sierra Leone, colony and protectorate, there are legislatures with a minority of elected members, but for the Northern Provinces of Nigeria the legislature acts in financial matters only. For the Gambia Protectorate the legislature of the Gambia legislates, for the Northern Territories of the Gold Goast the Governor, and so for Somaliland. The Legislative Council of Kenya legislates for the Kenya Protectorate.

Other territories are protected States in which the

British authority varies in extent. In Sarawak and British North Borneo, ruled by a British subject as rajah and a British chartered company respectively, the British Government does not interfere in internal administration, though it might do so in case of misrule of a serious character. In the Federated Malay States, and in less degree in the unfederated States, the Government acts through the local rulers, who are bound to act on the advice given to them except in matters of religion. In Zanzibar there is a duplication of a native Government, carried on under British advice and consular jurisdiction. In Tonga, a native Pacific kingdom, the local Government is in considerable measure autonomous, but, in cases of serious crime, consular jurisdiction is exercised over Europeans.

The mandated territories controlled by the Colonial Secretary are Tanganyika, which has a Legislative Council partly nominated, partly official ; the Cameroons, for the northern area of which the Governor of Nigeria legislates, and for the southern the Governor and Legislative Council legislate ; and Togoland, for which the Governor of the Gold Coast legislates. Palestine, since the abortive effort to create a Legislative Council in 1922–3, is legislated for by the High Commissioner, who has an advisory Council ; its future, under Article 22 of the League of Nations Covenant, should be independence, as in the case of Iraq. The only difference between the mandated territories and protectorates in legal position [1] is that British authority in regard to the former is subject to the terms of the mandate, and that a report must be made to the League Council for consideration by its Mandates Committee, which may comment on matters wherein violation of the mandate may be suspected.

[1] Mandated territories are governed by Orders in Council under the Foreign Jurisdiction Act, 1890.

In regard to these territories the authority exercised largely rests on the royal prerogative. That authorises the Crown to set up in colonies acquired by settlement a constitution analogous to the British including an elected legislative house, and such constitutions still exist in Bahamas, Bermuda, and Barbados. For conquered or ceded colonies, including those ceded by their inhabitants like Malta, the Crown may create any form of constitution, but, if a representative constitution is given, that is one including a house in which half the members are elected, the right to alter is lost unless expressly retained.[1] For other colonies Parliament has made provision, allowing the setting up of such constitutions as may be deemed proper ; this is the case with St. Vincent, Grenada, and Tobago, now united to Trinidad ;[2] with Jamaica,[3] British Guiana,[4] and Malta ;[5] with the Straits Settlements[6] and St. Helena,[7] formerly under the Government of India ; and with certain settled colonies, including the Falkland Islands.[8] For protectorates authority in fullest measure exists under the Foreign Jurisdiction Act, 1890.

All matters of importance concerning these territories are subject to the control of the Colonial Secretary, who advises the Crown as to disallowance of legislation, apart from the fact that important legislation should not be introduced without his prior approval or suggestion. Financial control is close, especially if Imperial grants are being given, and the Colonial Audit Department in London audits the accounts of most of the territories. Great progress has been made with the setting-up for the colonies and protectorates of unified services, the

---

[1] *Campbell* v. *Hall* (1774), 1 Cowp. 204 ; *Sammut* v. *Strickland,* [1938] A.C. 678.

[2] 39 & 40 Vict. c. 47.

[3] 29 & 30 Vict. c. 12.

[4] 18 & 19 Geo. V. c. 5.

[5] 26 Geo. V. & 1 Edw. VIII. c. 29.

[6] 29 & 30 Vict. c. 115.

[7] 3 & 4 Will. IV. c. 85, s. 112.

[8] 50 & 51 Vict. c. 54.

Chapter
XVII.

Administrative Service, the Legal, Medical, Forest, Agricultural, Veterinary, Police, etc.   Recruitment is shared by the Director of Recruitment and the Crown Agents for the Colonies, who, under the final authority of the Colonial Secretary, act as financial and business agents for the colonies and protectorates.

A large number of bodies in London serve purposes of advice and control.   There is a Colonial Advisory Medical Committee which dates in one aspect for 1909 ; a Colonial Survey and Geophysical Committee, dating from 1905 ; an Advisory Committee on Education in the Colonies, since 1929 ; an African Liquor Traffic Control Committee, since 1924 ; the Discovery Committee for Antarctic Research, since 1923 ; a Colonial Advisory Council of Agriculture and Animal Health ; a Colonial Development Advisory Committee, set up in 1929 to advise on the application of the funds rendered available by the Colonial Development Act, 1929 ; a Standing Financial Committee, since 1932, to consider financial matters affecting the colonies, etc., as a whole ; West African, East African, and Palestine Currency Boards ; a Bureau of Hygiene and Tropical Diseases ; and a Colonial Forest Resources Development Department.

The Imperial Institute since 1925 has been under the control of the Parliamentary Secretary of the Overseas Trade Department.   The Board of Governors includes Dominion representatives as well as representatives of the Colonial Office, which from 1907 to 1925 had been in management.

For Malaya and the Eastern African Dependencies there are Information Offices controlled by the Governments concerned under the authority of the Secretary of State.

From the courts of the colonies and other territories

appeals lie to the Privy Council,[1] whose functions have been discussed above. For the West Indies,[2] for the territories in West Africa,[3] and for those in Eastern Africa [4] an intermediate appeal court is provided.

3. *The India and Burma Offices*

The Secretary of State for India replaced in 1858 [5] the President of the Board of Control, who had exercised the powers of the Crown over the proceedings of the East India Company, when the control of Indian government was directly assumed by the Crown. The essential distinction between his position and that of the Colonial Secretary was the fact that, as a result of the past history of India, it was deemed right to associate with him in Indian government a Council of members with Indian experience, and that the control of Indian government was formally given to the Secretary of State in Council. The Government of India, therefore, despite its importance and the wide extent of its functions, was only the agency in India of the Secretary of State for India in Council, while in the colonies the Governor was invested with the executive power of the Crown, although the Colonial Secretary could direct him as regards its exercise. The final responsibility for India was very closely watched in England in the matter of tariff policy. It was deemed essential to forbid anything which might lessen the share of Lancashire in the Indian market, and a rather

[1] See Chap. XXI, § 3 (ii).

[2] West Indian Court of Appeal Act, 1919 (9 & 10 Geo. V. c. 47). Direct appeal lies as well as to the Court of Appeal

[3] West African Court of Appeal from 1928 : Gold Coast, Sierra Leone, Gambia, Ashanti, Nigeria.

[4] Eastern African Court of Appeal from 1921 : Kenya, Nyasaland, Uganda, Zanzibar, Tanganyika.

[5] 21 & 22 Vict. c. 106.

amusing constitutional wrangle occurred in 1876 [1] when the
Secretary of State was attacked for requiring the Indian
Government to revoke a duty on cotton importations,
and it was hotly contended by the Duke of Argyll among
others that he had reduced the Indian legislature to
complete subserviency. The minister retorted by citing
earlier actions by Liberal predecessors, which at least
showed that the Indian legislature had never been given
discretion in issues of any importance.

Reference has been made above [2] to the introduction
of the Morley-Minto reforms of 1907–9, to the far more
important Montagu-Chelmsford changes in 1917–21, and
to the great concessions of the Government of India Act,
1935,[3] which contemplates federation in 1940, and which
has given responsible government to the provinces. Under
it an important change has taken place in the status of
the Secretary of State. He no longer constitutes in
Council the fundamental authority for Indian government.
He is given advisers who are of wholly subordinate
character as compared with the former Council, whose
formal assent was necessary for expenditure of Indian
revenues, and the Government of India is vested in the
King and carried out in the central and local Governments
through the Governor-General and Governors. Over these
authorities the Secretary of State exercises a limited statutory control subject to Parliament. The issue of instruments
of instructions to the Governor-General and Governors
is, by an innovation, made subject to approval by both
houses of Parliament, and legislation by Orders in Council
in matters which the Act subjects to such procedure is

[1] 227 *Hansard*, 3 s. 1871 ff., 1964 ff., 1996 ff.; Monypenny and
Buckle, *Disraeli*, i. 1483-1509. On the Queen's title see *ibid.* ii. 790-98,
802-17.

[2] See Chap. III, § 12 (iii).

[3] 26 Geo. V. & 1 Edw. VIII. c. 2.

also subject to Parliamentary control, Orders having first to be submitted in draft to both houses.

By another innovation certain legislation passed in India by the Governor-General or the Governor over the head of his legislature has to be laid before Parliament, if possible before the assent of the Crown is accorded.

The recruitment and control of the Indian Civil Service and the Indian Police still rests with the Secretary of State, as well as the final voice in all issues of external relations and defence. He can also determine policy on any other issues if that is deemed necessary, and he is solely responsible for control of relations with the Indian States.

Burma, formerly a province of India, was separated from India contemporaneously with the coming into operation of provincial responsible government therein.[1] The territory is now a British possession but not a colony, and it enjoys a modified form of responsible government, except in regard to external relations and defence, which the Governor controls, while in certain other matters he has special responsibilities. The office of Secretary of State for Burma is held by the Secretary of State, since the co-ordination of Indian and Burman policy is clearly essentially a matter for one minister. The Parliamentary and Permanent Under-Secretaries also act for both territories.

India has since 1919 enjoyed the same status in the League of Nations as the Dominions despite the fact that its policy is dictated by the British Government, and even after federation external relations other than those between India and the Dominions will remain in British control. Burma has no place in the League, but has been represented at the Imperial Conference of 1937 on the same

[1] The Government of Burma Act, 1935 (26 Geo. V. & 1 Edw. VIII. c. 3).

footing as Southern Rhodesia, that is by the Premier as observer ; in fact this means little less than full membership, as the Conference is essentially advisory.

There is a High Commissioner for India in London who performs, under the control of the Government of India, the business functions formerly undertaken by the India Office.   He acts also for Burma.

CHAPTER XVIII

NATIONAL DEFENCE

1. *The Defence Ministries*

(i) The War Office

A VARIETY of reasons combined to maintain after the Napoleonic wars a state of remarkable confusion in regard to the administration of national defence.[1] The army had been accepted as a painful necessity in time of peace rather than a valuable safeguard, and the diversity of authority for its control was regarded, not as a fatal barrier to economy and efficiency but as a useful method of preventing the military power encroaching on the sphere of civil authority; the memory of the rule of Cromwell's major-generals seems to have long persisted. The Crown might have been expected to seek to attain a less unsatisfactory position, but its views were deeply affected by the fact that this effort would involve the co-operation of ministers, and this would bring about some perhaps serious limitation of the prerogative. Hence the medley of authorities was permitted to operate until its defects were distinctly and painfully revealed during the Crimean War, and reform became quite unavoidable.

Of the several authorities the Ordnance was the oldest. It reflected the time when the maintenance of forts and garrisons was the undisputed prerogative of the Crown; the department undertook necessarily the provision of

[1] Sir R. Biddulph, *Lord Cardwell*, chap. i.

guns and munitions of all kinds, and its activities in this
regard were extended to cover provisions for the needs of
the navy.   In the eighteenth century the Master-General
of the Ordnance was a minister of Cabinet rank ; he was
commander-in-chief of the artillery and engineers and
presided at the Board of Ordnance, which was given
the right to acquire lands for military purposes, while the
Ordnance Survey reflects a power now transferred to the
Minister of Agriculture.   The rise of responsible government saw the disappearance of the Master-General from
political importance, and the reforms of 1855 [1] ended the
history of the Board as a separate department.   Its powers
were given by statute to the Secretary of State, to whom
the Queen entrusted the seals of the War Department,
while the office of Commander-in-Chief passed into the
hands of the officer entrusted with command over the
infantry.

A second office which disappeared as such was that of
Secretary at War, which Lord Palmerston had held for
years in his youth.[2]   In the eighteenth century this officer
served to express the royal will in matters of army administration with a vague responsibility to Parliament which
was made more real in 1783 [3] when he was required to
prepare estimates for Parliament, transmit the money
voted to the Paymaster-General of the Forces, and to
settle annually the accounts of expenditure.   In 1793 the
King surrendered command-in-chief to the General Com-
manding-in-Chief, who became in matters of internal discipline and regulation the channel by which the royal
pleasure was communicated in lieu of the Secretary of War,
whose position was affected next year by the appointment

[1] 18 & 19 Vict. c. 117.

[2] Omond, *Parl. and the Army*, 1642–1904, pp. 66 ff. ; Clode, *Mil. Forces,*
ii. 690 ff.

[3] 22 Geo. III. c. 8 ; 23 Geo. III. c. 50.

of a third Secretary of State for War. The latter relieved the Secretary at War of the business of a definitely political character other than that connected with estimates, the preparation of the Mutiny Bill, the control of the execution of military law, and the safeguarding of the rights of the civil population against the army. Matters as to the principles of the employment and size of the forces now fell to the Secretary of State for War, who was essentially in the Cabinet, while the Secretary at War was not often there. The delimitation of functions between the Commander-in-Chief and the Secretary at War was roughly indicated, after a long controversy in 1810. In the reforms of 1855 the two offices were assigned to one holder, and in 1863 [1] the office of Secretary at War disappeared.

The reform scheme affected also the commissariat [2] which was a branch of the Treasury, and supplied at home and abroad food and forage, fuel and light, for the forces. The system was not as inefficient as might have been expected, but in December 1854 it was transferred to the War Office.

The Secretary of State for War, when created in 1794, was chiefly concerned with the immediate war issues of the day, but in 1801 colonial business came into his hands and remained there until 1854. His charge over war business then was for a prolonged period rather subsidiary to his interests in the colonies. The Home Secretary was charged with issues of home defence and countersigned commissions for all but Indian or colonial forces ; stores for the army needed by the Commander-in-Chief had to be secured through the Secretary at War and the Home Secretary from the Ordnance Board. The Secretary of State for War was responsible with the Cabinet for the decision as to the strength of the army, its employment

[1] 26 & 27 Vict. c. 12.   [2] Clode, ii. 193-203.

in colonial defence, and for communications with officers overseas. In war he was responsible for the measures taken other than as regards home defence, and communicated with the generals in the field. In 1854 the offices of Secretary of State for War and the Colonies were rendered distinct, and the former absorbed the functions of the departments above mentioned. Further, the War Office, now reorganised, took over the functions of the Board of General Officers [1] in respect of clothing and the Army Medical Department, so that a more or less unified control existed, the essential difficulty remaining being the independent position in practice enjoyed by the Commander-in-Chief, though his actions had to be defended if occasion arose in the Commons or Lords by the Secretary of State.

The position was unsatisfactory, though after 1861 there was no attempt to limit the responsibility of the Secretary of State even formally, for the supplementary patent reserving to the Commander-in-Chief military command and discipline, appointments and promotions, subject to the responsibility of the Secretary of State, disappeared.[2] The duties of that minister were onerous and complex, and a marked improvement in organisation was caused by Mr. Cardwell's division of his office [3] into three sections. The military department fell under the Commander-in-Chief, whose complete subordination to the Secretary of State was stated by Order in Council ; ordnance and finance were placed under the Surveyor-General and Financial Secretary, who might sit in the Commons and thus afford relief to their chief. The Secretary of State was represented by a Parliamentary Secretary in the House of Parliament, of which he was not a member.

---

[1] Appointed by royal warrant in 1714.
[2] Clode, ii. 350 ff., 738 f.
[3] 33 & 34 Vict. c. 17 ; Order in Council, June 4, 1870 ; *Parl. Pap.* C. 164.

In 1887 the office of Surveyor-General, which had failed to fulfil expectations, was abolished, and in 1888 the War Office business was divided into the military and civil sides, the Commander-in-Chief becoming responsible for advice on all military matters, while the Financial Secretary was charged definitely with all matters relating to expenditure, account, and audit, and the control of manufacturing departments. But the military department obviously was too great a burden for any one man, for he had not merely the duty of advising on military policy in every branch, but he had serious administrative functions, and his position remained anomalous, though an effort on the part of the Duke of Cambridge to revise the question of his position was immediately defeated by Mr. Childers in 1882,[1] for he was in direct communication as a matter of right with the Crown. A Commission under Lord Hartington,[2] therefore, reported in 1890 in favour of the disappearance of so anomalous a post ; the Secretary of State should be advised by military officers whose executive duties should not be so heavy as to interfere with their acting as a consultative body, and the Commander-in-Chief should be replaced by a Chief of Staff. The Queen deeply resented the report as striking at the royal prerogative,[3] and only in 1895 was it possible for Sir H. Campbell-Bannerman to secure the Duke of Cambridge's reluctant retirement,[4] largely, no doubt, because the Queen hoped that it might be possible to secure the vacant post for her son, the Duke of Connaught. The office, however, was given to Lord Wolseley with reduced powers. He was made the principal adviser of the Secretary of State on military questions, charged with the plans for offence and defence, collection of military information, appointments, promotions, honours,

---

[1] Omond, pp. 128 ff.
[2] *Parl. Pap.* C. 5979.
[3] *Letters*, 3 s., i. 582-4, 594.
[4] *Ibid.* ii. 504 ff., 512 f.

and rewards.[1] But the Adjutant-General took over charge of discipline, education and training, enlistment and discharge ; the Quartermaster-General, the supply of food and forage, fuel and light, transport and the administration of the non-combative services ; the Inspector-General of Ordnance, the provision of warlike stores and equipment in all its aspects ; and the Inspector-General of Fortifications became responsible for fortifications, barracks, military railways and telegraphs, and War Office lands.

The South African War tested, as had the Crimean War, the efficiency of the organisation, and found it largely wanting, and Lord Wolseley in 1901 [2] declared that it resulted in the Commander-in-Chief not having sufficient control, while the subordinate officers had not full responsibility. Lord Lansdowne replied, rather tartly, that the powers of the Commander-in-Chief were adequate, but had not been effectively exercised by the holder of that office. There was, however, little doubt that the system was defective, and that the plan by which the officers mentioned above sat as a rule weekly as a War Office Council to consider matters suggested by the Secretary of State, or proposed by individual members, while an Army Board under the Commander-in-Chief dealt with estimates, the higher promotions, and in war the details of mobilisation, was far from securing the best advice for the ministry. The report of the Royal Commission on the war in South Africa [3] stressed this defect. The solution was found by the expert Committee on the Reconstitution of the War Office appointed in 1903.[4] It recommended the application of the proposal of 1890, and in 1904 letters patent

[1] Order in Council, Nov. 21, 1895.
[2] *Parl. Pap.* Cd. 512 ; House of Lords, March 5, 1901.
[3] *Ibid.* Cd. 1789, pp. 132-43.　　　[4] *Ibid.* Cd. 1932, 1968, 2002.

were issued transferring all the authority of the Secretary of State and Commander-in-Chief to a Council composed of the Secretary of State, Parliamentary Under-Secretary, Financial Secretary, and four military members, to whom was added as Secretary to the Council the Permanent Under-Secretary of State. Various changes in the exact delimitation of functions of officers took place, and in 1937–8 the Council's composition was increased by the addition of a Director-General of the Territorial Army, whose importance was thus at last duly recognised, while a Director-General of Munitions took over the functions of the Master-General of the Ordnance.[1]

The position of the Secretary of State is one of final authority, for the Army Council is not in a position to decide anything against his ruling, and he is therefore master in his own house, subject to the control of the Cabinet and Parliament. His chief military adviser is the Chief of the Imperial General Staff, a body planned in 1907 and developed in importance by Lord Haldane. Together with the chiefs of staff of the other two services, he forms a committee of advice to the Government on defence taken as a whole.

(ii) The Air Ministry

The creation of the Secretaryship for Air was a product of the Great War, and followed upon the comparative failure to give satisfaction of two Air Boards, whose functions were limited in the main to supply. The ministry was based on the analogy of the War Office and the Army Council, and the Air Council as reconstituted in 1938 comprises the Secretary of State as President, the Parliamentary Under-Secretary as Vice-President, the Chief of the Air Staff and First Air Member, the Air Member for

[1] Orders in Council, Aug. 10, 1904 ; Aug. 2, 1910 ; Oct. 15, 1922 ; Dec. 17, 1931.

Personnel, the Air Member for Development and Production, the Air Member for Supply and Organisation, and the Permanent Under-Secretary as Secretary.[1] The Secretary of State holds the same position of authority towards the other members as the Secretary of State for War towards the Army Council. He appoints the Air members, except the Chief of Staff, who is appointed by the King.

(iii) The Admiralty

The history of the Admiralty differentiated it considerably from that of the War Office. It represents the old office of Lord High Admiral of England, which ceased to be exercised by an individual from 1708 save for a brief and not fortunate tenure by the Duke of Clarence in 1827–8. Up to 1832 the commissioners were concerned with certain aspects only of naval affairs, the appointment and promotion of officers, the movement of ships, and the general control of the policy of the navy. They had two Boards subordinate to them : the Navy Board dealt with pay and stores other than victuals and ordnance ; the Victualling Board provided meat, biscuit, and beer for the unfortunate sailors ; while the Treasurer of the Navy had a distinct office, paying over the sums which he obtained from the Treasury on the direction of the Navy Board, of which he was a member. In 1832 [2] Sir James Graham sensibly secured legislation placing the two Boards under the control of Lords of the Admiralty, and in 1835 [3] the office of Treasurer was abolished and his duties handed over to the Paymaster-General.

The relations of the Lords of the Admiralty were from the first necessarily unequal, though the letters patent

---

[1] 7 & 8 Geo. V. c. 31 s. 8 ; Order in Council, July 28, 1938. Two additional members may be added.

[2] 2 & 3 Will. IV. c. 40.   [3] 5 & 6 Will. IV. c. 35.

appointing commissioners to execute the office of Lord High Admiral and to perform the functions of the Navy and Victualling Boards did not distinguish between the rank and powers of members. As pointed out by Sir John Pakington [1] in giving evidence to a Select Committee of the Commons, the First Lord had a position quite distinct from the others as a member of the Cabinet. If the members disagreed with his views, he could carry the matter to the Cabinet and receive authority to secure the appointment of a new Board, whence would be omitted the names of those who were not in accord with his views. To make the matter absolutely clear, Orders in Council from January 14, 1869, have laid it down plainly that the First Lord is responsible to the Crown and Parliament for all the business of the Admiralty, while the other Lords are responsible to him for the work which he ascribes to them from time to time. There is thus no question of his pre-eminence, though the position of a minister towards technical experts of high qualifications must necessarily be difficult, and power to disregard their advice must always in some measure be dependent on ability, in case of their feeling it necessary to resign, to find other advisers whose status will command the respect of the navy and of the country.

Some difficulty seems to have arisen as to the position of members towards the First Lord, for in 1890 [2] there seems to have been prevalent the view that the First Lord should invite the opinions of members, that he could not expect to receive it unless asked for, and that each Lord was responsible only for the work assigned to him. The position of the First Sea Lord *vis-à-vis* his fellow Sea Lords was also uncertain, and some friction arose which

Chapter XVIII.

---

[1] *Report of Select Committee of the Commons*, 1861, p. 185.
[2] *Parl. Pap.* C. 5979, p. ix; App. i. pp. 8 f.

in 1904 evoked an Order in Council [1] of August 10 which assigned to the First, Second, and Fourth Sea Lords responsibility to the First Lord for so much of the general business of the navy and the movement, condition, and personnel of the fleet as might be assigned to them or each of them by the First Lord ; the Third Sea Lord and Controller was made responsible for the material of the navy, the Parliamentary Secretary for finance, while the duties of the Civil Lord and Permanent Secretary, who is added to the Board, were left to be defined from time to time. The distribution of business made by the First Lord on October 20 [2] marked the special position of the First Sea Lord. In matters of great importance he was to be consulted by the other Sea Lords, the Civil Lord, and the Secretaries, and, though these officers retained the right of direct access to the First Lord, the First Sea Lord was made in matters of this kind the necessary intermediary between the First Lord and the other commissioners.

As reconstituted in 1938, the Board of Admiralty includes the First Lord, the Parliamentary and Financial Secretary, and Civil Lord, with the Permanent Secretary as Secretary ; the naval members are the Chief of the Naval Staff, who is First Sea Lord ; the Chief of Naval Personnel, the Controller, the Chief of Supplies and Transport, and the Chief of the Naval Air Service, who are the Second, Third, Fourth, and Fifth Sea Lords ; and the Deputy and Assistant Chiefs of the Naval Staff. The addition of a Lord for the Air service marks the culmination of a long controversy between the Air Ministry and the Admiralty regarding the control of the aircraft employed to assist the navy. After much difficulty the Cabinet decided that the Admiralty must be allowed to control the aircraft whose services were indispensable to

[1] *Parl. Pap.* Cd. 2416.   [2] *Ibid.* Cd. 2417.

the effective operation of the naval forces under present conditions. The change became fully effective only on May 24, 1939, and it involved the Admiralty assuming responsibility for the shore stations on which the naval aircraft are based. It is anticipated that under the new régime co-operation between the services will be more cordial and effective than under the former régime.

(iv) The Ministry for the Co-ordination of Defence

The organisation of the co-ordination of defence was tardily undertaken in any comprehensive manner. It was natural that the issue of joint planning should command attention in and after the Crimean War, where combined action was conspicuous by its absence, as it had on occasion been in the Napoleonic struggle. The Hartington Commission on the Civil and Professional Administration of the Naval and Military Departments [1] had before it suggestions for the placing of the Admiralty and War Office under a single ministerial control in order to secure improved preparation for political contingencies and for joint action in the event of war. One project contemplated the creation of a single Minister of Defence who would be the supreme head of the two departments ; another would have placed at the head of either department a distinguished professional man, leaving it to a minister to deal with the expenditure and accounts of the two services and to act as a medium of communication between them. It was obvious that the objections, which have since been deemed sufficient to destroy the proposals for a single Minister of Defence, applied to either scheme, and both were rejected ; the effort to co-ordinate too such different services would be beyond the capacity of any

[1] *Parl. Pap.* C. 5979, p. viii.

single minister, and both services would suffer from the difficulty that in the Commons they would have no spokesman wholeheartedly eager to defend their interests. If the second scheme was intended to place the real responsibility for all except finance in the hands of professional men, it would sin against the rule that there must be a minister to accept responsibility from his place in Parliament. The Commission, therefore, contented itself with the sensible suggestion of the creation of a Naval and Military Council, which might be presided over by the Prime Minister, and would include the Parliamentary heads of the two services and their principal professional advisers. This Council would consider the estimates, so that the two services could compare the urgency of their respective demands, settle points at issue between the two departments, and discuss any matters of joint naval and military policy which the heads of the services thought to require discussion and decision.

The sound advice of the Commission resulted in the decision of the Liberal Government in 1895 to constitute a Council, and Lord Salisbury's administration adopted the project of its predecessor. The functions of the Council consisted in large measure of seeking to settle disputes on estimates between the War Office, the Admiralty, and the Treasury, but this limited sphere of operations was widened under Mr. Balfour's Premiership. He himself assumed the duty of regularly presiding and of determining what members should be summoned to the discussions, while in 1904 the Colonial Defence Committee, created in 1885 to consider problems of colonial defence, was made subordinate to it. To the meetings of the Committee of Imperial Defence were regularly invited the Secretary of State for War, the First Lord of the Admiralty, the heads of the Army General Staff, the First Sea Lord, and the heads

of the army and navy intelligence departments.[1] The
Chancellor of the Exchequer, the heads of the Foreign,
India, or Colonial Office, or other departments and representatives of the self-governing colonies, might be invited
when matters affecting their interests were concerned. The
estimates sank to secondary importance in its discussions,
the needs of Imperial defence taking first place, and the
departments were guided by its decisions in the character
and cost of their preparations. A permanent secretariat
was created and the records of discussions were carefully
kept.

This organisation served very important functions, with
changes only in personnel and the use in ever-increasing
measures of committees and sub-committees for the consideration of definite subjects. The Committee was always
an advisory body, but, when matters had therein attained
accord, the fact that the Prime Minister and the heads of
the departments concerned had agreed meant that action
would be taken in accord with its advice so far as the issues
lay in the hands of British departments. In regard to
colonies, later Dominions, possessing responsible government, of course, its position was purely advisory. It was
responsible for the preparation of the famous War Book[2]
which gave essential advice to the Dominions, no less
than to the colonies and protectorates, regarding the
measures to be taken there, as in the British Islands, in
the event of war, and it was at a meeting of the Committee
summoned *ad hoc* that Sir E. Grey in 1911 gave a full
statement of the essential issues of British foreign policy,
in a manner hitherto without parallel. Moreover, the
Committee's functions suggested the formation of the War
Cabinet, as elsewhere explained.

---

[1] 139 *Hansard*, 4 s. 619 ; 146 *ibid*. 62 ; Lord Londonderry, House of
Lords, March 14, 1934.　　　　　[2] Asquith, *The Genesis of the War*.

After the war and the return to more normal conditions, the Committee revived its full activities, but the experience of the war had not by any means killed the agitation for the subjection of the whole sphere of defence to a single minister, and in 1921 Mr. Churchill defended his combination of the offices of Secretary of State for War and Air by the argument that he thus co-ordinated the work of the two allied services. The Committee under Sir E. Geddes which recommended economies in all departments in 1922 advocated a single defence ministry.[1] The advice was not acted on, but a Committee recommendation of the Committee of Imperial Defence resulted in the creation of a special Chiefs of Staff Committee which was given the duty of collective advice on policy with a view to rendering the Committee of Imperial Defence a comprehensive view of British commitments. At the same time Mr. Baldwin, on becoming once more Premier, resumed the excellent practice, which had been in abeyance since 1920, of presiding personally over the Imperial Defence Committee. His reasons were of conclusive weight. There is great advantage in the Prime Minister being familiar with defence issues which must come for sanction before the Cabinet ; he cannot decide between conflicting claims on the estimates unless he knows precisely the matters at issue, and he must be prepared for the developments which must take place in the event of war. Since then the rule that the Prime Minister ought to be fully cognisant of the proceedings of the Committee has become accepted on every hand.[2]

The extent, however, of responsibilities for defence which was brought home to the public by the decision of the ministry which had seriously neglected defence, to rearm in 1936, seemed to many of its supporters as well as

---

[1] *Parl. Pap.* Cmd. 1589.   [2] 287 *H.C. Deb.* 5 s. 1321.

others excessive, and the demand for a ministry of defence was revived. It was once again unsuccessful, but the ministry yielded to the popular demand to the extent of appointing a Minister for the Co-ordination of Defence, the politician chosen being Sir Thomas Inskip.[1] The motive of the choice was clear ; it was not proposed to appoint a minister who would stand at the head of the defence departments, but to choose one who would work with the existing agencies and be of Parliamentary service in meeting criticisms with the skill which practice as Attorney-General had given the minister in a remarkable degree. The new minister was made deputy chairman both of the Imperial Defence Committee and of the Defence Policy and Requirements Committee of the Cabinet, and to him various duties were delegated. These include the general day-to-day supervision and control of the whole organisation and activity of the Imperial Defence Committee ; the co-ordination of executive action and of monthly progress reports to the Cabinet or any Committee thereof on the execution of the reconditioning plans ; discernment of any points not taken up or being pursued too slowly ; and, in consultation with the Premier or other ministers, as required, of appropriate measures for their rectification. He was given the right of personal consultation with the Chiefs of Staff together, including the right at discretion to summon under his chairmanship the Chiefs of Staff Committee ; the proposal that he should regularly convene that body was rejected, no doubt because it would have been regarded as an undue interference with the freedom of the technical experts to work out plans in conjunction, free from civilian suggestion or influence. He was, however, made chairman of the Principal Supply Officers Committee, a position especially appropriate to a

---

[1] *Parl. Pap.* Cmd. 5107, p. 14 ; 309 *H.C. Deb.* 5 s. 659.

minister who was expected to be busied in the efforts then being undertaken to make up for the great advantage possessed by Germany in the effective organisation of munitions production. The powers thus accorded resemble those recommended by the Committee in 1904, which favoured the appointment of a chairman other than the Prime Minister for the Committee of Imperial Defence. The appointment, though it certainly strengthened the defence of the ministry in Parliament, did not at the time or later satisfy critics, and in 1938 in particular the demand for a ministry of supply to enable Britain to rival Germany in war preparations, including the supply of aircraft, led to renewed pressure on the ministry, especially after the return of Mr. Chamberlain from his visit to Munich was marked by his insistence on the necessity of rearmament as an auxiliary to his policy of appeasement. Anxiety was caused also by the change in the outlook of ministers regarding aircraft preparations. Whereas Mr. Baldwin had insisted on the maintenance of parity in first-line aircraft, Mr. Chamberlain reduced this claim, insisting instead that such things as possibility of increase in production, quality of airmen, reserves of aircraft, and so on ought to be taken into consideration as well as mere numbers.

The danger of air attack, however, in 1938 compelled fresh developments, as the work of air-raid precautions, entrusted in the first place to the Home Office, proved to impose too serious a strain on that department. At the close of the year, after criticism of the presence in the Lords of the Secretary of State for Air had led to his supersession by a member of the Commons, and after the failure of Earl Winterton to strengthen the Home Office administration, the appointment of a new Lord Privy Seal was announced, with the duty of attending to civilian defence from air attack, and the Ministry of Labour was given the duty of dealing with National Service. It was inevitable that the work should be entrusted to it, for the control of unemployment rests with the ministry, and already it had information regarding the employment of large numbers of the community. The preparation of a compulsory register of all adults or all persons in the realm, though loudly demanded by a section of the supporters of the ministry, was rejected on the score that such a register would serve no very useful purpose, unless kept steadily up to date, while all that was wanted, the supply of an adequate number of volunteers for civilian defence, could be secured by voluntary registration, based on the distribution of some twenty millions of pamphlets.

The Committee of Imperial Defence continues to work largely through committees and sub-committees, including the Joint Planning Committee,[1] originally composed of the Directors of Plans of the three services to whom in 1936 were added three graduates of the Imperial Defence College, one from each department. The plans produced by the Committee are submitted to the Committee of Imperial Defence.

In addition to the Committee of Imperial Defence, the Cabinet in July 1935 created a Defence Policy and Requirements Committee,[2] whose business it is to keep the situation as to defence constantly under review in order to secure the co-ordination of defence arrangements and foreign policy, and to advise the Cabinet and the Committee of Imperial Defence in the light of the international and the financial situation as to any necessary changes in policy or in defence proposals. This body, unlike the Committee of Imperial Defence, was a Ministers' Committee proper, and was composed of the Prime Minister, the Foreign Secretary, the heads of the three service

---

[1] 309 *H.C. Deb.* 5 s. 660.　　　　[2] *Parl. Pap.* Cmd. 5107, p. 14.

departments, and other ministers, including the Chancellor of the Exchequer. It advised the Cabinet regarding the necessity of strengthening the forces in the Mediterranean in view of the Italian menace to British communications therein, and it developed the inevitable plans for the extension of the forces, so long neglected with disastrous results to British power in 1936–9.

The ministerial changes in January 1939 saw the Minister for the Co-ordination of Defence transferred to the Dominions Office, and his place given to Admiral of the Fleet Lord Chatfield, thus reversing the policy which had selected a civilian for that post. It was, however, provided that Mr. Morrison, whose removal from the Ministry of Agriculture had been compelled by widespread dissatisfaction with ministerial policy, would remain in the Cabinet, and would aid the Minister for the Co-ordination of Defence, answering for him in the Commons. Mr. Morrison was given membership of the Committee of Imperial Defence, and made chairman of the Principal Supply Officers Committee, and of the Ministerial Sub-Committee on Man-Power of the Committee of Imperial Defence, and President of the Oil Board. The two ministers have the aid of the staff of the Office and the Cabinet, including that of the Supply Board, recently strengthened, but the creation of a ministry of supply was steadfastly refused. Later Mr. Morrison was given charge of the Food Defence Plans Department, taking over the work from the President of the Board of Trade. The increased rate of rearmament after the Albanian crisis resulted in a concession to those ministerialists who demanded a ministry of supply. On April 20 Mr. Chamberlain announced the establishment under Mr. Burgin, then Minister of Transport, of a Ministry of Supply with Cabinet rank, to deal with the problems of army supply, to assume responsibility for certain stores of general use which the War Office already supplied to other departments, and to acquire and maintain reserves of essential metals and other raw materials. The Ministry of Supply Act provided for certain powers to be used if need be, including the right to demand priority for governmental orders, to requisition supplies if the former power proved insufficient, to settle questions of prices, to require protection of works, and to commandeer storage, among other things. The Civil Defence Act regularises the position of the Lord Privy Seal, and gives wide powers regarding safety against air raids, including the formation and execution of evacuation plans in the interest of children, mothers, cripples, and blind, with power to billet compulsorily. The ministry may also compel factory owners to provide effective safety precautions for their staffs.

2. *Civil Control over Defence Policy*

The obligation of defence officers to obey the instructions of the Civil Government is complete, for the ministry represents Parliament, and the defence forces are subordinate to the authorities which are placed over them by its authority. The question was never really in dispute in the controversies which were waged over the position of the Commander-in-Chief ; but the Duke of Cambridge was anxious to maintain a sphere of authority in which he should exercise unfettered discretion, though the responsibility therefor to Parliament must rest with the Secretary of State, and the Queen desired the right of being advised by a permanent officer who should not change with ministries.[1]

On the issue of the control of operations in the war a

[1] *Letters,* 3 s., ii. 504 ff.

very real difficulty appeared in the case of the Crimean War, for the ministry was very doubtful of the skill with which operations were being conducted, and the Cabinet would have liked to change the commander. But his position was defended by the Secretary of State, and the Cabinet acquiesced.[1] In the South African War some degree of difference of opinion was found to exist between the Queen and Lord Salisbury over the question whether Lord Roberts should be required to send home two officers who were deemed unsuited for further service in view of reverses which they had sustained. The Queen was reluctant to permit such intervention by the Cabinet, but Lord Salisbury insisted with justice that the decision could not be left to Lord Roberts alone. The errors of Generals in the field could not be taken upon them by the Cabinet, which was responsible to Parliament, even though it would be reluctant to interfere without substantial cause.[2]

In the course of the Great War the question of the position of the ministry and its Generals came under consideration, especially in the determination to remove Sir John French from the command in France in 1915.[3] The work done by him had been earnest and energetic, but it was not crowned with any particular success, and there seems no reason to doubt that it was a wise decision to suggest his retirement, though without, apparently, absolutely insisting upon it. The grant of a peerage and of the command-in-chief at home certainly softened the blow, and Sir D. Haig's selection in his place was probably essential to victory. It is curious that Lord Esher should have been so little aware of Sir H. Wilson's limitations as to suggest that he might be given the command in France.

[1] Cf. Bell, *Palmerston*, ii. 121 ff.
[2] Keith, *The British Cabinet System, 1830–1938*, p. 516.
[3] Esher, *Journals*, iii. 280-88, 290-93; Duff Cooper, *Haig*, i. 277 ff.; Spender, *Lord Oxford*, ii. 191.

The relations between the Cabinet and Lord Kitchener were far from easy, and various efforts were made to assure his retirement, Sir John French among others endeavouring to secure that he should be superseded by a civilian Secretary of State.[1] These efforts failed, and it was as Secretary of State that Lord Kitchener undertook the fatal mission to Russia, where his arrival might have helped to bring the power of Russia more effectively to bear on the war. His services in securing the creation of the great British armies clearly outweighed any other defects, and there is no reason to suppose that Mr. Lloyd George's tenure of the War Office effected any substantial improvement on what was in train. When Prime Minister, Mr. Lloyd George aimed consistently at securing the conduct of the war on the basis of transferring the main British effort from the western front to an eastern front. In that aim he had to face the steadfast opposition of Sir W. Robertson, Chief of the General Staff, and Sir D. Haig. The result was that, after a long course of manœuvres, the former was forced to resign his office, but the latter adhered to his principle that he could not resign so long as he felt competent to perform his work, and Mr. George was thus unable to secure his project of seeking a decision in the east.

Sir D. Haig, throughout the various discussions which led to the creation of a War Council at Versailles,[2] which proved ineffective as a mode of controlling the operations, remained ready to accept any system which preserved the constitutional position of the British command. He therefore agreed to orders being given by Sir H. Wilson as

---

[1] Cf. Esher, *Journals*, iii. 269, 275 ff., 278 f., 295 f. ; iv. 2, 4 f., 7 f., 16, 31 f.

[2] Duff Cooper, *Haig*, ii. 223 ff. ; Robertson, *Soldiers and Statesmen*, i. 214-37.

representing the Army Council,[1] and on no occasion
challenged the supreme authority of the Civil Government. Mr. George would gladly have rid himself of his
Commander-in-Chief during and after the operations at
Passchendaele in 1917,[2] which assuredly were prolonged
long after success should have been recognised as impossible. But he was unable to take this action ; he would
have had serious difficulty with his Cabinet, and the effect
on public opinion would have been disastrous to morale.
Unhappily he exercised his unquestionable right of supreme
control by refusing to send out sufficient forces to enable
the Commander-in-Chief to hold in adequate strength the
greater length of line in France which was insisted upon
by the Prime Minister on grounds no doubt of great
political weight, with the result that in March 1918 the
British army suffered a severe and most unfortunate defeat.
It is difficult to avoid the conclusion that the ministry
should either have superseded the Field-Marshal or have
supplied him with the troops which were hastily placed
at his disposal, many brought from distant theatres of war
where their services were not requisite. It must be admitted that the war did not reveal the evolution of any
correct technique for the best co-operation of military and
civil ability, and, so far as Mr. George did intervene, it
seems as if his initiative lacked success.

One complete fiasco, the Mesopotamian expedition,[3]
must be assigned to failure of control from the War Office
or Cabinet, failure of intelligent supervision by the India

---

[1] Cf. Esher, *Journals*, iv. 178, 180. The arrangement by which under
Order in Council Jan. 27, 1916, orders for military matters were issued by
the Chief of the General Staff under direct Cabinet control was constitutionally unobjectionable and preferable to Army Council orders. Contrast
Esher, *Journals*, iv. 179 f., 186. The system disappeared on Robertson's
retirement.

[2] Duff Cooper, *Haig*, ii. 133 ff. gives the best case for the episode.

[3] Royal Commission Report, 1917 ; Spender, *Lord Oxford*, ii. 294-6.

Office and the Government of India, failure of the Com- mander-in-Chief in India to appreciate the needs of the forces, and over-estimation by the General in local command of his prospects of success and under-estimation of the strength of the forces which could be brought against him.

The relation of individual soldiers and officers to the duties incumbent upon them was raised in a serious form in the Curragh incident elsewhere referred to.[1] It is clear that it is the duty of both officers and men loyally to carry out every duty assigned to them whether as regards a foreign enemy or as regards the suppression of disorder. No officer or man may ask for assurances as to orders which he may be required to obey either for safeguarding public property or the support of the civil power in the ordinary execution of its duty, or for the protection of the lives and property of the inhabitants in case of disturbance of the peace. These rules are the more incumbent because enlistment is voluntary, and officers and men should not enter a service unless ready to give faithful obedience.

3. *The Defence Forces*

(i) The Army

Several points of constitutional importance were raised during the reign of Queen Victoria. There had been given by 1803 [2] statutory power to the Crown to make articles of war effective even in peace and applying to all Imperial forces, and these, with the Mutiny Act which was enacted yearly, formed the basis for the government of the troops. In 1879 the articles of war and the Mutiny

---

[1] Oxford, *Fifty Years of Parliament*, ii. 151; Halévy, *Hist. 1905–15*, pp. 546-9.

[2] 43 Geo. III. c. 20.

Act were brought into a single measure,[1] and this was amended in 1881 under the style of Army Act. It is made effective each year by an Act which was originally the Army (Annual) Act, but is now the Army and Air Force (Annual) Act. This Act, though short, serves the purpose of putting in force the Army Act and the Air Force Act, which is under the Air Force (Constitution) Act, 1917, a close transcript of the Army Act; it makes also alterations and additions to these Acts. Thus the whole of these Acts may be considered by way of suggested amendments each year.

The Act retains the ancient preamble, modified to date, showing that a standing army is not lawful without consent of Parliament in time of peace, the desirability of the maintenance of an army, air force, and royal marines, specifying the numbers of the two former, but not of the marines, and the necessity of legal provision for the punishment of persons guilty of mutiny and other offences. It maintains the Army and Air Force Acts in force in the British Islands up to April 30 of the following year, and elsewhere up to July 31 of that year, and applies them to persons subject to military law or the Air Force Act, whether within or without the British dominions, thus governing their actions in foreign territory no less than on British territory. Persons subject to military law or Air Force law include others beside those who are included in the numbers specified, for the British forces in India, as distinct from the Indian army proper, which is governed by the law enacted by the Indian legislature,[2] are governed by the Army and Air Force Acts, and under special circumstances other forces raised by the Crown in British or British-controlled territory fall under the Act.

---

[1] For the advantages see Col. Stanley's speech, 243 *Hansard*, 3 s. 1910.
[2] Ridges, *Const. Hist.* (ed. Keith, 1939), pp. 366 f.

A constitutional issue of grave importance was raised in 1878 [1] when Indian troops were sent to Malta as a measure of defence in case war should break out with Russia over Turkey. It was vehemently contended that, if it was lawful to make such use of the forces, there was provided a means of stultifying the intention of Parliament which provided for the maintenance of so many troops for the safety of the United Kingdom and the defence of Her Majesty's possessions. It was indeed clear that to introduce the forces into the United Kingdom would definitely run counter to the meaning of the Army Act, but it was not by any means so clear that their use in Malta was forbidden. In any case it was stressed that the Government of India Act, 1858, forbade, except in the case of urgency, the employment of Indian revenues in the maintenance of Indian forces beyond the frontier of India without the consent of Parliament. Therefore in due course Parliament must be approached to find the money or to allow the sum to be met from Indian revenues, as had to be done later in the case of the Indian forces employed outside India in the Great War.[2]

A second issue of importance fell to be settled under George V as a result of the Statute of Westminster, 1931, which rendered it necessary, in case of legislation intended to apply within a Dominion, to which the Act applied, to obtain the request and consent of the Dominion to the enactment of the Act. As Canada, the Union of South Africa, and the Irish Free State were not willing to make such application, it became necessary to eliminate them from the application of the Army Act, and to secure provision by legislation in Canada and the Union, on the

---

[1] 240 *Hansard*, 3 s. 187, 213, 369, 515 ; Monypenny and Buckle, *Disraeli*, ii. 1157-60.

[2] For the position under the Government of India Act, 1935, see Keith, *Const. Hist. of India, 1600–1935*, p. 366.

model of the Visiting Forces (British Commonwealth) Act, 1933, of the United Kingdom, under which British forces in a Dominion, and Dominion forces in the United Kingdom, might be protected from interference by the local law, while permitted to be present therein.[1] The application, however, of military and Air Force law to British forces sent to a Dominion with the assent of the Dominion Government does not rest on the local legislation, but on the Army and Air Force (Annual) Act, which binds those subject to military or Air Force law, wherever they may be. As a matter of fact, during the Great War Canadian forces in special were maintained in Britain under the operation of Dominion legislation, which under the Army Act as it then stood had extraterritorial validity, just as it now has under the Statute of Westminster.

As constituted in 1939, the army includes the Royal Dragoons and Scots Greys as the sole remaining cavalry ; Royal Armoured Corps ; Royal Artillery, Field Artillery, and Anti-Aircraft and Coast Defence ; Royal Engineers ; Royal Corps of Signals ; Foot Guards ; Infantry of the Line ; Royal Army Service Corps ; Royal Army Medical Corps ; Army Dental Corps ; Army Educational Corps ; and Corps of Military Police.

Entry upon the army service is voluntary under normal conditions,[2] though in the Great War,[3] from 1916 to 1919 compulsion had to be applied to maintain the strength of the armed forces. The result was not reached without serious delay ; in the early period of the war there was no need for compulsion so far as numbers of men were concerned, but the voluntary procedure had the grave disadvantage that it permitted the enlistment of many trained

[1] Keith, *The Dominions as Sovereign States*, pp. 91 ff., 642 f.
[2] For the Conservative desire for compulsory service see Halévy, *Hist. 1905–15*, pp. 152 ff., 389 ff.
[3] Spender, *Lord Oxford*, ii. 202 ff. ; Esher, *Journals*, iv. 18 ff.

workers who would have been of greater use at home in production of munitions, coal-mining, shipbuilding, and so on. Later, when the failure of volunteers was apparent, the reluctance of ministers to adopt compulsion led to various devices, carried out under Lord Derby's guidance, to secure sufficient recruits. But this failed, and the policy of compulsion was carried with only the resignation of Sir John Simon, who resisted it on principle. Further legislation was found necessary to supplement the first Act, but it was decided not to risk extending the operation of the system in practice to Ireland ; it was not possible, it was felt, to accord the operation in war of Home Rule, and without it compulsory service would be resisted. The close of the war did not permit immediate release of the whole of the forces ; it was found necessary to legislate to secure a sufficient number of troops for the occupation of enemy territory pending the effective return of peace. But this was easily effected, after a serious outbreak of unrest in London among troops of long service, whom it was proposed to return to serve overseas, while newly enlisted men were being released to meet the convenience of their employers, had warned the ministry [1] of the grave danger which it was running by its complete disregard of the unfairness of continuing in service civilian soldiers who had faced such serious warfare.

Members of the regular forces are always subject to the Army or Air Force Act, as the case may be. Special importance, therefore, applies to their being properly enlisted in full understanding of the terms of service, and therefore attestation takes place before a justice of the peace or other magistrate, who must satisfy himself of the desire of the recruit to enlist and who requires him to take an

[1] The remarkable fact is that the policy adopted was due to the War Cabinet, which showed a complete ignorance of psychology.

oath of allegiance. Service is for such periods as are from time to time decided, part in the serving army, part in the reserve. The latter was regulated by the Reserve Forces Act, 1859, later by the Act of 1882.[1] The important constitutional provision therein contained is that the power to call out the reserve by proclamation on permanent service in case of imminent national danger must be exercised under control of Parliament, for the occasion must first be communicated to that body if sitting, and if not, must be declared in Council and notified in the proclamation calling out the forces, and Parliament must be called to meet within ten days from the proclamation, if it stands adjourned for a longer period. The members of the reserve fall under military or Air Force law when undergoing their annual training or when called out on permanent service. As a matter of convenience it was arranged, by the Act of 1882,[2] that a certain number of the reservists should be authorised to accept liability for service outside the United Kingdom without the issue of a proclamation, though their calling out must be notified to Parliament.[3] This rule is now for the time being superseded by the Reserve and Auxiliary Forces Act, 1939, described below.

In 1837 the old constitutional force, the Militia, was ineffectively organised, and the raising of the quotas from the districts under the control of the Lord-Lieutenants by ballot had been suspended in 1829. In 1852 the force was reconstituted on a voluntary basis, though the ballot was retained as a possible necessity, and in 1855 the Home Secretary was deprived of control in favour of the Secretary of State for War under the new position of that office. In

---

[1] 45 & 46 Vict. c. 48.

[2] Extended by the Reserve Forces Act, 1937 (1 Edw. VIII. & 1 Geo. VI. c. 16).

[3] There are also a Supplementary Reserve of skilled workers ; an Infantry Supplementary Reserve ; and a Supplementary Reserve of officers.

1871 the Army Regulation Act took away the authority Chapter
XVIII. of the Lord-Lieutenants, who were only authorised to present for first commissions. In 1882 the Militia Act consolidated the enactments applicable to the force. The Militia could be called out for embodiment in case of national danger, with the usual provision for summoning Parliament, if not sitting, within ten days. Otherwise the recruits underwent certain training, and when training with regular forces or embodied, were made subject to military law. A Militia officer was always so subject.

The Yeomanry were a volunteer corps of horsemen who were trained annually under military law, and who could be called upon to aid the civil power in case of rioting ; the Volunteers, as organised under Acts of 1863 and 1881, were in the main riflemen, with some light horse, artillery, and engineers, who fell under military law only when training with the regular forces or the Militia when so subject ; but unlike the Militia they could be called upon to serve outside the country, which was contrary to the historical position of the Militia as the local force.

The Territorial and Reserve Forces Act, 1907,[1] marked the carrying out of a plan matured by Lord Haldane to reorganise the forces of the Crown so as to provide an expeditionary army, and to have an effective territorial organisation which would be able to allow of the expansion of the army in case of war. The Volunteers and Yeomanry were merged in the Territorial Force, which in 1921 [2] was renamed the Territorial Army, and the Militia were transferred to the category of special reservists, as contrasted with the ordinary reservists who had served in the regular army ; to these the name Militia was restored in 1921, but the force was not then developed. The Territorial

---

[1] 7 Edw. VII. c. 9. See Haldane, *Autobiography*, and Maurice, *Haldane*, i.
[2] Territorial Army and Militia Act, 1921 (11 & 12 Geo. V. c. 37).

Army is formed by voluntary enlistment, originally either for home service only or for service outside the realm in case of war ; recruits now are required to accept liability for general service. In peace there is in the first year a special period of preliminary training if so provided by Order in Council, and a period of drill annually, and military law applies when serving with regular forces, or training, or embodied, or called to serve under a definite agreement. The Army Council may, and in certain cases must, embody the force if the army reserve is called out by proclamation, but there is in the Act of 1907 (s. 17) the usual requirement of notification to Parliament and its summoning if adjourned so as not to meet for more than ten days. A wider power is now given by the Reserve and Auxiliary Forces Act, 1939, noted below.[1] Parliament also must approve if it is desired to extend to thirty days the normal period[2] of training of the force, or to prescribe preliminary training.

For administration an essential feature is the creation of county associations presided over by the Lord-Lieutenant, whose business it is to stimulate recruiting, to secure buildings, and to provide ranges and areas for manœuvres. Commissions are granted on the recommendation of the President. For the regular forces commissions are obtainable either through the cadet colleges, to which admission is given by competitive examination ; through the Universities after graduation ; through the Supplementary Reserve of Officers ; or through the Territorial Army, certain units of which are marked out as officer-producing. Promotion from the ranks is also possible.

The purpose for which the Territorial Army was pre-

---

[1] The war danger produced National Defence Companies of ex-soldiers ; an Officers' Emergency Reserve ; and an Officer Cadet Reserve ; those joining are only under an obligation of honour to undertake service in war.

[2] Infantry 8-15, mounted 8-18 days.

pared has altered with the change of circumstances in Europe. The plan of the Government, as expounded on March 8, 1939, accepts the necessity of affording France [1] full aid, by air and sea, and by the despatch of an expeditionary force to arrive by prescribed times. The field army then contemplated was one of regular troops, four infantry and one armoured divisions ; of Territorials, nine infantry, three motorised, and two armoured divisions. Seven divisions of Territorials were to act as an anti-aircraft and coast defence force at home. A second strategic reserve had been created in the Middle East, based on Palestine ; oversea garrisons had been brought up to war strength, with increased enlistment from local residents, including Maltese and Ceylonese, for the first time in the latter case. The regular army strength in 1939–40 was fixed at 187,000, the Territorials at 250,000, while complete arrangements were made for immediate recruiting for all the defence services immediately on mobilisation.[2] Conscription in peace was then ruled out, much to the disappointment of French military opinion, which feared that, on the outbreak of war, France might be overwhelmed unless a large British force could be landed to make up in some degree for her weakness in man power.

But the policy of the ministry, though apparently definitive, speedily proved inadequate. On March 29 it was announced that the thirteen divisions of the Territorial Field Force would be duplicated, the number of that force being increased to 340,000. Voluntary recruitment

[1] Complete solidarity with France was announced by Mr. Chamberlain, Feb. 6 ; Lord Halifax, Feb. 23, 1939.

[2] The estimates for 1939–40 were £161,133,000, £66,232,000 to be borrowed from the defence loan, raised to £800,000,000 in lieu of £400,000,000 ; Defence Loans Act, 1939 (2 & 3 Geo. VI. c. 8). For the numbers of the regular army, 2 & 3 Geo. VI. c. 17.

was still insisted upon as sufficient.   But the Albanian
crisis and the pledges given to Greece and Rumania
strengthened the demand in France for proof of British
firmness of purpose, and on April 26 Mr. Chamberlain
announced his conversion to compulsory service in emergency.   His position was constitutionally very difficult.
He admitted that Mr. Baldwin had given in April 1936 a
pledge against conscription and that he himself had done
so on February 17, 1938.   He was inclined to minimise his
pledge of March 29, and the case on this head was not
improved by Lord Maugham's argument in the Lords,
which if taken seriously would deprive ministerial pledges
of any moral value, a position repugnant to popular
feeling if acceptable to legal ingenuity.   Mr. Attlee argued
that the ministry had broken faith, a view formally
accepted and enforced by the Labour Party Conference on
May 31, and suggested that, if a general election were
ruled out of possibility, a new Government should have
taken over responsibility.   In fact the proper course to be
followed [1] was clearly consultation with the opposition
parties with a view to form a truly national Government
including Opposition leaders and ministerialists who had
been sacrificed to the unwise and indeed immoral policy
of appeasement at the expense of the liberty and lives of
other peoples whom Britain was pledged to preserve.   But
Mr. Chamberlain declined to follow this more constitutional course, preferring to rely on the probability that
not only would he have his usual Commons majority, but
that the Labour party would not refuse to co-operate nor
would it use its industrial power to defeat conscription.
In fact both the executives of the trade unions and the
Labour Party Conference decided to co-operate, under
protest that the Government had broken faith and that

[1] Keith, *The Scotsman*, April 27, 1939.

voluntary means had not failed. The efforts of Labour were therefore devoted to securing concessions in the interests of those to be compulsorily trained, to safeguarding conscientious objectors, to securing that industrial compulsion would be avoided, and to insisting that the measure was for an emergency alone.

The Military Training Act, 1939,[1] though passed under the guillotine without an agreed time-table, was fairly well discussed, and Labour suggestions, as well as those of the Liberals, secured many improvements on a badly drafted and obscure measure. Under it youths between the ages of 20 and 21 normally resident in Great Britain become liable for military training for four years as militiamen, being deemed to have been enlisted under the Territorial and Reserve Forces Act, 1907. They will receive six months' continuous training after being called out, which takes place normally within a year of registration in the military training register of the Ministry of Labour ; thereafter they will serve for three and a half years as militiamen, doing such training as may be prescribed, unless they enter, with the permission of the Army Council, either the regular army or the regular air force, which they can do at any time, or unless they enter after the six months any of the reserve or auxiliary forces. Important concessions are made as regards calling up. The time may be accelerated for registration if so desired, and classes of youths may be allowed to postpone training, *e.g.* undergraduates and others in like position may be allowed to complete the courses of study on which they are engaged, while it was announced that agricultural workers, fishermen, and workers in anthracite mines would not be called up during the summer. Any individual whose request for permission to be trained earlier or later is declined, has

[1] 2 & 3 Geo. VI. c. 25.

his case determined by a Military Training Hardship Committee, of which large numbers have been appointed by the Ministry of Labour ; each is composed of two members selected from a panel including all the members of panels under the Unemployment Insurance Act, 1935, and is presided over by a chairman who will normally be a chairman of a court of referees under the Act. Appeal lies to the umpire or a deputy umpire under the Act, sitting with two assessors.

For conscientious objectors elaborate provision is made. In lieu of registration in the military training register, any person may apply for registration in the register of conscientious objectors, and this is provisionally accorded. The issue is finally decided either by a local tribunal or by an appellate tribunal ; there are two divisions of the latter, for England and Scotland, consisting of three members, the chairman chosen by the Lord Chancellor and the Lord President of the Court of Session respectively. The local tribunals consist of a county court judge, in Scotland a sheriff or sheriff substitute, and four members, all chosen by the Minister of Labour, with due regard to impartiality, and as regards one member of each kind of court after consultation with organised labour. The tribunal may on an application (1) grant unconditional inclusion in the register of conscientious objectors, which gives complete exemption ; (2) grant conditional exemption, which means that the person exempted must do civil work under civilian control, provided or approved by the Minister, for six months at rates of pay analogous to those of militiamen, unless the tribunal decides otherwise in the national interest when other work may be approved by it ; (3) order enrolment in the military training register for noncombatant duties only ; or (4) reject the application and order registration in the military training register.

Even, however, if registration as a conscientious objector is refused or not applied for, and any person refuses to perform military service on grounds of conscience, and is sentenced to three months' imprisonment or more, he can apply to the appellate tribunal, which may recommend his discharge on the expiry of his sentence, thus preventing further proceedings such as those which in the Great War made martyrs of certain conscientious objectors. If not satisfied that the ground of conscience existed, the tribunal may still recommend discharge, but require the objector to do civil work for a period up to six months as if he had been conditionally enrolled in the register of conscientious objectors. If he fails to do such work, he may be sentenced by a civil court to two years' imprisonment.

The view that a conscientious objection entitles a man to complete exemption from making any contribution to the welfare of the State, while retaining the right to become a Civil Servant, to acquire in due course the franchise,[1] etc., is one difficult morally to justify. The case of those who are willing to do civil work on militia pay is much easier to defend. If a conscientious objector is to suffer no disadvantage and to gain exemption from military service, the very strongest motive for becoming such an objector is provided, for it is clearly unfair that the average man who undergoes training should be allowed to be treated only on the same basis as he who refuses. No doubt this concession facilitated the passage of the Bill, but what is morally indefensible should not be done merely for convenience. The doctrine thus enunciated is of grave danger to the State.

It is equally unfortunate that efforts should have been

---

[1] A proposal to give the franchise to all trainees was rejected. Registration was popular, 229,046 registering by June 9; only some 3800 alleging conscientious objections.

made to excuse Dominion nationals normally resident in Great Britain from service. Mr. De Valera demanded that the British Government should not treat as British subjects any Irish nationals, a claim which was preposterous in view of the fact that Britain and the Dominions had accepted Eire as still part of the British Commonwealth, and British protection abroad was regularly extended to Irish nationals. Secondly, he contended that, under the International Protocol of 1930 relating to military obligations in certain cases of double nationality (Article 2), " if a person possesses the nationality of two or more States, and, under the law of any one of such States, has the right on attaining his majority, to renounce or decline the nationality of that State, he shall be exempt from military service in such State during his minority ". But, unfortunately for this argument, there is no provision whatever in the British Nationality and Status of Aliens Act, 1914–33, which permits a British subject at any age to lay aside that nationality on the ground that he is an Irish national. Moreover, the British Government has consistently denied that relations between itself and the Dominions are governed by the League Covenant or conventions concluded under its auspices.

But, though the British Government could not concede in terms the Irish claim, much was done to meet it. No Dominion national or person born in any part of the King's dominions outside Great Britain, or therein domiciled, or born or domiciled in any protectorate, or mandated territory, or territory under the suzerainty of the Crown, though resident in Great Britain, is liable to registration, if he has been resident in Great Britain for less than two years, or is residing only for educational purposes, or the circumstances of his residence are otherwise such as to show that he is residing for a temporary purpose only.[1] Few Dominion nationals will thus become liable, and, as they will be essentially permanent residents, it may be assumed that they will not desire to evade obligations of other residents in the country in which they have settled in their own interest.

The exemption of Northern Ireland from the Act was demanded by Mr. De Valera, and Mr. Chamberlain yielded. It is manifestly most unjust that the people of Northern Ireland, which receives large British subsidies and makes no proper contribution to Imperial charges, should escape conscription, and Mr. De Valera doubtless realised that, by securing exemption, he would strengthen his claim for the withdrawal of British forces and the union of the territory with Eire. In the long run it is impossible for the heavily burdened people of Great Britain to undertake the obligation of providing benefits for people who do not share their obligations. The decision may well mark a decisive moment in the history of Northern Ireland, whose Government has unquestionably shown itself oppressive and unfair to the minority.

The exemption of the Channel Islands from the operation of the Act is another anomaly which is hard to defend on any logical or moral ground. Power is taken to apply the measure to the Isle of Man, as is clearly proper.

By another derogation from the ordinary law, assurances were given in the Commons that the common law obligation of every soldier, as of every British subject, to aid the civil power in case of need would not be made applicable in practice to trainees in the six-months period of continuous service. It was also pointed out that it was accepted on all sides that soldiers were not expected to

---

[1] The power to apply the Act to persons not resident in Great Britain is given by s. 18, but Dominion Nationals and persons belonging to other parts of the Empire are exempt.

perform civil work, unless, of course, special obligations might be imposed under the Emergency Powers Act, 1920, in case of an internal crisis. The position laid down is intended to allay the fears that trainees might be used in case of industrial unrest as strike-breakers, performing work which normally would be performed by civilians.

Pay at 1s. 6d. a day, without deductions, was given to trainees under Labour pressure, with provision for wives and dependants and possible grants for special liabilities. The cost is high, £30,000,000 for works and equipment, £10,500,000 for the first year, rising to £26,500,000 in 1941. Those who advocate the permanent retention of such a system as part of the national policy are imposing a grave burden on the finances of the State, and doubtless involving a depreciation in the standard and extent of the social services.

To meet the wishes of those recruits who may prefer naval service,[1] the Act provides for the creation of a royal naval special reserve, in which men can serve for six months continuously in the first instance, and then for three and a half years. They fall under the terms of the Royal Naval Reserve (Volunteer) Act, 1859, with the necessary modifications.

The duration of the Act is three years, subject to earlier termination, if the necessity for it disappears, by Order in Council; it may be continued year by year on Orders based on addresses from either house of Parliament. Regulations on procedure may be made by the Minister of Labour, subject to annulment by resolution of either house within forty days. Consequential matters may be dealt with by Order in Council based on resolutions of both houses; in emergency, when Parliament is

---

[1] They can enter the Air Force Reserve or the Auxiliary Air Force, if they prefer, power to enlist under like conditions already existing.

prorogued or dissolved or both houses are adjourned for more than fourteen days, Orders may be made, but they expire twenty-eight days after the Commons first sit after the Order is made, unless approved by resolutions of both houses.

The purpose of this new move is to supply men to relieve the Territorial Army of part of the burden of anti-aircraft defence, to aid the mobilisation of the regular army, to add to the strength of the Territorial Army, and to provide a reserve supply of trained men. The immediate needs of the situation in 1939 rendered it desirable to simplify the procedure to call out the reserves and the auxiliary forces in whole or part, and this now can be done by the issue of an Order in Council under the Reserve and Auxiliary Forces Act, 1939,[1] conferring authority on the Admiralty or the Secretaries of State to call out such forces, if satisfied that their service is urgently required for ensuring preparedness for the defence of the realm against any external danger. The rules of the Reserve Forces Act, 1882 (s. 13), and of the Territorial and Reserve Forces Act, 1907 (s. 17) regarding the form of procedure by proclamation and Orders in Council declaring a state of imminent national danger or great emergency, and the summoning of Parliament if not in session, are not applicable. There is thus removed a constitutional safeguard of some importance, but the Act has only the same duration as the Military Training Act, 1939, and there are like provisions for issue of regulations and Orders in Council on consequential issues. Both Acts contain a novel provision requiring employers to reinstate in the same position as would have been theirs, had they not been called up, men affected by the Acts. The penalty for failure without sufficient cause so to act is a fine up to

[1] 2 & 3 Geo. VI. c. 24.

£50, and the employer may be ordered to pay up to twelve weeks' salary to the employee.

The additions thus made to the forces have led to certain changes. The posts of Inspectors-General of the Forces which existed before the Great War have been revived in a new form. The Inspector-General of Oversea Forces is entrusted with inspection of higher training of the regular and territorial field armies, of oversea garrisons, with consultation with the Indian military authorities, liaison with foreign staffs, and the co-ordination of all training preparations for the despatch of an expeditionary force. The Inspector-General of the Home Forces is responsible for the inspection of Militia and regular troops at depôts of anti-aircraft and coast defence and of Territorial Army units, and will make himself acquainted with command home defence schemes and maintain touch with the civil authorities responsible for anti-air raid protection duties and with the regional commissioners, who will be given important functions to act for the central Government in the event of the interruption of normal communications in time of war. To secure the following-up of orders and decisions in view of the greatly increased responsibilities of the War Office, a Director-General of Progress and Statistics was appointed in May.

In time of peace neither soldier nor officer can claim a right to resign at pleasure, though the Crown has an absolute right to discharge, and no redress can be obtained in respect of such action,[1] the public interest being deemed to demand that the Crown shall retain absolute freedom. So it was ruled in the case of a naval officer that an unauthorised resignation exposed him to arrest and court-martial.[2]

---

[1] *Tufnell, In re* (1876), 3 Ch.D. 164 ; *Dickson v. Combermere* (1863) 3 F. & F. 526 ; *Kynaston v. Att.-Gen.* (1933), 49 T.L.R. 300.

[2] *Cuming, ex parte* (1887), 19 Q.B.D. 13. Cf. *Hearson v. Churchill,* [1892], 2 Q.B. 144.

There are, however, provisions under which enlisted men can, within a short period, retire on payment of a reasonable [1] sum, a rule necessary to save the country from loss by reckless enlistments, and a compassionate discharge may be granted for sufficient cause, such as the necessity of releasing a boy whose services are needed at home. Normally a soldier is entitled to discharge at the termination of the period, for which he has agreed to serve, unless he desires to continue his service so as to earn pension, a privilege which may be granted at discretion, but which was widely extended in 1937–9 in view of the necessity of adding to the effective forces of the Crown. But in certain circumstances a soldier may be required to continue his service for a specified maximum period,[2] while of course fresh legislation in time of war will assuredly extend the periods of service of most soldiers.

(ii) The Air Force

In the case of the air arm the army had control over the Royal Flying Corps, the Admiralty over the Royal Naval Air Service, but the efforts of the Air Board under Lord Cowdray secured the provision of aeroplanes in sufficient number to justify the decision to pass the Air Force (Constitution) Act, 1917,[3] which gave authority to create an independent Air Force, and, on the analogy of the army, a system of regulations and law. Thus the Air Force Act and the King's Regulations are based on the corresponding instruments for the army. The principle of an Auxiliary Air Force and a R.A.F. Reserve was adopted by an Act of 1924.[4] The constitutional rules are similar to those

---

[1] Army Act, s. 81. This does not apply to trainees.
[2] *Ibid.* ss. 87, 88.   [3] 7 & 8 Geo. V. c. 51.
[4] 14 & 15 Geo. V. c. 15. See also Air Force Reserve (Pilots and Observers) Act, 1934. On March 9, 1939 it was announced that sections of the

applicable to the army, the Territorial and Reserve Forces
Act, 1907, and the Reserve Forces Act, 1882, having been
adapted by Orders in Council, October 9, 1924.

The risk of war in 1938–9 resulted in the creation of
the R.A.F. Civilian Wireless Reserve ; the R.A.F. Officers'
Emergency Reserve ; the R.A.F. Reserve Class E, which
excludes training in time of peace ; a Civil Air Guard open
to men and women ; and an Auxiliary Territorial Service
for the army and the air force recruited from women.
There is also the R.A.F. Volunteer Reserve, with entry at
age 18–25.

(iii) The Navy

The position of the navy differs in certain points. The
absence of any distrust of the force rendered annual legislation to keep it in being unnecessary, while the conditions
of naval service were such as to render such legislation
often absurd. Hence the Naval Discipline Act, as consolidated in 1866, has remained in lasting operation, with
amendments made from time to time. Officers are commissioned by the Admiralty, not under the royal sign-
manual which is used for commissions of the army and
the air force, though statutory authority exists to allow
the delegation of this work.[1] Enlistment is for a maximum
period with the possibility of extension of service which
is usually desired, in order to qualify for pension.

There are various forms of reserves, the Royal Naval
Reserve under the Royal Naval Reserve (Volunteer) Act,
1859 ; the Royal Fleet Reserve [2] under the Naval Reserve

Volunteer Reserve would be formed overseas, *e.g.* Hong-Kong, Malaya, East
Africa. The estimates for 1939–40 were £220,626,700, £142,000,000 being
taken from loan funds ; 118,000 men were allowed for.

[1] 25 & 26 Vict. c. 4; 165 *Hansard*, 3 s. 1483; Lee, *Edward VII.*, ii. 48
(use of stamp by King).

[2] In 1939 arrangements were made to enlist men prepared to join for
service when the reserve as a whole is not called out.

Act, 1900 ; and the Royal Naval Volunteer Reserve under the Naval Forces Act, 1903. In 1932 was constituted a Royal Naval Wireless Auxiliary Reserve, and in 1937 a Royal Naval Volunteer Supplementary Reserve, the latter of yacht owners and others willing to take commissions in war-time if asked to do so. The terms of service depend on the conditions of enlistment, which are governed by special Acts, but in the case of the Royal Naval Reserve the power is given to call out for service on shore or at sea for a period up to three years, which is extendible by proclamation to five years.

In 1937–9 arrangements were made under which the Admiralty is given authority over the fleet air arm separately from the Air Council. The Admiralty not merely controls the aircraft when afloat on aircraft carriers, but also when on shore.

The Royal Marines, a force of infantry and artillery, existing from 1755, was amalgamated into a single corps by Order in Council of October 11, 1923 ; a corps of Royal Marine Engineers was formed by Order of February 10, 1919. The force is subject, when serving on ships, to the Naval Discipline Act, otherwise to the Army Act, but unlike the regular army its numbers are not limited by Parliament, except by the restriction of the annual provisions made for them, their position being the same as in the case of the naval forces.

While in the Great War compulsion was used to maintain the strength of the army, in the case of the navy impressment of seafaring men, which is apparently still legal under the common law, was not resorted to.[1] Men liable for compulsory service could avoid such liability by

---

[1] *Broadfoot's Case* (1743), Foster, 154 ; *R.* v. *Tubbs* (1776), 2 Cowp. 517 ; *Anthony Barrow's Case* (1811), 14 East, 346, show the limits of the right of impressment.

volunteering for naval service, and great readiness was displayed by seafarers of many types to aid in the naval operations of mine-sweeping, despite the grave risk.

The war danger resulted in the opening of a R.N. Volunteer (Wireless) Reserve ; a R.N. Auxiliary Sick Berth Reserve ; and the Royal Marine Police Special Reserve ; while men with five years' service in the navy or marines, but not pensioners or reservists, were invited to register themselves for service in war-time only in one or other force. For women openings were offered in clerical and domestic capacities.

As the result of the new responsibilities of the Admiralty as regards air defence, a class of R.N. officers was constituted by Order in Council, February 24, 1938, and an air branch of the Royal Naval Volunteer Reserve was constituted by Order in Council of November 4, 1938.

By proclamations of September 28, 1938, the power to call out officers of the retired and emergency lists of the Royal Navy and Royal Marines and the special reserve of engineer officers of the Royal Navy, officers of the R.N. Reserve, and men of the R.N. Reserve and Royal Fleet Reserve, and officers and men of the Royal Naval Volunteer Reserve, and to extend the terms of service of seamen and marines then serving, was duly exercised. These proclamations were withdrawn on November 25, when the immediate crisis had passed.[1] As noted above, a simpler procedure is provided under the Reserve and Auxiliary Forces Act, 1939, and a Royal Naval Special Reserve is provided for by the Military Training Act, 1939 (s. 9).

[1] The sum allowed for 1939–40 was £145,779,000, £80,000,000 being taken from the defence loan.

4. *The Law and the Jurisdiction affecting the Defence Forces*

There are general principles of importance regulating the position of members of the defence forces and the civil courts. It has been recognised since 1689 that it is necessary that men of the defence forces shall be subjected to a special code of discipline, and therefore the naval service is subjected to the rules of the Naval Discipline Acts, 1866–1938, which penalise mutiny, desertion, absence without leave, disobedience to orders, waste or embezzlement of stores, improper loss of ships, misconduct regarding prize ships, and other naval misconduct as well as actions normally criminal. Offences are made, according to their character, triable by court-martial or summarily [1] by the officer in command of the ship; in 1915 authority was given to the Admiralty to establish disciplinary courts to deal with misconduct of officers in time of war. The procedure of courts-martial is regulated by the Acts and by general orders which must be approved by Order in Council. Provision is made for the appointment of a deputy judge advocate who sends a report of the proceedings to the Admiralty, but the carrying-out of sentences is not dependent on approval. The fact that a seaman is amenable to the Acts in no way affects his liability to be dealt with by a civil court for any offence therein triable.

The military forces were left in a different position which is still maintained, largely on constitutional grounds, for it is part of the theory of responsible government that Parliament must have the right to force any ministry from office by failure to enact the Army and Air Force (Annual)

Chapter XVIII.

---

[1] For an unsuccessful action against a captain on the score of improper exercise of this power, see *Jennings* v. *Shelley, The Times*, March 1, 1939; 55 T.L.R. 508, following on jurisdiction, *Heddon* v. *Evans* (1919), 35 T.L.R. 642.

Bill, which brings into operation the Army Act and the
Air Force Act for another year each, and appoints the
maximum number of the forces authorised to be maintained. In 1879 the provisions of the Mutiny Act and the
Article of War made thereunder were consolidated as the
Army Discipline and Regulation Act, which in turn was
repealed in 1881 and its provisions in an amended form
reissued as the Army Act, 1881. This measure, as amended
from time to time, by the annual Act, is reprinted as the
Army Act. The offences which are specifically military
include offences in relation to the enemy ; mutiny and
insubordination ; desertion and absence without leave ;
fraudulent enlistment ; offences in relation to prisoners, to
courts-martial, billeting, impressment of carriages, and so on.

Ordinary offences against the law may be tried by
courts-martial with the exception of murder, manslaughter,
treason, treason-felony, and rape committed in the United
Kingdom ; such offences committed elsewhere are triable
by court-martial on active service, or if the nearest civil
court is more than a hundred miles away. There are minor
limits on the exercise of civil jurisdiction against soldiers.
There are general, field general, and district courts-martial
with graded powers, and certain offences by officers and
men can be dealt with summarily, but in cases of importance the accused may choose trial by court-martial.
These courts are judges of law and fact, but sentences
need confirmation. In the United Kingdom the Judge
Advocate-General examines all proceedings and advises as
to confirmation of findings and sentences. The office was
political from 1806 to 1892 ; thereafter it was held until
1905 by the President of the Probate, Divorce, and Admiralty Division of the High Court; but since then it is a
Civil Service post with deputies ; at general courts-martial
a deputy must, and at districts courts-martial may, be ap-

pointed to watch the proceedings and forward them to the Judge Advocate-General ; up to 1860 he acted as prosecuting officer. Even after confirmation a petition may be preferred under King's Regulations. The rules of evidence for courts-martial as for naval courts-martial are as in English civil courts, and counsel may appear on either side.

If trial of a person subject to military law for a civil offence takes place in a civil court, no further trial is permissible by court-martial ; [1] if there is trial by a court-martial, civil trial is not illegal, but the punishment, if any, awarded by the court-martial must be taken into consideration in awarding punishment.[2]

The rules as to the army have been applied to the air force.

Those persons who are subject to naval, military, and air force law from time to time are defined by the Acts ; [3] there is a general distinction between regular forces always so subject, and forces which are subject only when engaged in training, or when placed on active service, or when attached to the regular forces.

From the proceedings of courts-martial no appeal lies to civil courts. They are, however, clearly bound to exercise their powers to secure that these courts shall not exceed their authority ; the writs, now orders, of *habeas corpus*, prohibition, and *certiorari* are available to rescue persons who have been falsely claimed as subject to the jurisdiction of courts-martial ; to prohibit such courts dealing with them ; and to quash proceedings.[4] But,

---

[1] Army Act, s. 162 (6).   [2] *Ibid.* s. 162 (1), (2).

[3] *Ibid.* ss. 175, 176 ; Air Force Act, ss. 175, 176 ; Naval Discipline Act, ss. 87-90 B.

[4] For *habeas corpus*, see *Wolfe Tone's Case* (1798), 27 St. Tr. 614. Cf. *Broadfoot's Case* (1743), Foster, 154 ; *Freyberger, Ex parte*, [1917] 2 K.B. 129 ; *Vecht* v. *Taylor* (1917), 116 L.T. 446 ; *Dawson* v. *Meuli* (1918), 118 L.T. 357 ; *Gschwind* v. *Huntington*, [1918] 2 K.B. 420.

where persons are subject to the law of one or other of
the forces, the right of the courts to intervene seems open
to grave doubt.   The possibility of dealing with alleged
cases of wrongful enlistment, which formerly existed, has
been taken away by legislation referring such issues to the
Army or Air Council.   Moreover, members of the defence
forces hold their positions at the royal pleasure, and no
action lies by them for alleged breach of contract or
dismissal without cause.[1]

An important point arises whether a subordinate has
any remedy against a superior who improperly causes his
arrest and trial.   In *Sutton* v. *Johnstone* [2] the latter was
tried for neglect of duty, cowardice, and disobedience to
orders, but was honourably acquitted by court-martial.   It
was, however, held by the Exchequer Chamber that he
could not retain the damages awarded in the court below
on the ground that he had not proved absence of reasonable and probable cause.   In *Dawkins* v. *Paulet* [3] it was
ruled by King's Bench that a subordinate has no redress
for acts done by a superior officer in the course of his duty,
even if he acts without reasonable, probable, and justifiable cause, but that he must have recourse to such redress
as may be allowed by the Articles of War.   Subsequent
cases [4] have not affected this decision, which may perhaps
be liable to be overruled only by the House of Lords
though it has been commented on unfavourably by the
High Court of the Commonwealth of Australia.[5]

---

[1] *Tufnell, In re* (1876), 3 Ch.D. 164 ; *Dickson* v. *Combermere* (*Viscount*),
(1863), 3 F. &. F. 527 ; *Grant* v. *Secretary of State for India* (1877), 2 C.P.D.
445 ; *Denning* v. *Secretary of State* (1920), 37 T.L.R. 138 ; *Leaman* v. *R.*
[1920] 3 K.B. 663.

[2] (1787), 1 Bro. P.C. 76.   [3] (1869), L.R. 5 Q.B. 94.

[4] *Dawkins* v. *Lord Rokeby* (1875), L.R. 7 H.L. 744 ; *Marks* v. *Frogley*,
[1898] 1 Q.B. 888 ; *Fraser* v. *Hamilton* (1917), 33 T.L.R. 431 ; *Fraser* v.
Balfour (1918), 34 T.L.R. 502 ; *Heddon* v. *Evans* (1919), 35 T.L.R. 642.

[5] *Gibbons* v. *Duffell* (1932), 47 C.L.R. 520.

A further difficulty arises how far an order of a superior justifies action by a subordinate which is otherwise illegal. It appears to be the case that an inferior will be held free from liability, if he obeys in good faith an order not manifestly illegal ; but the authority on this head is very small. In *R.* v. *Thomas* [1] a sailor, who, ordered to keep off boats from a ship, killed a man was held guilty of murder, but granted a pardon. In the Cape [2] a soldier was found not guilty because the order to fire was not patently illegal, and, when Mr. Sheehy Skeffington was murdered, [3] his actual executioners were not put on trial. In view of the gravity of refusal to obey orders in war, it may be that almost any case of obedience to orders would be held justifiable ; but the matter must not be pressed, for, if carried too far, it would result in permitting subordinates at the order of their immediate superior to shoot an officer of higher rank.

The forces of the Crown are necessarily available for employment in the maintenance of order internally in case of any sort of unrest. In the case of the army reserve special provision is formally made under which men may be called out in aid of the civil power by the Secretary of State or by the officer commanding in any town or district, on the requisition of a justice of the peace. The Home Secretary is the minister naturally appealed to by civil authorities in regions where disturbances beyond the power of the local forces to control are feared. In some cases aid may be obtained from the Metropolitan Police or a neighbouring force. Otherwise, the Secretary of State will

[1] Russell on Crimes (6th ed.), iii. 94 ; *Keighly* v. *Bell* (1866), 4 F. & F. at p. 790.

[2] *R.* v. *Smith* (1900), 17 Cape S.C.R. 561.

[3] *Parl. Pap.* Cd. 8376 (1916). Four men were tried for the murder of an Arab prisoner at Jaffa in Jan. 1939, but only one conviction was allowed to stand by the Court of Appeal : *inter arma silent leges.*

make the necessary requisition to the appropriate defence ministry. But in emergency local authorities may apply to the officer in command of the nearest force, notifying the Home Office at the same time. The mode of action to be followed in such cases has been on several occasions authoritatively laid down, especially in the case of the Featherstone riots,[1] where the use of military aid to prevent grave destruction of property under a Liberal Government was naturally severely attacked in Parliament and in the country, but was completely vindicated. In the famous Bristol riots of 1831, during the reform agitation, grave injury to property and ultimately serious loss of life were due to the failure not so much of the civil authorities, as was shown on the indictment of the mayor,[2] as of the officer commanding the military forces, who later committed suicide and who seems to have been mentally deranged at the time of the rioting. The military may, of course, act on their own initiative, but in England this is seldom necessary.

[1] *Parl. Pap.* C. 7234 (1894).
[2] *R.* v. *Pinney* (1832), 5 Car. & P. 254.

CHAPTER XIX

THE LEGISLATIVE AND JUDICIAL POWERS OF THE EXECUTIVE

1. *The Legislative Powers of the Executive*

THE grant by Parliament of authority to legislate to the Chapter
XIX. executive is not of recent origin. In 1603 [1] and 1710 [2] are recorded wide grants of power to deal with plague and quarantine and the Poor Law Commissioners were invested with the widest authority to make regulations for the management of the poor. There were wide delegations as to lodging-houses regulation by the local authorities in 1851,[3] as to ships by an Act of 1852, and as to the militia in the same year.[4] As early as 1855 the Metropolis Management Act authorised the removal of difficulties arising under the Act by Order in Council, and like authority was included in the Local Government Acts of 1888 and 1894. In 1854 alteration of provisions of the Merchant Shipping Act by Trinity House was permitted, and in 1875 alteration by the Secretary of State of provisions as to explosive substances. Other Acts permitted the bringing of a statute into operation by Order ; [5] the addition to a schedule of persons, places and things to which the Act was to apply ; [6]

---

[1] 1 Jac. I. c. 31.
[2] 9 Anne c. 2 ; *R.* v. *Harris* (1791), 4 T.R. 202.
[3] 14 & 15 Vict. c. 28, s. 9.
[4] 15 & 16 Vict. c. 44, s. 55 ; c. 50, s. 13.
[5] Copyright Act, 1852, ss. 2, 4.
[6] Salmon Fisheries (Scotland) Act, 1863, s. 4.

and modification of rules which are found impossible of performance or to work hardship.

Gradually there grew up the practice of providing safeguards for the validity of delegated legislation, so as to avoid question in the courts. In seventeen cases before 1900 occur clauses providing that the making of a rule or an order or the confirmation of a scheme shall be conclusive evidence that the requirements of the Act have been complied with; thus the Extradition Act, 1870, forbade Orders in Council bringing the Act into force to be questioned in any court. The classes of cases where rules and orders are expressed to have effect as if enacted in the Act fell into two classes, those where a department of state itself made the rule or order, and those in which it merely confirmed a scheme submitted by another body, commissioners, local authority or trustees, and thus superseded the procedure by private Act. But the power was in the early cases limited, and a wide authority to make regulations was first found in the Cremation Act, 1902, and the Air Navigation Act, 1919.

There was at the same time a tendency to save the expense of private Bills by securing a provisional order. Under that mode of operation an Act sponsored by a department gives legal force to an order or number of orders prepared by other authorities and approved by the department. This plan appears in growing frequency from 1870 onwards, but it in its turn gave way to a yet simpler procedure, under which a scheme is drawn up, submitted to a department, and with or without alterations confirmed by the department which, normally but not always, has to lay the scheme before Parliament for information, and possible intervention. The Light Railways Act, 1896, marks the beginning of an extensive use of this substitute for a Provisional Order Bill or a private Bill. In 1899 for

Scotland the Private Legislation Procedure (Scotland) Act secured the advantages of a procedure for private legislation based on that for Provisional Orders, thus saving promoters much time and money in any normal case.

In 1893 the issue of rules had become so regular a part of the work of the executive that it was felt imperative to make regulations to secure their due publication, and to provide for a regular procedure prior to enactment. This took the form of the Rules Publication Act, 1893, which requires that notice of the intention to make a statutory rule must be gazetted at least forty days before the rule is made, and during that period the draft is to be available for inspection, and any representations made by a public body must be duly considered before any rule is made. The Act, however, does not apply to any rules, regulations, and by-laws (orders are not within its terms) which are not required to be laid before Parliament at all, or which are required to be laid or to be laid in draft for a period before taking effect. Nor does the Act apply to rules made by the Board of Trade, the Local Government Board, or its successor the Minister of Health, in respect of matters taken over from it, the revenue departments, or the Post Office, or under the Contagious Diseases (Animals) Act, 1878, and amending Acts by the Board (now Minister) of Agriculture. To these exceptions rules of the Supreme Court were added in 1925. A further derogation from the effect of the Act was the authority given in case of urgency to issue provisional rules which took immediate effect. While such a procedure was clearly useful if the provisional rules were replaced early by rules made in the ordinary way, as in the case of the census in 1920–21, some departments were content to allow matters to remain as provisional ; thus some rules as to old-age pensions remained in provisional form from 1911 to 1920.

The practice of delegating legislative powers became regular in the war.   From 1914 to 1918 the Defence of the Realm Acts gave enormous powers of delegated legislation, and like authority was contained in the Acts creating, or authorising the creation of, the new ministries of Food, Labour, Shipping, National Service, Munitions, and Reconstruction.   The powers exercised under these grants were wide and far-reaching and deeply affected the life of the nation, but they were acquiesced in as the inevitable concomitants of a great war.   After the war the process had to continue.   Schemes of unemployment and health insurance, housing conditions, the reform of local government, the revision of the regulations as to transport, the regrouping of the railways, the rationalisation of the production of coal, had to be faced, and it was felt impossible to place on Parliament the duty of dealing with these matters in the ordinary way.   The ministers of Health, of Transport, and of Labour, and the Board of Trade had to be given widest discretion.   Thus in Acts passed between 1920 and 1930 five give power to the executive to remove difficulties in their operation, while between 1915 and 1929 twenty statutes authorised power to modify substantially the statute itself.

From 1929 the danger of too generous delegation of legislative power became the subject of discussion, and in October 1930 the Lord Chancellor set up a committee to consider " the powers exercised by or under the direction of ministers of the Crown by (*a*) delegated legislation, (*b*) judicial or quasi-judicial decision, and to report what safeguards are desirable or necessary to secure the constitutional principles of the supremacy of Parliament and the supremacy of the law ".   On November 2 appeared an indictment of the dangerous tendencies of the day in *The New Despotism*, by the Lord Chief Justice of England, and his criticisms were re-echoed in 1931 by Mr. Allen in *Bureaucracy Triumphant*, where he alluded to the tortuous processes of the official mind. Judicial consideration of the power of the executive in *Yaffe, Ex parte*[1] focused public opinion on the issue and removed in considerable measure public anxiety.

The question of the extent of the authority under delegated legislation had already come before the courts in *Institute of Patent Agents* v. *Lockwood*, which raised the question of the validity of certain rules as to payment of fees by such agents which the Board of Trade had made. The Act gave the same force to rules as if they had been enacted in the Act, and the House of Lords, overruling the Scottish Court of Session, ruled that full effect must be given to this provision and that the rules must in themselves be deemed to be binding.[2] This decision was carried rather further in two subsequent cases and its difficulties were canvassed, but the matter came into essential prominence in *Yaffe's Case*.[3] The Housing Act, 1925, provided that an order of the minister when made shall have effect as if enacted by this Act. A housing scheme was planned under the Act, but on the view of the Court of Appeal in another case[4] where it had granted a writ prohibiting the minister from proceeding to confirm a scheme, it was imperfect because it failed to specify precisely what was to be done with every parcel of land which it was proposed to acquire compulsorily. The minister, however, modified and confirmed as modified

---

[1] [1931] A.C. 494 ; [1930] 2 K.B. 90.
[2] *Institute of Patent Agents* v. *Lockwood*, [1894] A.C. 347. Cf. *London and General Bank, In re*, [1894] W.N. 155 ; *Baker* v. *Williams*, [1898] 1 Q.B. 23.
[3] [1931] A.C. 494.   [4] *Davis, Ex parte*, [1929] 1 K.B. 169.

the scheme, and it appears from the judgment of the Lords that even in its earlier form the scheme was within the power of the Act. But in the Divisional Court it was admitted by the Attorney-General that the scheme as submitted was *ultra vires*. The court, however, held that the order of the minister confirming the scheme was valid, but the Attorney-General went so far as to argue that anything done by the minister, if it purported to be done under the Act, was valid and could not be enquired into by the court. The Court of Appeal rejected his reasoning and decided that, as the scheme was not properly made, it could not be made effective by confirmation. The House of Lords allowed the validity of the scheme and would have accepted an invalid scheme if duly amended, but also declined to allow the proposition that the courts must accept anything purporting to be done under the Act. The decision of the Lords is no doubt not wholly beyond question as to its precise meaning, but the natural interpretation is that anything which is within the spirit of an Act can be validly laid down by rules if they are to have effect as if enacted, while matters outside the meaning of the Act cannot be so dealt with.

The criticism of the grant of too wide powers suggested by the decisions in *Davis's Case* and *Yaffe's Case* led to a new form of enactment in the Housing Act, 1930, the Land Drainage Act, 1930, and the Agricultural Marketing Act, 1931. Under the new procedure an application can be made within a specified time after the making of a confirming order to the High Court to question its validity, on the ground that it is not within the powers of the Act, or that any requirement of the Act has not been complied with. If the court is satisfied that the order is not within the powers of the Act, or that the interests of the applicant have been substantially prejudiced by the failure to comply with the requirements of the Act, it may quash the order. The remedy by which the use of *certiorari* is abolished, is clearly just ; it is wrong to hold up important housing schemes, as had been done by the procedure adopted.[1]

Steps were taken also to deal with the objections felt to the enactment that the making of an order should be conclusive evidence of compliance by the minister with any conditions laid down to govern its making. In the Land Drainage Bill in the Lords for " conclusive " was substituted " prima facie ",[2] and the confirmation by the minister under the Road Traffic Act, 1930, of an order establishing a parking place was made evidence only that the requirements of Section 90 of the Act had been complied with. On the other hand, the provision was allowed to stand in the Agricultural Marketing Act, 1931, which made no provision for review by the courts, but a scheme thereunder could not come into operation without the positive approval of Parliament, and opportunity was given to persons aggrieved to vote against its remaining in force at the poll of those affected.[3]

Yet another safeguard was provided for in the Local Government Act, 1929, the Road Traffic Act, 1930, and the Mental Treatment Act, 1930, which allow departmental modification of the Acts, for an affirmative resolution of Parliament was made necessary. A proposal to allow the houses to modify regulations under the Road Traffic Act was wisely negatived, in view of the fact that no procedure existed for settling cases where the two houses might differ in their views as to the changes to be made.[4] Under that Act the Highway Code fell to be specially approved by both houses, and in the Land Drainage Act, 1930, provision

---

[1] See also Poor Law Act, 1930, s. 142 ; Public Works Facilities Act, 1930, Sch. I. Pt. III. 2.   [2] 77 *H.L. Deb.* 5 s. 932.
[3] 21 & 22 Geo. V. c. 42, ss. 1 (8), 3.   [4] 76 *H.L. Deb.* 5 s. 321.

was made under which the minister must lay before Parliament a report giving particulars of any question referred to him and the reasons for his decision.

The dramatic crisis of 1931, however, resulted in the abandonment of the safeguards in emergency measures. The National Economy Act, 1931, went far beyond the principles of the Emergency Powers Act, 1920, elsewhere described, and gave power by Order in Council to reduce expenditure in certain services scheduled to the Act ; the power was to be exercised within a month, but the reductions could be restored only by Act of Parliament. It was admitted in both houses that necessity alone justified so drastic a measure. After the dissolution of Parliament further emergency Acts were passed ; the Abnormal Importations (Customs Duties) Act, 1931, which gave wide powers to the Board of Trade, and the Horticultural Products (Emergency Customs Duties) Act, 1931, which gave powers to the Minister of Agriculture and Fisheries, acting with the Treasury, to impose special duties. Both these Acts required subsequent affirmation by resolution of the Commons. These Acts were temporary, but the Import Duties Act, 1932, gave the Treasury power to remove duties imposed thereby on the recommendation of the Import Duties Advisory Committee set up under the Act after consultation with the department concerned. The Treasury was further authorised in like manner to place additional duties on articles of luxury or articles produced in substantial quantity in the United Kingdom. Moreover, exemption from the duties under the Act might be extended to mandated territories by Order in Council, while the Act itself gave it to colonies and protectorates. As regards the Dominions, India, and Southern Rhodesia power was given to the Treasury to provide for exemption or preference on the recommendation of the Secretary of

State. In the case of foreign countries like powers might be exercised on the recommendation of the Board of Trade, and that department with Treasury concurrence might place additional duties on imports from countries discriminating against British goods. The operation of duties imposed required confirmation by the Commons within twenty-eight Parliamentary days after making, while in the like period other orders might be annulled by resolution of the house. Unusual powers were also given under the Wheat Act, 1932.

The Committee on Ministers' Powers [1] reported in March 1932. They recognised delegation of power as inevitable, but they thought that the actual course of delegation had been haphazard and should be reconsidered. Whenever legislative power was delegated, the limits of the power should be clearly defined in the statute by which delegation was made. Parliament should not depart from the normal type of delegation without special need, nor without conscious consideration of the special grounds put forward as constituting the need, and it should grant powers of the exceptional type only on exceptional grounds.

The normal type in the view of the Committee is distinguished by the fact that the limits of the power delegated are so clearly defined as to be understood by Parliament, by the executive, and by the public, and can easily be enforced by the judiciary. Negatively, the type is marked by the fact that no power is delegated either (1) to legislate on matters of principle or to impose taxation, or (2) to amend Acts of Parliament, either the Act by which the powers are delegated or other Acts. Of such a power an excellent example exists in the authority of the Minister of Transport under the Road Traffic Act of 1930 to restrict or prohibit the driving of motor or other

[1] *Parl. Pap.* Cmd. 4060.

vehicles on specified roads on the application of a local authority. On the other hand, instances exist of too wide authority to legislate or even to tax ; the former is found repeated in the Poor Law Act of 1930 from the original Act of 1834, while power to tax is illustrated by the Safeguarding of Industries Act, 1921, and the legislation of 1931–2 above referred to. There are objections also to giving power to amend the Act creating the power, but in none of the instances between 1888 and 1929 was the power of much importance, the measures being intended to meet minor points of difficulty and to obviate hardship to local authorities. There is more difficulty as regards the power to amend other Acts, as in the case of the Juries Act, 1922, and the Mental Treatment Act, 1930. Objection also must be taken to vague powers such as those given to the Board of Trade by the Patents, Designs, and Trade Marks Acts, 1883 and 1888, or Part IV of the Road Traffic Act, 1930, which allows the minister to make orders on appeal binding on the Traffic Commissioners appointed under that Act ; the courts in fact have had to narrow the effect of the power to bring it within reasonable limits. It is also objectionable to provide that action by a minister shall be conclusive evidence that the requirements of an Act have been met, and that the order confirmed is within the powers of the Act.

On the other hand, against the incidental disadvantages of delegation must be set its merits. Pressure on Parliamentary time forbids discussion in detail of legislation, and to attempt to do so merely means that Parliament neglects essential duties. Further, many measures are so technical that they cannot effectively be discussed by members of Parliament ; they must be dealt with by experts on the topic. It is impossible to provide, in any such scheme of legislation as that regarding Health and

Unemployment Insurance, or trade boards, for all the contingencies, and regulations become essential. Flexibility again can best be attained by delegation which enables the ministry to adopt new proposals arising out of the rapid development, for instance, of mechanical road transport. Experiment again is permissible, and that is great benefit in cases like town-planning, where all is more or less in a state of flux. Emergency powers, whether general or special, may be essential; the Defence of the Realm Acts and the Emergency Power Act, 1920, are clearly measures which are unavoidable, as well as the powers given to the Minister of Agriculture and Fisheries to take drastic steps to deal at once with animal diseases and to prevent their spread.

The disadvantages are also clear. There is the danger of passing Acts in too summary a form, and leaving undue freedom to the executive. There is no doubt also that the facilities given to Parliament to scrutinise regulations is imperfect. In addition to the publicity afforded by the Rules Publication Act, 1893, there are in statutes delegating powers many provisions regarding the procedure to bring them before the notice of Parliament. These vary from mere laying before which gives Parliament information but no control, to laying with the power to Parliament to annul by resolution of either house; laying with requirement of an affirmation by both houses or in fiscal issues by the Commons; laying in draft and laying in draft with the provision that nothing is to become effective unless approved by resolution. But, while the Lords' procedure allows of effective action by a private member who wishes to secure that a regulation be annulled, it is less easy in the Commons, though such a motion can be divided upon after 11 P.M. But otherwise there is practically no other mode of criticism than by asking questions on the regulations. Another valid objection is that the regulations may be so wide as to exclude judicial intervention to save the subject from oppression, while it is true that the delegation may be so vague as to cause uneasiness and doubt. If illegal actions do take place, the immunities of the Crown render redress difficult, and, while efforts are made to give reasonable publicity and to consult beforehand interests likely to be affected, this is not always practicable, especially if the public in general is affected, and not some specific interests, which are duly organised.

Provision, however, exists which secures that in certain cases before making rules authorities must consult experts of some sort or another. This is so under the Merchant Shipping Acts as regards the Board of Trade ; under the factory legislation from 1901, as regards the Secretary of State ; under the Trade Boards Act, 1918, as regards the making of special orders by the Minister of Labour ; under the Electricity (Supply) Act, 1919, as regards confirmation of special orders by the Minister of Transport ; under the Seeds Act, 1920, as regards the making of rules by the Minister of Agriculture and Fisheries ; as regards making of regulations for London traffic by the Minister of Transport under the London Traffic Act, 1924 ; [1] as regards the making of certain regulations by the Minister of Labour under the Mining Industry Act, 1926 ; and so on. Even where no compulsion to consult exists, departments are normally ready to invite the co-operation of expert bodies of all kinds.

The Committee made recommendations for the safeguarding of the making of regulations at considerable length, but their views have never received acceptance, and may be regarded as unlikely of adoption. The in-

[1] The matter falls under the London Passenger Transport Act, 1933

clusion of powers of regulation-making remains unaltered in recent Acts, except that to a limited extent precautions have been taken to require approval by Parliament affirmatively.

It must be remembered that approval by Parliament may prove inadequate. Under the Unemployment Assistance Act, 1934, regulations made require Parliament's approval, but the first set made proved unsatisfactory in operation to many members of Parliament, and the opportunity was taken of a supplementary estimate to press the Minister of Labour to secure changes. He therefore made suggestions to the Board, which responded by asking Parliament [1] to suspend the operation of the regulations approved, while it produced another set [2] which were more fortunate. There is little doubt that great care was taken in framing the regulations, and that proper consultations were had. The difficulty was that it proved impossible correctly to picture how the regulations would operate in their application by many different officers in parts of the country where conditions were various.

One safeguard in regard to delegated legislation has the authority of the Committee on Ministers' Powers and is supported by common sense. It suggests that there should be appointed a Committee which should have the duty of considering all clauses in Bills delegating legislative power. The Committee would note whether the power was delegated in normal form with due allowance of opportunity for expert investigation and criticism, whether it purported to oust any possibility of legal challenge, and any other matter which appeared of interest to the public. It would be entitled, if it found anything abnormal, to require an explanation from the ministry concerned, and it would be entitled to call the attention of the house by a special

[1] 25 & 26 Geo. V. c. 6.   [2] S.R.O. 1936, No. 776.

report to anything which it deemed out of due course or
likely to introduce a dangerous innovation. It is difficult
to see why some such Committee should not have been
created already, and the reform is one of those which could
be made easily, if it were desired to provide a simple safeguard against the alleged dangers of the possession of the
bureaucracy of excessive powers. The fact that it has not
been set up may indicate that in practice the bureaucracy
has usually succeeded in sending out rules which are sufficiently reasonable to arouse no very grave opposition.

The effect, however, of the consideration given to the
issue may be traced in the Coal Act, 1938,[1] for under it the
powers of the Coal Commission to arrange for the reduction
of the number of coal-mining undertakings in any area
are to be exercised, not directly, but by means of a recommendation to the Board of Trade, followed by the making
of a Provisional Order by the Board, which of course presents full opportunity for representations by those affected
to the Select Committee to which the Order Confirmation
Bill, if opposed, will go.

2. *The Judicial and Quasi-Judicial Powers of the Executive*

One of the characteristic features of the constitutional
development of the nineteenth century was the recognition
by Parliament that the ordinary courts of law were not
well adapted to deal with certain types of question.
Various steps were taken to deal with such cases, one of
which remains remarkable. The Medical Act, 1858, gave
power to the General Medical Council to remove from the
register of medical practitioners the name of any such
practitioner judged by the Council, after due enquiry, to

[1] 1 & 2 Geo. VI. c. 52, s. 67.

have been guilty of infamous conduct in any professional respect. Such a removal deprives a doctor of his recognised status, and may be fatal to his chance of earning a livelihood. Nevertheless there is no redress available against such action, and it is not even possible for a doctor by voluntary request for removal of his name to avoid the action of the Council.[1] There has been criticism,[2] not without justice, of the character of this enactment, and, while the principle of control of registration of midwives is given to the Central Midwives Board by the Midwives Act, 1902, an appeal was allowed to the High Court. Equally when disciplinary control over solicitors was ascribed to the Discipline Committee of the Law Society, an appeal was allowed to the High Court by the solicitor affected.

In certain other cases appeals are given from decisions to tribunals constructed specially, which are independent of all control by the Government. Appeals against Inland Revenue valuations under the Finance (1909–10) Act, 1910, were given to referees appointed by the Lord Chief Justice, the Master of the Rolls, and the President of the Surveyors Institution, and under the Acquisition of Land (Assessment of Compensation) Act, 1919, appeals arising out of disputes over the price offered by Government departments or local authorities lie to one of a panel of arbitrators similarly appointed.[3]

In other cases, while ministers appoint tribunals, they are given functions to be carried out in a completely judicial spirit. Thus in 1873,[4] when the Railway and Canal Traffic Act was passed, advantage was taken to

Chapter
XIX.

---

[1] 21 & 22 Vict. c. 90 ; *R. v. General Medical Council* ; *Kynaston, Ex parte*, [1930] 1 K.B. 562.
[2] Memo. of Medical Practitioners' Union, Jan. 11, 1939.
[3] *West Midlands Joint Electricity Authority* v. *Pitt*, [1932] 2 K.B. 1.
[4] 36 & 37 Vict. c. 48.

substitute for the jurisdiction of the Common Pleas over matters arising under earlier Acts that of a court of three commissioners, one expert in law and one in railways business. In 1888, on the passing of a new Railway and Canal Traffic Act,[1] the court was remodelled and now consists of three members, one a judge assigned by the Lord Chancellor and two members selected formerly by the Board of Trade, now by the Home Secretary under the Ministry of Transport Act, 1919.[2] This body has power over questions of facilities to be given and arrangements for through traffic over different railway systems, and other disputes between railway companies. On points of law alone there lies an appeal to the Court of Appeal. To this body were assigned powers under the Mines (Working Facilities and Support) Act, 1923, and the Mining Industry Act, 1926, and the Coal Act, 1938 (s. 51), gives further power.

From this body jurisdiction over railway rates and charges was transferred under the Railways Act, 1921,[3] to the Railway Rates Tribunal, which is composed of three members appointed by the King on the advice of the Lord Chancellor, the President of the Board of Trade, and the Minister of Transport respectively, in order to secure legal knowledge, business experience, and knowledge of railway affairs. They are appointed for a term of years but may be reappointed, and their work is partly judicial but also partly administrative, for they have the widest powers over the determination of railway charges. On points of law appeal lies to the Court of Appeal or the Court of Session in Scotland.

The Chief Registrar of Friendly Societies is appointed by the Treasury, and holds office at pleasure. The parties

[1] 51 & 52 Vict. c. 25.   [2] 9 & 10 Geo. V. c. 50, s. 2.
[3] 11 & 12 Geo. V. c. 55, s. 20.

to a dispute affecting such a society may refer to him for an arbitral award, and he can state a case for the opinion of the High Court.[1] He has an important power of investigation of the affairs of societies and branches, and may order that a society or branch be dissolved.[2] He deals as Industrial Assurance Commissioner with disputes under the Industrial Assurance Act, 1923, and certain powers are conferred on him by the Trade Union Act, 1913, and the Trade Disputes and Trade Unions Act, 1927.

The Special Commissioners of Income Tax are appointed by the Treasury under the Income Tax Act, 1918, and hold office at pleasure. They have appellate jurisdiction in income tax and sur-tax cases, and can be required to state a case for the High Court on a point of law. The position of this body is peculiarly anomalous, for, though public servants, they adjudicate in a spirit of remarkable independence between the Crown and the taxpayer, and their reputation for fairness is high.[3]

The Board of Referees also deals with certain income tax issues. They are appointed by the Treasury from business and professional men specially competent to deal with the issues in question, and have as chairman a King's Counsel.

These tribunals are in the main concerned with very definite legal points, which experience of the matters concerned enables them to handle more effectively than the ordinary court of law. In the case of other tribunals their purpose is more definitely to determine in first instance or on appeal justiciable issues arising out of the work of Government departments involving a much greater discretionary element than income tax issues. Tribunals of this kind were necessary for the working of

[1] 59 & 60 Vict. c. 25, s. 68.   [2] *Ibid.* s. 80.
[3] *Parl. Pap.* Cmd. 615 (1920) para. 359.

the Unemployment Insurance Acts ;[1] a claim in such cases is submitted to an insurance officer appointed by the Minister of Labour, who may reject it, if it is due in his opinion to a Labour dispute, appeal in that case lying to the Court of Referees ; or he may admit the claim or refer it to that court, which consists of an equal number of representatives of employers and insured contributors under a chairman appointed by the ministry. Final appeal is allowed to the umpire appointed by the Crown. It is clear, that if the umpire could be influenced by the ministry, the value of the appeal would largely disappear, but by convention the umpire is left, even in vital matters, free to judge according to the best of his ability.

Under the War Pensions Act, 1921,[2] an appeal was given from an award to the Pensions Appeal Tribunal appointed by the Lord Chancellor. Appeal was so provided under the Widows', Orphans', and Old Age Contributory Pensions Act, 1925,[3] to a referee or referees from a panel of barristers and solicitors appointed by the National Health Joint Committee, whence no appeal lay save that a case might be stated for the High Court on a point of law.

In certain cases, instead of giving powers to officers who are indeed appointed by ministers, but in practice are allowed to work freely, the power is given to ministers themselves to make decisions which are judicial in a few cases, but in the main are quasi-judicial. The essential difference between the cases is that a judicial decision is one based on the application of a definitely prescribed law to a given set of circumstances, while a quasi-judicial decision involves a statutory authority to use his adminis-

---

[1] 10 & 11 Geo. V. c. 30 ; 20 & 21 Geo. V. c. 16 ; now 25 & 26 Geo. V. c. 8.
[2] 11 & 12 Geo. V. c. 49, s. 4.
[3] See now 26 Geo. V. & 1 Edw. VIII. c. 33 ; for voluntary contributions, 1 Edw. VIII. & 1 Geo. VI. c. 39.

trative discretion, and to be guided by his views of public policy after hearing the facts and ascertaining, if necessary, the bearing of the law on the facts as ascertained.

In the Public Health Act, 1875, by Section 268 a definitely judicial function was imposed on the Local Government Board, for it was required to adjudicate between persons aggrieved by orders of the Board to pay expenses incurred by local authorities.[1] So also under the Law of Property Act, 1922,[2] judicial authority was given to the Minister of Agriculture and Fisheries regarding the computation of compensation for extinguishment of manorial rights. Judicial also is the function of determining what is insurable employment under the National Health Insurance Act, and an appeal lies on a point of law to a judge assigned by the Lord Chancellor whose decision is final.[3] The minister may, instead of deciding, refer the issue to the judge. In the case of education the Board was given power to decide disputes between voluntary school managers and local authorities regarding the maintenance of such schools. In the leading case of *Board of Education* v. *Rice*[4] it was held that the functions of the Board were judicial, and that it had not duly dealt with the dispute so that *mandamus* lay to it to do so.

Cases of quasi-judicial decision are numerous. Thus by Section 10 of the Education Act, 1921, the Board of Education must decide if a school is necessary or not, due regard being paid to the interests of secular instruction, the wishes of parents and the education of their children, and economy of the rates. Clearly the weighing of these considerations requires the exercise of judicial qualities;

[1] *R.* v. *Local Government Board* (1882), 10 Q.B.D. 309.
[2] 12 & 13 Geo. V. c. 16, s. 139.
[3] 14 & 15 Geo V. c. 38, s. 89 ; 26 Geo. V. & 1 Edw. VIII. c. 32, ss. 161-4, 176. The work is done by a specially delegated officer.
[4] [1911] A.C. 179.

equally clearly the decision is a matter of policy and will be dictated ultimately in large measure by the general outlook of the minister. But the Board proceeds judicially in so far as it arranges for a public enquiry at which the wishes and opinions of those concerned are noted, and a report thereon with recommendations is made to the Board. A copy of this report must be supplied to any local education authority concerned, but the final decision is that of the Board.

Again, the Minister of Health [1] is bound to decide any disputes which may arise between the medical officer of health of a district and the officer of a county regarding information to be supplied to the latter by the former. The minister must give both officers an opportunity to present their views, and thereafter he decides on his opinion of what is best in the interests of medical administration. The matter arises in a very similar form regarding clearance orders made by a local authority. In such cases a public enquiry is held at which persons affected are authorised to present their views ; the officer who holds the enquiry reports to the minister, who decides in his discretion what he should do. The principles affecting such issues were laid down in *Local Government Board* v. *Arlidge*,[2] under the Housing, Town Planning, etc., Act, 1909. Being aggrieved by a closing order in respect of a dwelling-house, Mr. Arlidge appealed to the Local Government Board, which held a local enquiry but dismissed the appeal. The House of Lords upheld the action of the Board, dismissing the contention which was accepted by the Court of Appeal, that the appellant was entitled to have the report of the inspector revealed to him. The arguments apart from this decision for disclosure or non-

---

[1] 9 Edw. VII. c. 44, s. 69 (2), (3) ; Local Government Act, 1933, s. 113.
[2] [1915] A.C. 120.

disclosure are evenly balanced, but the official view is that
the report is a confidential matter which is but one of the
materials on which the minister makes up his mind, and
that publication would serve no useful purpose, for it
might mislead the public regarding the grounds for the
decision of the minister. Moreover in practice, no doubt,
if publication were resolved on, the reports would be made
mainly formal, and the inspector would give separately
and confidentially his own personal views. Though, however, the report is confidential, the procedure in these cases
must be fair. In *Errington* v. *Minister of Health* [1] the
minister had confirmed a clearance order ; at the public
enquiry the persons affected had put forward evidence to
show that the buildings in question could be reconditioned,
but after it the minister by his officials received fresh
evidence from those upholding the making of the order
without disclosing it to the parties affected, and viewed
the premises in the presence of the former but not of the
latter. On this ground the confirmation was quashed.
On the other hand, in the case of the *Brighton Corporation
(Everton Place Area) Order*, 1937,[2] the owner of certain
land in a clearance area which the corporation had decided
to acquire compulsorily attended at the enquiry and undertook to comply with a clearance order, submitting a plan
for the redevelopment of the land when cleared. The
minister confirmed the order, and it was contended that
he should, before doing so, have called upon the owner to
make further observations regarding his plan. That was
ruled to be unnecessary, as, the facts having been before
the minister, he was under no obligation to prefer his offer
and to compel the local authority to make a demolition
order in place of a compulsory purchase order. The
position of an inspector who holds enquiries for the

[1] [1935] 1 K.B. 349.   [2] (1938), 54 T.L.R. 637.

Minister of Transport under Section 81 of the Road Traffic
Act, 1930, is precisely similar ; he is a mere agent of the
minister, as pointed out by Avory, J., in *R.* v. *Minister of
Transport*; *Southend Express Carriers Ltd., Ex parte.*[1] It
is clearly a case for the discretion of Parliament whether
such matters are given to ministers to decide or assigned
to the courts, as was done by the Mines (Working Facilities
and Support) Act, 1923, when under private ownership it
became necessary to give assistance to mining concerns
to obtain the right to work minerals held in private ownership, when the owner was unwilling to agree on reasonable
terms.   The advantage of judicial action in such cases
was shown to be held by Parliament when three years
later it extended the authority given, and as regards the
question of railway rates the tribunal chosen is essentially
judicial in outlook and functioning.

It will be noted that in many cases these decisions,
whether taken by the minister or by courts, partake of
the nature of legislation. The making, for instance, of a
closing order or clearance or demolition order is not
a judicial decision as to existing rights ; it is legislative
in essence, as was recognised in *Yaffe's Case,*[2] and it is
this characteristic which renders it especially appropriate
that authority should be given to a minister responsible
to Parliament.

Between the purely judicial and quasi-judicial decisions
the distinction has been already noted. In both cases
there must be a dispute with presentation of their cases
by the parties ; there is normally the necessity of finding
facts with the aid of arguments, unless the facts are
agreed ; but thereafter they differ. In judicial cases there
must be a disputed point of law to be discussed, or at
least a point of law, and the decision is based on a finding

[1] *The Times*, Dec. 18, 1931.   [2] [1931] A.C. 494.

of facts and the application thereto of the law, after any dispute thereon has been decided by the court. In quasi-judicial decisions no point of law may be involved, and the decision is determined by the free choice of the minister as a matter of administrative discretion.

There are, however, certain principles of natural justice or of the national sense of justice, which ought to govern all decisions, and the Committee on Ministers' Powers expressly recommended that they should be stressed in dealing with quasi-judicial decisions. The most obvious is that a man should not be judge in his own case. The remotest pecuniary interest, it is clear, should debar a judge from deciding a case, unless it be disclosed to the party concerned ; in *Dimes* v. *Grand Junction Canal* [1] relief given by the Lord Chancellor to a company in which he had an interest of some thousand pounds was set aside by the House of Lords after consulting the judges. This case, however, is rare, but the principle applies wherever there is cause for bias, and it has been applied to negative borough justices deciding a matter in which they had actively taken sides in the proceedings of the borough council of which they were members.[2] The matter, however, cannot be pressed unduly, for the Lord Chancellor sits to hear appeals from the colonies which affect policy of which he himself has, or may have, to take part in the Cabinet. Nor is it clear that it is against public interest that a minister should be empowered to further a policy approved by Parliament in quasi-judicial decisions.

On the other hand, plainly no decision should be

[1] (1852), 3 H.L.C. 759. Cf. *R.* v. *Hendon Rural Council* ; *Chorley, Ex parte,* [1933] 2 K.B. 696.

[2] *R.* v. *Rand* (1866), L.R. 1 Q.B. 230 ; *R.* v. *Sunderland Justices,* [1901] 2 K.B 352 ; *R.* v. *Sussex Justices* ; *McCarthy, Ex parte* (1924), 93 L.J.K.B. 129.

made unless the party affected has been given a full
opportunity to state his case, and has been informed of
the case which he has to meet. But it cannot be held
necessary to import into the procedure of ministerial
decisions the necessity of oral hearings [1] or the technical
rules of English law which in many respects are unquestionably out of date and ill-adapted to further the end of
a rapid and effective decision. Nor is it essential, as we
have seen, that the minister should disclose to the parties
the report of his inspector, and it remains uncertain
whether or not he should be required to do so.[2] On the
other hand, it seems essential that the reasons for ministerial decisions should be given clearly and definitely, for
the information of the parties, and that, where they are
of general interest, they should be published, just as
decisions of the umpire on unemployment payments are
periodically issued. The objection that the findings are
thus rendered more open to criticism is not of much
weight; a decision against a man's interest not given
with explanation of reasons is on the whole more annoying
and much more suggestive of failure of the minister to
appreciate the points which have been raised.

The Committee on Ministers' Powers advised that,
whenever a judicial decision proper fell to be made by a
minister, there should be an appeal from his decision to
a judge of the High Court under a summary procedure,
but that no appeal should normally lie on facts. From
administrative decisions, whether they involved a judicial
element or not, they held that no appeal should lie. In
cases where judicial issues were involved, the Committee

---

[1] *Local Government Board* v. *Arlidge*, [1915] A.C. 120. Cf. *Marriott* v.
Minister of Health, [1937] 1 K.B. 128.

[2] Cf. *Offer* v. *Minister of Health*, [1936] 1 K.B. 40 ; *Denby & Sons, Ltd.*
v. *Minister of Health*, [1936] 1 K.B. 337 with *Parl. Pap.* Cmd. 4060,
pp. 100-107.

favoured recourse to the ordinary courts, but, if there were special reasons, there might be set up a ministerial tribunal which, though appointed by the minister, should be independent in the exercise of its functions, as in the case of the referee, who decides under the Import Duties Act, 1932, questions as to the value of goods subjected to duty. In that case the Lord Chancellor appoints, no official of the Government may be appointed, nor is appeal allowed either on law or facts.

The Committee reported against the proposal of creating a system of administrative law, but they proposed that, apart from the jurisdiction exercised over ministerial decision under the ordinary powers of the courts, there should be allowed an appeal proper from every judicial decision on points of law. The report was singularly strong against the idea of a regularised system of administrative courts, which it regarded as inconsistent with the sovereignty of Parliament and the supremacy of the law. Such a system would involve the abolition of supervisory and appeal powers of the ordinary courts over ministerial decisions, and would result in the withdrawal to a great extent of those judicial activities which are inseparable from administration from the influence of public opinion. It insisted, instead, that the essence of the English system was that the ordinary courts could deal with any actual or probable breach of the law committed by any servant of the Crown. This they deemed to distinguish fully the English legal system from French *droit administratif*. But the obvious difficulty remains that the French system secures to the citizens a very substantial amount of redress for official actions whether they involve or not an actual breach of law. In England, it is clear that under the existing rules remedies against the Crown are neither simple, cheap, nor effective. The point of the proposal seems to have been misunderstood by the Committee. What was clearly intended was to give the proceedings of ministerial decisions a more judicial character, and to make them better instruments for decisions than they now are.

There are in fact sound reasons for entrusting many issues to ministerial decisions. The process is simple as a rule, and cheap and normally much faster than that of a court. There is no need to adhere to obsolescent standards of evidence, nor to observe meticulously the rule of following precedent in cases where it appears that on the whole innovation would better serve the public interest. To be inveterate in error may be necessary for the House of Lords, but it is undesirable to adopt that precedent for ministerial disposition. The history of the treatment of workmen's compensation is a melancholy one, and it is difficult to deny that the House of Lords has on occasion delivered judgments which no ingenuity can satisfactorily reconcile, while the expense of appeals is rather scandalous, far more money often being spent in a case which yields no general guidance whatever than would have been awarded in compensation to the dependants of the dead man. Moreover, the number of appeals on the statutes which affect wide circles of people, such as the pensions for widows, orphans, and in old age provided in 1926, is so great as to render reference to the ordinary courts out of the question. But, while there is everything to be said for administrative tribunals, there are reforms which are necessary if the system is not to involve danger. The doctrine that full opportunity should be given to those affected to present their cases, and that the matter should not be decided on evidence submitted behind their backs, is essential. But it is also desirable that the personnel who decide issues should be definitely appointed for that purpose, and should have some legal training, and that they should be understood to be definitely performing their functions in a judicial spirit free from ministerial pressure. Those who urge further systematisation of the system would allow appeals from their rulings to a supreme administrative court [1] which would be composed of Civil servants with legal qualifications who would be free from the possible bias which must mark a tribunal attached to any single department.

The right of the ordinary courts to decide questions whether ministers act within the limit of their judicial powers must remain in principle. All that can be required in this direction is that the system of operation of this control shall be simplified and expedited. There is nothing very difficult in this if the reform were once agreed to be essential. The House of Lords might be asked to decide without the slow business of approach through the lower courts,[2] or a single judge might be set aside in the High Court for this business, or a special tribunal might be created consisting of Civil servants and a judge. Those who advocate administrative courts would give to the final appeal tribunal the power to deal also with issues of *ultra vires*.

It is easy, of course, to regard the judicial activities of the executive as a dangerous example of bureaucratic usurpation of power, especially when combined with the wide legislative authority given to the executive by many statutes. But in the main the process is one that is natural and inevitable with the evolution of modern needs, and what is necessary is not to seek to stay a process which has great advantages, but so to limit and regularise it that such risks as may be involved in it shall be

---

[1] Cf. Mr. Robson's proposal rejected in Cmd. 4060, p. 110.
[2] H. J. Laski, *Parl. Govt.* pp. 358 ff.

minimised.[1]   Thus in the case of the Coal Act, 1938, it is patently proper that appeals as to valuations made by the Regional Valuation Boards of interests to be acquired by the Commission should lie in an effective way, and a referee selected by the Board of Trade from a panel is certainly a fit and proper mode of disposing of an issue.[2]   Moreover, protection against ignoring of any provision of the Act or the Registration Act or of rules made thereunder is accorded by permitting application to be made within six weeks of the notice of the certificate of valuation given by the Board to the High Court.[3]

The imposition of penalties by Marketing Boards and other similar bodies, not under governmental control, has raised serious problems, and the Courts have intervened to correct errors of law.[4]   But the general principle that such procedure is desirable, and in view of the elective character of such Boards defensible, is maintained by a Departmental Committee[5] which recommends that for each scheme a small disciplinary board of not more than five persons, including an independent chairman with legal qualifications and experience, should be appointed by the minister.   For the herring industry scheme district disciplinary tribunals seem inevitable ; otherwise the purpose of the scheme would be frustrated, for the ordinary courts could not perform the work effectively.

[1] The desirability of making proceedings before judicial tribunals like the Court of Referees fully privileged for purposes of the law of libel is obvious : contrast *Collins* v. *Henry Whiteway & Co., Ltd.*, [1927] 2 K.B. 378.

[2] 1 & 2 Geo. VI. c. 52, sch. 3, s. 12.

[3] *Ibid.* s. 17.

[4] *R. & W. Paul, Ltd.* v. *Wheat Commission*, [1937] A.C. 139 ; *Ferrier* v. *Scottish Milk Marketing Board*, [1937] A.C. 126.

[5] *Parl. Pap.* Cmd. 5980.

CHAPTER XX

THE CIVIL SERVICE

1. *The Recruitment of the Service*

THE comparatively limited sphere of administration at the accession of Queen Victoria rendered it possible for the Government to be carried on with the aid of a Civil Service of no very great character or competence. Ministers themselves did not resent doing much work that was of no real importance, and the tradition persisted long in the Foreign Office where Lord Palmerston treated his subordinates as mere clerks and was duly hated by them in return. Lord Salisbury to the end did not desire to have advice tendered to him on issues of importance, did his work remote from his staff, and hardly knew any of them personally. In other departments matters might be much better. But the appointments were made by patronage pure and simple. The chances of promotion were uncertain, because merit might easily be overlooked in order to confer a favour on a political friend who desired advancement for a protégé, and this uncertainty rendered men unwilling to seek proficiency when it was uncertain if it would be rewarded. The use of patronage to fill customs, excise, and postal offices had been so serious that Mr. Burke secured their disfranchisement in 1782 [1] and the disability was removed only in 1868. The pressure of scientific discovery

---

[1] They desired disfranchisement as Lord North and his opponents were pressing them to vote for them, see 22 Geo. III. c. 41 ; 31 & 32 Vict. c. 73.

and of wider aims for the operations of government resulted in consciousness of the defects of the machinery
of administration, and Jeremy Bentham preached energetically from 1810 onwards the necessity of drastic reform.
How slow men were to move may be seen from the fact
that the Treasury instruction that clerks appointed to the
principal offices in all departments should possess a competent knowledge of book-keeping, by double entry was
ignored. The fact that it was given must be recorded
as significant of the failure of the Treasury to grasp the
nature of the problem to be faced. There was one redeem-
ing feature in the arrangements. The respect for property
which was so dominant a feature in the English mind
rendered men reluctant to remove from office any person
once appointed thereto, provided he did not offend by
political hostility or prove utterly dishonest. Hence a
change of ministry might well deny an aspirant promotion
for which he was fit, but it did not mean the wholesale
extrusion of Civil servants to make way for protégés of
the new ministry, and Britain was thus saved the grave
injustices of the spoils system which flourished in the
United States, and was thence borrowed under responsible
government by Canada, where it persisted unchecked into
the present century.

Competition as a means of securing comparative
efficiency had been suggested in the Charter Act of 1833,
which renewed the charter of the East India Company.
The conditions of successful work in India had induced
in 1813 the creation of a special school at Haileybury
for the preparation for their work in India of those
nominated to be Civil servants, and the plan of subjecting
them to strict examinations had been in part resorted to.
There was too much desire for patronage among the
members of the governing body of the company to allow

of full effect being given to the proposals of the Act of 1833, but the energy of Mr. Macaulay [1] succeeded in securing in the last Charter Act of 1853 complete adoption of the principle of admission by competitive examination to the Indian Civil Service. In the meantime essential steps towards reform had been taken in England. In November 1848 the Treasury had inaugurated an enquiry into the system of organisation of the Treasury and other departments, and it was conducted with great care by Sir Charles Trevelyan, who had had Indian experience, and Sir Stafford Northcote. The report with comments by experts was presented to Parliament in 1854. The report covered the essential principle that choice of clerks should be carried out, not by patronage but by competitive examination. It was asserted emphatically that the possession of higher capacities in youth was marked by greater success in later life. It was also laid down that there should be a differentiation between the kinds of work to be performed, distinguishing the intellectual from the mechanical and routine, that each work should be done by persons best suited for it, and that there should be distinct examinations for this purpose. The principle was one which appealed to the spirit of the time, and the Civil Service was thus enabled to escape the absurd position which long prevailed and still in some measure prevails in the Dominions, where it is held that all Civil servants should enter by one examination which must be low enough to admit youths of inferior education, while the salaries paid to entrants render the services unattractive to all the University graduates, and the country loses their services. Lastly, the report adopted the view that the test for entry should not be one based on the work of the departments individually. Rather a broad education

[1] Cf. 128 *Hansard*, 3 s. 754 ff.

of the type given in Oxford and Cambridge was deemed the best foundation for the work of any office. Readiness of comprehension, the gift of dealing with people, readiness to take the initiative and to assume responsibility, are indeed qualities which in practice emerge easily from the education which is given in the Universities, and, while in the earlier period regard was had too exclusively to Greek, Latin, and the studies based thereon, the admission of scientific studies as entitled to equal honour has promoted a more even division of posts. The general principle, however, has been held by later expert opinion to be fully justified, and to require modification but not abandonment. The recommendation involved the proposal to create a single independent authority to examine candidates and the requirement of a period of probation from those appointed.

The report was received with disapproval by all who stood to lose by the abolition of patronage, but Mr. Gladstone accepted it, as he held that the upper classes would, from their superior educational and other qualities, be assured of securing the higher administrative posts. The Queen was sceptical.[1] The Civil Service Commission created in 1855 was given power to examine persons proposed to be appointed and, if satisfied of their suitability for the posts for which they were proposed, it could give a certificate, whereupon the minister could appoint, subject to six months' probation. But persons of mature age with special qualifications were exempted from the necessity of a certificate. In 1859 the position of the Commission was much strengthened by the enactment that a pension for work as a Civil servant could normally only be obtained by one who had entered the service with a certificate. An Order in Council of June 4, 1870, com-

[1] *Letters*, 1 s. iii. 9, 11.

pleted the position. It made competition the all but invariable rule throughout the service, but allowed the Commission, if it thought fit, to dispense with such an examination ; it exempted certain offices, where direct appointment by the Crown applied, from certification ; it enabled a department which desired to dispense with certification after examination for a special post to secure certification if the Treasury and Commission agreed. The Treasury was now given formal powers to approve the rules made by the Commission and departments for testing candidates, the periods at which examinations should be held, the number of vacancies, and so forth. The new régime eliminated the old authority of the head of a department to dispense with a certificate at his discretion, and ended the system of competition from a limited number of nominees which had been enjoined in 1860 and which, as worked, had often proved a farce. It was, however, made clear that promotion of officers once in the service was not affected, remaining in the hands of the heads of the departments, and that menial and temporary posts were not included in the requirement of examination.

The system thus established was often submitted to further investigation, as by the Playfair Commission of 1875, the Ridley Commission of 1886–90, the Macdonnell Commission of 1912–14,[1] the Gladstone Committee of 1918, and the Royal Commission of 1929.[2] The question of greatest difficulty which has emerged is naturally that of classification. The simple division between intellectual and routine work made by the report of 1854 is not one which can be carried out simply, and the young persons recruited by the lower form of examination naturally proved to include many who were intellectually capable

---

[1] *Parl. Pap.* Cd. 7338 (1914). [2] *Ibid.* Cmd. 3909.

of much more than the work for which they were nominally recruited. Moreover, the growth of social services of all kinds added enormously to the complexity of the kinds of work to be done. In an office such as was the Colonial Office there might be no great difficulty in dividing the work between the First and the Second Divisions, though there would remain the question whether it was wholly desirable that the First Division should remain closed to the members of the other division, but in the newer ministries such as those of Health or Pensions this simple distinction could not work. Hence there developed a complex series of divisions which varied and still vary. In 1920, following on the report of the National Whitley Council on the Organisation of the Civil Service, an attempt was made to reduce comparative chaos to some sort of order, and thence emerged, apart from the industrial workers, manipulative staff, messengers, etc., a system of general classes, divided into administrative, executive, clerical, women clerical (formerly writing) assistants, and shorthand typists, together with departmental classes of executive, clerical, unestablished clerical, and unestablished typing, a position justified no doubt in a certain degree but lacking all simplicity. To these must be added inspectorates,[1] professional, scientific and technical staffs,[2] subordinate supervisory and technical staffs, and the assessors, collectors, and clerks to commissioners of taxes.

2. *The Administrative Class*

Of these classes the most important constitutionally is the administrative, which includes only some 1200 posts. This class is concerned with the formation of policy so as to ensure continuity and due consideration of all aspects

---

[1] About 2500 strong.   [2] About 7000 strong.

of difficult questions. Vacillation, uncertainty, and incon-
sistency are assuredly marks of bad administration. There
is need not merely to apply to particular cases the principles already laid down by Parliament or under the prerogative, but to study proposals for the alteration of the
existing law in the light of emergent circumstances. There
is variation between departments ; the Board of Education and the Ministry of Health are called upon to maintain
good relations with the local authorities, a matter which
does not concern the Customs or Excise or the Admiralty.
In some departments, again, the work involves the weighing
of rival technical opinions and the taking of decisions on
such issues. The qualifications of men able to undertake
such tasks must be high, and this is the cause and justification of recruitment by an examination which is based in
each subject on the best honours standards of the British
Universities. The Foreign Office and Diplomatic Service
still in some measure stand apart ; up to 1919 entry was
denied to all those who had not a private income of £400
a year and could not afford to work abroad for a couple
of years as Diplomatic attachés without pay. This rule
was then abrogated, but entrance is still restricted by the
necessity of approval by a Board of Selection ; those admitted to consideration must pass a competitive examination in which special importance attaches to a knowledge
of French, German, and another foreign language. There
is no doubt that, prior to the change, the qualifications of
the services fell definitely below those of the rest of the
administrative staffs. This is attested by the melancholy account of their abilities given to the Queen by Lord Salisbury
in 1886, when explaining the ineffective character of British diplomacy, and the same general belief in the modified
capacity of the services is shown by Lord Esher in 1920.[1]

---

[1] *Journals*, iv. 258.

The problem of the type of examination best suited to secure suitable men has been long investigated with no very clear results. One innovation is the *viva voce* interview which is awarded the very high figure of 300 marks. It is alleged that the interview is too much directed towards bringing out social rather than other qualities, and it is at least plain that the number of marks allocated to this very dubious test is excessive. Improvement in it seems essential if dangerous results are not to be feared.[1]

The most recent criticisms [2] of the administrative class recognise its high qualities, but stress two defects. It is said that the traditional attitude of the departments is not to stir up issues unless it is absolutely necessary, and that accordingly initiative is stifled. It is stressed also that the class is derived so exclusively from a particular type that it fails to appreciate issues outside the experience of its social *milieu*. Thus, for instance, penal reform has seldom been suggested by those dealing with it ; reforms therein have been suggested from outside. This verdict may be questioned to some extent, for Sir S. Hoare's far-reaching schemes of alteration of the criminal law and treatment of prisoners appear to suggest official inspiration, even if due allowance is accorded for the personal interest and initiative of the minister. The slow history of army reform is also adduced, and more convincingly the failure to alter the many anomalies of workers' compensation. The delay of a decade in revision of the cost of living index by the Ministry of Labour is a reasonable example of the unwillingness of the official mind to move from the established routine. Possibly too the objections of the Treasury to a vast scheme of public works intended to grapple with the difficulties of depressed areas and so on may be the outcome of the

[1] Finer, *Modern Govt.* ii. 1311-14.
[2] H. J. Laski, *Parl. Govt.* pp. 325 ff.

inhibitions of the official mind. It may be admitted that members of the administrative class are not from personal contacts deeply aware of the hardship involved to bright lads in the reduction of scholarships or the inequalities of the unemployment allowances or the peculiar dangers of the occupation of miners.

It is not, however, certain how much that is undesirable is to be traced to such causes, and still less is it easy to see how the position can be seriously remedied. The most promising idea is the introduction of persons of ability with a different social experience as a means of influencing thought, but no device can well be imagined which will do much in this regard. Another suggestion involves the bringing of departments into more effective touch with the people. Unemployment assistance was too closely in the hands of officials without contact with the trade unions or the unemployed. Each department might have advisory committees attached to it which would help the department to understand the people and people to appreciate the difficulties and problems of the department. It must, however, be remembered that the Civil Service cannot be expected to do more than represent the prevailing attitude of the public, and that for it to go before the bent of public opinion might do more harm than good. There have been administrators who have earned the reputation of desiring to urge on their ministers to move at a pace which is out of touch with public feeling, and who therefore are dangerous to a ministry.

In some cases, no doubt, there is sound reason for complaint of class consciousness still injurious to the best use of talent in the public service.[1] There is no excuse to be found for the long-continued attitude of the Treasury to the Foreign service; thus the suggestion of the Ridley

[1] Harold Nicolson, in *The British Civil Servant*, pp. 47-64.

Commission of 1890 that the income qualification should
be abolished was defeated more by the Treasury than the
Foreign Office itself. Even now the existence of a selection Board acts as a deterrent to entrants, even if the
Board actually is not unduly influenced by the obvious
social status or attainments of the would-be candidates.
Some allowance in the past was no doubt necessary for
the social demands of the Courts of Vienna, Petersburg,
Berlin, Rome, and even Paris, and there is still in foreign
capitals a certain advantage in Britain being represented
by members of the aristocracy or others with the prestige
of Eton. Still, it is clear that further democratisation of
the service is desirable if it is to command full public
favour, and the obvious solution of the problem is presented by the fusion of the Diplomatic and Consular services, which would increase the capacity and value of both.
Moreover, the position would be further improved if there
were devised for the instruction and testing of members
of the new service a staff college analogous to that at
Camberley. Those who were admitted to its courses in
finance and economics would be tested and pass out with a
distinction analogous to that enjoyed by graduates from
the staff college, and there would be afforded a possibility
of the promotion of men, not by accident or by personal
friendship or by reason that they can be trusted not to
do anything very active or likely to cause trouble, but
because they have shown skill and intelligence in dealing
with the type of problem which has become of ever-
increasing importance to the interests of the Commonwealth.

3. *Other Classes*

For the non-administrative classes of the service there
are examinations of differing kinds. The executive class

with similar officers, such as assistant inspectors of Inland Revenue, number about 16,000 and are recruited at age 18–19 on what is a Higher School standard ; the clerical classes, say 60,000 strong, represent the standard of the School Leaving Certificate, and are recruited between age 16–17 ; below these standards there are examinations in part competitive, in part merely test, for the definitely lower branches of the service, which include women clerical assistants, typists, counter clerks, sorters, telegraphists, postmen, telephonists, messengers, warehousemen, cleaners, and so on.[1]

There are various avenues of promotion, though entry thus into the administrative class is not easy. The executive class have a number of well-paid posts available ; clerical class employees may aspire to the executive class or that of higher clerical officer. In the other or manipulative classes there are opportunities to reach the clerical classes by special examinations confined to such candidates. There are also in the classes themselves supervisory posts which are normally reached by seniority. The question of promotion, which caused much difficulty, was eventually simplified by an investigation by a committee of the National Whitley Council which led to the institution of annual reports [2] in a prescribed form by officers holding supervisory positions on those under them. The classes established are A, denoting above average fitness for promotion ; B, denoting average fitness ; and C, below average. The work of promotion is given to promotion Boards made up of senior officers who naturally rely largely on these reports. The essential difficulty lies in equating the work of different supervisors, for they naturally differ greatly

---

[1] The numbers in these classes vary ; excluding industrial staffs on April 1, 1938, all Government staffs numbered 376,491 (women, 101,406) : Cmd. 5815.

[2] Finer, *Modern Govt.* ii. 1346 ff.

in their judgments of what makes for suitability for
promotion, and the system has not produced wide satisfaction. The point, no doubt, in which it most clearly
fails is that it does not conduce to the special promotion
of those young officers who have had to enter the lower
branches of the service through inability to remain at
school long enough to advance to University standards.
They may, by study later and by taking degrees or producing research work of real merit, show to outsiders that
they possess capacities beyond those normal in the grade
in which they work, but they seldom seem to secure any
advantage in their service from qualifications which should
be more effectively recognised. The difficulty here is that
there is always much jealousy among fellow-workers at
the special promotion of another worker, and that the
jealousy will certainly not be lessened if the promotion
seems to be made because of work done outside the normal
departmental routine. As against the gain to the State
of advancing a young officer of promise must be set the
loss due to the creation of discontent among many members
of the service. It must be accepted as inevitable that in
the Civil Service, as outside it, much ability does not
receive what would be a due reward.

A problem of considerable difficulty is caused by the
position of technical officers in relation to the administrative branch. The objection to the existing system,
which has often been pressed, is that there is insufficient
scope for the technical officers to put their views with
personal force before the minister. Much difference no
doubt exists between departments in the degree of attention paid to expert advice, and at times expert officers
have succeeded largely in having their policy taken up
by the administrative staff. On the other hand, when the
Bridgeman Committee investigated the conditions of the

Post Office, it was impressed by the fact that the engineer-
in-chief received only £1650 a year as compared with the
£3000 of the Secretary, and it was also satisfied that the
system by which the administrative staff determined
issues on technical advice without the actual participation
of the experts was defective. The result was the creation
of a functional Board for the Post Office including the
Postmaster-General and his assistant, the Director-General
who replaces the Secretary, his deputy, the Comptroller and
Accountant-General, the Engineer-in-Chief, the Directors
of Establishment and Personnel, of Telegraphs and Tele-
phones, and of Postal Services, and the Public Relations
Officer. The position of the Director-General is now that
of *primus inter pares* charged with ensuring continuity and
the smooth working of the general system of administration. The new scheme obviously prevents the complaint
that technical advice is overruled without due cause, and
like arrangements may be desirable in other departments
of State. Already, it must be added, very wide use of
skilled advice in technical matters is made in such departments as the Colonial Office, where control of local administration involves the use of the best technical advice.

4. *The Employment of Women*

The employment of women in the Civil Service has
long raised problems which are not yet solved in their
entirety. The admission of women was consequent on the
taking over of operatives of the Telephone Company in
1870 ; there followed their employment tentatively in the
Post Office, in various branches, while the Board of Education began to employ a certain number. Certain posts as
inspectors of schools and factories were created, and the
Labour Exchanges and National Health Insurance schemes

in 1909 and 1910 presented opportunities for further employment, in clerical posts and in inspectorates, the candidates being selected by nomination and interview. But in 1914 there were only about 3000 in the Post Office, 300 in other departments, and 600 typists, and beyond promotion to the rank of supervisors no further advancement seemed possible. The war brought enormous opportunities for women to work, to replace men who were needed for war purposes, to staff the many new offices, munitions, food, national service, war savings, and so forth. Some 200,000 women thus found work, and their enfranchisement in 1918 was accompanied by the Sex Disqualification (Removal) Act, 1919, which opened to them nearly every branch of the Civil Service. The Reorganisation Committee of that year ascribed to women large blocks of routine and repetitive work, for which women are known to be well adapted, but it contemplated that admission to the administrative class and the executive class should be by special entry, and little was done to accord such entry. Parliament, however, was moved to intervene, and in 1925 the ordinary administrative examination was opened to females. There followed a prolonged struggle by women's organisations to compel the placing of women on the same footing as men in the service in lieu of the policy favoured in the Post Office and the Ministry of Pensions of separating the male and female staffs and presenting separate vacancies for each. In 1929 the issue was referred to a Royal Commission with other questions, and the report of 1931 approved the principle of complete equality of opportunity.

There remain certain matters which are regarded as grievances by women. The Diplomatic and Foreign services were left closed to women and, while the Colonial Office and Dominions Office were opened experimentally

at the end of 1938, the Foreign Office and Diplomatic
service remain closed. There are strong arguments against
opening in either case. Matters being as they are, women
are no doubt less well suited for the purpose of acquiring
essential information in foreign capitals, for they cannot
enter into social relations on a footing of equality with
foreign diplomats. But it is a more important objection
that foreign countries do not desire to receive women
diplomats, and to offer them would result in hesitation or
refusal to receive. There is further the issue of equal pay
for equal work, which the House of Commons has affirmed
in 1936, but which the ministry has not thought fit to make
effective. The reasons for differentiation are really obvious.
They rest on the assumption, which is normally correct,
that a man has dependants to keep to a greater extent than
a woman, and that as a matter of social welfare it is in the
interest of the country that a man should work and marry
and that his wife should be able to make a home and rear
children. The dangers of a falling population are now
recognised in many circles, and the absorption of large
numbers of women in Civil Service avocations need not be
encouraged by giving them rates of pay which would attract
men. Women point out that they are supported in their
demand for equal pay by men in the service, but the patent
reason therefor is not that the men wish the women to have
equal pay, but that they know equality of pay will secure
for them preference in regard to those types of work where
there is competition between women and men. In those
kinds of work especially suited for women, such as typing
and shorthand and routine manipulative processes, there
is clearly no need to increase pay for women, as there is
already a full supply of applicants, most of whom enter
the service with the natural intention of leaving it as soon
as a suitable chance of marriage offers itself.

A third issue of interest is the demand that women should be allowed to remain in their posts after marriage. The chief objection to this proposal lies in the fact that, in view of the difficulty of finding posts for many women who are compelled to work for their living, it is unfair that a woman should continue in work after she has obtained the advantages and security of marriage. The right of the Treasury to allow retention of office after marriage covers all that is essential ; the wishes of postal officials has been expressed on occasion by a clear majority in favour of the present system by which retirement on marriage with a gratuity is requisite. Insufficient consideration is given by the mostly unmarried advocates of retention of women on marriage that it is not in the public interest that Civil servants should be burdened with extraneous obligations to the extent that a woman who has a home to look after is burdened.

5. *Political Rights*

The political rights of Civil servants is a topic which raises serious difficulties. The former rule which debarred Civil servants from voting was necessary and salutary, but its abrogation became proper when the diffusion of the franchise diminished the risk of undue pressure on the State. The question, however, has appeared in a somewhat different light with the very great extension of the service in recent years and the political activities of dockyard workers, employees in munition works, postmen, and so on. The danger from this source is so far not generally deemed worthy of action. The position might, however, be radically altered if the introduction of State socialism added largely to the numbers of workers in State service. Even as it is, there is little doubt that the service voters are numerous enough to influence members of the Commons to bring pressure to bear on the ministry for ever-increasing concessions to the services. As regards activities of a definitely political character, the traditions of the Civil Service require that it should be free in the eyes of the public from any suspicion of being actuated by motives of partisan politics. The Civil servant, it is felt, should not be permitted by political action to inflict damage on the public service in its authority, dignity, and reputation for impartial performance of duty. Employees, therefore, under the Order in Council of 1910, were required to take no overt part in public political affairs. The departmental rules vary, but it is clearly improper for any public servant to become the secretary of a political society or club, and uniformed servants in the Post Office are forbidden to canvass or take part in other political activities while in uniform. Moreover, it is improper for a Civil servant to serve on a committee whose purpose is the return of a particular candidate to the Commons, or to prefer such a result.

The necessity of political impartiality has been accentuated by the development of the taking of important decisions affecting the public by executive departments exercising in effect legislative powers under delegation and authorised to decide issues thence arising. It is clear that it would be most unfortunate if it were felt that those exercising this wide authority were acting under the influence of some political theory, and so confidence in their impartiality was lost. It is thus obvious that the maintenance of the rule that standing for Parliament involves retirement from the public service [1] is in the best interests of the country, and that relaxation is possible only in the

Chapter XX.

---

[1] Order in Council, Nov. 29, 1884 ; for relaxation for industrial staffs of defence departments, Order, July 25, 1927. General rule of avoidance of political activity, Treasury Minute, Feb. 27, 1928.

case of industrial workers in certain instances, such as those in the dockyards, though even this concession is not altogether easy to approve, as a matter of logic and principle. It is also clear that it would be against the interest of the State that Civil servants who retire to take up candidatures should be entitled to reinstatement if defeated ; still more objectionable would be acceptance of the suggestion that a man who has served in the Commons and been defeated should be allowed to revert to his former post. Anything of this kind would result in the conviction that the Civil service was being brought into politics.

In the case of service on municipal bodies the position differs, because such bodies are often not really marked by divisions on national political lines. But those departments which, like the Ministry of Health, are in close relations with municipal authorities are well advised in forbidding their servants to take upon themselves the responsibilities of membership. It is not merely that the work of a member of many local bodies would make a serious demand on the time of the officer and interfere with his normal hours of employment, but that his impartiality might be affected by the interest he had in municipal developments.

6. *Legal Status*

The relations between the Crown and its servants have been made clear by a number of judicial decisions which have negatived the idea that a Civil servant, unless expressly provided by statute, holds on any tenure save of the pleasure of the Crown.[1] It is therefore possible for a

---

[1] *Dunn* v. *The Queen*, [1896] 1 Q.B. 116 ; *Shenton* v. *Stuart*, [1895] A.C. 229 ; *Kynaston* v. *Att.-Gen.* (1933), 49 T.L.R. 300. Salaries cannot be assigned or taken in execution : *Flarty* v. *Odlum* (1790), 3 T.R. 681 ; *Apthorpe* v.

Civil servant to be dismissed at any time without cause assigned or notice, and the exercise of the discretion of the Crown would not be questioned in any court. Nor has the Civil servant any right of action against the Crown for alleged breach of contract or for pay or pension, for a pension is made a matter of discretion on the part of the Treasury.[1] In practice the power of dismissal rests with the head of the department, and by a tradition of prolonged standing dismissal, after the period of probation has been served, is a penalty inflicted only for gross misconduct or for absolute incompetence. Lesser defects are met, if at all, by inducing earlier retirement than normal or transfer to other work ; the power without any harshness, to require resignation on pension at sixty, aids in maintaining a certain flow of promotion and securing the removal of officials of second-rate talents. But it is not open to dispute that there is normally a security of tenure which has no parallel in business life in any branch.

7. *Pay and Conditions of Service*

Questions of pay and conditions of service were for many years left to individual negotiation with the departments and the Treasury, or were dealt with by associations of Civil servants which sprang up gradually, especially in the Post Office. The situation took on a new aspect after the Great War, when the increase of the numbers of the

Apthorpe (1887), 12 P.D. 192 ; *Mulvenna* v. *Admiralty*, [1926] S.C. 842, unless the office is a sinecure : *Grenfell* v. *Windsor* (*Dean*) (1840), 2 Beav. 544. But if a bankrupt is allowed to remain in office, the head of his department may allow a part of his salary to go to the trustee : *Ward, In re*, [1897] 1 Q.B. 266. So as regards a pension : *Lupton, In re*, [1912] 1 K.B. 107 ; Bankruptcy Act, 1914, s. 51 ; *Garrett, In re*, [1930] 2 Ch. 137 ; Police Pensions Act, 1921.

[1] *Nixon* v. *Att.-Gen.*, [1931] A.C. 184. A pension may be assigned or taken in execution : *Huggins, In re* (1882), 21 Ch.D. 85 ; *Willcock* v. *Terrell* (1878), 3 Ex.D. 323 ; *Lucas* v. *Harris* (1886), 18 Q.B.D. 127.

service and the growth of trade unionism outside it produced an energetic demand that the Government should
adopt, in its relations with its servants, the principles
which it advocated in the case of other employers. In 1917
the Whitley Report on relations between employers and
employed was regarded by Civil servants as presenting an
ideal to be aimed at, and after the war a National Provisional Joint Committee of thirty members, representing
equally the official and staff views, reported on the constitution, objects, and functions of a National Council and
Departmental Councils for the Civil Service. The Government approved and both kinds of Council were created.
The National Council consists of 54 members equally
divided. The official side includes high officials of the
departments ; the staff side is selected by Civil Service
groups or associations specified in the constitution of the
Council ; the experiment of employing as members of the
official side members of Parliament was tried but not
found satisfactory. It is in fact plain that such members
would tend to become the object of undesirable pressure
to induce them to give their support to the views of
the staff side, whose representatives are usually whole-
time officers of associations or serving Civil servants of
ability.

The National Council deals with general issues, while
the Departmental Councils, which are varied in constitution to accord with the special conditions of the different
branches of the service, are concerned with special problems and are expected to refer to the National Council,
which is not a court of appeal from the Departmental
Councils, issues of general character. The sphere of operation of the Councils is wide. They may consider issues of
the general provisions regarding recruitment, hours, tenure,
and remuneration ; encouragement of the further educa-

tion of Civil servants and their training in higher administration and organisation ; the improvement of official
machinery and the provision of opportunities for the full
consideration of suggestions on these heads by members
of the staff; and proposed legislation in its bearing on
the position of Civil servants in relation to their employment.   The National Council may deal with promotion and
remuneration of Civil servants on salaries up to £700,
the Departmental Councils with those up to £500.   The
activities of the National Council resulted in the regrading
and reorganisation of the Civil Service, and codification of
the superannuation regulations, and provision for a diploma
of Public Administration in the University of London.   The
National Council, however, has been criticised as too large,
and it is said that its procedure is ineffective.   But the
Departmental Councils have won greater praise ; they can
discuss allegations that the principles of promotion have
been violated, and the staff side can bring up cases of
disciplinary action.   No doubt the system in these cases
is a safeguard against any too flagrant favouritism, though
no doubt it helps to block the way to the accelerated promotion of the abler men, lest discontent may be caused.
It is claimed also that small but valuable improvements
on the conduct of business in the Admiralty, Post Office,
and Customs and Excise departments have been achieved
by suggestions from these councils.   The recommendations
of the Councils are not absolutely binding on the Government or the heads of departments.   It is clear that to give
them full force would be to interfere with the responsibility
of ministers and of the Treasury in particular to Parliament, and therefore it is recognised that they have advisory force only.   But the normal practice is to give them
effect.

For remuneration and conditions of work therewith

connected a Civil Service Conciliation and Arbitration
Board was set up in 1917. Its operations were intermitted from 1922 to 1925, but it was then revived in the
form of the Industrial Court constituted by the President
of that court aided by a representative of either side ; [1]
its authority extends to claims by classes of employees on
scales up to £700 a year, but by consent it may deal with
other classes.[2] By its awards very large concessions have
been made to Civil servants both as regards remuneration
and otherwise. The advantages of a simple and regular
system of dealing with claims are obvious ; the one
danger is that too great a burden may be placed on the
public revenue. There is probably some tendency on the
part of the court to make too little allowance for the great
benefits which accrue to Civil servants in the way of
security and permanence of tenure of office, sick leave
with pay, and superannuation. The complaints that the
Civil Service is underpaid are shown to have little foundation in view of the very large number of applicants for
any vacancies, whether in the higher or lower ranks.
The complete uncertainty of other forms of employment
negatives, in the view of most Civil servants, the advantages which may be gained by men of special ability
therein.

The position of Civil servants demands from them a
high standard of personal integrity in regard to the
carrying out of their duties, and exceptions on the whole
are very rare. Among higher officials for many years
the only serious cases have been those of Mr. Gregory
and Sir C. Bullock, in both of which error of judgment

[1] The panels whence members are taken are provided by the Minister
of Labour representing the Chancellor of the Exchequer and the staff
side.

[2] Rules of Procedure of the Industrial Court for Civil Service Arbitrations,
Nov. 28, 1928.

alone was in question, and their removal from the service with the authority of the Prime Minister [1] shows how high is the standard of personal integrity demanded. In the lower ranks occasional instances of misuse of authority in respect of aliens who desire to remain in Britain or to be naturalised are alone recorded beside efforts to use knowledge of revenue procedure to defraud the income tax authorities. Civil servants are criminally liable for oppression [2] or breach of trust,[3] fraud or imposition, or in certain cases neglect [4] in respect of their legal duties. The Official Secrets Acts, 1911 and 1920,[5] the Prevention of Corruption Acts, 1906 and 1916,[6] and the Honours (Prevention of Abuses) Act, 1925, apply to them, while postal officials are subject to special liabilities in respect of disclosure of telegrams, etc.[7] They are personally liable in tort for any illegal action, though they will be indemnified by the State if their action was taken under official sanction, and in good faith. They have, however, the protection of the Public Authorities Protection Act, 1893, and they are not liable for statements otherwise libellous in reports to superiors.[8]

As loyalty to the State is essential, the failure in duty on the part of some members of the Civil Service in the General Strike of 1926 necessitated action to enforce this

---

[1] H. J. Laski, *Parl. Govt.* pp. 435, 438.

[2] *R.* v. *Williams* (1762), 3 Burr. 1317. For good faith as a defence, *R.* v. *Young* (1758), 1 Burr. 557.

[3] *R.* v. *Baxter* (1851), 5 Cox C.C. 302.

[4] Cf. *R.* v. *Pinney* (1832), 3 St. Tr. (N.S.), 11, 510 ; *R.* v. *Eyre* (1868), Finlason, Rep. 55, 58. For stealing property, see 6 & 7 Geo. V. c. 50, s. 17 (2) ; 15 & 16 Geo. V. c. 86, s. 24, Sch. II. ; for extortion, *Lee* v. *Dangar, Grant & Co.*, [1892] 2 Q.B. 337.

[5] *R.* v. *Simington*, [1921] 1 K.B. 451 ; *R.* v. *Crisp and Homewood* (1919), 83 J.P. 121.

[6] *R.* v. *Evans* (1923), 17 Cr. App. R. 121

[7] Post Office Act, 1908, ss. 55-8, 69, 89 ; Telegraph Act, 1868, s. 20.

[8] *M. Isaacs & Sons, Ltd.* v. *Cook*, [1925] 2 K.B. 391.

obligation. The Trade Disputes and Trade Unions Act, 1927,[1] therefore made provision that a Civil servant may not be a member or representative of organisations whose primary object is to increase the remuneration of Civil servants unless their membership is confined to persons employed by the Crown and they are not affiliated to organisations of different composition, nor have political objects nor are affiliated to a political party. Despite the objections of the Labour party to this enactment, it does not seem possible to take any exception to it, or to assert that it can be justifiable for Civil servants to be liable to be called out on strike. Their obligations to the State place them in a position quite different from that of ordinary workers, and those who claim the right to strike are clearly bound to withdraw from an employment in which that right cannot properly be exercised.

8. *Criticisms of the Service*

Criticisms of the Civil Service are inevitable and numerous. It suffers clearly from certain inevitable tendencies. It offers to men a career of safety which many, through obligations demanding such safety, have to place above adventure, and men once appointed find it increasingly difficult to make up their minds to risk change, even when they discover that they have no real chance of exerting their full capacity under official conditions of work. Hence a very large proportion of Civil servants tend to fall into a routine which enables them to turn their talents to other interests. The high proportion of upper-grade Civil servants who show literary or artistic ability is a sign that for them the activities of their offices are not adequate expressions of their capacities. In the

[1] S. 5; Civil Service (Approved Associations) Regulations, 1927.

lower grade the tendency to develop into mere machines, performing regular and uninteresting tasks with accuracy but without enthusiasm, is inevitable. There is, as in all business, much work to be done which requires no intellectual effort, and which brings out no valuable characteristics. Though there is a certain efflux of men from the Civil Service, few attain high position in business or finance, and this is probably due not so much to devotion to the State as to the fact that the qualities developed in Civil servants are not those of active initiation and readiness to take risks and to rely on one's individual judgment, which do much to assure success in business life. There are, on the other hand, a substantial number of Civil servants in the higher grades who are devoted to their work because it is for the State, and who are ready to sacrifice excellent opportunities elsewhere in their anxiety to do good work for their country. But it must be admitted that these men often find in the organisation of the departments grave obstacles to making effective their ideals, and that they tend to become discouraged and at length to resign themselves to the inevitable. Instances of successful Civil servants who impressed their personality on their departments and secured the carrying out of policies in which they were enthusiasts are few and far between, and, as in the case of Sir R. Morant, there were special circumstances which aided their success.

The tendency of officials is to develop routine and to cultivate rigidity of procedure. The excuse and in part justification of this attitude is the necessity of answering complaints by the public ; there must be a due record kept to show why action in any case was taken, and precautions must be adopted to secure that all similar cases are dealt with on the same basis, so that the minister may not have to admit errors for which he must take responsibility in his department. But there can be little doubt that the tendency to routine is apt to be encouraged and red-tape methods develop and are persisted in long after they should have been obsolete. There is the standing example of the Foreign Office, in which clerical work of no value whatever as a training in diplomacy was enforced on the junior members of the staff until Sir E. Crowe [1] insisted on breaking away from tradition and examining the methods by which, in the Colonial and other offices, the junior members of the staff were trained to form and express opinions on official papers from the very first.

There is no doubt in certain cases a tendency to assume a measure of assertion of authority in dealings with the public. This is most noteworthy in certain lower spheres of authority, in the ranks of the police, of tax officials, of licensers of automobiles or testers of capacity to drive them, of Post Office officials in the smaller offices, of agricultural research authorities, and so forth ; there is a tendency to show in their attitude to the public a measure of arrogance which is resented. But the extent of this authoritarianism is kept in check by the existence of a healthy and energetic public opinion and the existence of Parliament. Nor, with rare exceptions, is it found in the higher grades, so far as the public is concerned.

There is always the danger of departmentalism among Civil servants. Each great department has valuable traditions, and most of them regard themselves as specially well fitted to perform any function assigned to them and are reluctant to transfer any part of their work to other hands. There have been struggles to decide to what department should appertain the care of affairs of the Middle East ; the issue of unemployment assistance has aspects interesting the ministries of Health and Labour alike ; the education

[1] Tilley and Gaselee, *The Foreign Office*, pp. 124 f., 135.

of peccant children concerns the Home Office and the Board of Education ; a long and bitter struggle was waged as to the control of the aircraft needed by the fleet ; the Foreign and Colonial offices often differed in view between the need of considering foreign relations and of conciliating colonial interests in the period before the rise to full statute of the Dominions. To the Colonial Secretary used to fall the task of explaining why Britain could not, on account of foreign policy considerations of paramount weight, accord to Canadian fishermen the full measure of support desired by the Dominion, and of convincing Australia that there could be no question of proclaiming the New Hebrides a British possession in disregard of French rights therein. The feuds of the Treasury with the spending departments were no doubt due in principle to the desire of the Treasury to save the public revenues from rash spending. But no one can seriously doubt that the Treasury developed a technique of opposition to all suggestions of increased expenditure which became a departmental habit and precluded the calm consideration of proposals, so that any suggestion had to be weighed seriously by departmental chiefs with a view to decide whether it was worth while trying to secure the assent of the Treasury, in the assurance that it would in the long run be requisite for success to induce the minister himself to take up the issue with the Chancellor of the Exchequer or the Prime Minister himself.

The qualities of integrity and regularity of process which mark the service are nevertheless widely felt not to be sufficient to secure the best ends of the country, and this has led to the development of the form of control of issues of public importance by bodies which are expected to preserve what is best in the public service system while giving greater scope to individuality and initiative.

9. *The Semi-Public Services*

Bodies of this kind are the Central Electricity Commission, the Electricity Commissioners, the London Passenger Transport Board, the Port of London Authority, and the British Broadcasting Corporation.[1]

The Central Electricity Board was created under the Electricity (Supply) Act, 1926, for the purpose of forming the National Grid system and supplying electricity in bulk to retailers of that commodity. The staff of some 1300 is mainly technical, but recruitment by competition has not been adopted. There seems no sufficient ground for this failure. It must be remembered that competition has the advantage of offering a fair chance to all members of the public, and these bodies are all supported by public authority ; they are under no risks of loss and have not the right which appertains to employers who risk their fortunes to choose their own employees at will. Competition also automatically sets a high standard of efficiency, prevents mere favouritism, and the due form of competition to test ability of technicians is a problem solved by the Civil Service Commission. The Board dispenses also with formal classifications of staff, has a contributory pension system, offers encouragement to junior members to suggest improvements, and claims to have developed a fortunate *esprit de corps*. The rates of salaries it pays are not published, and are largely fixed on consideration of individual merits ; the chairman receives £7000 a year, which is double the pay of the Secretary to the Treasury.

The Electricity Commissioners exercise the functions of the Ministry of Transport in respect of the control of the Electricity Board and the various electricity supply undertakings throughout the country, whether private

[1] H. Finer in *The British Civil Servant*, pp. 127-64.

companies or local authorities. The matters affected are the constitution, the financing, the area of, and the prices charged by the undertakings. Their main energies seem directed towards the reduction of generating stations within the divisions which they have prescribed and the co-ordination of individual undertakings. There are five commissioners appointed by the minister of Transport, and their staff, which is small, is dealt with practically on Civil Service lines, with regular grades and orderly promotion.

The London Passenger Transport Board is in a position of special importance, because it is charged with the care of transport in a large and most important area. It employs an administrative and clerical staff of some 5000, and 72,000 weekly wage workers. The chairman, vice-chairman, and five other members of the Board are appointed by trustees for various interests under the London Passenger Transport Act, 1933, and the chairman and vice-Chairman have salaries of £12,500 and £10,000 respectively. The staff is not recruited by competitive examination, but there is a contributory pensions scheme and a plan for intensive training of picked employees from age 18 to 28 with the prospect of attaining high rank at an early date. Establishment officers are employed who show interest in the like activities of corresponding officers in the Civil Service, and the favouritism shown by private employers is less marked. The strike among employees at the time of the coronation of 1937 revealed the staff in its worst aspect ; it was a deliberate attempt to hold the public to ransom, and investigation showed that there was no substance in most of the claims put forward, while one and all would have easily been remedied by adoption of the normal procedure provided for such cases. The strike revealed how little sense of public duty exists in employees even of a body which is mainly concerned with the public

interest and is wholly devoid of any desire to earn high
profits for selfish share-owners.

The Port of London Authority, established under the
Port of London Act, 1908, employs some 4500 persons in
posts analogous to the Civil Service ; there is a qualifying
examination conducted by the London Chamber of Com-
merce, and thereafter the grades are filled by promotion.
The authority offers very considerable security of employment, is generous in leave and holidays, does not treat
its staff dictatorially, and gives definite scales of salary
with increments and pensions. It has no difficulty in keeping its employees, who are satisfied with their treatment
and prospects.

The British Broadcasting Corporation has come in for
more investigation and criticism than any other of these
public agencies. The Board [1] is appointed by the Prime
Minister and Postmaster-General for a period up to five
years, and criticisms have been offered of the nominees
on the score that they have been persons without any
specially obvious qualification for work so serious as that
given to the corporation. The Ullswater Committee recommended the increase of the Board to seven, but it is
clear that in any case a very wide measure of authority
must rest with the Director-General. Under Sir John
Reith certain characteristics of a régime otherwise enter-
prising and original excited public criticism. The effort
was made to manage staff questions on principles quite
different from those of the Civil Service, secrecy being
observed on salaries and no effort being made to use competition as the basis of appointment. Moreover, arbitrary
removals of officers were alleged, and there was recorded
a serious error of judgment in the effort of the Director-
General to prevent a libel action being brought by a

[1] *Parl. Pap.* Cmd. 5329. For the annual report, see Cmd. 5668.

member of the staff who persisted in it, and won a resound-
ing victory.[1] The situation has now, largely as the result
of the discussions in Parliament, been remedied by the
establishment of the right of the staff to organise, which
must mean greater security of tenure.

Various criticisms are offered with justice. It is clear
that there is far too little public information regarding the
proceedings of these bodies, and they are exempt from the
financial scrutiny which the Comptroller and Auditor-
General and the Committee of Public Accounts provide in
the case of Government departments. At least regular
enquiries might be made by Royal Commissions whose
evidence might be published. This would certainly minimise the chance of gross favouritism and undesirable
methods of treating the staff. Secondly, there is no doubt
justification for the claim that, as the public pays directly
or indirectly for the work of these bodies, it is entitled to
be assured that the maximum quality is secured in their
employees. The plan of avoiding competition for entry is
unquestionably open to the suspicion that it unduly narrows
the field from which men and women can be drawn, and
thus lowers the standard of efficiency, while actual methods
of recruitment followed are all subject to the risk of intro-
ducing the evils of nepotism. The fact that none of these
authorities except the B.B.C. finds it convenient to make
use of the talents of graduates suggests that they are
missing important possibilities of improving their administrative staff. Mere promotion of the existing staff may
make for its contentment, but the body exists not merely
to content a number of members of the staff but for the
best interests of the public. Thirdly, there is no doubt
that the payment of very high salaries to the chief officials
of these bodies is open to criticism. The payment of such

[1] *Parl. Pap.* Cmd. 5337.

salaries is perfectly proper in commercial business because those who receive them are bound to take risks, but they are out of place when the only risks taken are faced by the public. There is no sound proof that large salaries are necessary in cases such as these where there is immunity from those vicissitudes and dangers which in private affairs may properly be rewarded by high pay.

PART VII

THE JUDICIARY AND ITS FUNCTIONS

CHAPTER XXI

THE JUDICIARY

1. *The Supreme Court of Justice*

IT was not until 1873 that any substantial changes were introduced in the confused system of jurisdictions which had been evolved by historical causes. The three great common law courts were those of Queen's Bench, Common Pleas, and the Exchequer. The King's Bench was the oldest and ranked the highest of the courts of common law ; it bore its name as a relic of the time when the King was thought to be present in person. It could deal with any class of cases between private persons, and there were certain matters which specially appertained to it. It could issue the writ of *mandamus* to magistrates or other persons under statutory or other obligation to perform certain acts ; it could deal with proceedings initiated by the law officers of the Crown in the nature of the ancient writ *quo warranto* investigating the right to the enjoyment of an office or the validity of a charter. Criminal informations came before it and to it were assigned certain matters under the poor law.

The Common Bench was competent to deal with any suit between private persons, and was the proper court for certain proceedings which survived the abolition of the real actions and of the procedure by fines and recoveries, which disappeared just before the accession of Queen Victoria. It had also appellate jurisdiction from the decisions of revising barristers on the claim to the franchise and in questions of law arising out of disputed returns under the Parliamentary Elections Act, 1868.

The Court of Exchequer lost in 1841 its equitable jurisdiction, and thereafter remained, on the one hand, a court of revenue concerned with the rights of the Crown against the subject, and on the other a court of pleas between subjects, save only those which were special to the other common law courts. Distinction between the courts was obsolete in principle, the judges were men of similar education and attainments, but the rigidity of procedure was such that it was impossible to relieve one court when it was overburdened with work by transfer to another.

Over against the common law courts were others with different origin. The Court of Chancery represented the equitable jurisdiction of the Lord Chancellor, which was used to redress the unfairness of the full application of the common law, and which had established itself as against the efforts of Sir E. Coke to destroy it through the favour of James I. The common law courts had adopted some principles of equity, but they had failed to apply them with full effect, and the just administration of the law demanded the maintenance of the Chancery or of some substitute for it.

In 1830 each of the common law courts had a staff of four, the chief justice and three puisne judges in King's Bench and Common Pleas, a chief baron, and three barons in the Exchequer. In that year a fourth judge was added to each court, and in 1868 a fifth. The Lord Chancellor was the original Court of Chancery, but he had been supplemented by an assistant, the Master of the Rolls, whose name reminds us that he was once in charge mainly of the records, and from 1813 a Vice-Chancellor. When

the equity jurisdiction of the Exchequer disappeared in
1841,[1] it was necessary to add two further Vice-Chancellors.

Another court of quite distinct character was that of
Admiralty which can be traced back to the jurisdiction
conferred on the Lord High Admiral, which had been
defined in Acts of Richard II.[2] In 1840[3] it was presided
over by a single judge, but in that year it was provided
that the ecclesiastical judge known as the Dean of Arches
might sit for the judge, and in fact the post was held by
the Dean, who *ex officio* was normally expert in legal
ideas remote from those of the common law.

At the beginning of the Queen's reign, the ecclesiastical
courts discussed elsewhere still dealt with wills of personal
as opposed to real property, the administration of the
estates of persons who died intestate, and matrimonial
causes. In the latter sphere they had power to grant
judicial separation of spouses but not to terminate a
marriage by divorce. When in 1857 the decision to permit
divorce in a complete form was arrived at, thus saving
persons aggrieved the cost and delay of a divorce by
private Act of Parliament, a new Court of Divorce and
Matrimonial Causes was set up to which the whole of the
jurisdiction of the ecclesiastical courts in these matters
was transferred, and at the same time there was created
a Court of Probate : one judge held both these courts.

For Bankruptcy there was a special court to which in
1831 were assigned a chief and three judges ; in 1847 the
chief judge disappeared and the duty of review, given
originally to three of the four judges, was conferred on a
Vice-Chancellor, and in 1851 on the new Lords Justices of
Appeal. From 1847 to 1861 there existed a Court for the
Relief of Insolvent Debtors whose function it was to deal

---

[1] 5 Vict. c. 5.   [2] 13 Rich. II. c. 5 ; 15 Rich. II. c. 3.
[3] 3 & 4 Vict. c. 65 ; for further jurisdiction, see 24 & 25 Vict. c. 10.

with cases of non-traders, but in 1861 this distinction was swept away.

Of these courts the King's Bench alone had criminal jurisdiction, though not in very frequent exercise ; that of the Admiralty, by a series of statutes culminating in 1861, had become exercisable in the ordinary courts by the usual English procedure.

Appeal lay from the courts of common law to the Exchequer Chamber, which was composed of the judges of the courts other than that from which appeal was being brought, and which was constituted in 1830.[1]   In the case of Chancery the only appeal court was the Lord Chancellor himself, and from his decision appeal lay to the House of Lords.   In 1851 [2] two Lords Justices of Appeal were created to sit with or without the Chancellor as an intermediate court of appeal.

From the Admiralty appeal was assigned to the Crown in Council in 1832,[3] superseding the delegates who used to hear ecclesiastical and Admiralty appeals ; in 1833 [4] the Judicial Committee of the Privy Council was given the work.   From the Probate Court appeal lay directly to the House of Lords,[5] and from the Court for Divorce and Matrimonial Causes appeal lay to the full court, which consisted of the Chancellor, the chiefs and senior puisne judges of the common law courts, and the judge of the Probate Court.   Their decision was final, except that, if a dissolution of marriage was decreed, appeal lay to the House of Lords.[6]

The common law courts were centralised at Westminster, and to bring justice, civil and criminal, to those concerned, it was necessary that the judges should go on

[1] 11 Geo. IV. & 1 Will. IV. c. 70, s. 8.
[2] 14 & 15 Vict. c. 83.   [3] 2 & 3 Will. IV. c. 92.
[4] 3 & 4 Will. IV. c. 41.   [5] 20 & 21 Vict. c. 77, s. 39.
[6] 20 & 21 Vict. c. 85, ss. 55, 56.

circuit. They were authorised to do so by commissions of assize, to which *nisi prius* was an incident, of oyer and terminer, and of gaol delivery, the former giving civil, the two latter criminal jurisdiction. The commission of assize was in its origin intended for the trial of real actions under the old procedure, but they were authorised to try other issues, and the juries summoned to Westminster to deal therewith were summoned conditionally, *nisi prius*, unless before the date of summons the justices of assize had come to the county. The difference between the other commissions depended originally on the fact that under oyer and terminer the justices dealt with criminals presented by a grand jury, while authority to deliver the gaols permitted them to dispose of those already in custody. For Middlesex and the London suburbs in Kent, Surrey, and Essex standing criminal commissions were issued for the trial of criminals, and thus was constituted the Central Criminal Court.[1] Prior to the accession of the Queen, a report had been sent to the sovereign of the case of any prisoner sentenced to death at that court, and the Crown in Council took the decision. Of that duty the Queen was relieved by statute.[2]

There was no system of appeal from criminal trials on indictment. If error appeared on the record, which, it must be remembered, contained neither the evidence nor the summing-up by the judge, the matter might be taken by writ of error to King's Bench, and thence to the Exchequer Chamber and the House of Lords. Or, if a conviction were recorded, the presiding judge might at his discretion reserve a point of law for the Court for Crown Cases Reserved, whose decision was final. This court[3] was set up formally in 1848, and consisted of the judges of the common law

---

[1] 4 & 5 Will. IV. c. 36. [2] 7 Will. IV. & 1 Vict. c. 77.
[3] 11 & 12 Vict. c. 78.

courts or any five of them, one being a chief of one of the
courts.   It was a formal recognition of a practice which had
developed, under which a judge consulted some of the other
judges if a matter of difficulty arose.

In the case of misdemeanour the prisoner was less unfairly treated, because since 1673 [1] it had been held that
motion might be made for a new trial on the score that there
had been misreception of evidence, that the judge had
misdirected the jury, or that the verdict was against weight
of the evidence. Otherwise all that could be done was
to apply to the Home Secretary for the exercise of the
prerogative of mercy.

To these jurisdictions must be added those of the
Common Pleas at Lancaster and the Court of Pleas at
Durham.   As a relic of the *jura regalia* once conferred on
the holders of these counties palatine, these courts exercised
a jurisdiction distinct from the courts at Westminster.

Sir R. Palmer in 1867 urged the appointment of a Royal
Commission to secure a reorganisation of the courts which
would improve, simplify, and diminish the cost and delays
of justice. The Commission reported in 1869,[2] and in 1873
Lord Selbourne brought forward and passed his Judicature
Act. This measure created a Supreme Court of Judicature,
divided into a High Court and a Court of Appeal. To the
former were assigned all the jurisdiction of the three courts
of common law, of the Chancery, of the courts of Probate,
Divorce and Matrimonial Causes, and the Admiralty, the
courts held under commissions of assize, oyer and terminer
and gaol delivery, and the Lancaster and Durham courts
of Pleas. To these jurisdictions were added in 1883 that
of the Court of Bankruptcy, and the power of the London
Court of Bankruptcy set up in 1869 was also merged in that

---

[1] Cf. *R.* v. *Duncan* (1881), 7 Q.B.D. 198.
[2] Cf. Lord Cairns (1875), 223 *Hansard*, 5 s. 574.

of the High Court. The High Court at first sat in five Chapter
divisions, but in 1881 the old common law courts were XXI.
consolidated into a single division known as Queen's
Bench.

The reform involved two immediate improvements on
previous practice. Any judge may sit in a court belonging
to any division, Chancery, King's Bench, or Probate,
Divorce, and Admiralty, and any relief which any of the
old courts could have given can be given by the judge
or division, and any ground of claim or defence can be
recognised. Where there were conflicting rules of admiralty, common law, or equity, the one to be followed
was laid down, and, in the absence of precise definition,
equity was to prevail. Those matters in which equitable
doctrines had been especially applied were expressly
assigned to Chancery.

The Court of Appeal was given appellate jurisdiction
from the High Court, and in addition from jurisdictions
outside the High Court, in lunacy, in bankruptcy, in cases
arising in the Chancery courts of Lancaster and Durham,
and until 1896 in the Court of the Vice-Warden of the
Stannaries; in that year the court was abolished and its
powers passed to the county court. In 1934 appeals
generally from county courts [1] were given to the Court
of Appeal, which already had been given appellate jurisdiction in the important class of workmen's compensation
cases.

The creation of a Court of Criminal Appeal [2] was obviously a natural complement to the improvement of appellate jurisdiction, but, though advocated by Sir H. James
and others as early as 1882, it was difficult to secure any
decision in its favour. But the unjust condemnation of
Adolf Beck in 1896 for an offence committed by a certain

---

[1] 24 & 25 Geo. V. c. 53.   [2] 7 Edw. VII. c. 23 ; 8 Edw. VII. c. 46.

Smith was repeated in 1904, but fortunately error was suspected and Smith was arrested and confessed his guilt.[1] It
was made clear that the conviction in 1896 might have
been avoided if the accused had been allowed to show
that he was not identical with Smith, as held by the
police, but the court ruled the evidence out of order.
Further, at that time the accused could not give evidence
in his own defence, for only in 1898 was Lord Halsbury,
for once throwing off conservatism, able to secure for
prisoners the right to give evidence in their own behalf,
while not forcing them to go into the witness box.[2] The
reform was bitterly opposed by many who believed that
unfair counsel would use the opportunity of cross examination to convict criminals out of their own mouths,
but in practice the advantage of the Act to the accused
has been palpable, and Beck might well have been
saved if he had been able to tell his own tale. A Royal
Commission was set up to go into the case, and it was
content to recommend that judges should be compelled to
state a case on request, instead of acting on their own
judgment as in the past ; but Parliament was induced by
the Liberal Government to take a broader view.

Appeal now lies against a conviction on indictment,
criminal information, or coroner's inquisition, on a point
of law ; on a question of fact or mixed law and fact on the
certificate of the trial judge, or with the leave of the court ;
on a point of the sentence, where not fixed by law, with
the leave of the court. In a case of a question of law,
if the Attorney-General certifies that it is in the public
interest that the decision of the court should be further
considered, there is an appeal to the House of Lords. Few
such certificates have been given, and then essentially for
the purpose of determining precisely what degree of proof

[1] *Parl. Pap.* Cd. 2315.   [2] 61 & 62 Vict. c. 36.

is necessary for securing convictions and points of no less Chapter XXI. importance.[1]   The Court of Criminal Appeal is not bound by the views of the Court of Appeal on the issue whether an action civilly legal is criminal ; but in the one case, where a vehement difference of opinion has taken place, namely on the right of an association to threaten to black-list a firm accused of departure from agreed action unless a fine is paid, the view of the House of Lords has been obtained to overrule that of the Court of Criminal Appeal.[2] It may therefore be presumed that normally cases of differ-ence of view will not be left unsolved.

The court is constituted of the Lord Chief Justice and the judges of King's Bench, any three to form a quorum. The prerogative of mercy is unaffected by the Act, but the Home Secretary may refer a case submitted to him to the court, except in the case of a petition against a sentence of death, or obtain the opinion of the court on any point arising out of the petition.

It has been necessary with the growth of business to add to the numbers of members of the High Court from time to time.   In order to facilitate the dealing with com-mercial cases, a special Commercial Court has been set up as part of the King's Bench, and in it under rules of court, procedure is more expeditious and the right of appeal restricted.

As constituted in 1939, the King's Bench was manned by the Lord Chief Justice and 19 puisne judges, the Chancery Division by the Lord Chancellor and 5 judges, the Probate, Divorce and Admiralty Division by a Presi-dent and 4 judges.[3]   Proposals to abolish this division as a distinct division, and to require judges of the King's

---

[1] *Woolmington v. Director of Public Prosecutions*, [1935] A.C. 462 ; *Andrews v. Director of Public Prosecutions*, [1937] A.C. 576.

[2] *R. v. Denyer*, [1926] 2 K.B. 258, corrected by *Thorne v. Motor Trade Assocn.*, [1937] A.C. 797.   [3] 1 & 2 Geo. VI. c. 2.

Bench to undertake its duties, were hotly criticised by the
Bar, and attention was drawn to the inconvenience of not
entrusting the conduct of divorce cases to judges specially
expert, and the objection to interfering with the international status which had been obtained by the Admiralty
Division and which might be seriously affected by the
taking over of its work by King's Bench.

The Court of Appeal consists of the Master of the
Rolls, who since 1881 has been a judge of appeal only,
and 8 [1] Lords Justices of Appeal. It normally sits in
divisions of 3 justices, though for some purposes 2 suffice.
Ex-Lords Chancellors or Lords of Appeal in Ordinary may
since 1891 sit, if invited by the Lord Chancellor, who
may also invite any judge or ex-judge of the High Court
to act.

The commissions for circuits are issued as before 1875,
but a commissioner is deemed to constitute a court of the
High Court and has all the powers of a judge sitting at
Westminster. Power was also given in 1875 to alter the
circuits by Order in Council, and later Acts, now consolidated in the Supreme Court of Judicature (Consolidation)
Act, 1925, allowed new grouping of counties for the purpose
of assizes. Important reforms were made under these
powers, and there are now eight circuits, assizes being
held in winter (January), summer (May), and autumn
(October).

In 1875 [2] authority was also given for making rules of
court. The rule making authority as established under
the Act of 1925 is made up of the Lord Chancellor, Lord
Chief Justice, Master of the Rolls, four judges, two
barristers, and two solicitors appointed by the Lord
Chancellor. Its activities are the basis of the existing code
of rules of the Supreme Court, which, though procedural,

---

[1] 1 & 2 Geo. VI. c. 67.   [2] See now 15 & 16 Geo. V. c. 49, s. 99.

deeply affect the extent of jurisdiction of the Court and the nature of the relief which can be granted.

A council of judges [1] of the Supreme Court is required to meet annually to consider the working of the Judicature Act and of the rules made under it, and defects and proposed amendments in the administration of justice, and to report thereon to the Home Secretary for the consideration of the executive, but this function has not proved to be of much importance. What has been accomplished has been due rather to the promotion of reform by a committee appointed by the Lord Chancellor which has successively dealt with a number of difficult points of law, whence have resulted Acts of very considerable importance. Of these the most valuable to the subject has been that [2] which confers the right to recover, for the benefit of the estate of a dead man, damages which would have been awarded to an injured person who had survived his injury, but which formerly disappeared on death under the operation of the maxim *actio personalis moritur cum persona*.

2. *The House of Lords and the Trial of Peers*

One extraordinary original jurisdiction is left to the House of Lords, which has preserved it by reason presumably of the general dislike of the Conservative party for any diminution of the privileges of the peerage than for any rational ground.

As a remnant of its ancient powers, a peer accused of treason, felony, or misprision of treason or felony, is

[1] 15 & 16 Geo. V. c. 49, s. 210.

[2] Law Reform (Miscellaneous Provisions) Act, 1934 (24 & 25 Geo. V. c. 41) ; *Rose* v. *Ford*, [1937] A.C. 826. See also Law Reform (Married Women and Tortfeasors) Act, 1935 (25 & 26 Geo. V. c. 30) : *Barber* v. *Pigden*, [1937] 1 K.B. 664.

entitled to trial by his peers. If Parliament is not in
session the accused is tried in the Court of the Lord High
Steward, appointed by the Crown to hold the trial; in case
of treason or misprision thereof he must summon all peers
who are entitled to sit and vote. He presides and decides
points of law, though the judges may be summoned to
advise, and the verdict is that of all the peers, who must
be unanimous and number twelve for a conviction.

If Parliament is in session the Lord High Steward
presides, but only as *primus inter pares*, and a majority
decides, all peers being eligible to attend and vote. The
former type of trial last occurred in 1686 when Lord
Delamere was tried for treason. But after long disuse the
latter form was revived in 1901 for the trial of Earl Russell,
who had committed bigamy, his first marriage having been
ineffectively dissolved by a divorce in the United States
which was without value in an English court, as the peer
was never domiciled in the State of the divorce. The
judges were summoned, and the Lords of Appeal took part
in the trial, which resulted in a conviction and a light
sentence.[1] In 1935 the necessity of such a trial arose in
Lord de Clifford's case,[2] where manslaughter was alleged,
though not proved. The expense of the proceeding was
inexcusable, apart from the invidiousness of the different
mode of trials of a peer and a commoner, but a Bill to
terminate the abuse failed to be taken up by the Government with sufficient energy to secure it being carried
through Parliament. It was not explained why in any
case the trial was not arranged when Parliament was
not in session, when the proceedings could have been far
simpler and much public money saved. The maintenance
of a foolish anomaly must be deprecated; an acquittal
of a peer which was deemed unjust might easily have

[1] [1901] A.C 446.   [2] *H.L. Pap.* 12, 1935–6.

serious repercussions on the whole position of the peerage, Chapter
XXI. and peers guilty of crime should have no privilege to save them from just punishment after the verdict of an impartial jury.

3. *The Courts of Final Appeal*

(i) The House of Lords

The House of Lords as the final court of appeal for almost all causes from the courts of England, Scotland, and Ireland was, at the beginning of the Victorian era, not a body of very imposing character, owing to the paucity of peers with sufficient judicial experience to render them well qualified to act as final interpreters of the law. On the other hand it was already the practice for peers without legal qualifications to abstain from taking part in the determination of causes, though no formal exclusion existed,[1] nor has been created. The effort to strengthen the Lords for judicial purposes by the addition of life peers failed in the case of Sir James Parke,[2] but the grant to him of a hereditary peerage provided the house with one additional experienced lawyer.

It is not surprising, therefore, if Lord Selborne in his effort in 1873 to secure a coherent jurisdiction endeavoured to create a Court of Appeal which would take the place of the Lords as a court. The proposal was accepted by Parliament, and the only exception which was made was the exclusion of Scottish and Irish appeals on the ground that the lawyers of these countries had not been consulted. In the Commons the exception was removed, but the Lords would not agree, and the Act as passed excluded these appeals, but was not to take effect in any event until

---

[1] *Lord Kinross, In re*, [1905] A.C. 468, which permits peers to practice before the Lords in appeal causes.

[2] *Wensleydale Peerage Case* (1856), 5 H.L.C. 958.

November 1875. In the meantime the change of Government brought Lord Cairns into the office of Lord Chancellor, and he was not so keen a supporter of immediate abolition of the power of the Lords as his predecessor. He did, however, introduce a Bill in 1874 to terminate even Scottish and Irish Appeals, but the Commons did not deal with it owing to preoccupation with the Public Worship Regulation Bill, and in 1875 the Lords repented of their attitude and Lord Cairns had to secure the passing of a Bill suspending the operation of the Act of 1873 until 1876. In 1876, however, the policy adopted was different ; the Lords was to be retained as a court of appeal, but it was to be strengthened and its procedure was in some degree to be modified to enable it to perform more effectively its judicial functions.[1] Hence provision was made that no appeal might be heard unless there were present not less than three Lords of Appeal, and that term was defined to mean the Chancellor for the time being, the Lords of Appeal in Ordinary, and any peer of Parliament who had held high judicial office. Such office was defined to include the Chancellorship, a paid judgeship of the Judicial Committee, and a judgeship of one of the superior courts of Great Britain and Ireland. The Lords of Appeal in Ordinary were created with life peerages, and their number now stands at seven. The innovation afforded the Lords indispensable assistance, and at the same time it was provided that the Lords of Appeal could hear causes in the name of the house during a dissolution or prorogation. It was thus made statutory that on these occasions no peers not Lords of Appeal might exercise judicial functions. It is now the rule that no appeal lies in civil cases [2] save by leave of the Court of Appeal or the house itself.

---

[1] Monypenny and Buckle, *Disraeli*, ii. 594, 715, 812.
[2] 24 & 25 Geo. V. c. 40. For criminal appeals see p. 282 *ante*.

The forms of a sitting of the Lords are still preserved and a decision results in a declaration on motion that it be ordered and adjudged. Members naturally are free to express their own opinions separately, and the result, therefore, may be reached by a bare majority of three to two when five Lords sit, as usual, and these three may arrive at the like result but on differing grounds. There are, no doubt, objections that the final decision should thus lose much weight, but the rule is fixed. More objectionable is the fact that the House of Lords regards itself as bound by its own decisions [1] so that, even when matters come to light which were not before the court when a decision was arrived at, it is practically impossible to depart from the earlier ruling, though ingenuity may be shown in distinguishing the new cause ; this has been notably the case in workmen's insurance problems. The practice becomes, naturally, especially open to criticism when, as may happen, the decision is arrived at by equality of voices, the rule being that if on appeal there is no majority in the Lords, the judgment below not only stands, as is inevitable, but it attains the value of a judgment of the Lords.[2] When it is remembered that not only may the Supreme Court of the United States vary its judgments on sufficient emergent cause, but that the Judicial Committee of the Privy Council follows a like plan,[3] the rigidity of the Lords is open to question. The argument that it is expedient that the law should be altered by legislative action, not by judicial initiative, and that the practice of the Supreme Court is due to the rigidity of the federal constitution, is not conclusive.

[1] *London Street Tramways Co.* v. *London County Council*, [1898] A.C. 375.
[2] *R.* v. *Millis* (1844), 10 Cl. & F. 554 ; Dicey and Keith, *Conflict of Laws* (1932), p. 742.
[3] *Read* v. *Bishop of Lincoln*, [1892] A.C. at p. 654 ; *Transferred Civil Servants (Ireland) Compensation, In re*, [1929] A.C. 242.

(ii) The Privy Council

For the rest of the Empire the final court of appeal remains the Judicial Committee of the Privy Council, which represents the authority of the King in Council which for England was destroyed by the Long Parliament, but left intact for the lands overseas. In 1833 [1] the admiralty and ecclesiastical appeals in England were assigned to the Judicial Committee, then formally constituted, with a view to assure that appeals should be dealt with essentially by men of judicial experience. Under the previous régime appeals might be disposed of by any members of the Council summoned to hear them, and no doubt in many cases issues were dealt with rather from the point of general expediency than of strict law. The Committee now constituted consisted of the Lord Chancellor, the Lord President, and former holders of either office, the holders of certain high judicial offices and past holders thereof, and two persons nominated by the Crown, a clause made use of to admit Lord Oxford and Asquith to the Committee. Two privy councillors who had held high judicial office in India were added with salaries of £400 a year, whose services were regularly employed in hearing Indian appeals. The quorum was fixed at four, later reduced to three, but five judges sit for the more important cases. Permission was given in 1915 for the Committee to sit in two or more divisions simultaneously if desirable, and this is now often done.

Later changes [2] in the composition of the Committee strengthened it in two directions. The Lords of Appeal in Ordinary were added in 1876, and all seven are now available for service thereon ; the two final courts of appeal

[1] 3 & 4 Will. IV. c. 41.
[2] 50 & 51 Vict. c. 70 ; 58 & 59 Vict. c. 44 ; 3 & 4 Geo. V. c. 21 ; 19 Geo. V. c. 8 ; 18 & 19 Geo. V. c. 26.

thus contain an important identity of personnel and their views become more accordant. Further, by a series of statutes from 1895 to 1929 the right of judges and ex-judges of the highest courts of the Dominions and the Australian States and of the colonies to sit as members of the Committee if made members of the Privy Council is established, while for India special provision was made in 1929 for the presence in the Committee of two salaried judges with Indian experience ; the retiring age for these judges alone is seventy-two. In 1840 the Church Dis-cipline Act provided that in ecclesiastical causes under the Act archbishops and bishops, if privy councillors, should be members of the Committee, but the Appellate Jurisdiction Act, 1876, reduced them to the position of assessors. The attendance of Dominion judges on Dominion appeals has necessarily, in the absence of any provision for salaries being made, proved to be sporadic, though the Chief Justice of Canada or Australia has on occasion sat.

The conception of a single court of appeal for the whole Empire was discussed in 1901 at a conference at which the self-governing colonies were represented. It was advo-cated from time to time by Lord Haldane, and received consideration by the Imperial Conference of 1921 when the issue was brought up by Mr. Hughes for Australia.[1] But the project has never commanded wide support. In the view of the English bar it is not desired to have ex-traneous aid in deciding cases from the courts of England, Scotland, and Northern Ireland, and the feeling in the Dominions is that, if change is made, it should rather lie in the direction of the total extinction of appeals outside the country concerned.[2] It is argued that the cost of such

[1] Keith, *The Dominions as Sovereign States*, p. 398.
[2] Cf. H. Hughes, *Judicial Autonomy in the British Commonwealth of Nations* (1931).

appeals is very high, so that poor litigants suffer, while
rich corporations are able to pursue appeals or, by threat
thereof, induce compromises ; it is insisted that such
appeals delay justice, an argument which is certainly
unanswerable ; that they indicate that Dominion judges
are of inferior calibre, and by doing so tend to depress the
local courts both in their own and the public estimation ;
that the Judicial Committee, because of lack of knowledge
of local conditions, sometimes misconceives situations and
gives unsound judgments ; that the Committee regards
things from the point of view of a very conservative and
capitalistic outlook ; and that in any case the growth of
national autonomy in the Dominions is inconsistent with
the resort to the Privy Council. The idea that there is a
valuable bond of Empire in the feeling that redress can
always be obtained from the Crown is denied any validity,
for the Committee is no more than a court. The result of
these and other considerations was that in the Commonwealth of Australia Constitution as agreed upon in Australia
appeals on the constitution of the Commonwealth or the
States were not to be allowed unless the public interest
of some other part of Her Majesty's dominions were involved. Against this Mr. Chamberlain urged the advantages of uniform interpretation of law as a basis for that
unity of action which would lead to a real federation of
the Empire. But the delegates held that no patriotism
was inspired by thought of the Privy Council, that kinship
and a common sense of duty were the true links of Empire,
and that unity of action was in no way bound up with
uniformity of interpretation of law. In the end a compromise was reached ; while the appeal was left open in
general, it was cut off in matters involving the constitutional relations of the Commonwealth and States and of
the States *inter se*, though, on a certificate by the High

Court of the Commonwealth, appeal even in these cases might be permitted ; the view taken in the Commonwealth, however, negatived use of this power save in a single instance,[1] and the result in that case was that no further certificate was given. Appeals on such issues could, however, still come from the State courts under the Orders in Council regulating appeals thence, issued under the authority of the Judicial Committee Act, 1844, but to obviate conflict of decisions between the Judicial Committee and the High Court, which actually arose [2] on the right of the States to levy income tax on the salaries of federal officials, the Commonwealth Parliament removed from the Supreme Courts of the States jurisdiction over such issues.

In the case of the Commonwealth, therefore, appeal in constitutional cases lies only where no issue of powers *inter se* arises. The federal Parliament may by reserved Bill [3] further limit the appeal from the High Court, but this has not yet been done. Moreover, under the power of the alteration of the constitution given by Section 128 thereof the appeal, even from State courts, might be taken away under the usual form of constitutional amendment, which requires ultimately the assent of the majority of the voters in the Commonwealth and of the voters in at least four States.

In the case of the Union of South Africa under the South Africa Act, 1909,[4] appeal lies only from the Appellate Division of the Supreme Court by special leave from the Privy Council, and this leave is very seldom given, as the law of the Union is Roman-Dutch law in which the Privy Council is not especially expert, and as the Union does

---

[1] *Att.-Gen. for Commonwealth of Australia* v. *Colonial Sugar Refining Co.*, [1914] A.C. 237.

[2] *Webb* v. *Outrim*, [1907] A.C. 81 ; *Baxter* v. *Taxation Commrs.* (1907), 4 C.L.R. 1087.   [3] S. 74.   [4] S. 106.

not desire appeals to be heard. The question of the abolition of the appeal is under consideration. In the case of Canada, on the other hand, right of appeal in criminal causes from both federal and provincial courts was formally abolished in 1933 under the authority of the Statute of Westminster, 1931, which freed the Dominions from the restrictions on legislative power imposed by the Colonial Laws Validity Act, 1865, and allowed the Parliament to cut off the appeal provided by the Judicial Committee Act, 1844, which had invalidated an earlier effort [1] to abolish all criminal appeals. The civil appeal from the provincial and federal courts alike remains operative, because it is impossible for the various governments to concur in a policy of abolition. The special rights of language and education of Quebec might be endangered if the appeal were abandoned, and the provinces fear that the Supreme Court judges might come to regard issues raised from the view of the federal Government, whose appointees they are.

From all other territories, the colonies, protectorates, and even the mandated territories appeal lies either with or without the special leave of the Privy Council on terms specified in local legislation, or more usually by Orders in Council with the force of statute law. Even for the Dominions there are advantages in the interpretation by one court of the rules of English common law and of the meaning of British statutes, which are operative in the oversea territories, and of statutes on subjects of common interest in which the Dominions have followed the terms of British Acts which, like the Sale of Goods Act [2] or that on Negotiable Instruments, have been re-enacted in the

---

[1] *Nadan* v. *R.*, [1926] A.C. 482 ; *British Coal Corporation* v. *R.*, [1935] A.C. 500 ; Canadian Act, Criminal Code Amendment Act, 1933, s. 17.

[2] *Grant* v. *Australian Knitting Mills*, [1936] A.C. 85.

Dominions. In the case of the colonies and protectorates, the Privy Council serves an important purpose in preserving the supremacy of British legislation and of the prerogative, while, though it refuses to act as a court of appeal in criminal cases,[1] it will intervene to prevent grave injustice by neglect of the essential forms of procedure. For India it performs like functions, and is of special importance in seeking to preserve uniformity of law, for, unless and until it is so provided by Indian legislation, the functions of the Federal Court do not extend to deal with causes not involving federal issues, and it does not serve as a general court of appeal from the provinces as does the Supreme Court in Canada and the High Court in Australia.[2]

The Privy Council advises the King as a Council, and the Judicial Committee's advice must be approved by the King in Council to give it effect, but by a convention of the constitution the report of the Committee is always approved. The reasons for the report are not embodied in the Order in Council but are given separately. Under an Order in Council of 1627, repeated in 1878, the rule is that there is no publication, official or private, of the mode in which the votes went if the Committee is not unanimous. The decisions, therefore, carry with them the additional force which is implicit in unanimity, though in many cases such unanimity may be artificial. The question, however, was definitely raised in 1911 at the Imperial Conference, and, though a resolution in favour of allowing the publication of dissentient opinions was accepted, on consultation there was agreement among the Dominion Governments[3] that it was on the whole desirable to adhere to the former practice of apparent unanimity. It

---

[1] *Knowles* v. *R.*, [1930] A.C. 366 ; *Lawrence* v. *R.*, [1933] A.C. 699 ; *Ras Behari Lal* v. *King-Emperor* (1933), L.R. 60 Ind. App. 354.

[2] Keith, *Constitutional History of India*, chap. x. § 19.

[3] Keith, *Imperial Unity and the Dominions*, p. 382.

can fairly be argued that as regards the colonies and minor dependencies at least there are substantial advantages in the fact that a pronouncement by the sovereign should carry with it all the additional weight of unanimity.

The Council, as already noted, does not feel bound to adhere absolutely to earlier pronouncements, if these were arrived at without due consideration of other facts and arguments which later are adduced. But of course it refrains from change of opinion save in cases of importance.

Where the Privy Council differs in view from the House of Lords, there is possibility of conflict of opinion in oversea courts, whether the Privy Council judgment or that of the Lords should be accepted. The rule appears to be that these courts must follow the Privy Council if its judgment is of later date than that of the Lords, but that, if the Lords' judgment is of later date and rests on an interpretation of the common law or statute different from the view of the Committee, the Lords' view should be followed.[1] Where neither the Committee nor the Lords has laid down a rule, the opinion of the Court of Appeal deserves serious weight.

4. *The Courts of Inferior Jurisdiction*

(i) Civil Jurisdiction

At the accession of Queen Victoria civil justice was normally to be had only by an action commenced at Westminster and tried there, or begun there and tried under a commission of assize on circuit. The ancient county court had ceased in fact to exercise any jurisdiction, and only in certain places were there local courts with some sub-

---

[1] *Trimble* v. *Hill* (1879), 5 App. Cas. 342 ; *Robins* v. *National Trust Co.*, [1927] A.C. 515 ; *Brooker* v. *Thos. Borthwick & Sons.*, [1933] A.C. 669 ; *Will* v. *Bank of Montreal* (1921), 3 D.L.R. 526 ; *Negro* v. *Pietro's Bread Co.*, [1933] Ont. R. 112 ; Keith, *The Dominions as Sovereign States*, p. 394.

stantial amount of jurisdiction, such as the Lord Mayor's Court at London (now merged with another court into the Mayor's and City of London Court), the Passage Court of Liverpool, the Hundred Court of Record of Salford, the Chancellor's Court in the University of Oxford, and a number of others, most of which were obsolescent if not obsolete. In addition to these courts a number of other places had obtained courts of request, a title reminiscent of the ancient Court of Requests at Whitehall, which had expired under the Commonwealth.

In 1846 was begun the creation of a new type of county courts which were intended to allow of the collection without undue difficulty of small debts under a uniform mode of procedure. These courts proved themselves popular, and their jurisdiction was steadily extended so as to relieve the High Court of unnecessary concern with litigation where the amount at stake was fairly small. In 1888 the various statutes conferring extended powers were consolidated, and in 1934 [1] there was a further consolidation and extension of powers.[2] The recourse to these county courts is furthered by the rule that those who go unnecessarily to the High Court may, even if successful, only be awarded costs on the county court scale. Appeal was made originally to the High Court, but since 1934 to the Court of Appeal. The judges are appointed and may be removed from office by the Lord Chancellor and there is a normal age limit of seventy-two. In 1938 there was given a substantial increase in salary. Promotion from a county court to the High Court is extremely rare, but the quality of the judicial work done by these courts is very high.

[1] County Court Act, 1934 (24 & 25 Geo. V. c. 53).
[2] 1 & 2 Geo. VI. c. 63, s. 16, extends from £100 to £200 the limit of jurisdicton in certain cases including contract and tort. The High Court can punish contempt of orders of a county court : *R.* v. *Edwards* ; *Welsh Church Commrs., Ex parte* (1933), 49 T.L.R. 383.

(ii) Criminal Jurisdiction

Inferior criminal jurisdiction is exercised by justices
of the peace trying indictable offences at Quarter Sessions,
or exercising a summary jurisdiction. There is a commission of peace for each county ; on it are placed all the
judges of the High Court, all Privy Councillors, and such
persons as may be appointed by the King, who acts through
the Lord Chancellor. He in turn is advised by the Lord-
Lieutenant, who is aided by a committee in order to secure
that justices shall not be chosen from one class of the population only, but he may make appointments without such
advice, and he is in no way bound to accept all the suggestions made. The Lord-Lieutenant is the chief of the
justices and is now regularly the *custos rotulorum*, keeper
of the records for the county.

The jurisdiction of justices was simplified and made
more satisfactory by legislation of 1848 and by the Summary
Jurisdiction Act, 1879, while further extensions and modifications have been made by recent legislation. In some
cases offences can be summarily tried by a single justice,
or by two justices sitting as a court of petty sessions. In
other cases summary trial is impossible ; a single justice,
or justices in petty sessions, may hold a preliminary
examination where a man is suspected of having committed
such an offence, and either dismiss the case or secure the
appearance of the accused for trial by committing him to
prison or by requiring bail for his appearance before the
suitable court. The offence may be triable at Quarter
Sessions, or may be reserved for trial by a judge of the High
Court sitting under commission on circuit. In certain
offences the accused has the option to be tried summarily
by justices at petty sessions, or to be committed for trial
at Quarter Sessions or at the next assize.

At Quarter Sessions the justices sit four times a year to hear and decide cases of indictable offences, with the aid of a jury. They act also, through a special committee, as a court of appeal from convictions by justices sitting in exercise of summary jurisdiction ; the committee system was arranged by the Summary Jurisdiction (Appeals) Act, 1933, to meet criticisms of ineffective operation of the appeal system. In the same spirit in 1938 steps were taken to facilitate the practice of having as chairman a person with legal qualifications ; chairmen elected by the justices without such qualifications have been criticised as ineffective in presiding over the justices who form the court, and as being unduly under the control of the clerk in regard to legal points. Appeals also lie to Quarter Sessions in matters of rating, of licensing, and of determination of the legal settlement of paupers, so as to assign to the proper authority responsibility in respect of maintenance. In case of trial on indictment, the person convicted has a right of appeal to the Court of Criminal Appeal under the Act of 1907, while in rating and licensing matters a demand may be made that a case be stated for the opinion of the High Court. In addition the High Court may be moved to intervene by *certiorari* to quash orders when the justices have acted without jurisdiction, or by *mandamus* to require justices to perform some action which they have omitted or refused to do.

In the boroughs there are certain differences from the counties. Some have no separate commission, and fall under the jurisdiction of the justices for the county. Others have a commission but no Quarter Sessions, so that their justices exercise only summary jurisdiction. Others have Quarter Sessions, but the justices do not sit ; the judge is a recorder, appointed by the Crown on the advice of the Home Secretary and removable on his

recommendation ; he is normally a barrister in good practice
and an effective judge, and the tendency is for towns to
seek to be given recorders where there is a substantial
amount of serious crime.

At the accession of Queen Victoria, there was considerable complexity of jurisdictions in the London area ; there
were distinct commissions for the City of London, the City
of Westminster, and the Liberty of the Tower, while other
areas fell under one or other of the county commissions,
for Middlesex, Kent, Surrey, and Essex.　In 1839 and
1840 [1] therefore were created stipendiary magistrates,
salaried, and placed on the commission of the peace for
each of the four counties, and for Hertfordshire, Westminster, and the Liberty of the Tower.　They act singly,
but each has the powers of two justices when that number
is required for any legal act.　Their remuneration is defrayed partly by Middlesex, partly by Imperial funds.

In a few other towns stipendiary magistrates exist, paid
wholly by the locality.　They are all appointed and removed
on the advice of the Home Secretary.　The extension of
such appointments is probably a desirable reform.

For the administrative county of London there are
Quarter Sessions held twice a month, and the bench of
justices is presided over by a paid chairman or deputy.
A certain measure of friction has at times been noted
between Quarter Sessions and the stipendiary magistrates,
who consider that in certain classes of offences, especially
those committed by motorists, the justices are too apt to reduce sentences, even if they do not quash sentences outright.

On the whole there has been a gradual hardening of
opinion among those familiar with the proceedings of unpaid justices of the peace that their performance of their

[1] 2 & 3 Vict. c. 71 ; 3 & 4 Vict. c. 84.　In 1939 there were 13 courts, 27
magistrates.

work, though well meant and often energetic, is not wholly satisfactory. Too many justices remain on the bench beyond the age when they are competent to act effectively, whereas stipendiary magistrates are expected to retire at age seventy-two. Further, justices are too apt to fall under the influence of the clerk attached to the court, who is normally a solicitor familiar with the routine of the law, but without any special judicial capacity and without judicial responsibility. The substitution of paid magistrates has been recommended.

Under recent developments [1] the offences of children and young persons have been tried in special children's courts, in which justices of special qualification are expected to sit, and special arrangements have been made also for dealing without undue publicity with matrimonial disputes.[2] In such cases the court is constituted of three justices, of whom one should be a man, one a woman, and publication of the proceedings is drastically restricted on the analogy of the restrictions imposed in the case of High Court proceedings in divorce,[3] nullity, etc., suits, while as in the case of children's courts the proceedings are conducted without the general public being permitted access to the court.

(iii) The Coroner's Court

The exceptional jurisdiction of the coroner has been considerably affected by recent legislation. Until 1888 he was elected by the freeholders in the county court, but the Local Government Act of that year made the appointing authority the county council, save in boroughs with separate Quarter Sessions where the population exceeds

[1] Children and Young Persons Act, 1933 (23 & 24 Geo. V. c. 12).

[2] Summary Procedure (Domestic Proceedings) Act, 1937 (1 Edw. VIII. & 1 Geo. VI. c. 58).

[3] Judicial Proceedings (Regulation of Reports) Act, 1926 (16 & 17 Geo. V. c. 61).

10,000, when the borough council appoints. In 1926 [1] the Coroners (Amendment) Act restricted eligibility for the office to barristers, solicitors, and medical practitioners, and abolished franchise coroners other than the King's coroner, the coroner of the royal household, and the coroners for the Scilly Islands and for the City of London. The latter has the duty of holding inquests into fires at which a verdict of arson may be returned. A coroner may be removed for misconduct by the Lord Chancellor.

The essential criminal function of a coroner is to hold an inquest in cases of suspicious death. He sits then with a jury, formerly of from 12 to 23, now, under the Act of 1926, of from 7 to 11. The proceedings in such cases are on oath, but the strict rules of judicial evidence are not always observed, and some coroners conduct a roving enquiry, which may on occasion reveal facts useful to the police, but which often certainly only causes annoyance to relatives. If the jury with not more than two dissentients finds a verdict of murder or manslaughter against any person, the coroner must commit for trial, but, though this is not absolutely essential, it is usual to take proceedings before the justices and to act on their committal; if they do not commit, the prisoner will almost certainly be discharged before the petty jury. If the coroner knows that proceedings are being taken before justices, he now may and does adjourn the case and thus prevents that duplication of proceedings which elicited dislike of the older procedure. The proposal that further limits should be placed on the action of coroners has some strong arguments in its favour, but these are not decisive. The only other important duty of a coroner is the holding of inquests into treasure trove; his former powers as to wreck and to royal fish were taken away in 1887.

[1] 16 & 17 Geo. V. c. 59; Coroners Act, 1887 (50 & 51 Vict. c. 71).

5. *The Legal Profession*

Nothing is more conservative than the legal profession, and, as a result, the relation of barristers and solicitors is much as it was in 1837. The right of audience in the superior tribunals has been preserved for members of the Bar, while solicitors have been allowed to appear in the inferior courts in which barristers also may plead. The usurpation of the function of solicitors by unauthorised persons has been penalised, and thus the monopoly of the profession has been strengthened. At the same time there have been continuous efforts to improve the qualifications of members of the profession. Service as an articled clerk, normally for five years, secures familiarity with the actual work of a solicitor, and the passing of a preliminary, an intermediate and a final examination secure a reasonably high standard of attainment. Since 1878 the examinations have been held under the management of the Law Society, founded in 1831 to look after the interests of the profession. It started in 1903 a much-improved system of legal education to supplant that in force since 1833, and secured the aid of local law societies, and in 1922 the general rule was laid down that, before taking the final examination, an articled clerk should attend for a year a law school provided or approved by the Society. Admission to the rank of solicitor, after due service and passing the examinations, is given at discretion by the Master of the Rolls, and to practise as such a solicitor must take out each year a practising certificate, paying therefor the fee prescribed. Women became eligible in 1919 [1] for treatment on the same terms as men.

Solicitors are officers of court, and as such are subject

[1] 9 & 10 Geo. V. c. 71.

to summary orders by the court in case of misconduct.[1]

In 1888 [2] a Discipline Committee of the Law Society appointed by the Master of the Rolls was authorised to report to the court on charges brought against solicitors. In 1919 [3] power was given to a committee of the Law Society to strike off the rolls, subject to appeal to the court.

In the case of barristers admission remains in the hands of the four Inns of Court, as represented by the benchers, who are the governing body of each, and whose number is maintained by co-option. It rests with the benchers to remove from the rank of barrister-at-law persons who have proved unworthy ; the step is rarely taken, though a case occurred in 1938, a conviction for a criminal offence being later recorded against him. It is possible that against refusal to admit or removal an appeal might lie to the judges of the High Court.

The Inns include barristers and students seeking admission to the Bar. The rules for admission include the formal keeping of terms, twelve in all, there being four a year, and the passing of examinations. The Council of Legal Education, which has existed since 1852, includes representatives of the Inns and has done much to advance the cause of education. Since 1894 there is a General Council of the Bar elected by barristers, which is the accredited representative of the English Bar and charged with the promotion of its interests ; it is a repository of the technical and complex etiquette of the Bar.

The distinction between solicitors and barristers has

---

[1] Cf. *Brendon* v. *Spiro*, [1938] 1 K.B. 176 ; *Myers* v. *Rothfield*, [1938] 3 A.E.R. 498.

[2] 51 & 52 Vict. c. 65.

[3] 9 & 10 Geo. V. c. 56, s. 5 ; *Solicitors, In re* ; *Marshall, Ex parte*, [1938] 1 K.B. 616. No appeal lies from refusal of the Committee to make any order : *Solicitor, In re*, [1934] 2 K.B. 463.

been abolished in many oversea territories and its maintenance in England has at times been criticised. There is
no doubt that it is one of the factors of the chief defect
of English law, its extreme costliness which renders poor
litigants liable to lose their cases for lack of funds to carry
them to the highest courts or to obtain the services of the
ablest of the counsel. It can hardly be denied that the
cost of justice is often prohibitory, but it is nothing new,
and there is naturally grave reluctance to disturb an
arrangement which is so profitable to solicitors and counsel
alike. Yet it is one of the factors which induce business
men in their contracts to stipulate for arbitration. The
system, no doubt, makes for greater development of legal
principles, for barristers are constantly dealing with such
issues.

In 1837 there existed a distinction between the serjeants and other barristers ; [1] the former were appointed
from the latter of sixteen years' standing by writ of
summons under the great seal issued by the King in
Council. They alone had audience on the Court of Common
Pleas until the court was thrown open for others to
practise in, by an Act of 1846.[2] In 1851 [3] any barrister of
fifteen years' standing might be appointed to the new rank
of Lord Justice of Appeal in Chancery, and under the
Judicature Act, 1873,[4] the rule, which until then had
been observed, of appointing judges from the rank of
serjeants disappeared ; any barrister of ten years' standing
might be appointed a judge of the High Court, while for
the Court of Appeal fifteen years' standing, or service for
not less than a year in the High Court, was provided.
The order of serjeants, thereafter, ceased to be added to

---

[1] Pulling, *Order of the Coif.*   [2] 9 & 10 Vict. c. 54.
[3] 14 & 15 Vict. c. 83, s. 1.   See 15 & 16 Geo. V. c. 49, s. 9.
[4] 36 & 37 Vict. c. 66, s. 8.

and the surviving members of the fraternity sold Serjeants' Inn in Chancery Lane in 1877.

Between barristers a distinction exists, for barristers of some standing and success in practice may apply to the Lord Chancellor for permission to become King's Counsel. Those who take this rank are in general debarred from appearance without a junior counsel being briefed with them. Permission to appear in cases against the interests of the Crown is now accorded as of course. Women became eligible under the Sex Disqualification (Removal) Act, 1919. Neither the profession of solicitor nor barrister has so far appealed widely to women as a means of earning a livelihood.

The influence of the profession on the enactment of procedure rules is secured by the use of the Bar Council to put forward names of persons suitable to fill the two places reserved on the Rule Committee of the Supreme Court.

It is one of the characteristic features of the legal system that the judges are selected from the Bar. There is thus no chance of the introduction of a judge with a mind not trained in the normal legal manner to upset the traditional point of view ; even judges who have been supporters of Labour in politics seem soon to acquire the normal Conservative standpoint, and an occasional exception to the ordinary type, like the late Mr. Justice McCardie, can hardly be said to be welcomed. On the other hand, there are clear advantages in the solidarity between bench and Bar, and the high standard of judicial integrity is certainly aided by the fact that judges are conscious that they are under the continuous scrutiny of men with like experience, some of whom may have even declined to sacrifice their high earnings at the Bar for the security of a judgeship.

CHAPTER XXII

THE FUNCTIONS OF THE JUDICIARY AND THE
CHARACTERISTICS OF ENGLISH JUDICIAL PROCEDURE

1. *The Interpretation of the Law*

THE courts intervene to declare the meaning of the law Chapter XXII. only on the initiative of persons affected by its prescriptions. In the Dominions, Canada has found it desirable to develop the right of the Crown to obtain the advice of the courts on the constitutionality of legislation without waiting for instances of its operation, and the raising of the issue by private persons.[1] But in Australia the High Court has negatived any desire to play the rôle of interpreter *in vacuo*,[2] and, though the rules of court of England provide for declaratory judgments,[3] the action of the High Court thereunder is essentially restricted. The court will only make a declaration where a real and not an academic or fictitious issue is involved, such as the validity or otherwise of a contract, which a defendant threatened to enforce, or the claim of defendants to be entitled to send sewage into the plaintiff's sewer without his consent, or the necessity of giving information under the provisions as to land taxation of the Finance Act of 1910. On the other hand, the court will not make a

---

[1] *Att.-Gen. for Ontario* v. *Att.-Gen. for Canada*, [1912] A.C. 591.

[2] Keith, *The Dominions as Sovereign States*, pp. 374, 451.

[3] *Guaranty Trust Co. of New York* v. *Hannay & Co.*, [1915] 2 K.B. 537 ; *Russian Commercial, etc., Bank* v. *British Bank for Foreign Trade*, [1921] A.C. 438.

Chapter
XXII.

declaration of right where it is endeavoured in this way to avoid the necessity, under the procedure by petition of right, of obtaining the royal fiat.[1]   Thus in the vast majority of cases the courts interpret the law only in so far as it becomes necessary to do so in deciding rights of individuals or companies.

Interpretation means inevitably legislation in some degree, and that degree is marked where it is the common law that falls to be interpreted, for in a sense the common law is the creation of the judges.   The classical modern instance of such creation may be seen in the case of the invention of the doctrine of common employment, under, which a worker cannot recover damages from an employer if he is injured by the fault of a fellow-servant.   There was admittedly, when *Priestley* v. *Fowler* [2] came up in 1837 for decision, no ruling either way on record and the court had to decide on principle, and held that it was entitled to take into account the results of a decision either way. Unluckily [3] it decided that a worker impliedly agrees to accept the risks naturally incidental to his employment, and that injury through the negligence of a fellow-worker is a normal risk.   The decision is characteristic of the mentality of the time, and it is a striking example of the love for precedent that it has never been abrogated as in itself unjust and oppressive.   On the other hand, later, in 1893,[4] a more enlightened morality led to the decision that negligence towards a helpless invalid in one's charge might constitute manslaughter.   But, where no case of suffering was concerned, the House of Lords had declined

[1] *Bombay and Persia Steam Navigation Co.* v. *Maclay*, [1920] 3 K.B. 402.

[2] 3 M. & W. 1.   For judicial comment see *Wilson's and Clyde Coal Co.* v. *English*, [1938] A. C. 57.

[3] *Radcliffe* v. *Ribble Motor Services, Ltd.* (1939), 55 T.L.R. 459.

[4] *R.* v. *Instan*, [1893] 1 Q.B. 451.

in *Derry* v. *Peek*[1] to convert into a legal obligation one clearly moral.

In dealing with statute law the courts have a more limited authority than in interpreting the common law. They claim no authority to ignore the terms of a statute, even if it results in the statute being rendered meaningless, and a man who has once failed to pay rates, through having been excused payment through poverty, has been held to be disqualified for good because the statute refers to payment of all poor rates.[2] Nor can the courts ascribe to the legislature principles of public policy, so that they can extend or modify the application of any Act under the influence of the supposed meaning of the legislature.[3] Its views of public policy must be gathered from the terms it thinks fit to use. If, of course, there is real ambiguity in the words of an Act, then the courts are compelled to have regard to matters not contained therein, such as the purpose for which the legislation seems to have been passed, and like considerations. But the courts will not rewrite Acts; if the legislature insists on laying down provisions that are in fact unworkable, the courts will still give them legal effect, leaving it to the legislature to amend its errors in the light of the strictures of the courts.

One broad function is assumed by the courts, the application of the paramount doctrine of public policy to avoid actions in themselves not *prima facie* illegal. The most interesting application of this doctrine was in the famous case of *Egerton* v. *Earl Brownlow*,[4] where the House of Lords refused to follow the opinions of the judges, who were asked to advise, but decided that a

[1] (1889), 14 App. Cas. 337. For a new doctrine of public mischief, see *R.* v. *Manley*, [1933] 1 K.B. 529.

[2] *Abel* v. *Lee* (1871), L.R. 6 C.P. 365.

[3] *Gwynne* v. *Burnell* (1840), 7 Cl. & F. 696.   [4] (1853), 4 H.L.C. 1.

condition in a will which provided that a beneficiary should forfeit an interest if he failed to secure a certain title was invalid. Parke, B., for instance, was prepared to recognise the operation of the principle in cases of covenants in restraint of marriage or trade, but refused to extend the principle beyond limits already admitted. Despite the rejection of this limitation by the Lords, the tendency to limit continued, and it was applied in *Griffith* v. *Earl of Dudley*[1] to deny that it was possible to declare void a contract taking the employee out of the operation of the Employers' Liability Act, 1880, and Lord Halsbury in *Janson* v. *Driefontein Consolidated Mines, Ltd.*,[2] denied that any court can invent a new head of public policy. In *Ertel Bieber & Co.* v. *Rio Tinto Co.*[3] Lord Dunedin insisted that he was not inventing any new type. But this view has not been too rigidly insisted upon. In *Horwood* v. *Millar's Timber, etc., Co., Ltd.*,[4] the doctrine of restraint of trade was pressed to the extent of holding it illegal for a moneylender to bargain in lending money that the borrower should engage not to determine his employment or move from his house without the lender's assent and not to borrow money or sell or pledge his property. Moreover, there has been a steady modification of the idea of restraint of trade as making a contract illegal. The extent of the restraint in relation to the dealings and relations between the parties is now taken as a fundamental issue. While some judges are impressed by the objection to reducing the sanctity of contract by adducing public policy as stressed by Jessel, M.R.,[5] others have stressed rather the rule that the law shall not encourage things contrary to the public interest. A great

---

[1] (1882), 9 Q.B.D. 357. [2] [1902] A.C. 484.
[3] [1918] A.C. 260. [4] [1917] 1 K.B. 305.
[5] *Printing, etc. Co.* v. *Sampson* (1875), 19 Eq. 462.

diversity of opinion was revealed on the vexed question whether it was against public policy to allow a man to be sued on a promise of marriage made after a decree *nisi* of divorce but before the decree was made absolute. The House of Lords [1] though not unanimously, decided that, the marriage tie having effectively been rendered unmeaning by the decree, the promise could not be regarded as really likely to prevent reconciliation, and that it should be upheld. On the other hand, after differences of judicial opinion, the Lords ruled that, even if a contract promises payment of money assured on the suicide of the person in question, nonetheless such money cannot be recovered for the benefit of his estate, for out of a crime public policy forbids the recovery of money, just as no relative of a murderer may secure benefit by reason of a murder which he has committed.[2] So, again, the courts will not enforce a promise of secrecy made by a firm to an employee who had revealed improper practices by employees as regards disclosure of his admissions, for to do so would offend public policy.[3] On the other hand, while public policy demands that collusion in divorce proceedings should be penalised by refusal of a divorce, that does not mean that a divorce should be refused merely because there was an apparent collusion, if a frank disclosure of the circumstances in which a wife accepted money to enable her to bring proceedings is made.[4] But the courts will do nothing to enforce a contract which involves the smuggling of whisky into the United States, if that is prohibited by the federal law, for that is contrary to public policy.[5] Nor is it against

[1] *Fender* v. *Mildmay*, [1938] A.C. 1.
[2] *Beresford* v. *Royal Insurance Co.*, [1938] A.C. 586.
[3] *Howard* v. *Odhams Press, Ltd.*, [1938] 1 K.B. 1.
[4] *Beattie* v. *Beattie*, [1938] P. 99.
[5] *Foster* v. *Driscoll*, [1929] 1 K.B. 470.

public policy for a husband to accept an engagement under which his wife receives payment so long as he is absent, for without more it is impossible to find anything in itself wrong in such an accord.

In its functions the rule of following precedents is binding on every court. An inferior court is bound by the decisions of any superior court, and a divisional court follows the rulings of such a court as a normal rule, though a judge sitting by himself may, if he will, refuse to regard himself bound by a decision of another judge, if on consideration he holds that some point has been misconceived by his colleague, or that some precedent has been overlooked, or some judicial principle misunderstood. It must, however, be remembered that courts which may not differ can distinguish, and that the distinction may be such as to be virtually equivalent to overruling the prior decision.

2. *Judicial Control of the Executive and other Authorities*

It is an essential duty of the executive government to obey the law of the land,[1] whether or not there is any means of compelling it to do so, and the judiciary has an absolute duty to restrain actions of the executive which are illegal. It cannot refrain from doing so because of any considerations of State convenience ;[2] the ancient doctrine of *Entick* v. *Carrington*[3] is perhaps hardly likely to be ignored in Britain itself, but it has been found desirable to remind colonial courts that they must give it full effect, even if it should be found that to do so may interfere with the convenience of the administration. In fact, as shown in discussing the rights of the subject, the courts have been

---

[1] *Eastern Trust Co.* v. *McKenzie, Mann & Co.*, [1915] A.C. 750.
[2] Cf. *Eshugbayi Eleko* v. *Nigerian Government*, [1931] A.C. 662.
[3] (1765), 19 St. Tr. 1029.

busy in recent years in reasserting the principle that Parliament alone can impose taxation, and the executive must not do so without precise authorisation ; [1] that interference with liberty must be strictly justified by law, and is not to be excused merely because the person affected might be treated by the Crown as an enemy, though it has not done so ; [2] or because, under earlier regulations made inoperative by the creation of the Irish Free State, arrest and deportation of an alleged revolutionary would have been legal.[3]

It rests with the courts to define and by doing so limit the prerogative power of the Crown, a term the extent of which has been a subject of some discussion in recent years. The current view, that the power of the Crown to deal as it thought fit with the property of alien enemies within British territory was a prerogative power, was questioned by Warrington, J., in the case of the *Tsar of Bulgaria's* [4] property, which the Crown proposed to treat as confiscated ; he suggested that prerogative applied only to British subjects. There was no possible justification in the use of the term for this narrow view. Prerogative is essentially the power which is appropriate to the King as opposed to his subjects and dealings as sovereign with his enemies. It has since been held that the right of angary, the taking or destruction in case of war of enemy property, is a prerogative right,[5] and general usage agrees. The power of the courts to deal with such rights was shown in a remarkable manner in the case of *The Zamora*,[6] which raised the question whether the prerogative was limited

---

[1] *Newcastle Breweries, Ltd.* v. *R.*, [1920] 1 K.B. 854.

[2] *Johnstone* v. *Pedlar*, [1921] 2 A.C. 162.

[3] *Home Secretary* v. *O'Brien*, [1923] A.C. 603.

[4] [1921] 1 Ch. 107.

[5] *Commercial and Estates Co. of Egypt* v. *Board of Trade*, [1925] 1 K.B. 271.

[6] [1916] 2 A.C. 77, 95, 96, overruling *The Fox* (1811), 1 Edw. 312-14.

by international law, or whether in violation of international law the King could by Order in Council lay down rules binding the court. That had been formerly ruled to be possible by no less an authority than Lord Stowell himself, and Professor Holland had accepted that view. But it was negatived by the Privy Council on appeal.

In *Attorney-General* v. *De Keyser's Royal Hotel*[1] the courts established definitely a very important principle regarding the royal power in time of war over the property of subjects. The matter at issue was the requisitioning of a hotel to accommodate the personnel of the headquarters of the Royal Air Force as it then existed, and the demand of the owners for compensation, which was declared not to be due as of right on the score of the existence of a prerogative to take possession of any subject's property for the defence of the realm in time of war. It was, however, provided by the Defence Act, 1842, that land might be taken for defence purposes, but on compensation being made. The power to take possession of land was also given by a regulation under the Defence of the Realm Consolidation Act, 1914. The House of Lords held that the prerogative had been superseded in this case by the statute of 1842, from which as regards compensation no derogation was made by the regulation, and that accordingly compensation must be paid as under the Act. The essence of the position, therefore, was that the power of Parliament was supreme, and, if it thought fit to regulate a subject-matter in a manner which seemed clearly to exclude the use of the prerogative power, effect must be given to its will. Though there remain difficult questions as to when the statute substitutes its provisions for prerogative, they did not arise in that case, which well illustrates the determination of the Lords to put strict adherence to law above

[1] [1920] A.C. 508.

the specious suggestion that the state of war fully justified reliance on the prerogative. It may be added that the old authorities did not really support strongly the contention that no compensation was due, there was obviously a very great difference between merely entering on land and fortifying it or otherwise using it in war, and taking possession of a large and profitable hotel.

The courts have also determined what statutes must be deemed to be intended to bind the Crown. The principle enunciated in 1891 [1] is that the Crown can be deprived of an existing prerogative or interest only by express terms or by necessary implication. But what necessary implication is may be disputed ; on one view, if an Act be made for the public good, for the advancement of religion and justice, and to prevent wrong and injury, then it must bind the Crown. It was held in the *De Keyser's Royal Hotel Case* that this principle might be adduced to strengthen the view that the prerogative was bound, and in *Attorney-General of Duchy of Lancaster* v. *Moresby* [2] it was ruled that tenants of the Crown ought to be given relief from compliance with covenants which was granted to ordinary tenants. More surprising was the decision in 1923 that the royal prerogative of payment in priority to ordinary creditors had been taken away from the Crown in respect of claims against companies.[3] The conclusion was based on the fact that, while certain Crown debts were given priority, nothing was said of the others. It may be doubted if the framers of the Companies (Consolidation) Act, 1908, had the slightest intention of thus taking away the general rule of priority of Crown debts, but at any rate the Lords held that they had. On the other hand, it is clear that it was rightly held in *The Mogileff (No. 2)* [4] that the general

---

[1] *Perry* v. *Eames* (1891), 60 L.J. Ch. 345.

[2] [1919] W.N. 69.

[3] *Food Controller* v. *Cork*, [1923] A.C. 647.

[4] [1922] P. 122.

principle that the Crown could not be sued without its
permission forbade the suggestion that it could be brought
under jurisdiction on an interpleader issue.

The courts have also the power and duty to decide
in any case of delegated legislative power the question
whether there is legal authority for the delegation. The
Great War and the passing of the Defence of the Realm
Acts, with the wide right of making regulations for securing
the public safety and the defence of the realm, rendered
it incumbent on the courts to declare their considered
opinion on the validity of delegations. The judicial view
was, while allowing wide scope to the power, to refuse to
admit its validity in the case of regulations which could not
reasonably be deemed to contribute to either the public
safety or defence. Thus it was ruled in *Chester* v. *Bateson* [1]
that a regulation forbidding any person from taking proceedings to recover possession of dwellings, where munition
workers were living, without the consent of the Minister
of Munitions was *ultra vires*. The ground was, of course,
that access to the courts was a right which could not
lightly be denied, but it must be admitted that the decision
has often been criticised. So also as regards the decision
in *Newcastle Breweries* v. *R.*,[2] where the regulation attacked
was one which prescribed that on being requisitioned compensation was to be assessed in respect of rum by a Royal
Commission on a certain basis, which involved a fair price.
But the matter was complicated by the fact that, in accordance with earlier legislation, the Act of 1914 amending the
Army Act expressly provided at length for the payment
for articles requisitioned at the market price. The same
doctrine that the legislature did not contemplate regulations not giving fair compensation for goods taken was
reasserted in *Central Control Board* v. *Cannon Brewery, Ltd.*[3]

[1] [1920] 1 K.B. 829.   [2] [1920] 1 K.B. 854.   [3] [1919] A.C. 744.

On the other hand, when the Restoration of Order in Ireland Act, 1920, was passed, it gave regulations made under it the same force as if enacted in the Act, and in *Brady's Case*,[1] Lawrence, L.C.J., held that a regulation empowering the Home Secretary to intern persons suspected of acting in a manner prejudicial to the restoration of order in Ireland must be given full effect according to its terms, despite the objection to the subject being thus deprived of access to the courts. The decision again has not gone without question, but no later decision on the issue became necessary.

The courts have, of course, the duty to decide, where delegated legislation is allowed and the delegation is valid, whether any acts impugned fall legitimately within the terms of the delegation. In *China Mutual Steam Navigation Co.* v. *Maclay* [2] the court held that a power to requisition shipping was not a power to requisition the services of the owners and their staff to earn profits for the Government by running the ships requisitioned. But, when it was provided that the Shipping Controller could give directions regarding the employment of ships and could prohibit any British ship going to sea without a licence, it was properly ruled that it was impossible to claim that any particular orders of the Controller was invalid on the ground that it could not reasonably be said to further the safety of the public or the defence of the realm.[3] The principle to be followed was that, if the regulation was a legal exercise of power, a particular application could not be questioned. In like manner it was ruled in *Sheffield Conservative Club* v. *Brighten* [4] that, when a regulation authorising the taking of land was valid, then no landowner could challenge the

taking of his land on the ground that it was not necessary
for the public safety. It is assumed, of course, that in
so taking the land the executive was acting in good faith,
and not for some unreasonable purpose. The courts in
effect cannot undertake to control the discretion of the
executive acting within the ambit of its authority ; it can
define that ambit, it can declare illegal acts done without
it, but it cannot attempt to discriminate as regards acts
which fall fairly within it. So in the case of Palestine the
Privy Council [1] ruled that the courts there could decide if
any action of the executive was outwith the powers of the
mandate, but not that they could decide in what manner
in detail the Crown should use the powers of the mandate.
Other instances of the powers of the courts to save the
subject from restrictions on personal liberty and from unjust
taxation are noted elsewhere, as well as the special position
of the courts towards the actions of courts-martial under
the Army and Air Force Acts and the Naval Discipline
Acts, and in the time of martial law.

In addition to control over executive and legislative
acts of the executive, the courts can control their judicial
or quasi-judicial acts. For this purpose they can use the
prerogative writs, now orders,[2] of *mandamus, certiorari,*
and prohibition.

Mandamus is an order to a body acting judicially or
quasi-judicially, but its exercise against the Crown or
ministers representing the Crown is very limited. The
theory of the writ is that it may be issued against individual
officers in respect of duties which are owed by them to the
subject as distinct from that which they owe to the Crown,
but that it will not issue against the Crown. In *R.* v.

---

[1] *Jerusalem and Jaffa District Governor* v. *Suleiman Murra*, [1926] A.C. 321.
[2] See Administration of Justice (Miscellaneous Provisions) Act, 1938 (1 &
2 Geo. VI. c. 63), s. 7.

Commissioners of Customs [1] it was said that the goods were in the possession of officers of the Crown ; a *mandamus* would be a *mandamus* to the Crown which the court could not grant, and in *R.* v. *Lords Commissioners of the Treasury,*[2] Cockburn, L.C.J., insisted that " this court cannot claim even in appearance to have any power to command the Crown ". The same doctrine was applied by Lord Esher, M.R., to the case of the Secretary of State for War, though the point was also stressed that in the matter at issue there was no question of any duty owed by that officer to a subject as opposed to his duty towards the Crown.[3] It has, however, been issued to call on the Board of Education to determine certain issues regarding the legal liabilities of local education authorities towards managers of schools, which the Board had purported to decide but which it had not dealt with effectively.[4] In any case the writ will not be issued if there is an effective remedy, *e.g.* an action in tort against the officer in default available, nor if the duty in question is one in which there is a discretion.

The writ of *prohibition* is used to forbid a body acting judicially to proceed in excess of its jurisdiction or in contradiction of the law. Its use according to Brett, L.J., cited in the leading case of *R.* v. *Electricity Commissioners,*[5] is proper whenever the legislature entrusts to any body of persons other than the superior courts the power of imposing an obligation upon individuals, if those persons admittedly attempt to exercise powers beyond those given to them, by Act of Parliament. In that case the commissioners had powers to make, after local enquiries, an

---

[1] (1836), 5 A. & E. 380.   [2] (1872), L.R. 7 Q.B. 387.

[3] *R.* v. *Secretary of State for War*, [1891] 2 Q.B. 326.

[4] *Board of Education* v. *Rice*, [1911] A.C. 179.

[5] [1924] 1 K.B. 171, citing *R.* v. *Local Government Board* (1882), 10 Q.B.D. 309, 321.

order for incorporation of joint electricity authorities. They thus had to affect the rights of existing companies, and the writ of prohibition was invoked against the scheme formulated by the commissioners, before it had been made the basis of an order by the commissioners. It was ruled that the remedy was available. The decision further was given that, while the Act provided that an order if confirmed by the Minister of Transport was to have effect as if enacted in the Act, that fact did not prevent prohibition being used before the order was made and confirmed. The argument that Parliament should be left to deal with the taking effect of the order as contemplated by the Act was rejected. Prohibition has also been issued to the Light Railway Commissioners and the Comptroller-General of Patents, but, when the Attorney-General used to hear appeals in patent cases, prohibition was refused to him ; [1] the duty has now been taken from him. Nor was it granted to an inspector of the Board of Trade in respect of his examination of the affairs of a company merely for the purpose of a report to the Board which alone could take action. The remedy was used under the Housing Act of 1925 to forbid consideration of an imperfect scheme by the Minister of Health,[2] but it was doubted in *Yaffe's Case* [3] whether the procedure was appropriate or whether it was not better to proceed by *certiorari* after the scheme was confirmed. The procedure has now been altered, so that neither remedy is used.

Prohibition lies of course to income tax commissioners and to assessment committees. But it cannot issue against martial law tribunals,[4] for these are not courts of law nor

---

[1] *Van Gelder's Patent, In re* (1888), 6 R.P.C. 22. For the appeal tribunal, one judge, see 22 & 23 Geo. V. c. 32, s. 12.

[2] *R. v. Minister of Health* ; *Davis, Ex parte*, [1929] 1 K.B. 619.

[3] [1931] A.C. 494.

[4] *Clifford and O'Sullivan, In re*, [1921] 2 A.C. 570.

are they charged with judicial functions in the legal sense of the term.

Certiorari is a remedy not limited to judicial acts or orders in a strict sense, but to acts or orders of a competent authority which has power to impose a liability or to give a decision which determines the rights of property of the persons affected. But this view of Lord Parmoor [1] must not be pressed too far ; there must be more than a mere administrative order in question. The writ has been allowed against the Board of Education, where it had failed to deal properly with the determination incumbent on it of the rights of a local education authority and school managers.[2] It was granted also against the Local Government Board in respect of an appeal against a closing order, but it must be noted that the point that the remedy was incompetent was not raised. It can be used against an auditor or the Minister of Transport.[3]

The position is different when a body with full legislative powers is in question. It has been held that neither prohibition nor *certiorari* lies to the Church Assembly nor to its Legislative Committee.[4] These bodies do not exercise judicial functions in any sense. Nor again does either remedy apply where the making of a provisional order by a Government department is to be confirmed in due course by an Act.[5] The grounds for this view are various ; essentially the doctrine is that the judiciary has no right to dictate to the legislature what legislation it will pass. Nor, it has been ruled, will the court prohibit action to carry a private Bill through Parliament, even if this action is

---

[1] *Local Government Board* v. *Arlidge*, [1915] A.C. 120, 140.

[2] *Board of Education* v. *Rice*, [1911] A.C. 179.

[3] *Roberts* v. *Cunningham* (1926), 42 T.L.R. 162 ; *R.* v. *Minister of Transport; Upminster Services, Ex parte* (1933), 50 T.L.R. 60 ; [1934] 1 K.B. 277.

[4] *R.* v. *Legislative Committee of Church Assembly*, [1928] 1 K.B. 411.

[5] *R.* v. *Hastings Local Board* (1865), 6 B. & S. 401.

in breach of an undertaking given to the court.[1]

The question has recently been raised [2] whether the standards of judicial activity are sufficiently in harmony with modern movements. Lawyers, it is argued, are educated in the atmosphere of the duty of protection of property and the maintenance of the existing social system under which the country has so long flourished that they cannot contemplate the possibility that it requires radical transformation, which indeed is long overdue. English lawyers would look askance at the idea of any student of legal theory such as Professor Dicey or Sir F. Pollock being raised to the judicial bench, and they have ceased to attempt to make any original contributions to jurisprudence. There is no doubt truth in the last contention ; what has been written by English lawyers is confined to treatises on the existing law, and breadth of view is sadly lacking.

It is claimed that in many fields of law the defects of British legal decisions are patently due to this devotion to the existing law as shown by precedents, and a failure to give effect to new legislation is asserted, and ascribed to the fact that all change in law by Parliament is approached from the point of view that it must be assumed that the legislature does not really intend to overturn established doctrines, so that it is legitimate to limit the effect of its legislation on that assumption. Thus the famous decision in the *Taff Vale Case*,[3] asserting the liability of trade unions for the torts of their agents, is held to be against the plain words of the statute. This, however, is dubious ; the words of the Act are really not free from ambiguity,[4] and there is no proof that Parliament contemplated such a state of affairs as then arose. The wide character of the

[1] *Att.-Gen.* v. *Manchester, etc., Railway* (1838), 1 R. & C. Cases, 436.
[2] H. J. Laski, *Parl. Govt.* pp. 362 ff.
[3] [1901] A.C. 426.
[4] Cf. Asquith, cited by Spender, *Great Britain*, pp. 774 f.

immunity which was given by the subsequent Act of 1906 Chapter XXII. cannot be said to be patently in the public interest. Trade unions, as the General Strike of 1926 showed, can fail in duty to the public weal. In the *Osborne Case* [1] it is hardly fair to speak of the profound bias of the judges against the paid representation of the trade unions in the Commons. There are serious objections to the doctrine that a member of Parliament should be the paid servant of a single interest in his constituency, unable to vote freely or as the best interests of the people demand, on pain of losing his means of livelihood. It is no doubt equally objectionable that other interests should similarly command the services of members, but it was certainly not wrong for the judges to put upon Parliament the duty of dealing with the issue and of providing pay for all members. In *Roberts* v. *Hopwood* [2] the decision of the House of Lords was not really one based on what they, as distinguished from the local authority in question, thought proper to pay to working men. The Lords were bound to intervene to prevent a majority on a local authority imposing an unfair burden on the rates paid by very many poor taxpayers by giving one set of working men favours not enjoyed by others. Nor is it relevant to suggest that they would not have ruled excessive the salary of the County Clerk of Lancashire ; they cannot act except on the initiative of some litigant. If Parliament wishes to take away property without compensation, it is quite easy for that to be made clear, and it becomes then possible to criticise the courts for hampering the operation of the Housing Acts by adhering to the doctrine that legislation should be construed as far as possible to avoid injustice of this sort. [3]

---

[1] [1910] A.C. 87.　　　　　[2] [1925] A.C. 578.

[3] The decision in *R. W. Paul, Ltd.*, v. *Wheat Commission*, [1937] A.C. 139, seems eminently fair.

But the truth is that the legislation would not have been passed if compensation had been denied.   There is nothing more obvious in the present temper of the British electorate than that frank confiscatory proposals would secure the defeat of the great majority of those Parliamentary candidates who put them forward.   It is the result of the diffusion of property among the people which in the crisis of 1931 made the hint that, if Labour were given power, the Post Office savings would be endangered one of extremely disastrous consequences to the Labour cause.   The decision of the Lords in *Yaffe's Case* [1] that the jurisdiction of the courts to prevent excess of action on the part of ministerial authorities was not excluded by anything in the legislation in question was the obvious mode of interpretation, just as in *R. W. Paul, Ltd.*, v. *Wheat Commission* [2] the Lords held that the usual rules as to the power of an arbitrator were not excluded from operation by the terms of the Wheat Act, 1932.   It would be indeed to be regretted if Parliament were to be allowed to pass statutes seemingly innocuous and the judges were to interpret them to deprive the subject of rights which he assumes to be his.   The Committee on Ministers' Powers [3] demanded with energy not merely the maintenance of the supervisory power of the courts, but also the right to bring an appeal from judicial decisions by the executive on points of law.

There is much more justification in the criticism of the manner in which judges show extreme tenderness to the various devices which the genius of Lincoln's Inn excogitates to defeat the legitimate efforts of the legislature to increase taxation on the very wealthy.   The decision in *Inland Revenue Commissioners* v. *Duke of Westminster* [4] and many other cases falls below any reasonable standard of inter-

[1] [1931] A.C. 494.
[2] [1937] A.C. 139.
[3] *Parl. Pap.* Cmd. 4060, p. 117.
[4] [1936] A.C. 1.

pretation of statute ; this attitude is no doubt a legacy
from old times, when there was general agreement to regard
taxation not as a proper payment for the benefits conferred
by the State, but as an unjust extraction of funds from
oppressed taxpayers. It can no doubt be supported on
precedent, but the time has long come when by statute
the presumption against the claims of the revenue should
be abolished. Unhappily Parliament shows itself under
normal conditions distinctly reluctant to strike at owners
of great wealth, from whom, it must be remembered, the
funds of one great political party now in power are in large
measure derived.

On the other hand, it is hardly fair to suggest that the
judgment of Astbury, J., in the matter of the General
Strike was either untimely or unsound.[1] His view is no
doubt open to criticism, but it is very far from clear that
that criticism is tenable, and there is no doubt that the
effort to treat that strike as a venial if not laudable action
is unwise. The refusal of the Trades Union Congress to
use its industrial power in 1938–9 to compel the ministry
to alter its political policy is a proof that the failure of the
strike has not been forgotten as a warning of the limited
scope of the right to withhold labour. Much more serious
is the suggestion that the judges are so prejudiced against
Communists that they are not always able to give them
a fair trial, and that they have acted unfairly in permitting
prolonged mass trials arising out of social or political
disturbances, as a result of which the juries are unable
to determine fairly the weight of evidence against any
particular individual or to remember the bearing of the
accumulation of detailed testimony on which they are
asked to pass judgment. The idea that in *Elias* v. *Pasmore*[2]
dangerous latitude was given by the dicta at least of

[1] Laski, p. 371.   [2] [1934] 2 K.B. 164.

Horridge, J., to police action seems of very dubious value ;
no doubt, where law is harsh, an unfair reliance on techni-
calities to escape its operation must be encouraged by the
courts, but in modern conditions the proper *modus operandi*
is to obtain changes of law if that is possible rather than
to seek to evade substantial justice by formalism. The
issue of the attitude of the courts to the freedom of the
subject is dealt with elsewhere, but on the whole it must
be said that the decision of the House of Lords in *R.* v.
Halliday [1] can hardly be called in question. The existence
of war does, and must, vitally alter conditions, and the
safety of the State remains a primary consideration, in
view of which the mere internment of aliens or subjects
has to be accepted at times as an unavoidable evil.

There is really no parallel to be drawn between the
attitude of British judges and that of the Supreme Court
of the United States to certain aspects of President Roosevelt's New Deal. The position assigned by the Constitution
of the United States places on the judges of that court
obligations of excessive weight and difficulty. The British
remedy for any narrowness of interpretation by the judges
is legislation ; if it is passed, there is no reason whatever
to suppose that the judges will not give it effect. But is
it any part of their duty to adopt a social philosophy,
which has not yet been affirmed by the legislature, and to
go in advance of the general feeling of the public ? The
answer seems clearly to be in the negative.

3. *Characteristics of English Judicial Procedure*

(i) Judicial Tenure and Independence

The vital change by which the Act of Settlement, 1701,
exempted the judges from subjection to the will of the

---

[1] [1917] A.C. 260 (*Zadig's Case*).

Crown is maintained under the rules that judges are ap- pointed during good behaviour and can only be removed by the Crown for misconduct, or on addresses from both houses of Parliament.[1] The possibility of either procedure being necessary under modern judicial standards is small ; the only recent judge who excited serious discussion in Parliament was Mr. Justice Grantham, whose offences were committed regarding the trial of election petitions which were entrusted by Parliament in 1868 to two judges. The rather obvious partisanship of the judge was, however, regarded as not of sufficient importance to justify the ministry giving facilities for the pronouncement of censure or for a motion for an address. On the whole, this impartiality as between political parties must be regarded as remarkable as well as most satisfactory, for judges on the whole are recruited from politicians who have served with distinction as members of the Commons and who receive judicial preferment as the reward of such services.

The appointment of puisne judges is made by the Crown on the recommendation of the Lord Chancellor acting in his dual capacity as a lawyer and a politician, though no doubt he informs the Prime Minister of his selections ; Lord Brougham seems to have secured royal assent before informing his chief. The other judges are selected by the Prime Minister for royal approval. No doubt he consults the Lord Chancellor, but the latter has no veto, though on occasion, as in the case of Sir L. Walton,[2] his influence is used to prevent the elevation to a high office of a law officer not deemed by the Chancellor of sufficient calibre. Normally, however, the claims of the Attorney-General are regarded as definitely justified, unless he prefers to remain in the field of politics, and to seek, if he does retire from the Commons, the woolsack. It is

[1] 15 & 16 Geo. V. c. 49, s. 12 (1).   [2] Fitzroy, *Memoirs*, i. 315.

true that, after the passing of the Judicature Act, 1873,
it was announced that it was no longer intended to maintain the position of the normal claim of the Attorney-
General, but Mr. Gladstone showed, in his attitude to
Sir H. James,[1] that he regarded his right to preferment
as beyond question, and he actually offered him the
Mastership of the Rolls, which was suited rather to a
member of the chancery Bar or a chancery judge.   The
rule of promotion has been regularly observed and is taken
for granted.   The choice of the Lord Chancellor is that of
the Prime Minister, and normally he is chosen for political
services coupled with some legal capacity.   Lord Birkenhead surprised his supporters by exhibiting in his judicial
capacity considerably greater powers than had been generally ascribed to him.   On the other hand, the appointment
of Lord Maugham was unexpected, for he had not been
politically active.   After appointment, however, he developed a marked political activity in defence of the Prime
Minister's repudiation of the binding character of the
League of Nations Covenant which was hardly expected
in a judge.   It is indeed plain that the position of the Lord
Chancellor is abnormal, and not wholly to be commended.

The independence of judges is secured in part by the
grant of substantial salaries, £5000 for puisne judges and
Lords Justices, £6000 for Lords of Appeal in Ordinary
and Master of the Rolls, £8000 for the Lord Chief Justice,
and £10,000, of which £4000 is in respect of his services
as Speaker in the House of Lords, for the Lord Chancellor ;
the President of the Probate, Divorce, and Admiralty
Division rather anomalously receives only £5000.   There
is no age limit, but a retiring allowance of £3500 affords
little excuse for judges to remain in office after physical
defects and mental decline render their presence there

[1] Askwith, *Lord James*, pp. 105 ff.

oppressive to litigants and counsel. The failure of Parliament to enact a retiring age has been due in part to
the amazing vitality of such men as Lord Halsbury, but
it is not justified in the case of the average judge, and a
retiring age of seventy-two is clearly demanded ; in the
Dominions, where possible, retirement at a fixed age is
compulsory.

Judicial independence is also furthered by the fact that
there is little promotion of judges, certainly not enough to
render any judge willing to impair his reputation for independence in order to secure the approval of the ministry
of the day in the hope of preferment. It is, it may be
added, more common in the case of chancery judges than
of common law judges, and the former have few opportunities, even if they were willing to take them, of acting
in a manner to gratify administrations. Nor, it is fair to
say, are Governments anxious to weaken the reputation
of the Bench for impartiality, though of course a Labour
Government will be expected to secure that a judge of
Labour views shall be appointed, when it is in office, as
in the case of Slesser, L.J.[1] So also Lord Sankey owed his
position as Lord Chancellor (1929–31) to his readiness to
work with a Labour ministry and the evidence he had
given of sympathy [2] with Labour views when serving on
the commission on the coal industry in 1919.

A further security for the integrity of the administration of justice is the rule of publicity, which normally
requires that all proceedings of importance in the working
of criminal and civil justice shall be held in open court,
and that only subsidiary matters of no interest to the
public shall be conducted in private. This was declared

---

[1] He supported the view that the General Strike was legal : Clynes,
Memoirs, ii. 84 f.

[2] His recommendations were plainly unsound and were rejected.

with emphasis in a case in which the court had treated as
a contempt the action of a party to a case in circulating to
persons interested details of proceedings for nullity of
marriage,[1] but the House of Lords found the procedure
irregular and improper. Secrecy of proceedings is permitted only where publicity would defeat the ends of
justice, as for instance where in trials for treason or treason
felony or breach of the Official Secrets Acts it is necessary
to reveal matters which it would be plainly contrary to
the public interest to divulge, and whose revelation would
defeat the end of the prosecution. Again in certain proceedings in domestic causes and lunacy matters, the court
may feel that secrecy is essential if the true facts are to
be elicited. But in general secrecy is illegitimate, and in
the same spirit the Judicial Committee of the Privy Council
disapproved of the action taken in a provincial court in
Canada where a divorce case was heard in a room marked
" private " out of the desire to avoid undue publicity.[2]
It is a different thing when it is a question of publication
of details of an intimate kind likely to deprave the morals
of youth, and in any case serving merely to gratify lower
instincts, and hence the press itself, whose more reputable
representatives suffered from the competition of newspapers of less scrupulous character, was influential in securing the prevention [3] of publication of details in divorce,
nullity, and other proceedings. Similarly steps were taken
in erecting children's courts to restrict publicity to the
minimum,[4] and a like principle has been followed regarding
publication of proceedings of courts dealing with domestic
relations.[5] Even in these cases there has been some criti-

---

[1] *Scott* v. *Scott*, [1913] A.C. 417.
[2] *McPherson* v. *McPherson*, [1936] A.C. 177.
[3] 16 & 17 Geo. V. c. 61.
[4] 23 & 24 Geo. V. c. 12, ss. 37, 47 (2).
[5] See p. 301, *ante* ; 1 Edw. VIII. & 1 Geo. VI. c. 58.

cism of secrecy, and there is wide agreement that all suppression of publication demands careful justification.

Similar questions arose regarding the suppression of names in cases of prosecutions for blackmail, and judges as a rule simply content themselves with indicating the view that names of prosecutors should not be published. It is obviously still more objectionable that the names of persons accused of contravention of motoring regulations should be suppressed, and the fact that this happened in the case of the wife of a metropolitan magistrate evoked unfavourable comment from the legal profession and press no less than from the public. Again, in cases where there is held a preliminary enquiry to decide whether a prosecution should be proceeded with, though publicity is not legally required, it is normally observed and desirable. It is clearly not enough that justice should be done ; it is important that it should be seen to be done, and any secrecy at once creates the rumour, normally quite wide of the mark, that things are being hushed up. That such an impression is unreasonable does not alter the public feeling, and no doubt if the practice were to spread there would be the necessity of legislating to negative proceedings being held except in open court.[1]

On the other hand, the immunity of judges from legal attack for actions done in the carrying out of their duties has been affirmed. The immunity from proceedings, civil or criminal alike, is justified in 1868 in the case of *Scott* v. *Stansfield*,[2] where the position of a county court judge was concerned, on the ground that the privilege was not one for the protection of a corrupt or malicious judge, but

[1] Cf. the Home Secretary's general disapproval of secrecy as to names of complainants save in blackmail cases, and of trials under an alias : March 9, 1939.

[2] (1868), L.R. 3 Exch. 220. Cf. *Fray* v. *Blackburn* (1863), 3 B. & S. 576, 578 ; *Kemp* v. *Neville* (1861), 16 C.B. (N.S.) 523.

for the benefit of the public, whose interest it was that
judges should be at liberty to exercise their functions with
independence and without fear of consequences.   This
applies to whatever they say in judicial proceedings, however irrelevant to the proceedings before them.   The
Court of Appeal in 1895,[1] in accord with an earlier ruling
of the Privy Council,[2] laid it down that " no action lies
for acts done or words spoken by a judge in the exercise
of his judicial office although his motive is malicious and
the acts or words are not done or spoken in the honest
exercise of his office ".   Further, it appears clear that a
judge of the Supreme Court will be deemed to be acting
in the exercise of his office, even if he is actually exceeding
his jurisdiction.

This immunity has been extended to judges of inferior
courts, including coroners and courts-martial,[3] but in their
case it seems that the immunity does not apply to these
judges if they are acting outside the limits of their jurisdiction.[4]   It seems, however, that even in such a case the
judge will enjoy immunity if his action was induced by
his belief in the existence of facts which would have, if
true, given him jurisdiction, though in fact these facts
were not real.   In the case of justices of the peace, their
immunity when acting within their jurisdiction in un-
qualified,[5] but even in respect of their non-judicial acts
they enjoy a qualified and limited protection by the
Justices' Protection Act, 1848.   This position is justified,
it is held, by the onerous character of the judicial functions
of such justices, and the fact that they act gratuitously
in the public interest.

[1] *Anderson* v. *Gorrie*, [1895], 1 Q.B. 668.
[2] *Haggard* v. *Pelicier Frères*, [1892] A.C. 61, 68.
[3] *Dawkins* v. *Lord Rokeby* (1873), L.R. 8 Q.B. 255.
[4] *Houlden* v. *Smith* (1850), 14 Q.B. at p. 851 *per* Patteson, J.
[5] *Law* v. *Llewellyn*, [1906] 1 K.B. 487.

(ii) Contempt of Court

Judges are further protected from criticism by the law of contempt of court. It is obvious that the power to commit to prison or fine on this score is necessary to prevent the occurrence of such incidents as the throwing of missiles at judges or attempts to assault them. A court must have power to punish those who brawl therein, or seek to interrupt the proceedings, or to intimidate witnesses, or parties, or counsel, or the court itself. Moreover it must act *proprio motu* and without delay, if its jurisdiction is to be effective. The matter is different when the question is whether some publication tends to impede the due course of justice. Here it is plain that the publication may be obviously improper in that it may affect the minds of the jury or the witnesses and prevent their carrying out their functions in proper manner. The exercise of the power of the court summarily to intervene in such cases cannot well be denied, even if the cases raised are often somewhat thin,[1] and sometimes are possibly inspired by a desire to secure sympathy for accused persons and so indirectly to influence juries in their favour.

There is much greater difficulty regarding the use of the power of the courts in respect of comments on judges and their conduct of cases. It is frankly not undesirable that the press should be free to criticise the views of judges,[2] and, so long as they do not impute any corrupt motive or malice, it seems undesirable that they should run the risk of action taken by the judges themselves without the protection to innocence presented by the safe-

[1] *R.* v. *Lawson ; Nodder, Ex parte* (1937), 81 S.J. 280 ; *R.* v. *Fitzhugh ; Livingston, Ex parte* (1937), 81 S.J. 258 ; *Application of de Reding, In re, The Times,* June 14, 1939.

[2] *E.g.* Mr. Justice Grantham's prejudice in deciding electoral petitions ; Yarmouth Election Petition, May 4, 1906, and the remarks of Mr. Asquith ; Feb. 8, 1911 ; 21 *H.C. Deb.* 5 s. 291.

guard of a jury trial. The power to publish might easily
be misused with a view to prevent honest criticism of the
acts of judges.[1] It has so been used in the colonies, where
judges have resented comments on their different modes
of dealing with criminals whose actions are looked at in
different lights by public opinion.[2] In their case the Privy
Council has asserted the right of honest criticism, and it
may be that such a right will never be denied in English
courts. Yet it does seem desirable that, where judges
deem themselves improperly attacked, the prosecution
should be undertaken by the Crown and the trial should
be by jury and not before the parties affected. The rule
that no man should be judge in his own cause is sound,
and need not be restricted to civil proceedings. It is, on
the whole, better that criticism should be free than that
judges should be too jealously protected from comment.
There is no perfection of wisdom even on the judicial bench,
and resentment of foolish extra-judicial utterances is only
increased when it is found that they cannot without risk
be made the subject of any reference in the press. It must
be remembered that under the rules of the Commons
judicial conduct cannot be attacked except on a formal
motion, which means that the conduct of the superior
judges is virtually never commented upon seriously in the
Commons.

(iii) The Jury System

An essential characteristic of English judicial procedure
is the free use of juries to elucidate facts. In the case of
criminal proceedings the system has remained unaltered
except in one important aspect. The functions of grand
juries throughout the nineteenth century was to approve

[1] *R.* v. *New Statesman*; *New Statesman*, Feb. 18, 1928, H. J. Laski,
Parl. Govt. pp. 368 f.

[2] *McLeod* v. *St. Aubyn*, [1899] A.C. 549 ; *Ambard* v. *Att.-Gen. of Trinidad*,
[1936] A.C. 322.

or to reject accusations brought before them by finding a true bill of indictment or ignoring it. They could accept such indictments from private individuals as well as from justices, and to some extent this power on the part of individuals was abused, for which a remedy was found by statutory restriction of action on the part of private individuals. But the services of the grand jury were approved by many judges, and at times by ignoring a bill they saved innocent accused much hardship. The objection, however, was naturally taken that the grand jury involved a waste of time and duplication of work, for before them sufficient cause had to be adduced to justify them in finding a true bill. The experience of the war period was thought to show that they were unnecessary, and in 1925 it was provided that they need not be summoned to quarter-sessions if all the prisoners pleaded guilty. In 1933,[1] despite much judicial dissent, the drastic step was taken of abolishing their use, not only at quarter-sessions but also at assizes, with negligible exceptions for the cases of treasons committed overseas, oppressions of governors, and breaches of the Official Secrets Acts. The result therefore is that indictments are preferred before petty juries only if the prisoner has been committed for trial by justices or the coroner, or if permission is given by a judge,[2] or pursuant to the order of a judicial officer under the Perjury Act, 1911. The change has not gone without criticism, but it has saved individuals, who were formerly liable to summons in the capacity of grand jurors, some trouble ; on the other hand, the opportunity of addressing the grand jury and making remarks on criminal issues generally has disappeared, to the regret of some experienced judges.

[1] 23 & 24 Geo. V. c. 36, s. 1.
[2] *R.* v. *Rothfield* (1937), 26 Cr. App. R. 103.

The civil jury has suffered the same fate of restriction in use. In 1933 [1] it was provided that, instead of the old system under which in a common law action a party had normally the right to demand a jury, a jury is granted only on application, as a rule, where the case is one of libel, slander, malicious prosecution, false imprisonment, seduction, breach of promise of marriage, and in other actions, including running-down cases, if a charge of fraud is made against a party and he claims a jury. But in these cases a judge may none the less decline to allow a jury, if the trial requires any prolonged examination of documents or accounts or any scientific or local investigation which cannot conveniently be made with a jury. In all other cases the discretion of the judge is unrestricted, and different questions of fact in the same case may be dealt with in different ways. It may be doubted if this innovation is wholly for the best. It must be remembered that litigants are usually far more satisfied with decisions of juries than a decision of a single judge, and that, even if it is probable that a judge is more competent than a jury — and in many cases there is nothing in a judicial life or training to give any certainty on this score — nevertheless the fact that a jury decision will be more welcome to public opinion should be given weight. In the Dominions, where there have been relaxations in the use of juries, experience shows that appeals from judges are more numerous, as a rule, than appeals from jury decisions, and that the latter are regarded as more satisfactory than the former.

In the Dominions,[2] as always in Scotland, majority verdicts of juries are sometimes accepted under conditions provided by law. In England this has not yet been adopted as a principle. It is true that accord is clearly often arti-

---

[1] 23 & 24 Geo. V. c. 36, s. 6.
[2] Keith, *The Dominions as Sovereign States*, pp. 572-5.

ficial,[1] and that it means that doubters have been induced to agree to the majority by the force of personality of one or more of the majority, but in criminal causes the requirement is of service to the prisoner, for, if the jury cannot in a reasonable time achieve agreement, a new trial must be had, and, after a second disagreement the prosecution is in practice dropped. In civil cases the parties may agree to accept a majority verdict. The suggestion that has been made that English law should be altered to admit in criminal cases of the Scottish verdict of " not proven " is open to grave objection. Such a verdict enables a lazy or timid jury to avoid making up its mind one way or another, and leaves the accused free indeed and not liable to further trial, but under a stigma which prevents his resenting aspersions on his innocence.

4. *Other Functions of the Judiciary*

Closely connected with, but logically distinct from, the judicial functions of the judges are their authorities in regard to the management and distribution of property, as in the administration of trusts and of charities, the liquidation of companies, and proceedings in bankruptcy. So the foreclosure of mortgages and in a different field the grant of decrees of divorce, separation, nullity of marriage, restitution of conjugal rights, and so forth are not on precisely the same footing as ordinary judgments. Reference has been made above to their power to declare rights, which is not freely used ; in 1928 the proposal that the judges should give advisory opinions on certain rating matters was strongly opposed, and the idea was abandoned by the ministry.

One definite power of legislative character is that

[1] Cf. *R.* v. *Mills* (1939), 55 T.L.R. 590.

already alluded to, the making of rules of court. The
power thus to define the extent of jurisdiction to be exercised is of very remarkable importance, and it is not without difficulties, for the extension of the jurisdiction of the
High Court in contract in 1920 was so wide in terms that
much indignation was raised in Scotland, and efforts were
made to induce the Scottish courts to refuse to give effect
under the Judgments Extension Act, 1868, to the judgment thus rendered by the English court.[1] Fortunately,
this attempt failed, but the matter was adjusted by the
alteration of the rule of court, so as not to apply to a case
where the defendant is resident in Scotland.

Apart from the general rules of court, special power
exists for the making of rules for the Probate, Divorce,
and Admiralty Division of the High Court.

[1] Dicey and Keith, *Conflict of Laws* (1932), p. 250.

PART VIII
THE STATE AND THE PEOPLE

CHAPTER XXIII

ALLEGIANCE AND THE STATUS OF SUBJECTS AND ALIENS

1. *Allegiance and Nationality*

ALLEGIANCE is the personal relation which binds the sub- ject to the Crown, and by the preamble to the Statute of Westminster, 1931, it is accorded recognition as the point in which there is connection between all the subjects of the King, although they live in territories each of which has complete autonomy, so that it is no longer possible to speak of the Dominions as belonging to the United Kingdom. Allegiance in the case of British subjects is styled natural, and it can be made to cease only in definite ways; it is in no degree dependent on any profession thereof; an oath of allegiance is indeed required of a number of officials, judges, members of the defence forces, and clergymen of the Church of England, but the taking of the oath has no effect on the allegiance.

Allegiance is also due from all persons locally within the authority of the Crown. The point became of importance during the South African War, when it was discussed whether an alien who had been resident in British territory which was seized by the Boer forces, was guilty of a treasonable action in assisting these forces. It was ruled [1] that the fact of occupation made no difference; a resident alien was bound so to act that the Crown should not be harmed by reason of his admission to the privilege

---

[1] *De Jager* v. *Att.-Gen. of Natal*, [1907] A.C. 329.

341

of residence on British soil. So in the Great War it was ruled in *R.* v. *Ahlers* [1] that it was treason for an alien to take any steps in aid of his countrymen on the outbreak of war, which involved hostility to the Crown, though in that case guilt was not found to exist.

The nature of allegiance came under discussion in 1886 in the *Stepney Election Petition*,[2] for the issue there revived an old problem and solved it in a manner which was not wholly expected. It had been ruled by the judges of England [3] that when the Scottish King became also King of England, in 1603, all those who were born his subjects in Scotland after the date of his accession were *ipso facto* his English subjects. The question now arose as regards Hanover, for the accession of a woman to the throne severed the union of the two crowns then existing. It was now ruled that Hanoverians who were born there while William IV combined the thrones were British subjects, but that they ceased to be so on the accession of Queen Victoria.

A problem not yet judicially solved has presented itself from the legislation regarding Irish citizenship enacted by the Irish Free State and continued in being under the Constitution of Eire. It is the intention of that legislation to deprive the citizens of Ireland of British nationality and to give them the status of Irish nationals only throughout the world.[4] But it is not clear that the legislation is effective for this purpose, so long as for external purposes, such as the making of treaties, the King of the United Kingdom is asked to act for the State of Eire. It seems, therefore, that the citizens of Eire still owe natural allegiance to the

---

[1] [1915] 1 K.B. 616.
[2] *Isaacson* v. *Durant* (1886), 17 Q.B.D. 54.
[3] *Calvin's Case* (1608), 7 Co. Rep. 1.
[4] Keith, *Letters on Imperial Relations, 1916–35*, pp. 150-56; *Current Imperial and International Problems, 1935–6*, pp. 35 f., 47 ff.

King. No doubt it was this consideration among others which resulted in the decision of the United Kingdom and the Dominions to record their agreement after the passing of the Constitution of Eire that the Constitution was consistent with membership by Eire of the British Commonwealth of Nations. There is no doubt that Canadian nationality and Union of South Africa nationality is perfectly consistent with allegiance.

The law of nationality, as it stood in 1837, provided that birth on British territory carried with it nationality, that a person born abroad of a British father was also a British subject, and a child of a son born abroad, but in *De Geer* v. *Stone* [1] it was definitely laid down that there could be no further descent of nationality, severed from birth on British territory, and from this rule no departure was made until 1918. In 1844, however, the acquisition by aliens of British nationality, if they desired to settle in Britain, was facilitated. A more comprehensive measure, however, was enacted in 1870. [2] Under it the law stood that, after five years' residence in the United Kingdom, an alien might be granted a certificate of naturalisation. This did not necessarily involve loss of a foreign nationality, but a person naturalised could not claim British protection in his original country. The child of a naturalised father or widowed mother who lived with its parent in the United Kingdom, or with the father, if residing in the service of the Crown outside the realm, obtained naturalisation. But it was ruled that the child if over age at the time of the parent's naturalisation or if born abroad after it, did not attain British nationality. By an innovation, the wife of a British subject became a British subject, and by marriage to an alien husband a woman acquired,

---

[1] (1882). 22 Ch.D. 243. See 4 Geo. II. c. 21, s. 1 ; 13 Geo. III. c. 21.
[2] 33 & 34 Vict. c. 14.

in the view of British law, his nationality. Power was given to a foreigner who had become by birth British to divest himself of that nationality on attaining full age by a declaration of alienage ; in the Great War it was made clear that this right was not available for exercise during hostilities,[1] so as to exempt the person in question from any military service obligation incumbent on him. A British subject was given by the new Act the right to sever his allegiance by voluntarily becoming naturalised, while of full age in a foreign country ; but in *Lynch's Case* [2] in the South African War it was very properly ruled that no British subject could thus in time of war change his nationality to that of the enemy State, and that the effort to become a national thereof might be treated as treason.

The state of the law remained unaltered until 1914, when an Act, the terms of which had been fully discussed with the Dominions at the Imperial Conference of 1911, was passed. It was then desired to diminish the number of persons who lived permanently abroad but under the existing law could claim British nationality by descent, for the existence of such persons with double nationality was felt to be anomalous and objectionable. On the other hand, it was desired to eliminate a difficulty which had been found to exist in respect of persons who were living in protectorates like Southern Rhodesia, which were virtually colonies but which were still in law foreign territory, birth in which did not convey nationality.[3] The existing law would soon be ineffectual to give descendants of settlers British status. Thirdly, it was held to be desirable to get

---

[1] In the case of an enemy, see *Freyberger, Ex parte*, [1917] 2 K.B. 129 ; of a neutral, *Vecht* v. *Taylor* (1917), 116 L.T. 446 ; *Dawson* v. *Meuli* (1918), 118 L.T. 357 ; *Gschwind* v. *Huntington*, [1918] 2 K.B. 420.

[2] [1903] 1 K.B. 444.

[3] So also a citizen of Palestine is not a British subject : *R.* v. *Ketter* (1939), 55 T.L.R. 449.

rid of the anomaly by which persons naturalised in the Dominions and other oversea territories were indeed British subjects within these limits but were aliens in the United Kingdom. But two important deviations from the position thus attained were soon found to be necessary. In the first place, it proved that a number of naturalised subjects were disloyal during the war and used their British nationality as a cover for conduct injurious to the British Crown, and so it was necessary to give power to the Home Secretary to revoke, on due cause, such grants.[1] Secondly, the loyalty of oversea Britons living in such places as Argentina produced the desire to permit such people and their descendants the means of retaining indefinitely British nationality, if they really desired to do so.[2]

British nationality is normally attained by birth on British territory, with the negligible exception of children born in foreign embassies or children of enemy aliens born on British territory occupied by enemy forces. Birth on board a British ship has like effect, but not birth on a foreign ship in British territorial waters.

Children born out of British territory are normally aliens, but there are important exceptions. Thus, if the father was born on British territory, or on territory in which the Crown exercises extraterritorial jurisdiction (*e.g.* China or a British protectorate), or was a naturalised British subject, or was a British subject through annexation of territory (*e.g.* the Transvaal, Orange Free State, or Cyprus), or was a servant of the Crown and a British subject, then the child, though born abroad, is a natural-born British subject. Otherwise, if the birth of a child is registered within a year after birth at a British consulate, and if after reaching age twenty-one he makes a

---

[1] 8 & 9 Geo. V. c. 38, amending 4 & 5 Geo. V. c. 17.
[2] 12 & 13 Geo. V. c. 44.

declaration of retention of British nationality, renouncing at the same time, if the local law permits, any other nationality, he becomes confirmed as a British national.

Naturalisation is obtainable after a total of five years' residence within the eight years before application, the last year having been in the United Kingdom. The applicant must declare intention to reside in the British dominions or to serve the Crown. Knowledge of English or, in the case of Canada, French, or, in the Union of South Africa, Afrikaans, and good character are required. The Dominions and colonies and India are enabled to grant on like conditions certificates which are of validity in the whole of the Empire except Eire, which stands aloof.

The Home Secretary may include the name of any minor child of the person naturalised in his certificate, but such a child on reaching age twenty-one may make a declaration of alienage. He may also give a certificate of naturalisation at his discretion to persons of dubious nationality, and may waive conditions usually exacted in the case of women who have lost British status by marriage but desire to regain it after dissolution of marriage.

Naturalised persons have all the rights of natural-born British subjects, including the right to become Privy Councillors.[1] But a naturalised person may be deprived of nationality, if he obtained naturalisation by fraud or misrepresentation, or if he is by act or speech disloyal. In that case the Home Secretary may deprive his wife and minor children of nationality, but, if he does not, the wife may make within six months a declaration of alienage for herself and children.

The position of women was modified by the Act of 1914 to declare that wives of aliens were aliens, not as

---

[1] *R.* v. *Speyer*, [1916] 2 K.B. 858.

before subjects of their husbands' States, a matter which was outwith the scope of British law. In 1918 permission was given to a woman British by birth to resume that nationality if her husband became an alien enemy. After strong efforts by feminists to obtain complete independence of women as regards nationality, in 1933 [1] an Act was passed under which a British woman does not acquire the status of an alien, unless by marriage she obtains the nationality of her husband. This removed a serious grievance due to the United States Act of 1922, which terminated the acquisition of United States citizenship by women on marriage. Such women were unable to claim entry to America as citizens, nor could they be included in the quota of British immigrants, for they were not British. In the second place, if a woman's husband becomes an alien after marriage, she only loses her British nationality if she acquires that of her husband, and even then she can within a year make a declaration of retention of British status. Thirdly, a woman does not obtain naturalisation automatically on the naturalisation of her husband, but must signify her desire to do so within a year. Those who demand complete retention by a woman of her own nationality run counter to sound sense. It is not desirable in marriage that the spouses would have distinct loyalties, and serious inconvenience results in war-time from the presence of aliens in British homes. Much of the agitation is due to indiscriminate advocates of a meaningless equality ; applied to children the result would be chaotic and impossible.

If a British subject loses nationality by naturalisation in a foreign country, or by declaration of alienage, or other-wise, minor children lose that nationality if they acquire the nationality of their father ; but this rule does not

[1] 23 & 24 Geo. V. c. 49.

apply to the children of a widow who, on remarriage, acquires foreign nationality. But children who thus lose British nationality may reacquire it by declaration within one year after coming of age.[1]

The death of a husband or dissolution of marriage by divorce does not automatically change the nationality of a woman in the eyes of British law. On the declaration, however, of nullity of marriage, it may be assumed that the nationality of the woman is restored to its former condition.[2]

Annexation [3] of territory by the Crown confers, in default of other arrangements made by the Crown, British nationality on all subjects of the previous Government who do not evacuate the territory ; and conversely, cession of British territory severs the bond of allegiance. In practice, provisions are made, as in the case of the cession of Jubaland and of the Dindings, to safeguard the nationality of such British subjects as desire to retain it. The power to make a declaration of alienage is given also to those persons who, though born out of the Dominions of the Crown, are British subjects by virtue of the extension of that nationality by the Act of 1922.

2. *The Status of Subjects*

Among British subjects there are few differences of status now recognised by law. The privileges of the peerage have been noted; they include the right of male peers, if of age, to sit in the House of Lords, and peers and peeresses are entitled in case of treason or felony to trial by the House of Lords under special conditions noted else-

---

[1] Act of 1914, s. 12.   [2] *Ibid.* s. 11.
[3] *Doe d. Thomas* v. *Acklam* (1824), 2 B. & C. 779 ; *Doe d. Auchmuty* v. *Mulcaster* (1826), 5 B. & C. 777 ; *Bruce, In re* (1832), 1 L.J. Exc. 153.

where. But it was ruled in *Lady Rhondda's Case*,[1] largely as the result of the intervention of Lord Birkenhead, by the Committee of Privileges of the Lords, that a woman, a peeress in her own right, could not sit or vote in the House, despite the wide terms of the Sex Disqualification (Removal) Act, 1919, and the normal process of legislating to alter that position has been left unused, because of reluctance to tamper in any detail with the House of Lords, pending a possible reconstruction of that chamber.

As we have seen, political rights in respect of Parliament were denied to women, until the Representation of the People Act, 1918, removed the barriers to the vote, though not on an equality with men, until, by an Act of 1928,[2] full equality was given. The Sex Disqualification (Removal) Act, 1919, swept away all obstacles to women holding any office or public function, admitting them to juries, to incorporated societies, including the Inns of Court, to the office of solicitor on conditions similar to those affecting men, and to the Civil Service, with reservations in certain cases. The Universities were authorised to admit women to degrees notwithstanding any provisions to the contrary in their statutes or charters.

That feminist aims were wholly achieved by the Act is not the case, for a section of the movement resents not merely the slow rate of progress of women in the higher ranks of the Civil Service, and the small extent of their employment in the police force, but protests against all differentiation in factory and other legislation between men and women. It is, however, most improbable that this standpoint will secure much support.

[1] [1922] 2 A.C. 339.
[2] 7 & 8 Geo. V. c. 64 ; 18 & 19 Geo. V. c. 12. Parliament was opened to women by the Parliament (Qualification of Women) Act, 1918 (8 & 9 Geo. V. c. 47).

3. *The Status of Aliens*

British generosity to aliens rendered entry normally easy, though from 1793 onwards difficulties caused by the Napoleonic wars led to the enactment of an Alien Act which authorised surveillance of aliens and the deportation of suspected aliens. In 1826 these restrictions disappeared, and, although reimposed in 1836, and in 1848 for a time, the powers were left in abeyance. It was only in 1905 [1] that the growth of the alien population in certain London areas and the presence among them of a number of un-satisfactory elements, coupled with the suggestion in Labour circles that aliens were obtaining posts which should be reserved for British subjects, led to the passing of an important Aliens Act. It was made possible for the Home Secretary to prevent the entrance into the United Kingdom of aliens unable to support themselves or their dependants, or who were lunatic or idiots, or suffer-ing from disease and likely to become a charge upon the rates, or who had been convicted of an extradition offence in a foreign country, or who had been the subject in the United Kingdom of an expulsion order. Expulsion orders can be made against aliens convicted of crime and recom-mended for deportation by the court before which they are tried, or who have been reported by a magistrate within twelve months of their last entry to have been receiving public assistance, or to have been living in in-sanitary conditions, or to have been sentenced in a foreign country for an extradition offence. These provisions have been found useful in practice. But much wider authority was conferred by the Aliens Restriction Act, 1914, which expressly authorised in war or national emergency the con-trol of the entry of aliens, their deportation, the restriction

---

[1] Cf. Spender, *Campbell-Bannerman*, ii. 170 f., for his criticism.

of their place of residence, their registration, the supervision of their movements, their arrest, detention, and
search of their premises in specified circumstances. The
powers given were naturally widely employed during the
war.

On the restoration of peace the Aliens Restriction
(Amendment) Act, 1919,[1] continued in use the powers of
the executive to issue Orders in Council; the Act of 1905
was repealed, but the essence of its provisions was continued in operation by Order in Council. Certain disabilities on aliens mark the result of war conditions. The
right to hold land was originally denied to aliens, but the
power to lease, though only up to twenty-one years, was
given in 1844. Full power to hold land and to enjoy
almost complete civil rights was accorded by the Naturalisation Act, 1870, and repeated in the British Nationality
and Status of Aliens Act, 1914. There was excluded, however, the right to own in whole or part a British ship, but
this did not exclude the ownership of such a ship by a
company which is duly registered as British, though the
members of the company may be aliens by nationality.
The same rule applies to an airship. An alien is also
excluded from holding a pilotage certificate or acting as
master or chief officer of a merchant ship, or as skipper
or second hand of a fishing vessel. An alien's change of
name is controlled, and an alien, while after ten years'
residence he may be called upon to serve on a jury, may
be challenged on that ground alone. The right of an alien
accused of crime to be tried by a jury *de medietate linguae*
was abrogated in 1870. Aliens otherwise are not eligible
for the franchise, political or municipal, nor membership
of public governmental bodies, including Parliament, nor

---

[1] 9 & 10 Geo. V. c. 92; Orders in Council, March 25, Dec. 3, 1920;
March 12, 1923; July 24, 1925.

for the Civil Service. On the other hand, they may be admitted to the army and air force, but not to commissioned rank. There is, of course, no hardship in these rules, for naturalisation is open without undue difficulty to any alien of good character who desires to identify himself with the interests of the United Kingdom.

The position of aliens who are subjects of Powers at war with the Crown was of little importance throughout the Victorian epoch, but was forced into prominence during the Great War. It was ruled that aliens in these circumstances were liable to be treated as prisoners of war ; [1] it may be that their property might be confiscated, though in practice such action would be very improbable. Their right to sue is suspended during war, unless with royal licence, formal or implied. But they may be sued, and in that case they can appeal from decisions against them, and exercise such rights as are necessary to enable full justice to be done.[2] Difficult issues were raised regarding the position of companies which were of British registration but were under the control of alien enemies.

By the outbreak of war commercial and financial relations and intercourse between British subjects and residents on British territory and persons of any nationality voluntarily residing or carrying on business in an enemy country become illegal unless by royal licence.[3] Contracts with such persons become suspended in operation, and are dissolved if they involve intercourse with the enemy during the war in any way. Otherwise, when war ceases, they revive and may be enforced. But the position at the end of the Great War was elaborately regulated by the treaties of peace, which were given statutory

---

[1] *Forman, Ex parte* (1917), 87 L.J.K.B. 43.
[2] *Porter* v. *Freudenberg*, [1915] 1 K.B. 857.
[3] Dicey & Keith, *Conflict of Laws* (1932), pp. 905-9.

validity. The property of ex-enemy aliens was made available to the British Crown in discharge of part of the liabilities undertaken by way of reparation by the defeated States. Mixed Arbitration Tribunals were entrusted with the disposal of the conflicting rights, which, therefore, did not come before the ordinary courts.

It was found necessary during the war to give an extended meaning by statute to the conception, enemy alien, so that it might include for trading purposes enemy nationals, and certain persons with enemy connections, though not actually resident on enemy territory. The old rules framed under the simple commercial conditions of the Napoleonic wars proved quite inadequate to cope with the complications of modern business and financial life.

The actual principles affecting the admission of aliens have varied with emergent conditions. Unemployment has resulted in the drastic curtailment of immigrants who may interfere with the obtaining of work by British subjects. The former British rule of affording asylum to refugees has had to be seriously curtailed owing to the danger of the subversive efforts of certain refugees — for this reason M. Trotsky was refused admission by the Labour ministry [1] — and of aliens taking the places of British workers, but under the recent conditions of Europe as affecting Jews and non-Aryans, some relaxation has been allowed,[2] especially in cases where assurance is possible that those admitted have capital which will enable them to maintain themselves, and give work to British subjects. After the anti-Jewish campaign in Germany, Czechoslovakia, Poland, Hungary, and Rumania, which followed the collapse of the democracies at Munich, a number of refugees was accepted on the understanding

[1] In 1929 ; Clynes, *Memoirs*, ii. 115 f.
[2] Mr. Lloyd, House of Commons, March 21, 1939.

that their stay would be only temporary, prior to arrangements being made for their removal and settlement in
the United States, Palestine, or other countries. It was
recognised, of course, that the demand made by Germany
that room should be found in other countries for Jews,
expelled without being allowed to take their property with
them, was indefensible, but humanitarian considerations
were pressed in favour of relaxation of restrictions.

Temporary permits to enter Britain are more freely
given, especially for domestic servants or young people
desiring courses of instruction of various kinds or to learn
British business methods. These admissions are justified
by the advantage accruing to Britain.

CHAPTER XXIV

THE SECURITY OF THE STATE AND CLAIMS BY AND AGAINST THE CROWN

1. *The Security of the State*

IN the main in England questions of maintaining order are in the hands of the police forces, sheriffs, mayors, magistrates, justices of the peace, and others. In time of unrest their duties may be onerous ; reference has been made elsewhere to the use of the defence forces of the Crown to secure order, an action which occasionally has aroused serious political repercussions, as in the case of the incident at the Curragh in 1914.[1] The famous Bristol riots [2] revealed a regrettable failure to perform his duty on the part of the officer commanding the forces, who died by his own hand while the incident was being investigated, while the mayor after trial was found not to have been guilty of criminal failure. The responsibilities of military officers in acting in suppression of unrest are serious ; they should if possible act with civil co-operation, but an officer must make his own decision as to firing on a mob against the views of a magistrate if he thinks it necessary, though in such a case he must be prepared to justify his action. If there be no magistrate available, or one refuses to act for any reason, a military officer must act on his own initiative.[3] The ghastly toll of destruction and death

---

[1] Spender, *Lord Oxford*, ii. 41 ff.

[2] *R.* v. *Pinney* (1832), 3 B. & Ad. 947.   [3] *Parl. Pap.* C. 7234.

in the Gordon riots of 1780 was due to the failure of the military to act in the absence of orders from the magistrates until the King took the initiative and secured the issue of orders to the forces.[1]

It was not until 1920 that it was felt necessary to confer upon the executive a general power of action in the case of emergencies. The Emergency Powers Act was evoked by the gravity of labour unrest which threatened to express itself in a strike intended to paralyse the normal operations of the economic system of the country, and thus to compel the Government to concede the demands of miners and other workers. A proclamation of emergency may be issued by the Crown, whenever it appears that action has been taken or immediately threatened by any person or body of persons, which is calculated to deprive the community, or any substantial portion of the community, of the essentials of life by interfering with the supply and distribution of food, water, fuel, or light, or with the means of locomotion. Only actions on an extensive scale are aimed at, but the discretion of the Crown is absolute. It is, however, subject to the control of Parliament, and a proclamation lasts only for a month but may be renewed. If Parliament will not sit within five days of issue, it must be recalled by proclamation within five days. While a proclamation is in force the Crown, by Order in Council, may make regulations for securing to the community the essentials of life and may confer powers on any person for this purpose. But the Act forbids any form of compulsory military service or of industrial conscription, nor may any regulation make an offence of the mere act of striking or of peaceful persuasion to strike. Offences against the regulations may be tried by courts of summary jurisdiction, but there can be no

[1] May, *Const. Hist.* ii. 24 ff.; *Parl. Hist.* xxi. 690 ff. (June 19, 1780).

variation of criminal procedure, nor may fine or imprison- ment be imposed without trial. Regulations, to be valid, must be confirmed by both houses of Parliament within seven days of being made. They may be added to, altered, or revoked by resolutions of both houses, but without prejudice to action already taken thereunder. It will be seen that the restrictions on the use of arbitrary power are very far-reaching, and that the essential feature is the constant reference to Parliament for authority to act. No better safeguards can clearly be adduced, and the absence of power to set up extraordinary tribunals compares effectively with the exercise of martial law elsewhere.

A proclamation of emergency was issued in 1921, and again in 1924, but was then soon revoked. In 1926, on the other hand, there was need for a valuable code of regulations, which greatly facilitated the defeat of the dangerous General Strike, without involving serious conflicts between strikers and police. The strike was marred by several deliberate attempts at train-wrecking, but these were punished under the ordinary law, and remission of sentences was not given so early as to remove the deterrent effect of the punishment of so ghastly a crime, which incidentally alienated much public sympathy from the strikers.

In the case of Ireland much more drastic action had to be taken under the Restoration of Order in Ireland Act, 1920, which gave full powers of subordinate legislation on the analogy of the Defence of the Realm Consolidation Act, 1914, whose expiration after the war had been held to render new legislation necessary. It is clear that, once peace was restored, the unfettered powers in England and Scotland of the executive would have been deeply resented, while their continuation in Ireland was explained and justified by the waging there of a civil war.

There are, in addition, a number of standing powers which can be used in case of unrest, including the control of aviation, commandeering and use of aerodromes and aircraft, placing restrictions on aliens, billeting of defence forces, calling out of reserves and auxiliary forces, taking control of railway transport, etc.

Offences against the State are penalised in a variety of ways. The most serious crime is treason, which was defined in the Treason Act of 1352 and extended in part by judicial interpretation, in part by additional legislation, to cover an ever widening area. The Act of 1352 [1] stigmatised as treason the compassing or imagining the death of the King, of his consort, and heir ; the levying of war against the King in his realm ; adherence to his enemies ; the violation of his wife, of his eldest daughter, while unmarried, or the wife of his eldest son ; the counterfeiting of the great seal, the privy seal, or coinage ; the issue of false coinage ; and the killing of certain high officers in the discharge of their office. The judges added to this list any act directed to the deposition or imprisonment of the King or to the control of his person ; any measure concerted with foreigners for the invasion of the realm, or the going abroad for such purpose.[2] Mere riots were treated on occasion as treason if they were of a public or general nature.[3] The passing of the Riot Act [4] allowed non-political riots to be treated as mere felonies. By statute attempts to make the King change his counsels or to intimidate either house of Parliament were made treason.[5] It is also treason to question the title of the legitimate successor to the Crown under the Acts regulat-

---

[1] 25 Edw. III. st. 5, c. 2.

[2] *R.* v. *Hardy* (1794), 24 St. Tr. 199, 1379; *R.* v. *Horne Tooke* (1794), 25 St. Tr. 1, 725.

[3] *Dammaree's Case* (1710), 15 St. Tr. 521.   [4] 1 Geo. I. st. 2, c. 5.

[5] 36 Geo. III. c. 7 ; 57 Geo. III. c. 6.

ing it.[1] Of these treasons those regarding the seals, the coinage, and the royal officers are now abandoned. But the others remain, and there are no accessories in treason. All alike are guilty. But, as in the case of felonies, forfeiture disappeared in 1870, and hanging has been the mode of inflicting the penalty of death when awarded since 1814. It is still the rule that there must be two witnesses to one overt act of treason, or one to each overt act of the same head of treason.[2]

It has been ruled that to attempt to obtain naturalisation overseas during war in the foreign country which is at war is treason,[3] and treason is committed by adhering to the King's enemies overseas as by planning in Germany an attack to be carried out in Ireland.[4]

Misprision of treason is constituted by the concealment or keeping secret of any high treason ; knowledge must be shown, both of the treason and the persons concerned ; disclosure must be made to some magistrate or person in authority.[5] The penalty is imprisonment for life.

A modification of the law was, very sensibly, introduced in 1848 by the Treason Felony Act, which rendered it possible to treat in a milder way, not involving the death penalty, though penal servitude for life might be awarded, acts not directly directed against the life of the King. Thus a conspiracy to deprive the King of his Irish realm,[6] to levy war for that end,[7] or the storing of arms,[8] were proceeded against in the Fenian troubles as treason-

---

[1] 1 Anne, st. 2, c. 21 ; 6 Anne, c. 41, ss. 1, 3.
[2] 7 & 8 Will. III. c. 3 ; it permits challenge of 35 jurors.
[3] *R.* v. *Lynch*, [1903] 1 K.B. 444.
[4] *R.* v. *Casement*, [1917] 1 K.B. 98.
[5] *R.* v. *Thistlewood* (1820), 33 St. Tr. 681.
[6] *R.* v. *Gallagher* (1883), 15 Cox C.C. 291, 317.
[7] *Mulcahy* v. *R.* (1868), L.R. 3 H.L. 306.
[8] *R.* v. *Davitt* (1870), 11 Cox C.C. 676.

felony. Levying war against the sovereign in the United Kingdom or elsewhere is in like case ; [1] and, as in treason, there are no accessories ; all are principals. It is no objection to trial under the Act that the matters charged amount to treason, but trial involves exclusion of further proceedings as for treason.

Important services to the safety of the country against spies and persons who corrupt servants of the Crown, and these servants, is rendered by the Official Secrets Acts of 1911 and 1920, the former replacing an Act of 1889. Penalties are imposed on people who approach prohibited places or sketch such places, or who take copies of pro-hibited documents, or communicate sketches or copies or receive them. Such acts are felonies. It is a misdemeanour carelessly to part with sketches or information to unauthor-ised persons, or to retain them unduly long. It is also illegal to harbour spies, to wear unauthorised uniform in order to obtain admission to prohibited places, to make false declarations to that end, to forge passports or permits, to pretend to be a governmental officer or an employee of such an officer ; to communicate with foreign agents with a view to prejudice the State, or to interfere with the police or defence forces for such a purpose. The interception of telegrams and letters is provided for, and control of those who receive letters for others, while pro-vision is made to obtain information regarding spies. The value of the anti-spy system seems to have been remarkable on the outbreak of war.

A serious issue has, however, arisen under Section 6 of the Act of 1920, which authorises the asking a person who has disclosed information of a confidential official character for the source of his information. In *Lewis* v. *Cattle* [2] in 1938 it was held that a journalist, who had given a descrip-

---

[1] *R.* v. *Meaney* (1867), Ir. R. 1 C.L. 500.   [2] [1938] 2 K.B. 454.

tion of a person wanted by the police, apparently taken from a document circulated by one police station to another, and who refused to state the source of his information, could rightly be convicted. As the information was clearly of no very serious character, it was urged that the Act in this respect had been accepted by Parliament under a misunderstanding as to its intention. It had been supposed to be aimed at spies and matter connected therewith, and the minister in charge had made light of the idea that it could be used generally. The Home Secretary was very keenly pressed on this head and proved to be ready to secure by executive action that the Act should not be employed outside its sphere of dealing with information whose betrayal might be a source of danger, but this mere promise was received without satisfaction, and efforts to obtain legislation to narrow the ambit of the Act were determined on, resulting in a fairly satisfactory amendment, the power being confined to cases of espionage (1939).

Other offences against the State are mentioned elsewhere. Riot, rout, and unlawful assembly are fully provided against, and in their case, as in that of sedition, the width of governmental authority is patently so large that the powers might be abused by a Government which desired to achieve ends unpopular with a considerable element in the country. The offence of inciting soldiers or sailors to mutiny was penalised under an Act of 1797, and a simpler and easier method of procedure, as well as an extension of the law, was brought about by the Incitement to Disaffection Act, 1934.[1] The Police Act, 1919,

---

[1] For the excitement thereby created, see *Thomas* v. *Sawkins*, [1935] 2 K.B. 249, which asserts the right of the police to enter a meeting if they have reason to believe that in their absence there may be a breach of the peace or seditious utterance. This is much wiser than their inaction during the Fascist misconduct at their Olympia meeting.

had already made it an offence to excite disaffection in that force, whose loyalty had failed during the great strike among the London police in 1918, which revealed the force as determined to take advantage of the necessities of the country to extort unjust advantages for themselves. The doubt as to the trustworthiness of the force then engendered has never been dispelled, and has been a factor in the growing lack of confidence in the ranks of the Labour party in the impartiality of the administration of justice in England.

2. *Act of State*

It is the most striking sign of the rule of law that the defence of Act of State has been limited within the most narrow confines. It would have been easy to extend the system and to deny authority of the courts over matters essentially of high political character, but the practice of the courts has left this plea as technically valid only in certain instances. The plea was repelled decisively by the Privy Council when an effort was made to meet by it an action for damages arising out of destruction of property carried out by order of a naval officer acting under instructions to give effect to a *modus vivendi* with France regarding the Newfoundland fisheries. It was ruled, as it had already been ruled in regard to actions by governors in the colonies, that the courts must examine into them, and decide whether what was done could be justified under the powers of the Crown and that they could not be concluded by the plea of Act of State.[1]

The plea is available when an action is done outside British territory causing damage to the person or property of an alien, the action being either authorised *ab initio* or

---

[1] *Walker* v. *Baird*, [1892] A.C. 491 ; *Musgrave* v. *Pulido* (1879), 5 App. Cas. 102.

ratified *ex post facto* by the Crown. Thus in *Buron* v.
Denman [1] the action of a naval officer in destroying the
property of a slave trader in Africa was held to be safeguarded by ratification. It is also available if an attempt
were made to punish any person for killing or injuring
enemy aliens when authorised to do so by the Crown ;
the internment of such aliens by the Crown is an act for
which no *habeas corpus* proceedings lie.[2] In like manner
the British courts would not punish acts done in time of
war by enemy aliens on British territory ; such matters
lie outside the contemplation of municipal law.

The plea is also effective in respect of actions done even
against British subjects in connection with the taking
possession by the Crown of territories not British.[3] No
action lies against the Crown in the English courts, nor
can the local Government be sued. Nor is any claim valid
against either on the score of succession to former rights
and liabilities ; the rights the Crown may enforce, but it
is free to repudiate liabilities not essentially bound up with
the rights. This doctrine has been applied equally as
regards the annexation of the South African Republic,[4] and
the annexations by the East India Company or the Crown
of Indian States.[5]

One issue only is doubtful ; it seems to have been
suggested that in protectorates acts can be justified against
British subjects as Acts of State, but the doctrine appears
unsound on principle and of very slight authority.[6]

---

[1] (1848), 2 Ex. 167.
[2] *Forman, Ex parte* (1917), 34 T.L.R. 4.
[3] *West Rand Central Gold Mining Co.* v. *R.*, [1905] 2 K.B. 391.
[4] *Vereeniging Municipality* v. *Vereeniging Estates Ltd.*, [1919] T.P.D.
159 ; *Randjeslaagte Syndicate* v. *The Govt.*, [1908] T.S. 404.
[5] *Ex-Rajah of Coorg* v. *East India Co.* (1860), 29 Beav. 300.
[6] Anson, *The Crown* (ed. Keith), i. 320.

3. *Claims by and against the Crown*

The Crown still possesses certain valuable rights with regard to its relations with the public in matters affecting its claims, whether in private business or in respect of governmental activities. Thus an information at the instance of the Crown or of the Duke of Cornwall lies *in rem* to have the title of the Crown to property in its possession confirmed or its right to property held by a subject declared ; it lies also *in personam* to obtain payment of a debt due to the Crown or in respect of intrusion on royal hereditaments. In proceedings to recover penalties in customs matters the debtor may be arrested on a *capias* issued by authority of the Attorney-General and approved by a judge, and he must then give bail if he is to be released. In claims by Inland Revenue authorities the proceedings may begin with the issue of a *subpoena* addressed to the debtor.

As a concession mainly to those persons against whom the Crown has claims, it was provided in 1933 [1] that the debts due to the Crown might be recovered by ordinary writ of summons and proceedings taken in the county courts subject to the limitation of their powers. The same Act made the really important concession that the rules of costs applicable between subjects should in general be applied between the Crown and subjects, thus ending wholly the anomaly by which, as a general principle, the Crown did not pay nor receive costs in ordinary cases. But, in view of the fact that the Attorney-General or a Government department may have to be made a party to proceedings for formal purposes, in deciding as to costs courts are to pay attention to the existence of this obliga-

---

[1] Administration of Justice (Miscellaneous Provisions) Act, 1933, s. 7. See generally Crown Suits Act, 1865.

tion, and any other party to the case may be ordered to pay the costs of the Crown, a provision clearly necessary in the interests of the public.

The Crown may by writ of extent seize the body, lands, chattels, or things in action of a debtor, if there is risk of the loss of the debt. Where a Crown debtor has died, the writ *diem clausit extremum* can be employed ; where a debt is founded on a record *scire facias* as well as information lies.

The Attorney-General in right of the Crown may claim a trial at Bar of any information,[1] has a general right of reply in Exchequer cases, and other privileges.

In cases of claim in contract against the Crown, the remedy available is now petition of right, which is regulated by statute and has in practice replaced older remedies. The petition procedure is available, not merely to recover sums due under, or damages for breach of, contract, but also to recover compensation for the occupation of land taken under the authority of the Defence Act, 1842, and like measures.[2] It may be used to recover lands, chattels, or moneys which have come into the power of the Crown, as in the case of detention of goods in the customs,[3] or to obtain compensation for failure to restore ; to obtain money payable under a Crown grant and any like claim.[4] The exact limits to its operation are still not finally determined.

The procedure [5] is by way of a petition presented through the Home Secretary, who advises the grant or

[1] The Court has discretion to refuse under 1 & 2 Geo. VI. c. 63.

[2] *Thomas* v. *R.* (1874), L.R. 10 Q.B. 31 ; *Att.-Gen.* v. *De Keyser's Royal Hotel*, [1920] A.C. 508.

[3] *Buckland* v. *R.*, [1933] 1 K.B. 767.

[4] *Kildare County Council* v. *R.*, [1909] 2 I.R. 199, 232.

[5] Petitions of Right Act, 1860 (23 & 24 Vict. c. 34). No petition lies if the obligation is that of another government : *Att.-Gen.* v. *Great Southern Railway of Ireland*, [1925] A.C. 754.

withholding of the royal fiat " Let right be done ".   The
Attorney-General may be consulted in any case.   It is
clearly impossible to compel the Home Secretary to grant
a fiat, but it is clear that it must not arbitrarily be withheld.   If a fiat is granted, then the petition is lodged with
the Treasury solicitor and the Crown must plead or demur.
The action in general proceeds on the lines of an ordinary
action, but amendment of a petition is not permitted in
any point of substance,[1] for it would patently be unfair
to deprive the Crown indirectly of its right to grant or
refuse a fiat.   Moreover, the petitioner cannot compel full
disclosure of documents by the Crown, while he must, of
course, make full disclosure.   If the award is against the
Crown, no execution thereon is possible, but the Treasury
may pay out of any funds which Parliament may appropriate for the purpose.   It is clear that the control of the
Commons cannot be evaded under the English procedure.
Costs are in the discretion of the court.

This is the only form in which contractual and like
claims against the Crown can be pursued.   It was decided
as early as 1786 in *Macbeath* v. *Haldimand* [2] that a servant
of the Crown cannot be made personally liable in contract,
and various devices to overcome this difficulty have failed
to attain success.[3]   It is impossible to obtain a *mandamus*
against the Treasury to compel payment, and a declaratory
action to have a sum declared payable is also improper.[4]

In a number of cases, efforts made to extend the use
of the remedy have failed.   Thus it has been ruled that,
where by treaty the Crown obtains payments, whether
for wrongs done by way of confiscation of property in

[1] *Badman Bros.* v. *The King*, [1924] 1 K.B. 74.
[2] (1786), 1 T.R. 172.   An officer may, of course, pledge his own credit :
Samuel Bros. Ltd. v. *Whetherly*, [1908] 1 K.B. 184.
[3] *Dunn* v. *Macdonald*, [1897] 1 Q.B. 555.
[4] *Bombay and Persia Steam Navigation Co.* v *Maclay*, [1920] 3 K.B. 402.

France, or in respect of debts owed in China, or as com- pensation for damage done by Germany in the Great War, there is no right in those who are morally entitled to payment of the sums obtained to obtain orders against the Crown.[1] The Crown might conceivably act as trustee for the claimants, but it will not be presumed to have done so-and-so. Even if a bounty is granted for war services, the Secretary of State will not be compelled to pay to the objects of the bounty.[2]

The position of Civil servants and other servants of the Crown is regulated by the principle that they hold office at pleasure unless statutory authority exists to provide otherwise. No petition of right, therefore, can be maintained in respect of any alleged breach of contract of employment, and as regards pensions the grant is always discretionary. The question whether a servant could claim pay which had accrued due, but had not been paid, by petition of right has not been settled; it is very dubious if the Crown would ever fail to pay anything due. Moreover, it is idle to attempt to sue personally a superior officer by whom the immediate appointment is made, for in view of the fact that the Crown cannot be sued in contract, there is no ground for a claim based on alleged warranty of authority.

As regards torts the immunity of the Crown is absolute, and, as the Crown can do no wrong, the officials, who do wrong, have to bear the brunt. There is, of course, no great hardship in this for an officer who has acted under instructions from his superiors, for he will be defended at the cost of the Crown, and any damages awarded against him will be refunded to him. On the other hand, illegal

---

[1] *Baron de Bode's Case* (1846), 8 Q.B. 208; *Rustomjee* v. *The Queen* (1876), 1 Q.B.D. 487; *Civilian War Claimants' Assocn.* v. *R.*, [1932] A.C. 14.
[2] *Gidley* v. *Lord Palmerston* (1822), 3 Brod. & B. 275.

acts, not done in due course, will not be defended and
the officer will have to meet costs and damages from his
own pocket.   There is thus a reasonable probability that
officials will seek to keep within the law.   On the other
hand, members of the public have a grievance in that it
may happen that a judgment against a subordinate will
never be met, and juries in awarding damages would be
more generous if they knew that the sums would always
be defrayed from public funds.

The issue was definitely decided in *Canterbury* v.
Attorney-General [1] when Viscount Canterbury claimed for
damage done to his property, when Speaker of the
Commons, by the fire which, through the negligence of
the servants of the Crown, burned down the houses of
Parliament.   It was refused, and the like doctrine has
been adhered to consistently.

On the other hand, liability against the officer responsible is regularly enforced. [2]   The head of a department,
however, is not responsible for the acts of his subordinates,
for they are not his employees, [3] but that does not apply
if he has personally instructed the performance of the
actions impugned.   He may, however, incur responsibility
if he definitely omits to give suitable instructions to his
subordinates in consequence of which a tort is committed. [4]

Exceptions to these rules are statutory and not numerous.   The Board of Trade was made liable to suit, to

---

[1] *Canterbury* v. *Att.-Gen.* (1842), 1 Ph. 306 ; *Tobin* v. *R.* (1864), 16 C.B.
(N.S.), 310.

[2] *Money* v. *Leach* (1765), 3 Burr. 1742 ; *Brasyer* v. *Maclean* (1875),
L.R. 6 P.C. 398.   Contrast failure in actions against ministers : *Raleigh* v.
Goschen, [1898] 1 Ch. 73 ; *Macgregor* v. *Lord Advocate*, [1921] S.C. 847 ;
Gilleghan v. *Minister of Health*, [1932] 1 Ch. 86 ; *Mackenzie-King* v. *Air Coun-
cil*, [1927] 2 K.B. 517 ; *Bainbridge* v. *Postmaster-General*, [1906] 1 K.B. 178.

[3] *Whitfield* v. *Lord Despencer* (1778), 2 Cowp. 754 ; *Mersey Docks Trustees*
v. *Gibbs* (1864-6), L.R. 1 H.L. 124.

[4] *Mee* v. *Cruickshank* (1902), 82 L.T. 708.

please shipowners, if its officers improperly detained a
vessel on the plea that it was unfit to go to sea, a provision
no doubt intended to prevent undue vigilance in enforcing
measures for the safety of seamen in the days when shipowners were often indifferent to risk to life when profits
were concerned.[1] The Minister of Transport[2] can be sued
in contract and tort as well as sue, and he is responsible
for the acts and defaults of the officers, servants, and
agents of the ministry, no doubt in so far as they act
within the scope of their employment within the rules of
the ordinary law as to torts of subordinates. The Road
Traffic Act, 1930,[3] makes special provision for criminal
responsibility on the part of servants of Government departments. Mere incorporation of a Government department for certain purposes of suit does not involve any
general liability to suit in contract or tort.

There is a special case of liability in contract and tort
in matters not essentially of Government, as opposed to
commercial, character inherited by the Secretary of State
for India from the East India Company but transferred
under the Government of India Act, 1935, in a modified
form. The newly created Secretary of State for Burma
was placed by the Government of Burma Act, 1935, in
an analogous position.

It must be noted that liability of the Crown in England
is confined to matters over which authority is vested in
the Government there. Thus claims in respect of matters
in the Irish Free State ceased on the transfer of authority
to be capable of enforcement against the Crown in England.
In Scotland, and by statute in the Dominions, colonies,
etc., suits can in several cases be brought direct against

---

[1] Merchant Shipping Act, 1894, s. 460; *Thomson* v. *Farrer* (1882),
9 Q.B.D. 272.

[2] Ministry of Transport Act, 1919, s. 26.   [3] S. 121 (2).

the Government, and it is often suggested that like facilities should be provided in the United Kingdom. But, though long under consideration,[1] and though a Bill was drafted to show the changes necessary to effect this end, it was not taken up by any Government, and, though the Committee on Ministers' Powers [2] called attention to the fact that in France remedies in favour of the subject were more effective than in England, ministers remained indifferent, the one improvement conceded being the Act of 1933,[3] whose terms have been already in part recorded. It is striking that the further power therein given to simplify procedure under the prerogative writs were only in 1939 [4] carried into operation. It should be noted also that not only in France is a remedy given against illegal actions of officials, but that in many cases the improper use of legal powers (*détournement de pouvoir*) [5] is equally made subject to judicial intervention, a position of matters which is not even suggested in England.

4. *The Privileges of the Crown in Litigation*

In principle it rests with the Crown to determine what documents under its control may be permitted to be used in judicial proceedings. This was established in 1841 [6] in the case of correspondence between the Court of Directors of the East India Company and the Board of Control, the precursor of the India Office, and it had already been so decided regarding correspondence with the Colonial Secretary.[7] In the same spirit it has been ruled that letters

---

[1] *Parl. Pap.* Cmd. 2842.   [2] *Ibid.* Cmd. 4060, p. 112.
[3] Administration of Justice (Miscellaneous Provisions) Act, 1933.
[4] *Ibid.* 1938, s. 7.
[5] F. J. Port, *Administrative Law*, pp. 315 ff.
[6] *Smith* v. *East India Co.* (1841), 1 Ph. 50.
[7] *Anderson* v. *Hamilton* (1816), 8 Price 244 n.

from one firm to another containing confidential information from the Admiralty must not be disclosed, if the
information cannot be revealed without injury to public
interests.[1]

There are clear disadvantages in pressing too far the
claim of right to withhold disclosure, and the courts recently have been alert to indicate the limits of immunity.
The privilege must be claimed by the head of the department and it need not necessarily be asserted personally.[2]
In a suitable case a letter from the Minister of Transport
has been duly accepted. But it is not sufficient that
privilege should be claimed vaguely for a set of documents
as such ; the minister must, it would seem, apply his
mind to the actual documents in question, and claim on
full knowledge. If the court is not satisfied with the mode
in which the claim is put forward, it is within its power
to inspect for itself the documents in question and on the
result of that inspection to decide how far the Crown's
claim to withhold can be justified.[3] In Dominion cases
there has been a marked tendency of late to minimise the
claim of immunity.[4]

The Crown is further privileged in that communications
made on official business by one civil or other servant to
another cannot be made the basis of an action for slander
or libel, and a like privilege applies to the reports of the
Official Receivers in Bankruptcy.[5] In like manner the

---

[1] *Asiatic Petroleum Co., Ltd.* v. *Anglo-Persian Oil Co., Ltd.*, [1916] 1 K.B.
822.

[2] *Williams* v. *Star Newspaper Co., Ltd.* (1908), 24 T.L.R. 297 ; *Ankin* v.
L.N.E.R. Co., [1930] 1 K.B. 527.

[3] *Spigelmann* v. *Hocker* (1933), 50 T.L.R. 87 ; *Carmichael* v. *Scottish
Co-operative Wholesale Soc., Ltd.*, [1934] Sc. L.T. 138.

[4] *Robinson* v. *State of South Australia* (No. 2), [1931] A.C. 704.

[5] *Chatterton* v. *Secretary of State for India*, [1895] 2 Q.B. 189 ; *Burr* v.
Smith, [1909] 2 K.B. 306 ; *Isaacs & Sons* v. *Cook*, [1925] 2 K.B. 391 ; *Bottomley*
v. *Brougham*, [1908] 1 K.B. 584.

Director of Public Prosecutions [1] need not disclose the source of information on which he acts in a case. There is also the rule that servants of the Crown cannot be required to give evidence if that will be prejudicial to the public interest ; [2] this has been applied to the Lord Chamberlain, a Secretary of State, who is also by statute given immunity under the Foreign Enlistment Act, 1870, and an inspector of the Board of Trade. In *Rowell* v. *Pratt* [3] the principle was extended to apply exclusion from production in evidence to returns made by growers of potatoes to the organisation set up under the Agricultural Marketing Act, 1931. Proceedings by administrative tribunals have not been accorded so favoured a position as those of the courts. [4]

All public authorities, including servants of the Crown, are entitled to the protection of the Public Authorities Protection Act, 1893, under which suit in respect of any official act or any neglect or default in the execution of any statutory or public duty must be brought within six months of the act, neglect, or default, or, in the case of a continuing act, of its cessation. The officer affected must be allowed to tender amends, and, if an action is commenced after tender or payment into court, the claimant cannot recover damages unless the award in his favour exceeds the sum tendered or paid in. If successful, the official may be awarded costs as between solicitor and client. It will be seen, therefore, that the scales are somewhat weighted against the plaintiff. The most unsatisfactory point is the question of time which may work real

[1] *Marks* v. *Beyfus* (1890), 25 Q.B.D. 494.

[2] *West* v. *West* (1911), 27 T.L.R. 476 ; *Gibson* v. *Caledonian Railway Co.* (1896), 33 Sc. L.R. 638 ; *Irwin* v. *Grey* (1862), 3 F. & F. 635.

[3] [1938] A.C. 101.

[4] *Collins* v. *Henry Whitehead & Co.*, [1927] 2 K.B. 378 ; *Mason* v. *Brewis Bros.*, [1938] 2 A.E.R. 420.

injustice,[1] for the court is not given the right to extend at
its discretion when strict insistence thereon must work injustice.   But the limit does not apply to proceedings by
way of *certiorari*,[2] nor to a malicious prosecution.[3]   The
Wheat Commission [4] has been ruled to an authority for the
purposes of the Act, but if a port authority takes action
as a matter of contract, not really of the exercise of its
statutory powers, it has no protection.[5]

[1] *Harnett* v. *Fisher*, [1927] A.C. 574 ; *Freeborn* v. *Leeming*, [1926] 1 K.B.
160 ; *Copper Export Assocn.* v. *Mersey Docks* (1932), 48 T.L.R. 542.

[2] *R.* v. *London County Council*; *Swan & Edgar, Ex parte* (1929), 45
T.L.R. 512.   See also Preface.

[3] *Harten* v. *London County Council* (1929), 45 T.L.R. 318.

[4] *Paul Ltd.* v. *Wheat Commission*, [1937] A.C. 139 ; *Amour* v. *Scottish
Milk Marketing Board*, [1938] Sc. L.R. 347.   But not a railway company :
Swain v. *Southern Railway*, [1939] 1 K.B. 77.

[5] *The Ronald West*, [1937] P. 212.

CHAPTER XXV

THE RIGHTS OF THE SUBJECT AND THE RULE OF LAW

1. *The Fundamental Character of the Rights of the Subject*

In framing the constitution of the Irish Free State in 1922
an interesting attempt was made by the makers of the
instrument to secure a number of fundamental rights, on
the model of the list included in the constitution of the
United States. These included the liberty of the subject ;
the inviolability of his domicile ; freedom of conscience and
the free profession and practice of religion, subject to public
order and morality ; the right of free expression of opinion ;
the right to assemble peaceably and without arms ; the
right to form associations ; and the right to free elementary education. In the revised Constitution of Eire [1]
these rights were repeated and reinforced by a further set
of principles, which were differentiated from the former
by the fact that they are not intended to be enforced by
the courts, whereas the former are designed for application
in the judgments passed by the courts on the value of
legislation.

Under the Free State, however, the excellent principles
enunciated proved impossible of observance. It was found
necessary to reduce their operation in practice by drastic
legislation under which personal liberty, the right to form
associations, the right to assemble, and the right to the

---

[1] Art. 45, as opposed to Arts. 40-44. Cf. Keith, *The Dominions as Sovereign
States*, p. 557.

free expression of opinion were violated wholesale by a constitutional amendment, which, passed by Mr. Cosgrave's Government, was bitterly attacked by that of Mr. De Valera, but revived and made use of by the latter when he secured power in 1932. The powers in question do not figure in the Constitution of Eire, but the constitution gives ample scope for renewal of the former authority if there should appear to the Government of the day sufficient reason for reverting to it.

In the United Kingdom, on the other hand, the last period since 1837 has seen no desire to convert the principles affecting the liberty of the subject into formal laws. It is true that there is the technical difficulty in the United Kingdom that, as Parliament is wholly sovereign, it would be impossible to enact laws which could not be overridden by a subsequent law. But this is not absolutely conclusive of the issue. The Statute of Westminster, 1931, lays down a principle regarding the restriction of Imperial legislative power for the Dominions, which requires, in any Act which is to be treated as affecting them, that there shall be included a statement that the Act has been passed with the consent of the Dominions mentioned therein. An Imperial Act could provide certain fundamental principles and require that, in interpreting measures passed subsequently, it should be held that these principles were to be regarded as governing the interpretation, unless it was stated to the contrary in the Act. But whether this device would have any legal result must remain doubtful; the courts might and almost certainly would [1] simply rule that a later Act overrides an earlier, and that the device was ineffective to accomplish any end.

The liberties and rights of the subject, therefore, must

---

[1] *Vauxhall Estates, Ltd.* v. *Liverpool Corpn.*, [1932] 1 K.B. 733; *Ellen Street Estates, Ltd.* v. *Minister of Health*, [1934] 1 K.B. 590.

rest in the United Kingdom on the fundamental principles
of law, and they are therefore assigned by Professor Dicey [1]
to the rule of law regarded by him as an essential characteristic of the British constitution, and his theory forms part
of the accepted doctrines of British law.

The characteristics of the rule of law are three, representing different aspects of the same facts. It involves, in
the first place, the absolute supremacy or predominance of
regular law as opposed to the influence of arbitrary power,
and excludes the existence of arbitrariness of prerogative,
or even of wide discretionary authority on the part of the
Government. A man may be punished for a breach of the
law, but he can be punished for nothing else. Secondly,
it denotes equality before the law, or the equal subjection
of all classes to the ordinary law of the land administered
by the ordinary law courts ; the rule of law excludes the
idea of any exemption of officials or others from the duty
of obedience to the law which governs other citizens or
from the jurisdiction of the ordinary tribunals ; there can
be nothing really corresponding to the administrative law
(*droit administratif*) or the administrative tribunals (*tribu-
naux administratifs*) of France. The idea that affairs and
disputes in which the Government or its servants are
concerned are beyond the sphere of the civil courts, and
must be dealt with by special and more or less official
bodies, is fundamentally inconsistent with English traditions and customs. Thirdly, the rules which in foreign
countries naturally form part of the constitutional code
are not the sources but the consequences of the rights
of individuals, as defined and enforced by the courts; the
principles of private law have been by the action of the
courts and Parliament so extended as to determine the
position of the Crown and of its servants ; thus the con-

[1] Cf. Keith, *Const. Law* (1939), pp. 31 ff.

stitution is the result of the ordinary law of the land.

There have been criticisms of this view, but it has received the emphatic endorsement of the Committee on Ministers' Powers in 1932, in citing his discussion of the development of administrative law in England [1] " His conclusion was that, although modern legislation had conferred upon the Cabinet, or upon servants of the Crown who might be influenced or guided by the Cabinet, a considerable amount of judicial or quasi-judicial authority, the fact that the ordinary law courts could deal with any actual and probable breach of the law committed by any servant of the Crown still preserved that rule of law which was fatal to the existence of true *droit administratif*. In our opinion Professor Dicey's conclusion is no less true to-day than it was in 1915."

The criticisms [2] addressed to these principles seem to rest on failure to realise the facts. The objection to the repudiation of arbitrariness ignores the fact that the meaning of the claim is that the spirit of British law utterly repudiates the state of affairs which prevails in Germany to-day, when the executive is armed with absolute authority over the lives and fortunes of citizens and can, without any possibility of judicial control, arrest them, place them in concentration camps, and there procure their death. These acts are no doubt legal under the authority conceded by the legislature to the executive, and the system by which nothing may appear in the press which is not approved by the executive is equally legal, and it is equally legal that any assembly of citizens to criticise the executive is criminal. But the term " rule of law " has no meaning in such circumstances, and Professor Dicey's meaning was made clear by his famous contrast

---

[1] *Parl. Pap.* Cmd. 4060, p. 111 ; Dicey, L.Q.R. xxxi. 148.

[2] Jennings, *The Law and the Constitution*, pp. 295 ff.

between the liberty of the person under *habeas corpus* in England and the treatment to which Voltaire was subjected, legally no doubt under the law of France.

It is claimed that this conception of the rule of law merely reflects Whig ideas of 1886 and that it ignores the true problems which then had not emerged into full consideration, poverty and disease and the new industrial system. But the remedy for these issues is not the grant of arbitrary power, and the subjection of the owner of property to the mercy of any kind of authority with powers of confiscation at will to be exercised uncontrolled by the courts. It lies in the laying down by Parliament or by executive authorities, with confirmation by Parliament, of carefully defined rules, which can be enforced by the executive, subject to the control of the courts if they go beyond their powers. This is a principle which demands still the fullest respect ; that democratic Governments should limit as drastically as possible arbitrary action by executive authorities is the best hope of avoiding their destruction by Fascist or Communist oppositions.

There is, in the second place, a very important sense recognised by the Committee on Ministers' Powers in the doctrine of equality before the law, the meaning of which is perfectly clear. It embodies the essential doctrine that, with minimal exceptions, for any legal wrong inflicted by an official there is redress against that official in the ordinary courts, the judges of which are independent in every real sense of the Government of the day. It is open to argue, though British opinion is not prepared to accept the argument, that the French system for the obtaining of redress against official misconduct affords better results, but it is useless to ignore a fundamental principle as existent.

Thirdly, the view that the rights of the subject are the

result of declarations by the courts and not of constitutional legislation is a simple statement of facts, and, as
has been noted above, the history of such rights in the
Irish Free State suggests that they are better protected
by their treatment in the English practice than in the
more modern Continental form. The rights given by the
Weimar constitution are things of the past ; those given
by the British constitution have a more abiding value,
because they rest on fundamental legal conceptions, which
cannot easily be disposed of by legislation and which courts
will not depart from without legislation.

The term " rule of law " has therefore a fundamental
meaning, which is that given to it by Professor Dicey. It
negatives autocracy whether Fascist or Communist ; it
negatives the assumption into the hands of the executive
of wide and arbitrary powers ; it assumes the existence of
democratic control of a system which works through an
impartial law, and it explains the security of the rights
of British subjects.

Historically the securing of the rights now accorded
may be traced to a variety of causes. The early development of the legal doctrine of trespass was of great importance as assuring an effective vindication by the courts of
intrusion on individual rights. A further advantage was
due to the development of the prerogative writs and the
extension by statute of the advantages of *habeas corpus*.
The use of juries proved a fundamental feature in the
technique of protection of the individual from unjust prosecution by the executive, and a not less important service
was rendered by their employment in cases where false
imprisonment or malicious arrest was alleged. The gain was
added to by the refusal of the courts to admit the immunity
of the highest officers of the executive from their jurisdiction,
and by their denial of the validity of any doctrine of State

necessity. Moreover, the right to property was reinforced by the principle of the courts, which accepted the view that the interpretation of statutes should be based on the assumption that legislation does not take away vested rights without express provision. It has been contended that the habit of mind of judges in enforcing the last-named doctrine is now a source of obstruction rather than of public advantage. There seems no truth in this contention ; it is not for judges to interpret law on a basis of progressive extension of its meaning by their discretion ; the duty of such change is incumbent on the legislature, which is fully cognisant of the attitude of the judiciary, and which undoubtedly relies upon it to maintain its existing outlook in such matters.

2. *Personal Liberty*

The principle of personal freedom is that it can normally be restricted only by a judicial sentence pronounced under circumstances ensuring a considerable measure of just treatment, in respect of a definite breach of law, whether common law or statute. It is, of course, true that in many cases measures of restraint are legal. Parents or guardians have certain rights of restriction of the actions of those in their charge ; children placed in approved schools, lunatics confined under reception orders,[1] persons suffering from infectious diseases, habitual drunkards sent to homes for inebriates by judicial order, as well as prisoners awaiting trial or after conviction, are instances in point. But to reduce as completely as is possible the risk of illegal interference, the rights of private persons to arrest are confined to cases in which a felony has been committed, in which offences of certain kinds have been

[1] *Harnett* v. *Bond and Adam*, [1925] A.C. 669.

committed against himself or his household, or in which a breach of the peace is occurring. A police constable normally arrests only on a warrant granted by a magistrate, but he may arrest on reasonable suspicion of a felony, even if one has not in fact been committed, to prevent a breach of the peace, or when a breach has been committed, to prevent the commission, or after the commission, of many different crimes. His action, however, has to be followed by the bringing of the accused before the magistrates at as early a time as practicable, and, in order to diminish detention where not essential, the power to give bail has been accorded to senior officials of the police.[1] Magistrates who decide to commit for trial are normally expected to give bail, which should be reasonable, having regard to the danger, if any, of the prisoner absconding to evade trial, and his financial circumstances. If bail is refused, application can be made to a High Court judge. If a sentence of imprisonment is pronounced at Quarter Sessions, the prisoner who intends to appeal will normally be allowed bail, and so forth.

There has been little tendency on the part of the courts to reduce the freedom from undue police activity. It was decided indeed in 1935, in *Thomas* v. *Sawkins*,[2] that a police officer may enter private premises if he believes that a breach of the peace is imminent or other offence is about to be committed. This decision has been compared unfavourably with the pronouncement of the Home Secretary in 1934 in defending the inaction of the police on the occasion of a great Fascist rally at Olympia, which aroused great indignation through the violence with which ejection of those who ventured to ask questions was made,

---

[1] 42 & 43 Vict. c. 49, s. 38; 4 & 5 Geo. V. c. 58, s. 22; 15 & 16 Geo. V. c. 86, s. 45; for borough constables, see 45 & 46 Vict. c. 50, s. 227.

[2] [1935] 2 K.B. 249.

that the police could not enter without invitation unless
they had reason to believe that an actual breach of the
peace was being committed. It is, however, difficult not
to hold that the court was right, and the Home Secretary
wrong in his explication of the law, and it is unwise on
the contrast to base a suggestion that one view is officially
taken of Fascist and another of Communist propaganda.
Moreover, in *Davis* v. *Lisle*,[1] it has been ruled that, while
police officers may enter premises in order to make enquiries, they become trespassers if they fail to retire there-
from on request by the occupier. The wide powers of
arrest on suspicion under the Vagrancy Act, 1824, have
been drastically controlled by the courts, while the legislature was moved by the suicide of an unfortunate ex-
soldier, arrested for the venial offence of sleeping out of
doors without being in possession of visible means of
support, to an alteration of the law.

The attitude of the courts has, on the whole, been
marked of recent years by unwillingness to allow executive encroachment. The case of *Art O'Brien*[2] illustrates
their attitude. The accused was arrested and sent to the
Irish Free State, against the Government of which he was
asserted to be hostile, under authority contained in the
Restoration of Order in Ireland Act, 1920, and regulations
thereunder. But the court declared invalid the action
taken because the creation of the Irish Free State had
altered the legal position and declined to suppose that
a new regulation, hastily made by the executive, was
intended to alter the law as it existed at the time of the
arrest. Moreover, it surmounted the difficulty that, while
the arrest had taken place in England, the accused was

---

[1] [1936] 2 K.B. 435.
[2] *O'Brien, Ex parte*, [1923] 2 K.B. 361; *Home Secretary* v. *O'Brien*,
[1923] A.C. 603.

under detention out of England in a place not under the jurisdiction of the court, and it relied instead on the fact that the Home Secretary had in fact the power to secure the return of the accused to the jurisdiction of the court. Parliament, in consequence of the decision, recognising that actions might be brought by all those arrested and deported illegally, instead of legislating to deny them redress gave them in lieu just compensation to be awarded without further legal proceedings.

Not less striking was the decision in *Johnstone* v. *Pedlar* [1] that an alien, who was manifestly engaged in activities hostile to the Government in Ireland, was entitled to the full protection of the law, even though it might have been possible for the Crown to have withdrawn protection from him in view of his activities. The deliberate restriction of the ambit of the defence of Act of State is specially significant.

The necessities of war, undoubtedly, resulted in restriction of liberty. Not only could an interned enemy alien not obtain liberation under *habeas corpus* procedure, but regulations were made under the Defence of the Realm Act for detention of persons with hostile associations or of hostile origin. The leading case of *Zadig* [2] raised, in a very interesting degree, the question as to the power of making regulations under which detention was permitted without proof of crime, and Lord Shaw was decidedly anxious to reduce the power to a minimum, just as in *Sarno's Case* [3] Low, J., was anxious to assert the duty of judges to preserve the liberty of the subject. The majority in the Lords accepted the legality of the detention, and Lord Atkinson stressed the fact that neither the Habeas Corpus Acts or Magna Carta were being violated, as they

[1] [1921] 2 A.C. 262.   [2] *R. v. Halliday*, [1917] A.C. 260.
[3] *Sarno, Ex parte* (1916), 86 L.J.K.B. 62.

were subject to control by subsequent legislation. That really was not clear; the issue was whether the general principle of liberty enshrined in these Acts was duly over-ruled by regulations made under a vague statutory power. In time of peace the principle is clear, and the Government on June 6, 1923, accepted with pleasure from Lord Grey " the long-established principle of the constitution that the executive should not, without the previous and special authority of Parliament, exercise the power of arrest without bringing to trial by due process of law ".

The security of personal liberty is established partly by the civil action for damages for false imprisonment or malicious prosecution, in which a jury may award very high damages. On the occasion of the erroneous taking away of a woman, who was wrongly believed to be a person mentally unsound, the local authority hastily apologised and paid £500 compensation rather than meet an action, and the Home Secretary expressed regret that such an error could have been made. Even in the case of errone-ous detention by the police, the Home Secretary, while defending the legality of the action when within the law, has stressed the desirability of affording full protection, and changes in police procedure have been made to render errors less likely. A *cause célèbre* was that of Miss Savidge, whose prolonged questioning by the police resulted in investigation at the instigation of members of Parliament and in the issue of a report of a Royal Commission [1] which led to reaffirmation of the principles laid down by judicial authority regarding the limits within which questioning is permissible.

Liberation from custody, which is illegal, is best provided for by the Habeas Corpus Acts of 1679 and 1816. The course of their operation has shown the determination

[1] *Parl. Pap.* Cmd. 3231 (1928); 3297 (1929).

of judges not to allow their effect to be whittled away. As we have seen, the writ may be issued to a person who has power to secure the liberation of the person detained, though not himself having actual custody. Moreover, there is no appeal from the decision of the court thereon [1] nor on an order of discharge. But, on the other hand, appeal is permitted from the decision to grant or refuse the writ if the question is one of the custody of an infant,[2] and, where there is no criminal charge but, *e.g.*, custody is provided for under a legislative Ordinance overseas, an appeal lies from refusal to issue the writ,[3] but not from an order of discharge,[4] nor from an order which, without formally providing for discharge, determines the illegality of the detention in question.[5] Moreover, the defence of liberty is so applauded that he who seeks to vindicate it may go from judge to judge up to the highest tribunal.[6] Each must hear and deal with the application on the merits, irrespective of earlier refusals.

The procedure is based on an affidavit either by the prisoner or a person acting on his behalf showing probable grounds for the view that he is illegally detained. In the absence of urgency, a rule *nisi* is made by the Court of King's Bench or a judge in chambers, and a summons is served on the respondent, on the hearing of which the rule *nisi* is either discharged or made absolute, in which case the writ issues. Until 1862, the issue of the writ was possible to any colony or foreign dominion of the Crown, but, as the result of objections naturally taken in Canada to the exercise of this power, which by change of conditions

---

[1] *Woodhall, Ex parte* (1888), 20 Q.B.D. 832.
[2] *Barnardo* v. *Ford*, [1892] A.C. 326.
[3] *R.* v. *Crewe (Earl)* ; *Sekgome, Ex parte*, [1910] 2 K.B. 576.
[4] *Cox* v. *Hakes* (1890), 15 App. Cas. 506.
[5] *Home Secretary* v. *O'Brien*, [1923] A.C. 603.
[6] *Eshugbayi Eleko* v. *Nigerian Govt.*, [1928] A.C. 459.

had become inconvenient, the law was changed to forbid issue to such territories if there is therein a court capable of issuing the writ and securing its execution.[1] The writ cannot be issued to any person outside the jurisdiction of the court. But it lies to the Channel Islands and the Isle of Man, while Scotland has analogous provisions.

The use of the writ is of special interest in extradition proceedings, for it is the procedure under which a person committed for extradition by a magistrate is enabled to obtain the ruling of the High Court on the legality of what has been done. The High Court will decide whether the magistrate has acted within his field of jurisdiction, but not, as a rule at least, whether his decision has been correct either in law or on fact ; [2] but there remains the power of the Secretary of State at his discretion to refuse extradition.   There are analogous provisions regarding fugitive criminals from other parts of the Dominions and other territories under the control of the Crown, and *habeas corpus* proceedings are available to try the legality of the detention in England of prisoners in transit from one part of the Dominions to another.[3] It is in this way that due regard is secured from the rule that offenders may not be surrendered for political offences,[4] while it has been established that a person may be extradited for an offence committed through an agent abroad while the principal was in England.[5]

The value of the Acts has been proved by their application to confinement not under criminal charges.   Thus,

---

[1] 25 & 26 Vict. c. 20 ; *R.* v. *Crewe*, [1910] 2 K.B. 576.
[2] *R.* v. *Brixton Prison*, [1924] 1 K.B. 455 ; *R.* v. *Vyner*, 68 J.P. 142, 143 ; *R.* v. *Brixton Prison Governor ; Bidwell, Ex parte*, [1937] 1 K.B. 305.
[3] *Canadian Prisoners' Case* (1839), 3 St. Tr. (N.S.) 963.
[4] *Castioni, In re*, [1891] 1 Q.B. 149.
[5] *R.* v. *Nillins* (1884), 53 L.J.M.C. 157 ; *R.* v. *Godfrey*, [1923] 1 K.B. 24.

just as slavery in England was declared invalid in *Sommer-*
sett's Case,[1] so it was ruled that a husband has no right
to detain the person of a wife,[2] and that a parent may
recover a child from a home.[3]

In time of war it is normally necessary to legislate as
during the Great War to prevent the full operation of
habeas corpus proceedings, and in addition to measures
taken under the Defence of the Realm Acts an Indemnity
Act was passed in 1920, on the analogy of earlier Acts,
which gave the widest scope of indemnity of actions done
for war purposes, with certain safeguards.

The proceedings of the courts appointed under the
Army and Air Force Acts and the Naval Discipline Act
which authorise arrest and imprisonment are subject to
the intervention of the civil courts by *certiorari* and prohibition, and the officers who sit on them may in case of
usurpation of authority have to answer suits for assault,
false imprisonment, or be indicted for these offences or
manslaughter or murder.

A further measure of safety for liberty is to be found
in the illegality of the use of general warrants [4] to search
for the author or printer of publications alleged to be
criminal, and there is a like prohibition of such warrants
to search for papers [5] whereon a charge of sedition or
blasphemy may be founded. On the other hand, there is
statutory authority to search for papers under the Official
Secrets Act, under the Incitement to Disaffection Act,
1934, to search in premises for stolen goods, or for goods
which infringe the Merchandise Marks Act, 1887, for
blasphemous and obscene libels, counterfeit coins, forged

[1] (1772) 20 St. Tr. 1.
[2] *R.* v. *Jackson* (1891), 1 Q.B. 671.
[3] *Barnardo* v. *Ford*, [1892] A.C. 326.
[4] *Wilkes* v. *Wood* (1763), 19 St. Tr. 1153.
[5] *Entick* v. *Carrington* (1765), 19 St. Tr. 1030.

documents, explosive substances, and so forth. In the case of serious crime it is the custom of the police under common law, even if the arrest is without warrant, to search the persons accused. It appears also from *Elias* v. *Pasmore* [1] that, in case of lawful arrest, it is permissible to search the premises of those arrested and to seize all material relevant to the prosecution of any person for any offence. The dictum of Horridge, J., that " the interests of state excuse the seizure, otherwise unlawful, of documents or articles in the possession or control of the person arrested, if subsequently it should appear in fact that they are evidence of a crime committed by anyone ", is declared [2] to legalise the general warrant by authorising the police, if they can offer ground for the arrest of any person, to search the premises of the organisation with which he is connected with the object of finding evidence, not necessarily affecting him, but of a nature liable to incriminate others against whom they have no charge to make. But the claim seems to be too wide. The accused there was arrested on the premises, which were searched, and the documents discovered in the search, while not used against him, were successfully used in a prosecution for incitement to disaffection. It is clear that the documents were evidence of criminal activities, and it is difficult to see what principle of the right of liberty demands that police, who make a search of premises in which they have made a legal arrest, should be debarred from examining the documents therein, primarily for the purpose of discovering evidence against the person arrested, but secondarily, as in the case in question, with a view to finding evidence of the identity of any person who instigated the accused to illegal steps. Instead we may note that the action was

---

[1] [1934] 2 K.B. 164.
[2] H. J. Laski, *Parl. Govt.* p. 378.

successful in securing the return of the documents taken, once they had served the purpose of evidence against the accused.

There is, no doubt, every ground for vigilance, and the Council for Civil Liberties is wise in taking every care to assert the needs of meeting firmly every tendency to eliminate safeguards. But it is not wise to stress cases where there is clear evidence of illegal action, and of deliberate violation of the law. Incitement to disaffection is not a very laudable form of agitation.

3. *Martial Law*

One aspect of personal liberty, formerly of importance, revived in interest as a result of the outbreak among the native population of Jamaica in 1865. The question was there raised of the powers of the executive to deal with offenders when martial law has been proclaimed. In Jamaica there was undoubtedly serious misconduct in the suppression of the rising, a large number of executions being carried out with but scant proof of guilt, and in some cases accompanied by much cruelty, disgraceful to the British name. One matter, however, especially raised the question of illegality, for one of the outstanding opponents of the Government was arrested in an area where martial law was not in force, and sent to an area where it was, tried and executed, there being singularly insufficient evidence to convict him. The proceedings reflected grave discredit on the governor, who was recalled after a commission had been sent out from England to report, and was never again employed, though he ultimately obtained a pension which he had not earned. His position had been safeguarded, as far as possible, by a local Act of Indemnity, and it therefore proved impossible for persons unjustly treated to secure damages from him in England, since under English law no action lies for a tort committed overseas if it has been there indemnified.[1] An effort was made to bring the governor to book under the statutes penalising criminal actions by governors,[2] but the jury refused to find a true bill, and a like effort to secure punishment of others concerned under the Offences against the Person Act, 1861, penalising murder or manslaughter committed out of England, also failed for a like reason.[3] The charges, however, in both cases laid down important principles of the common law.

The question still left doubtful is not the right of the Crown, its servants, and subjects generally, to use any force necessary to repress disorder, insurrection, and armed rebellion, but the extent of that right. Has the Crown a special prerogative which enables it to act in advance of an emergency in general, apart from the right [4] to requisition ships in an actual emergency ? The answer seems to be in the negative. Again, has the Crown a special prerogative which authorises it to set up military courts to deal summarily with offenders, when martial law has been proclaimed or put in operation ? Or is it simply the case that the Crown, as part of its right to suppress disorder, can, when it is necessary to do so, set up bodies of officers styled courts, or courts-martial, with instructions to inflict summary punishment as part of the measures essential for destroying the rebellion ? If the former view were correct, it would seem natural that the courts so established would be assimilated in legal position

---

[1] *Phillips* v. *Eyre* (1869), L.R. 4 Q.B. 225 ; (1870), 6 Q.B. 1 ; Keith, *The Dominions as Sovereign States*, p. 560.

[2] *R.* v. *Eyre* (1868), L.R. 3 Q.B. 487.

[3] *R.* v. *Eyre*, charge by Blackburn J. (Finlason's Rep.) ; *R.* v. *Nelson and Brand* (1867), Cockburn's charge.

[4] *The Broadmayne*, [1916] P. 64.

to courts-martial under the Army Act, and be subject, if
they exceeded their jurisdiction, to control by the civil
courts. In fact, however, we have the authority of the
House of Lords [1] for the view that neither *certiorari* nor
prohibition lies, because the proceedings are executive,
not judicial. We may, therefore, dismiss the theory of a
prerogative to establish courts in the legal sense of the
term. The further question whether there is a right to
proclaim martial law can probably best be answered by
saying that it is not illegal for the Crown to notify the
existence of conditions which call upon it to exercise
to the fullest its authority to maintain order. An Irish
statute,[2] following on the revolutionary movement in
Ireland in 1798–9, refers to the acknowledged prerogative
of His Majesty for the public safety to resort to the exercise
of martial law against open enemies or traitors. The
ambiguity [3] of the Petition of Right, 1628, in forbidding
commissions to exercise martial law in time of war does
not afford guidance in any way, for the reference may
merely imply that the Crown might, in time of insurrection
or war, discipline its forces by courts-martial. There is
Irish authority in *Egan* v. *Macready* [4] for the view that a
definite prerogative exists to proclaim martial law but
that it can be limited by statute and that it had been
limited by the Restoration of Order in Ireland Act, 1920,
but that decision is hardly of great weight.

The decision of the Privy Council in *Marais's Case* [5]
raised much controversy by the view taken of the right
of civil courts to interfere in martial law proceedings.
The court was presided over by the Lord Chancellor, who

---

[1] *Sullivan and O'Clifford, In re*, [1921] 2 A.C. 570.

[2] 39 Geo. III. c. 11.

[3] Cockburn, L.C.J., in *R.* v. *Nelson*, charge, p. 59, stresses Coke's and
Blackstone's silence as negativing martial law in peace.

[4] [1921] 1 I.R. 265.   [5] [1902] A.C. 109.

of course was interested in the decision because a different result would have severely affected the position of the ministry in relation to the conduct of the war in South Africa. The Chief Justice of the Cape of Good Hope, who sat on the appeal, was known to have a different view, and the authority of the decision is, therefore, less than could be expected. It was laid down that in actual war civil courts had no authority to call in question the action of military courts. It is not an authority for any such right in a mere case of insurrection not amounting to war, and it is not an authority for the validity of sentences imposed by martial law courts after the outbreak or war is over. In the case of South Africa martial law sentences were carefully ratified by local law,[1] and the same plan was adopted in the Union of South Africa later in every case in which martial law was exercised for the purpose of putting down unrest on the mines and for suppressing rebellion in the Union.

In the Irish rebellion the courts acted on the view that they must not interfere with martial law proceedings,[2] and the like view was taken during the rebellion against the provisional Government established under the treaty of 1921 with the United Kingdom.[3] The objection that the provisional forces were not regular governmental forces was rejected, but it was asserted that it lay with the courts themselves to decide if there existed such a state of war as to justify their abstention from intervention,[4] and that, failing indemnification, it would be open for the courts after the end of the period of martial law to pass

---

[1] Cape Acts, Nos. 6 of 1900 ; 4 of 1902. See Keith, *The Sovereignty of the British Dominions*, pp. 558-61.

[2] *R.* v. *Allen*, [1921] 2 I.R. 241 ; *R.* (*Garde*) v. *Strickland*, [1921] 2 I.R. 317 ; *R.* (*Ronayne and Mulcahy*) v. *Strickland*, *ibid.* 333.

[3] *R.* (*Childers*) v. *Adjutant-General of Provisional Forces*, [1923] 1 I.R. 5.

[4] *R.* (*Garde*) v. *Strickland*, [1921] 2 I.R. 317, 329.

judgment on the legality of the actions done.[1] The criterion
in such cases would be the necessity of action rather than
its reasonableness, but it must be a very difficult matter
to assess necessity *ex post facto*, and indemnification is both
prudent and wise. It must not, of course, be thought that
soldiers acting under martial law can commit any excesses
they please unscathed. For the murder of Mr. Sheehy
Skeffington, Captain Bowen-Colthurst was tried and found
guilty by court-martial but insane ; and it was announced
in December in Palestine that, while the conduct of the
troops was normally excellent, four soldiers had been
placed on trial for alleged murder of a martial law prisoner.[2]
No doubt obedience to orders would normally excuse a
soldier's action, while leaving his chief responsible.

4. *Freedom of Speech and the Liberty of the Press*

Democracy demands for its true exercise the widest
possible freedom of criticism, and this right exists in
Britain under the doctrine that a man may say or write
anything so long as it does not constitute slander or libel,
is not blasphemous, obscene, or seditious. These qualifications are of course essential, but the interpretation placed
upon them must largely decide the extent of freedom of
expression both for individuals and the press.

False defamatory words if spoken constitute slander,
if written libel, and words are defamatory if they are
" calculated to convey an imputation on the plaintiff,
injurious to him in his trade, or holding him up to contempt, hatred or ridicule ".[3] Libel may be conveyed by

[1] *Higgins* v. *Willis*, [1921] 2 I.R. 386 ; *R. (O'Brien)* v. *Military Governor*, [1924] 1 I.R. 32.
[2] The Court of Appeal eventually upheld one conviction only, with a reduced sentence, Jan. 26, 1939.
[3] *Capital and Counties Bank* v. *Henty* (1882), 7 App. Cas. at p. 771.

an advertisement[1] and a talking film[2] is libel, not slander.
The rule that special damages must be proved in case of
slander does not apply where words impute crime,[3] or
contagious or infectious disease, or disparage a man in
the way of his profession, office, or trade, but to give a
cause of action it is not enough that defamatory words
may adversely affect a plaintiff in his business ; the language used must be such as affects him therein.[4] By an
Act of 1891 imputations on the chastity of women were
also made actionable without proof of special damage.
But it is not defamatory to state that a person has given
information to the police, for that is the duty of a good
citizen, and it appears not even to be defamatory to add
that an informer is disloyal to members of the club on
whose premises the offence reported occurred.[5] It is even
possible, in the view of the House of Lords, overruling the
Court of Appeal,[6] to make suggestions of discreditable
treatment in money matters of a servant. There are very
considerable difficulties in the position of the press, where
for instance inaccurate information is sent in by corre-
spondents normally trustworthy or photographs of the
wrong persons are published. Efforts to secure limitation
of actions to cases where real damage is proved have been
discussed ; unquestionably there is a real tendency for
juries to award excessive damages against newspapers
without consideration of all the circumstances of the case.

For libels tending to breach of the peace, even if not
made known to a third party, criminal proceedings are
possible. In the case of an information the leave of a

[1] *Tolley* v. *Fry and Sons*, [1931] A.C. 333.
[2] *Youssoupoff* v. *Metro-Goldwyn-Mayer Pictures Ltd.* (1934), 50 T.L.R. 581.
[3] *Gray* v. *Jones* (1939), 55 T.L.R. 437.
[4] *De Stempel* v. *Dunkels*, [1938] 1 A.E.R. 238.
[5] *Byrne* v. *Deane*, [1937] 1 K.B. 818.
[6] *Sim* v. *Stretch* (1936), 52 T.L.R. 669.

judge of the King's Bench Division was necessary,[1] while
an indictment against a newspaper requires sanction of a
judge in chambers. The dissemination of a libel may in a
suitable case be prevented by an injunction.

By certain statutes criminal proceedings for libel are
expressly regulated. Lord Campbell's Act, 1843, makes
it a misdemeanour to publish, or to threaten to publish,
or to offer to prevent the publication of a libel in order
to extort money, or maliciously to publish a defamatory
libel knowing the same to be false, or without knowing its
falsity. The Larceny Act, 1861, made it felony to send a
letter demanding money without probable cause, or to
accuse or threaten to accuse another of certain crimes in
order to extort money.

In 1843 an important concession was made in regard
to the stringency of the law. Before that date it was held
that falsehood was not essential to guilt, and that crimin-
ality was for the judge to decide, not the jury, but Fox's
Act in 1792 allowed the jury to find the accused not guilty.
In 1843 the accused was allowed to prove the truth of the
defamatory statement and that it was for the public benefit
that it should be published, and the liability of the publisher
was diminished by permitting him to prove lack of knowledge and absence of carelessness on his part in publication.

In a large number of cases statements are privileged
so that action does not lie in respect thereof. Thus there is
absolute privilege for statements made by counsel, parties,
and witnesses in judicial proceedings [2] as well as for the
remarks of the judge. There is privilege for statements,
however untrue, made in Parliament,[3] and in documents
which are printed by order of Parliament. State com-

---

[1] Informations can now only be brought *ex officio* by the Attorney-
General: 1 & 2 Geo. VI. c. 63.

[2] Cf. *Royal Aquarium Co.* v. *Parkinson*, [1892] 1 Q.B. 451.

[3] See i. 317, 321, *ante*.

munications between government departments are privileged,[1] reports [2] in pursuance of military duty or proceedings on courts-martial, and fair reports of contemporary judicial proceedings,[3] even if the report deals with an incident really extraneous to the case itself. In other cases there is only qualified privilege, which may be displaced by proof of malice. That applies to communications made in the course of legal, moral, or social duty,[4] statements made in self-defence,[5] communications based on a common interest,[6] fair reports of Parliamentary debates, fair reports of proceedings at public meetings,[7] official or otherwise, and of documents published at governmental request. A report by employers to a labour exchange is libellous, if malice is proved.[8] The reports of the decisions of a domestic tribunal are not privileged.[9]

On matters of public interest if correctly stated fair comment is allowed.[10] There is no more important branch of the work of the press, for it can, by leading articles and by publication of letters from readers, powerfully affect public opinion for good or bad. There is happily a wide field open to discussion of the actions of politicians, and strong language is not rare, as can be seen from the comments on Mr. Winston Churchill's adherence to the Liberal cause in 1903, or on Mr. MacDonald and Mr. Thomas in 1931 when they left their colleagues and joined the Opposition, and in 1938 over the betrayal of Czechoslovakia tempers

[1] *Isaacs & Sons* v. *Cook*, [1925] 2 K.B. 391.
[2] *Dawkins* v. *Rokeby* (1875), 7 H.L. 544.
[3] *Kimber* v. *Press Assocn.* (1893), 62 L.J.Q.B. 152.
[4] *Watt* v. *Longsdon*, [1930] 1 K.B. 130.
[5] *Koenig* v. *Ritchie* (1862), 3 F. & F. 413.
[6] *Hunt* v. *G.N. Ry. Co.*, [1891] 2 Q.B. 191.
[7] 51 & 52 Vict. c. 64, s. 4 ; *De Normanville* v. *Hereford Times, Ltd.* (1936), 79 S.J. 796.
[8] *Mason* v. *Brewis Bros., Ltd.*, [1938] 2 A.E.R. 420.
[9] *Chapman* v. *Ellesmere*, [1932] 2 K.B. 431.
[10] *Wason* v. *Walter* (1868), L.R. 4 Q.B. 73.

and language ran high. But such things are salutary, and, on the other hand, it is forbidden to attack the moral integrity of opponents, or to make false statements of fact regarding them. There is a special penalisation by the Corrupt and Illegal Practices Prevention Act, 1895, of the unpleasing habit of publishing false statements of fact in relation to a person's character at an election.

There is a certain alleviation of the difficulties of the press [1] in the fact that an apology may be pleaded and absence of malice and gross negligence, and payment made into court.[2] Damages may also be mitigated by proof that the plaintiff has already recovered damages from another source.[3] A journalist guilty of criminal libel may be tried summarily and fined up to £50.[4]

By a rule of practice newspapers, when defendants, are not compelled to reveal the name of informants. But this does not apply to the writer of a signed letter in a paper, who may be examined not only as to the information he had when he wrote, but also as to the identity of his informants.[5]

The amount of damages to be awarded in cases of libel is largely at the discretion of the jury, for the House of Lords is not prepared to approve of the substitution of the judgment of the court for that of the jury.

Blasphemy consists in speaking or writing and publishing words vilifying or ridiculing God, Jesus Christ, the Holy Ghost, Old or New Testament, or Christianity in general, with intent to shock or insult believers, or to pervert and

---

[1] Papers or books to be published must bear the printer's name and address (32 & 33 Vict. c. 24), and newspaper proprietors must register their names at Somerset House (44 & 45 Vict. c. 60, s. 9).

[2] R.S.C. Ord. XXII. r. 1.   [3] 51 & 52 Vict. c. 64, s. 6.

[4] 44 & 45 Vict. c. 60, ss. 4, 5.

[5] *South Suburban Co-operative Society, Ltd.* v. *Orum and Croydon Advertiser, Ltd.*, [1937] 2 K.B. 690

Chapter XXV. mislead the ignorant and unwary.[1] It is not, however, blasphemy soberly and reverently to examine the truth of Christianity,[2] even if in theory[3] Christians may be liable to punishment if they deny the truth of the Christian religion. Nor is the habit of swearing in use to be punished. It is no doubt true that the formal expression of the law has lagged behind the advance of public opinion, but it is still common sense that it is undesirable to give any encouragement to blasphemy, and the feelings of large numbers of subjects can easily be injured by reckless attacks on Christian dogmas.

Obscenity raises different issues.[4] It covers matter likely to deprave and corrupt those whose minds are open to immoral influences and into whose hand the works in question are likely to fall. Intention to corrupt is not vital. What is *prima facie* obscene can be published, if it is for the public good as advantageous to literature, science, art, or religion, and the extent of publication is not in excess of what is needed. Power is given by Lord Campbell's Act, 1843, to search for and destroy books that are obscene in the hands of the publisher and bookseller. It is forbidden to send indecent matter by post, and the Postmaster can stop such matter in the post, nor may it be exhibited for sale, nor indecent words written on buildings, etc. In regard to judicial proceedings, the freedom of publication, formerly enjoyed on the plea of public interest, was overruled by the Judicial Proceedings (Regulation of Reports) Act, 1926, which forbids in regard to

[1] *R.* v. *Gott* (1922), 16 Cr. App. R. 87.
[2] *Shore* v. *Wilson* (1842), 9 Cl. & F. 355, 539 ; *R.* v. *Ramsay and Foote* (1883), 48 L.T. 733, 739 ; *Bowman* v. *Secular Society*, [1917] A.C. 406.
[3] 9 Will. III. c. 35.
[4] *R.* v. *Hicklin* (1868), L.R. 3 Q.B. at p. 371 ; *R.* v. *Bradlaugh* (1878), 3 Q.B.D. 569 ; *R.* v. *Barraclough*, [1906] 1 K.B. 201 ; *R.* v. *De Montalk* (1932), 23 Cr. App. R. 182.

judicial proceedings generally the publication of indecent medical details injurious to morals, and in regard to divorce proceedings, of anything save names of parties, charges, legal arguments, summing-up, and result. There are similar restrictions on publication of cases under the new procedure respecting domestic relations of 1937.[1]

Here again it has proved difficult to adapt the exercise of the control of indecency to accord with the change in the standards of the public, and the wide diffusion of knowledge on all sorts of matters which at one time would have appeared to be essentially obscene. Again, a stout defence is often put up on literary and artistic grounds on behalf of certain books and art publications, and regret expressed at the stupidity of magistrates, who insist on forming their own judgments and who ignore the fact that their views are out of date, and that they are suffering from mid-Victorian prudery. It is perhaps doubtful if the works defended are of much value of any kind, and the activity of the police in seeking to destroy the baser forms of literature is laudable.

Sedition [2] raises other problems. There is not the least doubt of the extraordinary breadth of the legal conception of sedition, which includes any publication tending to bring into hatred or contempt or to excite disaffection against the King, his heirs or successors, the Government and Constitution, either House of Parliament, or to excite attempts to alter the matters as established in Church or State otherwise than by lawful methods, or to raise discontent or disaffection, or to promote feelings of hostility between different classes of British subjects. Special powers to search for documents calculated to seduce members of

---

[1] Summary Procedure (Domestic Proceedings) Act, 1937.

[2] 60 Geo. III. & 1 Geo. IV. c. 8, s. 1 ; *R.* v. *Fussell* (1848), 6 St. Tr. N.S. 723; *R.* v. *Vincent* (1839), 3 *ibid.* 1037; *R.* v. *Collins* (1839), 9 Car. & P. 456; *R.* v. *Burns* (1886), 16 Cox C.C. 355.

the defence forces from their allegiance are given by the Incitement to Disaffection Act, 1934. Sedition of course may amount to treason or treason-felony, and be prosecuted as such.

It is clearly possible for such a crime as sedition to be made a danger to the liberty of the subject, if the courts show readiness to interpret in a broad sense the provisions of the law, and the complaint is made [1] that in the case of Communists or unemployed workers there is too great readiness to prosecute and obtain convictions for words or writings insufficient to justify drastic action. Repression, it is suggested, by driving discontent underground may make it more dangerous than if speech were allowed as a safety-valve. Exception was taken very widely in 1937 to a sentence of twelve months' imprisonment inflicted under the Incitement to Disaffection Act, 1934, on a student, who appears to have held out offers to a member of the Air Force to be disloyal to his obligations.[2] But though the sentence, half of which was remitted, was severe, there was at least evidence that the attempt was deliberate, and that of an educated youth. It is impossible to class such an act with wild menaces of half-educated men who are suffering from the disadvantages of unemployment. Prosecutions, on the whole, seem mainly to be directed against leaders such as those mentioned in *Elias* v. *Pasmore*,[3] and it can hardly be said that in such cases there is not real danger of causing disaffection, the results of which for members of the armed forces might prove to be very grave. It is always undesirable to let those who induce crime in others escape the results of their action. But it would no doubt be desirable if steps were

---

[1] H. J. Laski, *Parl. Govt.* pp. 376 ff.
[2] *R.* v. *Phillips, The Times,* March 10 and 15, 1937.
[3] [1934] 2 K.B. 164.

taken much more closely to define the crime of sedition. It is not wise to allow so vague a crime to remain without limitation, and it must be remembered that the older authorities on sedition, which come from the period of repression during the Napoleonic wars, go very far in limiting freedom of discussion of the Government.[1]

Protection to the public against depravation of morals by theatrical exhibitions is to a limited extent provided, formerly under the prerogative, but under statute by the Theatres Act, 1843. The Lord Chamberlain has jurisdiction to forbid the performance of plays, without his licence, at any theatre in Great Britain ; he can also at discretion forbid any public performance of a play if he deems such performance contrary to decorum, good manners, and public peace. An interesting example of the use of the power for diplomatic reasons is afforded by Edward VII's action in securing the temporary cessation of performance of *The Mikado* during a ceremonial visit of a Japanese prince to England.[2] Old plays, if altered, and new plays must be submitted to the Lord Chamberlain for licence ; they are read by an examiner of plays, who insists on excision of what he deems too vulgar or improper for even modern taste ; standards have inevitably so relaxed that words and lack of garments which would have been vetoed in the Victorian age are accepted as a matter of course. But some rules are kept ; the portrayal of Queen Victoria in a play was long forbidden. The Lord Chamberlain is also the licensing authority in the cities of London and Westminster, in Finsbury, Marylebone, and Tower Hamlets, and in Windsor, as the King there has a royal residence. In the counties [3] the power rests with the county council,

---

[1] *Drakard's Case* (1811), 31 St. Tr. 495.   Contrast *R.* v. *Aldred* (1909), 22 Cox C.C. 1.   [2] Lee, *Edward VII*, ii. 381 ff.

[3] Transferred by 51 & 52 Vict. c. 41, s. 7.

but the Universities of Oxford and Cambridge can in the interests of the morals of the youth in their charge forbid the performance there of unsuitable plays, but seemingly they do not do so.

The Lord Chamberlain is not invested with powers over the exhibition of cinematograph films,[1] and, despite suggestions in favour of an official control, that has not been created. On the other hand, there is a voluntary censorship and local authorities supplement it by banning at their discretion even films which have passed its scrutiny.

Attempts by the Government of the day to secure that there shall be reticence in the press regarding issues of political importance are recorded from the early times [2] of responsible government, and are inevitable. But it is obscure whether the remarkable silence of the press regarding the rumours current, and freely detailed in the American press, regarding the attitude of Edward VIII to Mrs. Simpson was in any degree due to governmental pressure, and the assertion that it was so due was denied.

But considerable uneasiness was caused when it was discovered that the Foreign Secretary on September 22, 1938, had used his influence with the United States Ambassador to secure the suppression from a cinematograph film of important statements on the Czechoslovak issue made by two publicists with the intention of giving the public a just view of Czechoslovak rights. The apologia of the Home Secretary on December 7 was far from satisfactory, and the inevitable suspicion has been suggested that other

---

[1] See now 23 & 24 Geo. V. c. 51, ss. 307, 308, sch. 11, as to powers of county and county borough councils.

[2] Cf. Palmerston's relations with the *Morning Chronicle* and the *Globe*; Bell, i. 257. Lord Aberdeen revealed to *The Times* the intention of Peel's Cabinet to repeal the corn laws; Monypenny and Buckle, *Disraeli*, i. 734 f. Mr. Asquith's resignation in Dec. 1916 was forced by a disclosure to *The Times*; Spender, ii. 263 ff.

action of the kind has been or may be taken, and that the country may be treated as in Fascist States where the citizen is allowed to learn only such news as suits the policy of the administration.[1]   No doubt such suppression of information is rendered more possible by the modern system, under which so many newspapers are under the control of a single group of interests,[2] so that divergent views have difficulty in obtaining expression.

Reference [3] has already been made to the dangers which were threatened to the freedom of the press by the improper use of the Official Secrets Acts, and the surrender on this point forced by protests from the press on the ministry.

The British Government controls the British Broadcasting Corporation; it can control all transmission in emergency, at any time a Government Department may require transmission of any matter, and the Postmaster-General may forbid transmission. For defence purposes the Postmaster-General will control the wire broadcasting by the relay companies, a Post Office telephone broadcasting service, and a wireless service, as explained on June 16, 1939. The power of the ministry in time of unrest is clearly very great, and important even in normal conditions.

---

[1] On March 9, 1939, a completely misleading communication as to more settled prospects in Europe was authorised by Mr. Chamberlain, which was completely falsified by March 14, and on April 6 he had to explain away his action in seeking to suppress an indiscreet remark of the First Lord of the Admiralty, which already had been broadcast. Complaint was justly made that the form "D" used in the warning to the press is that normally associated with the Official Secrets Acts. For the giving of inaccurate information on foreign affairs see p. 142, *ante*.

[2] Northcliffe Group (*Daily Mail, Evening News, Sunday Dispatch*); Sir H. Harmsworth Group ; Berry Group (*Daily Telegraph and Morning Post, Sunday Times*) ; Beaverbrook Group (*Daily Express, Evening Standard, Sunday Express*) ; Daily News Group (*News Chronicle, Star*). For the control exercised over journalists see G. E. R. Gedye, *New Statesman*, xvii. 978.

[3] See p. 361, *ante*.

5. *The Special Privileges of Members of Parliament*

It is patent that, if members of Parliament are to exercise effectively their function of criticism, they must acquire as full information as possible on issues of administration. They have habitually done so, and it is common knowledge that the questions and criticisms addressed to ministers derive much of their value from the sources whence they are drawn. Mr. Churchill's effective exposure of the governmental misstatements regarding aeroplane strength could only be based on a measure of official inspiration, and in domestic issues it is often patent that officials concerned with health, labour, or unemployment work have aided members to frame criticism and suggestion.

The fact, however, that Mr. D. Sandys, M.P., a Territorial officer, framed a question calling attention to deficiencies in anti-aircraft guns and other instruments in June 1938, led to the grave error of the Attorney-General in suggesting in a conversation that he might be required, under Section 6 of the Official Secrets Act, 1920, to reveal the sources of his information, with the risk of imprisonment if he did not do so. Further, the Army Council required him to appear before a Military Court of Inquiry on the issue. This was a patent breach of privilege, as the Committee of Privileges held, and as the Commons affirmed on July 11 and 19, for which responsibility rested with the Secretary of State for War. There arose, however, the far more vital question of the position of Mr. Sandys under the Official Secrets Acts, and that formed the subject of two reports [1] from a Select Committee on the Official Secrets Acts. One point indeed was cleared up, apart from the question of the rights of members. The provisions of Section 6 of the Act of 1920 were so patently contrary to

[1] *H.C. Pap.* 173, 1938 ; 101, 1939.

English legal principles in demanding that information should be given with the alternative of punishment, that, as a result of press agitation, the power was, in a Bill introduced into the Lords, confined to cases popularly styled espionage.

The Committee stressed the fact that, under the Acts themselves, it is an answer in any case to a charge of communicating or receiving information of an official character, without due authority, that communication was in the interest of the State; but that rule, while leaving it to a jury to decide in each case, does not specially help members of Parliament. On the other hand, members are called upon to exercise their traditional right and duty of criticising the executive. " Parliaments without parliamentary liberties ", said Pym, " are but a fair and plausible way into bondage ", and, as was said in the Commons' petition to James I respecting impositions,[1] " freedom of debate being once foreclosed, the essence of the liberty of Parliament is withal dissolved ". The Committee therefore accepted the broad view that the immunity of members from the criminal law in respect of acts done by them in the exercise of the functions of their office could not be confined to acts done within the four walls of the House, accepting the dictum of O'Connor, J., in the Ontario case of *R.* v. *Bunting*,[2] which has support from American decisions,[3] and stressing Lord Denman's dictum in *Stockdale* v. *Hansard* [4] that all the privileges that can be required for the energetic discharge by the members of the House of their duties must be conceded without a murmur. The Committee rejected the contention [5] that privilege affords no protection against

---

[1] 1 *Com. Journ.* 431.   [2] (1885), 7 Ont. R. at p. 563.
[3] *Coffin* v. *Coffin*, 4 Mass. 1 ; *Kilbourn* v. *Thompson*, 103 U.S. 168.
[4] (1839), 9 A. & E. at p. 115.
[5] Based on the dictum of Stephen, J., in *Bradlaugh* v. *Gossett* (1884), 12 Q.B.D. 284, that an ordinary crime committed in the Commons would not

criminal prosecution, which it held to be true only of arrest, and to be inapplicable to words spoken by a member as part of his duties as a member. It appears therefore that proceedings for action in Parliament would raise a question of privilege, and would hardly be attempted by the Crown.

This does not cover the question of the illegality of seeking or accepting information not duly authorised to be communicated. It might be difficult to prove such action if there had to be adduced evidence of statements by a member in Parliament, for the Commons could forbid the giving of evidence. But, apart from this, certain considerations may be borne in mind. Though there is no principle that any kind of official information may be properly revealed without authority to a member of Parliament, and certain kinds of information patently could not be so revealed, there remains much that may, without injury to the State, be communicated ; in the past members have shown discretion, and presumably in the future members are likely so to use their knowledge as to benefit the State, not injure it. Prosecutions for offences again require the authority of a departmental head, for whose action some minister must take responsibility in Parliament, so that hasty action is improbable. Further, the Attorney-General must consent to a prosecution ; he must use his discretion judicially, and that would involve his having due regard to the special position and duties of a member of Parliament, with whose traditions and privileges he is essentially familiar. Finally, if the House is in session, a member threatened by prosecution can appeal to it to

be withdrawn from the ordinary course of criminal justice. This would, no doubt, be true of murder or aggravated assault. But the same judge pointed out that " nothing said in Parliament by a member as such can be treated as an offence by the ordinary courts ", which accords with the action of the Lords in 1668 in reversing on a writ of error the judgment in Sir John Eliot's case ; 3 St. Tr. 294 ; 9 *Com. Journ.* 19-25.

treat the matter as one of privilege, and it is always open to the House to regard as a contempt of its authority any action which, without actually infringing any privilege of members, obstructs or impedes them in the discharge of their duty.

The Select Committee was not willing to recommend any effort to define privilege, agreeing with Blackstone [1] on the advantages of keeping privileges indefinite, and stressing the fact, declared by the Commons in 1621, that the privileges of Parliament are the birthright and inheritance of the subject, in whose interest they in truth exist. It felt that the matter should be left to the good sense of members in using discretion in framing questions or seeking information regarding matters which affect the safety of the realm, while ministers should remember that the powers conferred on the executive by the Official Secrets Acts must not be used in such a way as to impede members in discharging their Parliamentary duties. In the conclusions of the Committee the Commons concurred, while the Lords referred the issue as affecting themselves to a Committee.

It is clear that, with a warning regarding issues of defence or Cabinet proceedings or Budget disclosures, the Committee is not disposed to interfere with the freedom of members to accept information from official sources without assuring themselves that its giving has been authorised. It must be remembered that much information is actually given under formal or implied authority to members who place themselves in touch with governmental departments. A minister often feels that his actions are such that knowledge thereof will redound to the profit of his department. In other cases officials feel it in the public interest to inform members of matters affecting their departments, even if they risk loss of office or even prosecution. In some cases,

[1] 1 Com. 164.

Chapter
XXV.
no doubt, such action is motived by political partisanship, but this is not lightly to be assumed.

It must not, however, be thought that a member of Parliament can with impunity reveal in the Commons matters of secret character injurious to the welfare of the country. A member who thus acted might be suspended from the service of the House, imprisoned, or expelled absolutely, and the last punishment at least is severe. None the less it must be admitted that a possible danger exists in the wide ambit of privilege accepted by the Committee, but against this must be set the great advantage of the Commons serving as the supreme inquest of the nation.

There is a further difficulty in the question of the legal position of the press if it reports improper disclosures made in the Commons by a member. No doubt in such a case as the making of statements contrary to the public interest an immediate appeal to the press reporters would secure that nothing injurious would be printed.

6. *The Right of Public Meeting*

The existence of the right of public meeting is without special legal protection in English law. It follows merely from the general principle that men may meet and discuss and listen to speeches wherever they like so long as they violate no law. They may not invade private property, and they may not obstruct the roads, which are primarily intended for passage. The issue was made a matter of great public importance in 1888, when efforts were made to claim the right of holding meetings in Trafalgar Square, but it was ruled [1] that action of this sort involved com-

---

[1] *R.* v. *Graham* (1888), 16 Cox C.C. 420 ; *Lewis, Ex parte* (1888), 21 Q.B.D. 191.

mitting a nuisance, which could be punished by fine as a misdemeanour. It does not, however, suffice to make a meeting unlawful because it is held in a highway.[1] The use of public parks for meetings was specially contested in the case of Hyde Park, where great meetings were held in 1866–7 in respect of the Reform agitation.[2] The position was cleared up by the Parks Regulation Act, 1872 ; and by the Municipal Corporations Act, 1882, and the Local Government Act, 1888, power was given to boroughs and country councils to regulate these issues. The Metropolitan Police Act, 1839, and the Metropolitan Streets Act, 1867, authorised the police to control processions. Older legislation still forbids tumultuous petitioning and the assembly of people for political purposes in numbers over fifty within a mile of Westminster Hall when Parliament or the courts of law are in session.[3]

There are obvious dangers in the meeting of large bodies of people, lest they develop into illegal assemblies. It constitutes a riot if three or more persons assemble with a common purpose, even if that purpose be itself legal, with the intention of mutual support against any opposition to the execution of their aim, and in executing their end display force or violence, so as to alarm at least one person of reasonable firmness. It becomes a rout when persons so assembled make a motion to execute their purpose. The responsibility for riot damage rests with the police fund of the appropriate authority, which gives special importance to the prevention of serious rioting.

---

[1] *Burden* v. *Rigler*, [1911] 1 K.B. 335.

[2] Walpole, *History*, ii. 173, 197. There is no absolute right to meet on a common (*De Morgan* v. *Metropolitan Board of Works* (1880), 5 Q.B.D. 155), or the foreshore (*Brighton Corpn.* v. *Packham* (1908), 72 J.P. 318). Obstruction of a footpath is illegal : Highway Act, 1835, s. 72 ; *Homer* v. *Cadman* (1886), 16 Cox C.C. 51.

[3] 13 Car. II. st. 1, c. 5 ; 57 Geo. III. c. 19, s. 23.

The Riot Act [1] strengthens the common law by making
it felony for twelve or more persons, riotously assembled,
to fail to disperse when commanded by a magistrate,
sheriff, mayor, or justice within an hour after the reading
of a proclamation under the Act ; they may be forcibly
dispersed even at the cost of death or injury. Armed
opposition to the reading of a proclamation is also a felony.
The police magistrates, and, at the request of the police,
other persons, are bound to aid in the preservation of order.
It is the duty of magistrates to secure order, and out of
the rioting at Bristol during the Reform movement arose
a trial of great notoriety, that of the Mayor of Bristol,[2] for
failure to cope with the rioters. The use of military forces
on these occasions is wholly proper ; where possible the
Home Secretary is used as a channel of communication
with the War Office, but in case of need local authorities can
apply direct to the officer in command of the nearest troops,
and the officers themselves may take action, if the situation
is getting out of hand. The limits on the employment of
the military for these purposes were carefully investigated
by a commission on the Featherstone riots [3] which reported
in 1894. Military forces were in considerable numbers held
in readiness during the General Strike in 1926, and in less
degree have been used in many minor cases of serious unrest.

Persons who take part in an unlawful assembly [4] are
guilty of misdemeanour, and an assembly is unlawful if
three or more people (1) assemble to commit, or when
assembled do commit, a breach of the peace, or (2) assemble to commit a crime by open violence, or (3) assemble
for any common purpose, even if lawful, in such a manner,

---

[1] 1 Geo. I. st. 2, c. 5 ; *R.* v. *Child* (1831), 4 Car. & P. 442.

[2] *R.* v. *Pinney* (1832), 5 Car. & P. 254. Cf. *R.* v. *Neale* (1839), 9 Car. & P.
431.

[3] *Parl. Pap.* C. 7234 (1894) ; Spender, *Lord Oxford*, i. 82-5, 210.

[4] *R.* v. *Neale, u.s.*

e.g. through carrying arms, as to give ground to reasonable people that a breach of the peace may occur. Prosecutions of Chartists for unlawful assembly and sedition were by no means rare at the beginning of Queen Victoria's reign, and the offence is still regularly prosecuted. But grave difficulties have arisen, on which much judicial divergence of view has been recorded, with regard to the position of an assembly whose own conduct is orderly and proper but which is violently opposed. If any meeting becomes disorderly, it is clear that the police may legitimately order it to disperse, simply on the ground that it constitutes a public nuisance ; if the order is disobeyed, obedience may be enforced. If, again, the police have reason to fear that riotous assemblies and tumultuous petitions may be promoted, application may be made to a magistrate, who may call upon any persons likely to promote disorder to give security for good behaviour ; refusal to do so may be met by committal to prison : when this procedure was employed against Mr. T. Mann in 1933 it was the cause of considerable protest, but its legality was beyond doubt, though the authority was a statute of 34 Edward III. c. 1.

It is obvious that there is considerable danger to the right of public meeting through the attitude of a hostile mob attempting to interfere with the meeting and thus creating ground for the termination of the meeting by police order. In the case of *Beatty* v. *Gillbanks* [1] the Court of King's Bench seemed to afford some hope for the fair treatment of orderly persons threatened by mobs ; the conviction of a Salvation Army leader on a charge of unlawful assembly was considered ; two justices had ordered him and others to abstain from assembling to disturb the peace. On case stated, the court ruled that a man cannot

[1] (1882), 9 Q.B.D. 308. Cf. *R.* v. *Justices of Londonderry* (1891), 28 L.R. Ir. 440, 461.

be punished for doing a lawful act because he knows that his action will evoke illegal conduct on the part of others. It had been held in an earlier case in Ireland [1] that a constable was justified in taking away an orange lily from a lady who was wearing it under such circumstances as to cause excitement and tumult. But stress had been laid on the peculiar urgency of the occasion of action, and it was recognised that there was great danger of making the law of the mob, not the law of the land, supreme. In *Wise* v. *Dunning* [2] this risk seems to have been run, for it was ruled that a magistrate, if there was evidence to show that a breach of the peace might be committed, might bind over persons who were alleged to be intending to carry out a lawful purpose in an unlawful manner by holding meetings and using language slanderous of Roman Catholics, for such an assembly would be an unlawful assembly. It is difficult not to feel that this view can be so pressed as to make every holding of an assembly dependent on the will of those opposed to the views of the promoters ; if they threaten to raise a riot, the assembly may in effect be forbidden. No doubt if at an assembly disorder breaks out through the attacks of the opposition, the police may call on the assembly to disperse ; but it is clear that the proper course is to endeavour first of all to arrest the interrupters. No further light is shed on the subject by *Duncan* v. *Jones*,[3] for the point there decided was simply that a police officer may forbid the holding of a meeting at a specified place, if experience gives justification for the view that the sympathisers with the purpose of the assembly may proceed to a riotous action, and that resistance to his order constitutes obstructing him in the exercise of his duties.

[1] *Humphries* v. *Connor* (1864), 17 Ir. C.L.R. 1.
[2] [1902] 1 K.B. 167.   [3] [1936] 1 K.B. 218.

The question arises whether, if other persons or the Chapter
XXV. police interfere with members of a lawful assembly, they can assert by force their right to assemble. From the decision in *R.* v. *Ernest Jones* [1] it seems that they should strictly refrain from anything more than self-defence, and should retreat rather than cause a breach of the peace by standing their ground, their legal right being to bring an action for assault or false imprisonment or to initiate criminal proceedings on that score. Common sense shows that the prime duty of the police is to arrest the offenders, and save the members of the assembly from the necessity of self-help.

In certain cases it has been attempted by recent legislation to control disorder. In order to diminish violence at electoral meetings, in special the Public Meeting Act, 1908, made disorderly conduct at any public meeting punishable by fine or imprisonment, and in the case of a political meeting such conduct is an illegal practice within the meaning of the Corrupt and Illegal Practices Act, 1883. But the Act proved of singularly little effect because it was regarded as undemocratic to invite police to be present at such meetings, and candidates at political meetings preferred to be shouted down rather than be dubbed lacking in sportsmanship, though there is little democracy in the spectacle of a speaker vainly striving against organised noise to explain political issues to a supposedly intelligent electorate.

A further step was taken in 1936.[2] The use of processions as means of demonstrations had become more and more frequent latterly, though it is a technique which has never lacked admirers, but processions of the Fascist party had become the cause of much disorder, whether the provocation came from the Fascists or their opponents ; on

---

[1] (1848), 6 St. Tr. (N.S.) 783.   [2] 1 Edw. VIII. & 1 Geo. VI. c. 6.

both sides there was very scant sign of reason. Moreover, the wearing of uniforms by the Fascists had an unpleasing similarity to the like practice among their Italian namesakes and the Nazis in Germany, whose tactics they sought to rival. The Public Order Act, 1936, renders illegal the use of uniforms in public places or at public meetings, signifying association with any political organisation or the promotion of a political object, unless under a special permit by the chief officer of police with the consent of a Secretary of State. Quasi-military organisations organised to usurp the functions of the police or to display physical force for political objects were also rendered illegal. Outside the City of London and the Metropolitan Police area, the chief officer can apply to the borough or urban district council for an order forbidding meetings for three months or less ; the assent of the Home Secretary is necessary ; the Commissioners of the City Police and of the Metropolitan Police have the power of prohibition with like assent. It is made illegal to possess offensive weapons when attending public meetings or processions, and offensive conduct tending to a breach of the peace is forbidden. Further, the Public Meeting Act is slightly strengthened, for at the request of the chairman a constable may ask an interrupter his name and address, and if he refuses or there is reasonable supposition that he is giving false information, he may be arrested without a warrant. This provision seems to have had little effect.

It has been objected [1] to the Act of 1936 that the result is that, in order to deal with Fascist processions and meetings which were disorderly, it has been decided to restrict equally Socialist or Communist gatherings which were orderly. But it is probable that in many areas the power

[1] H. J. Laski, *Parl. Govt.* pp. 380 f. ; W. H. Thompson, *Civil Liberties*, p. 37.

is not undesirable, if not used too freely. It must be remembered that in parts of London a quite unreasonable burden has been imposed on the police of preventing collisions between rival parties, and that such incidents, besides distracting the police from other duties, afford opportunities for theft and other forms of nefarious action.

The Public Order Act supplements as regards illegal drilling or practising military evolutions older legislation which forbids such action without the authority of the King or a Lord-Lieutenant or two justices.[1]

The use of force, including the employment of defence units or men, to suppress disorder has formed the subject of investigation and definition.[2] The indiscriminate use of firearms has been censured, and it has been made clear that troops should show all forbearance, should fire only in case of clear necessity to end disorder, should concentrate fire on actual rioters and avoid random shooting, which under modern conditions as to firearms usually ends in the death of innocent passers-by. In the Irish Free State damages have been awarded for reckless killing, and the prosecution of the offenders has been urged by Hanna, J. In England investigation has normally cleared those who fired from suspicion of criminal recklessness.

7. *The Right of Association*

The basis of the right of association is simply the right of contract under common law, the right to form trusts for any lawful end, and the power to set up companies. In

---

[1] 60 Geo. III. & 1 Geo. IV. c. 1. The power to authorise is given to a Secretary of State or a deputed officer by 10 & 11 Geo. V. c. 43, s. 16.

[2] Cf. Belfast Riots Commission, 1886, *per* Day, J., in *Manual of Mil. Law* (1914), p. 231 ; *H.C. Pap.* 236, 1906, *per* Mr. Haldane (*ibid.* p. 226) ; Featherstone Riot Committee, C. 7234 ; Batchelor's Walk Shooting (1914), Cd. 7631 ; *Lynch* v. *Fitzgerald*, [1938] I.R. 382.

1824–5 the existing laws against combinations of workers were modified, but it was made clear that acts of force in seeking to achieve the ends of such combinations were unlawful and criminal. In 1851 [1] it was decided that it was criminal for workers to combine to induce other workers to leave the service of their employers, and in 1861 this was embodied in the Offences against the Person Act. In 1871 [2] a very great concession was made by Mr. Gladstone's Government. It was provided that the purposes of a trade union should not be deemed illegal because they were in restraint of trade, and that unions might, if registered, vest their property in trustees, and penalties were imposed on persons embezzling their funds. But the Act forbade legal proceedings to enforce directly any of the purposes of the union. In 1875 [3] the Conspiracy and Protection of Property Act repealed existing legislation making breach of contract, with a few necessary exceptions, criminal, and provided that an agreement to do any act should not be an indictable conspiracy if such an act done by one person would not be a crime unless such combination was expressly made criminal by statute. At the same time peaceful picketing by strikers with a view to influence other workers to refrain from working was legalised. In 1893, [4] however, it was ruled that an action for damages lay against those who induced tradesmen to break contracts or even to refuse to enter into contracts; there was older authority on the issue of procuring breach of contract, but it referred to special cases such as that of a singer. [5] Later, [6] it was suggested

---

[1] *R.* v. *Rowlands* (1851), 5 Cox C.C. 466 ff. ; *R.* v. *Duffield, ibid.* 431.
[2] Trade Union Act, 1871 (34 & 35 Vict. c. 31).
[3] Conspiracy and Protection of Property Act, 1875 (38 & 39 Vict. c. 86).
[4] *Temperton* v. *Russell,* [1893] 1 Q.B. 715.
[5] *Lumley* v. *Gye* (1853), 2 E. & B. 224.
[6] *Quinn* v. *Leathem,* [1901] A.C. 495.

that a combination to induce third parties not to deal with or work for any person was actionable if damage accrued to such party. Further, in the *Taff Vale Case* [1] it was ruled that a trade union, though unincorporated and thus not a person in law, could be held liable in tort for the actions of its officers in carrying on a strike. This result caused great consternation, and further difficulty arose from the fact that the courts, very naturally, gave a restrictive interpretation to the right of picketing, which had no doubt been abused.[2] The Liberal victory was undoubtedly helped by the Labour reaction to decisions which were considered by those affected to be directly aimed at the efforts of the workers to better their conditions.

The Liberal Government [3] therefore passed the Trade Disputes Act in 1906 without any effort at resistance by the Lords, though the measure was not that drafted for the Government with due care, but represented the form preferred by Labour and accepted by the Prime Minister in the Commons, not without regret on the part of the more orthodox Liberals. The Act amended the definition of peaceful picketing and made it dangerously wide, but its essential concession was to exempt trade unions from responsibility for torts of officers or members, even if not done in the furtherance of labour disputes.[4] It provides that no action will lie for any act done, in contemplation or furtherance of a trade dispute, by a combination of persons if the act could not be actionable if done without combination, and for any act which merely induces a breach of contract of employment or interferes with trade, business, or employment or the right of some other person

[1] [1901] A.C. 426.
[2] *Lyons* v. *Wilkins*, [1899] 1 Ch. 255 ; *Charnock* v. *Court*, [1899] 2 Ch. 35.
[3] Spender, *Campbell-Bannerman*, ii. 277-80.
[4] *Vacher* v. *London Society*, [1913] A.C. 107.

to dispose of his capital.   A certain alleviation of the
extreme character of this legislation was afforded by the
principle which allowed a member of a society to obtain
an injunction against the use of the funds of the society
for unauthorised ends and against his expulsion for object-
ing to such use.   It was thus possible for resistance to be
made to the attempt to enforce a political levy [1] on an
unwilling member, and though the collection of political
levies was sanctioned by legislation [2] in 1912, some protection was then accorded to the members unwilling to pay.

The position of the trade unions became of serious
importance in the post-war period, when efforts were made
to organise a general strike to influence the political
activity of the Government in 1920, but without success.
In 1926, however, the grave error of the General Strike
showed that some trade unionists were without regard for
the essential interests of the State.   It was, therefore,
found necessary to legislate in the public interests, and the
Trade Disputes and Trade Unions Act, 1927, declares
illegal any strike which has any object other than, or in
addition to, the furtherance of a trade dispute within the
trade or industry in which the strikers are engaged, and
is a strike designed or calculated to coerce the Government
either directly or by the infliction of hardship on the
community.   Workmen are deemed to be within the same
trade or industry if their wages and conditions of employment are determined by the same Joint Industrial Council,
Conciliation Board, or similar body.   Lock-outs are equally
penalised in analogous circumstances, and it is an offence
to take part in a strike or lock-out in such circumstances.
The provisions of the Act of 1906 then are inapplicable,
and it is made illegal to expel from a union or penalise a

[1] *Amalgamated Society* v. *Osborne*, [1910] A.C. 87.
[2] 2 & 3 Geo. V. c. 30.

person who refuses to take part in an illegal action. The Attorney-General is also authorised to apply for an injunction to prevent the use of union funds in supporting such a strike. The political levy was rendered more effectively optional by requiring a positive assertion of willingness to pay by the members as opposed to the former rule which placed on members the necessity of the unpopular initiative in contracting out. Returns of the political funds of the unions were made obligatory. As mentioned elsewhere, organisations of Civil servants to improve pay and service conditions must not be affiliated to outside bodies with political objects. Moreover, no local or other governmental authority may penalise or differentiate against employees because of membership or non-membership of a trade union.[1]

The Act was at the time of its passing severely attacked by Labour partisans and these attacks have often been renewed.[2] They can hardly be held to be justified ; a general strike is simply an effort to coerce the Crown, and at common law is probably illegal. It is a substitution of mob violence — for into that a strike rapidly degenerates — for the orderly process of the ballot, and it is the negation of democracy. It is therefore a procedure which can commend itself only to those who believe that the establishment of socialism can be brought about only by revolutionary violence, and who believe in the doctrine of force, because they despair of converting their fellow countrymen to their economic dogmas.

The association of trade unions with political ends is the more objectionable because the enormous power of the unions denies to men in very many cases the possibility of engaging in any skilled employment if they are

---

[1] *Att.-Gen.* v. *Birkenhead Corpn.* (1929), 93 J.P. 33.
[2] Clynes, *Memoirs*, ii. 80 ff. ; H. J. Laski, *Parl. Govt.* pp. 379 ff.

not members of a union. To compel a man to adhere to
one political faith, as the price of procuring a decent living,
is as objectionable in principle and practice as the old
system under which agricultural tenants had to share their
landlords' political views.

Difficult questions sometimes arise out of the proceedings of trade unions. The right of a member to prevent
illegal use of funds has been referred to, but a trade union
tribunal, dealing with issues of membership, is in the same
position as any other domestic tribunal and will be allowed
to decide questions, so long as it complies with the requirements of natural justice, which in effect means so long as
the member is given a fair hearing, even if the decision is
plainly biased.[1] Nor can any member sue for the benefits
promised him if they should be denied, and where he
cannot sue he cannot obtain an injunction.[2] The courts,
however, may pronounce on the validity of by-laws of the
union.[3]

There are difficulties as to the limits of actions taken
to eliminate competition among members of one trade.
It has been ruled that members of a shipping combine can
protect themselves against competition by a system of
rebates refused to shippers who use rival lines,[4] and it has,
more surprisingly,[5] been laid down that a trade association
may put on a stop list, and so penalise, members who
violate a price agreement, and that fines paid on threat
of being thus treated cannot be recovered as paid under
duress. The Court of Criminal Appeal[6] rather naturally

---

[1] Ross v. Electrical Trades Union (1937), 81 S.J. 650.
[2] Russell v. Amal. Soc., [1910] 1 K.B. 506.
[3] Gozney v. Bristol, &c., Soc., [1909] 1 K.B. 901 ; Cox v. National Union
(1928), 44 T.L.R. 345 ; Miller v. A. E. U., [1938] Ch. 669.
[4] Mogul Steamship Co. v. McGregor, [1892] A.C. 25.
[5] Hardie and Lane v. Chilton (No. 2), [1928] 2 K.B. 306.
[6] R. v. Denyer, [1926] 2 K.B. 258.

thought such a demand criminal, but that view has been overruled by the House of Lords.[1]

8. *The Right to Property*

The Victorian conviction of the rights of property was marked by the adoption of the principle that compensation for taking of property for public purposes, central or local, must be accompanied by generous compensation, including allowance for the mere fact of expropriation as an invasion on the normal right to have and hold free from interference. This may be seen not merely in the case of lands taken for defence purposes but in the Lands Clauses Consolidation Act, 1845, the Railways Clauses Consolidation Act, 1845, the Waterworks Clauses Act, 1847, and the Towns Improvement Clauses Act, 1847. In the same spirit, though it was clear that commissions in the army had been bought at prices which were plainly illegal, the Government in 1871[2] readily secured authority for the illegalities to be overlooked. Since then it has been the constant complaint that efforts to improve the condition of the country, especially as regards housing and town planning, have been gravely hampered by the need of paying compensation on excessive terms, though there have been efforts by legislation[3] to moderate the tribute exacted.

There may be noted also the tendency of the courts to regard with jealousy every effort to obtain from wealthy taxpayers an adequate contribution to the revenue. Instead of adopting the maxim, which is applied in interpreting Dominion constitutions, that the substance of legislation should be preferred to the form, it has been

---

[1] *Thorne* v. *Motor Trade Assocn.*, [1937] A.C. 797.

[2] May, *Const. Hist.* iii. 274 ff.

[3] Acquisition of Land (Assessment of Compensation) Act, 1919 (9 & 10 Geo. V. c. 57).

repeatedly decided [1] that any mode of evasion of taxation which can be made consistent with a strict interpretation of the law against the interests of the State is legitimate, and does not evoke even protests on moral grounds from the judiciary. Yet for men of great wealth to spend large sums on legal advice, in order to avoid substantial contributions to the State, seems hardly creditable. It is unfortunate also that no Government has taken the sensible resolve to put an end to the evasion of tax payment by men who derive their fortunes from Britain, but claim a formal domicil in the Channel Islands, or in some Dominion where death duties are low.

A more satisfactory side of the attitude of the courts was revealed by the decisions which negatived during the war period any right on the part of the Crown to levy what was essentially a tax under some other form. In *Attorney-General* v. *Wilts United Dairies* [2] the executive under authority derived from the Defence of the Realm Consolidation Act, 1914, prohibited milk-dealers purchasing milk in one area for export to another area, except under licence. For giving such licences a charge of 2d. a gallon was imposed. The House of Lords ruled that this was a levying of money for the use of the Crown without the sanction of Parliament, and that its imposition was *ultra vires* and illegal. It may be held that there was not much moral justification for the objections of the firm to pay what it had agreed to do, and ultimately the War Charges (Validity) Act, 1925, was passed in order to stop claims of this sort.

There has, however, arisen of late years a new form of compulsory levies which do not rest on contract alone.

[1] *Inland Revenue Commrs.* v. *Westminster (Duke)*, [1936] A.C. 1. In his budget speech, 1939, Sir J. Simon announced retrospective legislation against the grosser forms of evasion.

[2] (1922), 91 L.J. K.B. 897.

The schemes for marketing natural produce, which are operated under the Agricultural Marketing Act, 1931, have a certain element of voluntariness in so far that those who are to be affected by the scheme, when it has been formulated, are permitted the right to vote as to whether the scheme is to be accepted. But, once the scheme has been approved by a majority of those who are in the category of persons affected by it, it becomes binding on all who wish to continue to produce, *e.g.* milk, for other than mere domestic consumption. These organisations are empowered to fix contributions of various kinds to be met by the persons comprised by the scheme, and these sums become payable, and can be recovered in the courts from reluctant payers. Moreover, a certain authority to impose penalties on persons who do not comply with the terms of the schemes is also accorded. Of the general validity of schemes there is no doubt, but in the case of *Ferrier* v. *Scottish Milk Marketing Board* [1] the House of Lords, overruling the Court of Session, applied *inter alia* the rule that taxation must be directly enacted by Parliamentary authority to invalidate the action of the Board in calling upon producer-retailers of milk to contribute a sum towards making up the difference between the sums obtained by the Board for milk sold for manufacture and the price of milk sold for consumption as such. The Board had claimed that the right under the scheme to call on the producer-retailers to contribute towards the costs of operating the scheme covered this claim. It was, however, fairly plain that this was an unjustified stretching of the term " cost " ; it was a contribution, possibly legitimate in the view that the scheme was intended to be worked on a basis of pooling receipts and sharing them out, but patently not covered by the authority given.

[1] [1937] A.C. 126.

These Boards are clearly a serious innovation as regards property rights, since their creation compels people who have long been engaged in individual industry to join a system of pooling receipts and selling as directed by the Board ; but their necessity has on the whole rendered them acceptable, though not without criticism of the manner in which the Board are permitted to exercise quasi-judicial authority over those who are implicated by law therein.

PART IX
THE STATE AND RELIGION

CHAPTER XXVI

THE STATE AND RELIGION

1. *The Church of England*

IN 1837 the regeneration of the Church of England was Chapter XXVI.
in full swing. Parliament in 1818 [1] had contributed gener-
ously to the building of new churches to meet the growth
of population, and in 1836 the ecclesiastical commissioners
were incorporated for the purpose of carrying into effect
wide reforms recommended by a Commission set up in
1835 to make recommendations regarding the better
employment of the still very large revenues of the Church.
The undue cost of cathedral and collegiate churches was
retrenched and provision made for augmentation of small
livings, while Queen Anne's Bounty continued to render
much aid. In 1836 a very important Act provided for
the commutation of tithe into a rent charge upon land,
payable in money, but varying according to the average
price of corn for the last seven years. This commutation
was practically complete by 1851, replacing the utterly
outworn practice under which the tithe was collected in
kind.

Much more important constitutionally was the decision
in 1850 to revive the activity of the convocations which
had been intermitted since 1717,[2] when a controversy
over a sermon preached by the Bishop of Bangor on the

---

[1] 58 Geo. III. c. 45 ; 3 Geo. IV. c. 72.
[2] Hallam, *Const. Hist.* iii. 244 ff.

subject of religious toleration caused so much ferment
that the ministry promptly prorogued the convocation.
Thereafter, while regularly summoned, prorogation as
regularly followed, and only in 1850 was the practice of
allowing discussion resumed. In 1861 was resumed the
practice of permitting the making of canons. The statute
regulating the procedure is the Submission of the Clergy
Act, 1534,[1] which lays down the principles that convocations can meet only with the royal summons, can make
canons only with royal licence, and that canons have no
force without royal assent, nor can they bind the laity
without the approval of Parliament. The procedure takes
the form of an Order in Council for the writs to the archbishops, followed by the writs, in consequence of which
the archbishops procure the attendance of their bishops,
deans, and a proctor for each chapter, archdeacons, and
two proctors of the clergy for each diocese in Canterbury,
and for each archdeaconry in York ; the bishops form the
upper, the others the lower house in each province. The
convocations can be prorogued and dissolved by writs
under the great seal only ; normally they are summoned
and dissolved with Parliament, but in 1921 this rule was
departed from in order to allow of the functioning of the
Church Assembly, then newly created.[2]

The making of canons requires royal letters of business,
accompanied by a licence in the form of letters patent
giving power to make, subject to confirmation, and a canon
duly enacted, usually by both provinces, becomes law on
a royal licence to promulgate. Thus in 1861 it was desired
to alter the 62nd canon forbidding parents to be sponsors
for their children, and in 1887 to alter canons 62 and 102
regarding the hours for solemnising marriage, which Parliament had extended to 3 P.M. In 1872 the authority was

[1] 25 Henry VIII. c. 19.   [2] Fitzroy, *Memoirs*, ii. 743 f.

given to frame resolutions regarding a shorter form of Chapter XXVI.
service, and this was then enacted by Parliament in the
Act of Uniformity Amendment Act, 1872.

It was clear that the process meant the complete control [1] of ecclesiastical legislation by the Crown, and equally
clear that the laity had no voice in decisions. The defect
was made up by various devices which gave a consultative
voice to the laity, but the war led to a definite advance,
which transfers from Parliament most of its legislative
power in matters ecclesiastical, and renders it unlikely that
it will legislate on such matters except in the new way.
The Church of England Assembly (Powers) Act, 1919,
provides for the existence of a National Assembly, consisting of three houses : the House of Bishops comprises
the members of the upper houses of the two convocations,
the House of Clergy the members of the two lower houses,
and the House of Laity is elected by the lay members of
the Diocesan Conference, who themselves are elected by the
parochial church meetings to which communicants of
the Church are admitted. In 1937 permission was given
to co-opt not more than ten persons to serve as members
of the house.[2]

Measures may be passed by this body under a prescribed procedure. Any innovation touching doctrinal
formulae or the services or ceremonies of the Church, or
the administration of the sacraments or sacred rites thereof,
must be debated and voted upon by each house separately,
and must then be either accepted or rejected by the
Assembly in the terms in which it is finally proposed by
the House of Bishops. The Assembly or any house may
debate and formulate its judgment by resolution upon any

---

[1] *E.g.* in 1861 and 1865 permission to promulgate an alteration of the
29th canon was refused.
[2] House of Laity (Co-opted Members) Measure, 1937.

matter concerning the Church or otherwise of religious or public interest, but the Assembly may not issue any statement purporting to define the doctrine of the Church on any matter of theology. The powers of the Convocations remain intact, and the Assembly may not exercise any power or perform any function belonging to the bishops by virtue of episcopal status.

When legislation is intended, then the measure must be submitted by the Legislative Committee of the Assembly to an Ecclesiastical Committee of both houses of Parliament consisting of fifteen members chosen by the Lord Chancellor and fifteen chosen by the Speaker. This body reports to Parliament on the nature and legal effects of the measure and gives its views as to the expediency thereof, especially with relation to the constitutional rights of all His Majesty's subjects. This report is sent to the Legislative Committee, and then only, if it so requests, is the measure submitted with the report to Parliament, whereupon, if a resolution in both houses is passed in favour of its receiving the royal assent, it may be presented for that assent, which is given as for a public Bill in the terms : *Le roy le veult.*[1] Such a measure may repeal any Act of Parliament including the Church of England Assembly (Powers) Act itself, but it may not alter the constitution or powers and duties of the Ecclesiastical Committee nor the procedure in Parliament. This is a most remarkable grant of power, but it is explicable by the fact that both houses are fully apprised of the constitutional implications of the measure before it is voted upon.

Two cases are well known where this sanction by Parliament has been refused, in both cases by the Commons against the less strong Protestantism of the Lords ;

[1] Very oddly the assent is not recorded on the measures published.

in 1927 and 1928 alike the Commons refused to sanction the Prayer Book [1] as revised to meet romanising tendencies in the Church. The plea that the new version was necessary in any case, as the old was never literally obeyed, was met by the perfectly correct contention that there would be no difficulty in accepting nearly all the changes, but that it was not fair to force through changes which were inconsistent with the Protestant character of the Church as established under Elizabeth and the Stuarts. The promise that the bishops would see that the new book would be obeyed, and nothing not thereby allowed permitted, was met by the unanswerable argument that no steps whatever had been taken to exercise the powers of the bishops to put down the illegal practices disapproved by the report of the Royal Commission which had investigated the whole question.[2] It must be added that, despite the veto of Parliament, the new book has been permitted to be used by both the archbishops. The position is unfortunate, for breach of law by ministers of religion renders it difficult for them to censure breach of other laws and weakens their influence for good, especially in those cases where the majority of the congregation is opposed to Popish practices.

The new authority of the Assembly has greatly simplified ecclesiastical administration. It is now possible to create bishoprics, to erect chapters and deans for such bishoprics, to regulate cathedrals,[3] to deal effectively with the many and miscellaneous offices attached to ancient foundations, to increase the powers of the Ecclesiastical Commissioners [4] and those of Queen Anne's Bounty,[5] to

[1] Spender, *Great Britain*, pp. 688-90.
[2] Halévy, *Hist. 1905–15*, pp. 76 ff.
[3] Cathedrals Measure, 1931.
[4] Ecclesiastical Commissioners (Powers) Measures, 1936 and 1938.
[5] Queen Anne's Bounty (Powers) Measure, 1937.

regulate the right of presentation to benefices,[1] to lay
down rules for ensuring that incumbents shall fulfil their
duties reasonably,[2] to regulate the status of curates, etc.
Only by such an Assembly would it probably have been
possible to take steps to bring to an end the sale of rights
of presentation to benefices,[3] and to give to parishioners
a certain power to make representations regarding the
appointment of an incumbent.[4] The bishop must notify
the Parochial Church Council,[5] which has been constituted
under a measure of the Church Assembly to take over
most of the functions of the churchwardens and vestry,
and it[6] then considers the proposed presentation. If the
patron secures the assent of the churchwardens for his
nominee, he can present him to the bishop, with a request
for admission, institution, and induction. If not, he may
apply to the bishop, who may, and, if requested by the
patron or the Church Council, must consult a body of
advisers elected by the Diocesan Conference. If the bishop
refuses assent, he may be overruled by the archbishop.[7]
The churchwardens and Church Council may make representations regarding any transfer of the right to present.

Despite useful changes in substance, the organisation
of the Church has been retained. The archbishops of
Canterbury and of York, Primates of All England and of
England respectively, rule their provinces, but the number
of dioceses has steadily grown until they number 29 and
12 respectively ; the use of measures is naturally simpler

---

[1] Benefices (Diocesan Boards of Patronage) Measure, 1932.

[2] Benefices (Ecclesiastical Duties) Measure, 1926.

[3] Benefices (Transfer of Rights of Patronage) Measure, 1930 ; Benefices
(Purchase of Rights of Patronage) Measure, 1933.

[4] Benefices (Exercise of Rights of Presentation) Measure, 1931.

[5] Cf. *Stuart* v. *Haughley Parochial Church Council,* [1936] Ch. 32.

[6] If no Council exists, it must be created : *King* v. *Truro (Bp.),* [1937]
P. 36.

[7] Cf. *Notley* v. *Birmingham (Bp.),* [1931] 1 Ch. 529.

than statutory legislation as in the Bishoprics of Bradford and Coventry Act, 1918. The Archbishop of Canterbury retains his right to issue licences for marriage throughout England, while his brother of York may issue licences valid throughout his province. The former alone possesses the power to confer degrees, but this authority cannot be used to confer the right to registration by the General Medical Council as a practitioner.

To a bishop belongs the powers to confirm; to confer ordination; to consecrate churches and burial-grounds; and to take part in the institution of a clerk in holy orders to a rectory or vicarage. By his power to refuse to accept a person presented to him for admission to a benefice he can secure due educational qualities in the nominee, as well as morality and pecuniary solvency. From refusal to institute appeal lies to the archbishop.

Ordination may be to the status of a deacon, who differs from a priest because he may not consecrate the holy elements nor pronounce absolution. It is usual to serve as deacon for a year before becoming a priest. Priests and deacons alike, before ordination according to the form prescribed in the Book of Common Prayer, must assent to the Thirty-Nine Articles, the Book of Common Prayer, and the Ordination of Bishops, Priests, and Deacons, and make a declaration against simony in the manner prescribed in the Clerical Subscription Act, 1865. They must also take the oath of allegiance as prescribed in the Promissory Oaths Act, 1868. It was rendered possible by the Clerical Disabilities Act, 1870, for priests and deacons to relinquish orders, but they can regain them by a simple procedure.[1]

The beneficed clergy, vicars, rectors, perpetual curates enjoy tenure during good behaviour; the unbeneficed

[1] 24 & 25 Geo. V. No. 1.

clergy, curates stipendiary are paid by incumbents, as a
rule, and hold office at their discretion. But they must
be licensed by the bishop of the diocese, who may withhold
the licence ; [1] others are attached to the armed forces as
chaplains, or to gaols, asylums, and other institutions. In
the Great War the privilege of immunity from service was
accorded to clergymen in general. Disqualification for
membership of Parliament remains, but the Ministers of
Religion (Removal of Disqualifications) Act, 1925, permitted clergymen to become borough councillors, and
membership of the county, district, and parish councils
was always open. In the beginning of Queen Victoria's
reign [2] the evils of clerical negligence were reformed by
forbidding farming of more than eighty acres without the
licence of the bishop, or the carrying on of any other trade
or dealing for gain or profit, except under certain conditions, under pain of suspension or deprivation. A clergyman is not bound to serve on a jury,[3] and is protected
during divine service or a visitation from arrest under
civil, as opposed to criminal, process.[4] But his contracts
are subject to the ordinary law and he may be made a
bankrupt.[5]

The work of the bishops has been lightened by the
extension [6] of the power to appoint suffragan bishops, who
can perform ordinations, confirmations, etc., for bishops,
who apply to the Crown for their appointment. Under the
Bishops Resignation Act, 1869, coadjutor bishops may be
appointed to assist aged and infirm bishops in their duties.
By the Cathedrals Measure new regulations have been
made of the functions of the dean or provost, canons, and
other clergy, with considerable simplification, diminution

[1] Appeal lies to the archbishop ; 1 & 2 Vict. c. 106, s. 98.
[2] 1 & 2 Vict. c. 106, ss. 28, 29, 31.   [3] *Beecher's Case*, 4 Leon. 190.
[4] Phillimore, *Eccl. Law*, p. 475.   [5] 4 & 5 Geo. V. c. 59, s. 50.
[6] 51 & 52 Vict. c. 56 ; 26 Hen. VIII. c. 14.

of posts without serious duties, and more economical and effective employment of the funds available.

The difficult issue of faculties has been simplified by the Faculty Jurisdiction Measure, 1938, which provides for the appointment of an advisory committee by the bishop in each diocese ; with its advice the archdeacon may, if an application is made by the incumbent and churchwardens with approval of the parochial church council, for repairs or redecoration, permit action without a faculty or direct that one be applied for, while the chancellor of the diocese may act on like advice if the matter is unopposed. Of constitutional interest is the creation of a rule committee whose rules must be laid before Parliament and may be annulled by resolution of either house.

For the work of making the revenues of the Church more effectively available the Ecclesiastical Commission was created in 1836, and its constitution somewhat varied by later legislation. It decided the due incomes of archbishops and bishops, effected retrenchments in the establishments of the chapters, fixing the number and stipends of the canons and assistant ministers. The estates of the bishoprics and cathedrals assigned to their supervision left available further sums, which were treated as a common fund and applied to the endowment of new livings or the increase of emoluments of poor livings. In 1926 the Ecclesiastical Commissioners Measure gave powers as to the augmentation of archdeaconries, the endowment of new bishoprics, the payment of the costs of legal proceedings taken by bishops to enforce the law of the Church, and the upkeep of Lambeth Palace and other residences. The commissioners are the two archbishops, the bishops, the deans of Canterbury, St. Paul's, and Westminster, the Lord Chancellor, the Lord President of the Council, the First Lord of the Treasury, the Chancellor of the Exchequer, a

Secretary of State, and other distinguished churchmen, while the work is done by three Church Estates Commissioners. The revenue in 1937 was £3,284,000.

Queen Anne's Bounty enjoyed, under letters patent of November 3, 1704, the first-fruits and tenths which she sacrificed in favour of the Church ; these sums were the first year's profit of a bishopric or other ecclesiastical preferment, and tenths an annual levy on the rateable value of all benefices, formerly payable to the Pope but appropriated by Henry VIII. The governors of the Bounty used the fund for the purpose of building residences for clergy, meeting the cost of dilapidations or improvements, and in augmenting the stipends of poor benefices.

The issue of tithes had been laid to rest in large measure by the commutation of that intolerable burden when paid in kind. But the position of incumbents tended to become difficult when, under stress of agricultural conditions, there revived a feeling of resentment against the payment of tithes, and it was clear that it was unfair to leave to individual clergy the work of collection. Hence in 1925 the tithe rent charge attached to benefices was vested in Queen Anne's Bounty, which, from March 31, 1927, undertook the collection of tithes and disbursed to the clergy the sums to which they were entitled. Some of the difficulty arose from the fact that, owing to the utter dislocation arising from war conditions, it had been necessary to fix the amount payable on a basis which was said to work out too onerously for the payer. The years after 1927 saw the renewal of agitation and proved that it was definitely disadvantageous to the Church that considerable amounts of its revenue should be derived from this source. Hence a Royal Commission was set up in 1934 and the Tithe Act, 1936, adopted an interesting solution. Tithe rent charges were abolished from October 2, 1936. Those entitled to them were compensated by issue of stock to yield to clerical holders at the rate of £91 : 11 : 2 per £100 charge ; to lay owners, £105. The former payers of tithe were required to pay redemption annuities charged on the land. A Tithe Redemption Commission was set up to carry through this rather complex transaction, which relieves the Church of any connection with tithe, though at a price estimated at £17,500,000. It must be held that this settlement is a wise and a generous one to the Church, for the funds now at its disposal are freed from the injury done to it by the appearance in the courts of Queen Anne's Bounty seeking payments, and denounced as exercising un-Christian pressure on farmers unable to make a living owing to the failure of the agricultural policy of the ministry. It is not, of course, impossible that the decision was helped by the obvious danger to Conservative candidates for Parliament from wide discontent in districts whence the ministry was wont to draw support.

2. *The Ecclesiastical Courts*

The Ecclesiastical Courts Commission in 1832 [1] summarised under three heads the jurisdiction then exercised by the ecclesiastical courts. They dealt with the purely civil questions of testamentary causes, and suits for separation of spouses and nullity of marriage ; with matters partly spiritual, partly civil, such as suits for tithes, Church rates, seats, and faculties ; and spiritual matters, dealing, in the way of criminal suits *pro salute animae*, with offences by clergy such as neglect of duty, immorality, false doctrines, dilapidations, and with offences by the laity such as brawling, irreverent conduct in church or churchyard, violating churchyards, neglect to repair ecclesiastical

[1] *Historical App.*, to Ecclesiastical Courts Commission, i. 193.

buildings, incest, incontinence, and defamation. The punishments were monition, penance, excommunication, suspension *ab ingressu ecclesiae*, suspension from office, and deprivation. Excommunication under an Act of 1813 had lost its efficacy as a means of enforcing obedience to the order of an ecclesiastical court, as it had been deprived of its severe civil penalties and disabilities ; but as a spiritual censure for an ecclesiastical offence it remained in theory as a ground for a sentence to be inflicted by a civil court of imprisonment for a term not exceeding six months.[1]

The limitation of this jurisdiction by statute has been considerable. In 1855 [2] suits for defamation were taken from the ecclesiastical courts, in which they had been admittedly anomalous. In 1857 [3] the far more important step was taken of giving jurisdiction in probate and matrimonial causes, together with the newly recognised divorce, to special courts now united in the Probate, Divorce, and Admiralty Division of the High Court of Justice. In 1860 [4] suits for brawling against laymen were taken from ecclesiastical jurisdiction, and, as punishment of incest was quite unsatisfactory, it was made criminal in 1908.[5] The Act of 1868 abolished suits for Church rates, and the courts ruled that jurisdiction in perjury had by inference removed from Church courts,[6] and dilapidations were made to depend on an order made by a bishop.[7]

The activities of the court of the archdeacon, formerly not unimportant, were moribund in 1832, nor have they been revived. The normal court of jurisdiction, therefore,

[1] 53 Geo. III. c. 127.
[2] 18 & 19 Vict. c. 41.
[3] 20 & 21 Vict. cc. 77, 85.
[4] 23 & 24 Vict. c. 32.
[5] 8 Edw. VII. c. 45.
[6] *Phillimore* v. *Machon* (1876), 1 P.D. 481.
[7] 34 & 35 Vict. c. 43 ; it is replaced by the Ecclesiastical Dilapidations Measure, 1923 (24 & 25 Geo. V. No. 3).

became that of the bishop, usually held by his chancellor Chapter
XXVI. and vicar-general, whose patent was normally for life. But his jurisdiction over the clergy for ecclesiastical offences was drastically affected by the Church Discipline Act, 1840, which required the bishop of the diocese in which an offence was alleged to have been committed to appoint a commission of five to enquire into the allegation and to report ; the matter then was dealt with by the bishop of the diocese wherein the accused was beneficed, who might deal with the accused if the latter were willing ; if not, try him with three assessors, or — and this was normal — send the case to the court of the archbishop. The jurisdiction of the bishop was thus decidedly limited. By the Clergy Discipline Act, 1892, which superseded the Act of 1840 so far as regards the offences with which it deals,[1] the bishop was authorised to declare void a preferment where the beneficed clergyman had been found guilty on indictment, or had been shown to have been guilty of immoral conduct by the result of legal proceedings under conditions specified in the Act. He was empowered to appoint a tribunal in a prescribed manner to try a clergyman for offences against morality or ecclesiastical law, not being a question of doctrine or ritual, and, subject to an appeal to the court of the archbishop or to the King in Council, to sentence him to deprivation with incapacity to hold preferment, or to suspension. The difficulties and publicity of such procedure were painfully revealed in two notorious cases [2] and suggested strongly the devising of some method less likely to involve the Church in scandal.

The Public Worship Regulation Act, 1874, was passed by the intervention of Mr. Disraeli, against Mr. Gladstone's

---

[1] Simony falls under the Act of 1840 : *Beneficed Clerk* v. *Lee*, [1897] A.C. 226.

[2] *Wakeford* v. *Bishop of Lincoln*, [1921] 1 A.C. 821, and Mr. Davidson's case.

condemnation, for the purpose of putting down ritualism.[1]
The measure in fact was merely a procedure Act, and at
that not in the slightest degree an improvement on the
Act of 1840. It deals with ceremonial offences, and allows
representations to be made by an archdeacon, a church-
warden, or three aggrieved parishioners to the bishop.
The bishop must consider the representation and, if he
refuses to take any action, must give his reasons in writing
both to the complainants and the clerk ; if he thinks
proceedings necessary, he must either, with the agreement
of the parties, deal with the issue himself without appeal,
or send the representation to the judge appointed by the
two archbishops with the approval of the Crown. He may,
if he finds the representations made out, issue a monition
for the discontinuance of the wrongful act, and if necessary
may inhibit the accused ; deprivation follows on inhibition
continued for three years, and not relaxed, which is conditional on a written promise of amendment, and, on a
second inhibition issued on the same monition within three
years of relaxation. The decision of the judge might be
appealed against to the King in Council, and the Act was,
as might be expected, a complete failure.

A further jurisdiction was created by the Benefices Act,
1892, which authorised the bishop to refuse to institute or
admit a presentee to a benefice on the ground of physical
or mental infirmity, serious pecuniary embarrassment,
grave misconduct or neglect of duty, evil life, or having
caused grave moral scandal since ordination. Appeal lies
to the archbishop, sitting with a judge of the High Court,
who decides all points of law ; if he finds no fact sufficient
in law exists, then the archbishop must direct institution
or admission ; otherwise he determines at his discretion
whether institution or admission should be required. If

[1] Monypenny and Buckle, *Disraeli*, ii. 653-71, 742.

a bishop refuses to admit a proper person to a benefice, a judge may order admission, but in default the archbishop may be required to do so.[1]

It will be seen that much of the jurisdiction of the bishop as regards clergymen has been regulated by statutes limiting the normal jurisdiction of the consistorial court. It retains, however, authority in such matters as faculties for church ornaments and kindred issues. In the important matter of negligent performance of duties, the Benefices (Ecclesiastical Duties) Measure, 1926, provides for the determination of allegations, made against a clergyman, by a Commission, and authorises the bishop to inhibit if such negligence is proved.

From the decrees of the consistorial court held by the bishop's chancellor, appeal lies to the provincial courts of Canterbury and York. Over these the official principal of the archbishop presided, this officer in the case of Canterbury bearing the style of Dean of Arches, originally the style of the officer who presided over the court in Bow Church (Sancta Maria de Arcubus), which exercised the archbishop's jurisdiction over thirteen parishes of London, exempt from the jurisdiction of the Bishop of London, and thus peculiars of the archbishop. Until 1857 there was a prerogative court held at Doctors' Commons, which exercised the testamentary and matrimonial jurisdiction shared by the archbishop with the bishops' courts ; this disappeared in 1857, as did the prerogative court in York. The Act of 1874 made an important change in the position of the judges of Canterbury and York, for it gave the official principalship of each archbishop's court to the judge created under that Act.[2] Clearly this ensures that

[1] *Notley* v. *Bishop of Birmingham*, [1931] 1 Ch. 529.

[2] The judge of the provincial courts is thus Dean of the Court of Arches, Vicar-General for the Court of Peculiars and for granting marriage licences in the province, and Master of the Court of Faculties, with power to grant

a lawyer of considerable eminence will be available for such matters as come before the court, from which appeal lies to the King in Council.

There remains, however, a residual jurisdiction on the part of the archbishop exercised by the Archbishop of Canterbury in what is presumably a continuation of the former Court of Audience; in it Archbishop Benson determined in 1889 that he had jurisdiction to deal with complaints brought against the Bishop of Lincoln.[1]

3. *The Position of the Church in Ireland and Wales*

In 1869 the disestablishment of the *Irish Church* ended a long controversy. Just at the close of the reign of William IV, the Whig ministry had pushed forward schemes for the settlement of the controversy over the collection of tithes by the clergy of the Church coupled with the appropriation of the surplus revenues of the establishment for the moral and religious education of all classes of the people. The Church could claim only some 850,000 out of a population of nearly eight millions, and had an income of £865,525, while in 860 parishes there were less than fifty members.[2] But the Whigs failed wholly to overcome the resistance of the Lords to this act of justice, and they yielded in 1838, thus forfeiting the respect of many of their followers and leading directly to the ultimate triumph of their rivals. Tithes were commuted, as in England, for a fixed rent charge, and a Parliamentary grant given, while by a grant in 1845 to Maynooth College, for the training of Roman Catholic priests, some compensation was given to that Church.

ordinary and special marriage licences, and to appoint notaries public. A distinct commissary for the diocese exists.

[1] Roscoe, *Bishop of Lincoln's Case*.   [2] May, *Const. Hist.* ii. 294 ff.

The census of 1861 revealed that of the diminished population of 5,800,000 only 693,000 were members of the Church, and the movement to reconsider the establishment was started by Mr. Dillwyn, who, however, found no encouragement under Lord Palmerston's régime in seeking to raise a controversial issue. Mr. Gladstone was then not ready for action, but his views had changed by 1867, and in 1868 [1] he pressed forward with a resolution demanding disestablishment, despite the arguments of the ministry that such an issue should not be dealt with until it had been brought before the electorate. Mr. Gladstone, who never accepted the doctrine of the mandate, repudiated the idea and was successful in his resolution, and presented a Bill to prevent the creation of new life interests in the Church, which, though passed by the Commons over the heads of the Government, was rejected in the Lords. At the dissolution of the autumn, the issue was placed before the electors in the clearest form, and the verdict was conclusive. The English dissenters, Scottish Presbyterians, Irish Roman Catholics, and Liberals in general combined to attack an establishment which never had any justification. The Act passed in 1869 [2] dissolved the connection of the Churches of England and Ireland, and, provided that the latter should cease to be established by law, dissolved all existing ecclesiastical corporations, extinguished all rights of patronage, including those of the Crown, compensating private persons for their value, and terminated the connection of the episcopate with the House of Lords. Ecclesiastical jurisdictions and law as part of the law of the land were abolished, but the law was to continue to bind the members of the Church as part of a contract which they had accepted, and which

[1] Monypenny and Buckle, *Disraeli*, ii. 341 ff.
[2] 32 & 33 Vict. c. 42.

would stand until its terms were altered by a body representative of clergy and laity. A convention in 1870 established a general synod with a House of Bishops and a House of Representatives and declared the doctrines of the Church, which henceforth was able to control its own fortunes, free from the authority of the State. A Representative Church Body [1] was incorporated by letters patent of 1870 to hold property for the Church, while a Commission was set up to dispose of the transfer to that body of Church property, and a grant of £500,000, to deal with life interests, and to hold the residue for such purposes as Parliament might determine. The powers of the Commission were given to the Land Commission in 1881, and under the Government of Ireland Act, 1920, apportionment of the Irish Church Temporalities Fund was made as between Northern Ireland and the Irish Free State. The present Church constitution dates from 1926.

The causes which led to the disestablishment of the Church of Ireland affected strongly the position of the *Church of England in Wales*. The spread of nonconformity in the eighteenth century had been greatly aided by the fact that the clergy of the Church then seldom knew Welsh, and neglected wholesale their duties, so that the number of adherents of the Church sank to perhaps a quarter of the population. The disestablishment movement directed at the whole of the Church which Mr. Chamberlain favoured in 1885 had much greater vitality when applied to Wales. It was accepted in the Newcastle Programme of 1891, and in 1895 [2] the Government had a Bill for this purpose on hand when it was defeated on supply and resigned. In 1906 all the Welsh members

---

[1] Cf. *Corbally* v. *The Representative Body*, [1938] I.R. 35 ; *Lyster-Smythe's Estate, In re, ibid.* 231.

[2] Spender, *Campbell-Bannerman*, i. 161, 165, 167.

returned were solidly in favour of disestablishment, and a Bill for that purpose was duly introduced in 1909, but not further proceeded with after second reading, in view of the pressure on governmental time through the Finance Bill. The issue, however, was revived after the passing of the Parliament Act, 1911. The opposition of the English Church was mobilised with the utmost care, especially by Mr. F. E. Smith, who denounced the Bill as shocking the conscience of every Christian community in Europe, a dictum which may be compared with the verdict of the Archbishop in 1923, four years after the measure had taken effect : " Few, if any, now desire a return to the old order ". The essential reason for disestablishment [1] was that the Church was gravely unpopular with great numbers of the people, while, freed from that dislike, it was assured of a successful existence in friendly rivalry with other churches.

The Act [2] had, as a result of this opposition, to be passed by the procedure of the Parliament Act over the resistance of the Lords, but after the war there was general acceptance of its necessity, and by a fresh Act the original measure, whose operation had been postponed [3] when the war crisis arose, was brought into force on March 31, 1920. The bishops of the Welsh dioceses ceased to have any right to sit in the Lords or the clergy in convocations. The existing ecclesiastical jurisdictions and law ceased to exist as such, but power was given to a representative body to provide for the government of the Church ; to establish courts but without coercive jurisdiction and without appeal to the Privy Council ; and to enact ecclesiastical law. The existing law was made binding on members of the Church

---

[1] Halévy, *Hist. 1905–15*, pp. 433 f., 538 f. ; Spender, *Lord Oxford*, i. 93-5 (1895) ; ii. 299 (1910), 352, 353 f.

[2] 4 & 5 Geo. V. c. 91.

[3] 4 & 5 Geo. V. c. 88 ; 9 & 10 Geo. V. c. 65, s. 2.

as if they had contracted to obey it, and was to be enforced
in the Civil courts as far as it affected rights of property.[1]
The powers given have been used [2] to make it clear that
the Church courts are not bound by decisions in English
courts, including the Privy Council, in matters of faith,
discipline, and ceremonial. Property questions were handed
over to commissioners, with power to effect a division of
assets between the Church representative body and the
local authorities. That Commission is authorised to frame
rules of procedure which, if confirmed by Order in Council,
have legal effect, but it cannot constitute itself judge in
its own cause,[3] though in other matters committed to it
it can decide without appeal on law and fact alike.

4. *The Political Influence of the Churches*

The political importance of the Church of England
remained great throughout the Victorian epoch. The
Church gradually recovered in the early years of the reign
its moral soundness, and grew out of the defects which
had helped the growth of nonconformity. It had one
appeal of great force : it was the Church of the aristocracy,
of the great landed gentry, and of the Universities of
Oxford and Cambridge. Another appeal became of great
importance as time went on ; the teachings of the nonconformist churches, with their insistence on taking
literally their tenets, attracted large numbers of people,
but they rather repelled than otherwise the large numbers
of men who did not desire to abandon connection with
a church, but had no desire for active religious exercises.

---

[1] *Price* v. *Welsh Church Representative Body*, [1938] Ch. 434.

[2] April 20, 1922. Nonetheless the relations of the Churches are so close
that orphans of the clergy can be beneficiaries under a charity of 1809 :
Clergy Orphan Corpn. v. *Christopher*, [1933] 1 Ch. 267.

[3] *Wingrove* v. *Morgan*, [1934] Ch. 423.

Hence there was throughout the century a steady re-inforcement of the Church from the ranks of the middle classes, as they gained wealth and leisure, a process aided by the natural desire to join a church which was the faith of those whose social position they envied.

The nonconformist efforts were important in securing a strong backing for many important movements of reform, such as the abolition of slavery in the colonies, and it was in nonconformist circles that the Northern cause in the American civil war found the sympathy denied it in the upper classes. The political power of the movement showed itself in the disestablishment of the Irish Church and the opening of the Universities, which secured its adherence to the Liberal party, but it lost in coherence after the split among Liberals on the Home Rule issue. There was a remarkable revival in the last ministry of Lord Salisbury, and the ministry of Mr. Balfour,[1] due to the Education Acts of 1902–4, which gave wide privileges to the denominational schools, to the favour shown to the liquor trade by giving compensation for withdrawal of licences, and to the employment of Chinese in the South African mines under conditions akin to slavery ; and non-conformist influence did much to win the election of 1906. But, though 180 dissenters sat [2] in the Commons, it proved impossible to secure any amelioration of the position, and the revival of the Home Rule issue affected some diminution of unity. This was carried much further by the Liberal split under Mr. Lloyd George, for he had been the idol of Welsh Nonconformity and of many English non-conformists, and the strength of the movement has manifestly declined from the political standpoint. The power of the Church of England has no doubt increased in so far

[1] Spender, *Campbell-Bannerman*, ii. 64, 76 f., 81, 137 f., 282, 338 f.
[2] Halévy, *Hist. 1905–15*, pp. 63 ff.

as it has not, since the disestablishment of the Welsh
Church, any serious hostility to face, but this is largely
due to the lack of interest in Christianity of any sort
among great masses of the people, who are content to use
the Church, if at all, for baptisms, marriages, and burials.
The Church remains, however, a definitely Conservative
force ; here and there, the extravagances of its Anglo-
Catholic section tell against that party by evoking local
opposition and driving members of the Church to turn to
nonconformity. The nonconformist movement equally has
suffered from the growth of religious indifference, which
has driven the Wesleyan Methodist, the Primitive Methodist, and the United Methodist churches to a unity con-
summated in 1932. The Congregationalists and Baptists
have also formed closer relations among their churches to
combat the growth of indifference to religion among the
people.

The close relation between Church and State has
naturally resulted in the possibility of the use of the
patronage of the State to secure a definite attitude in
the Church. The most interesting feature of this attitude
in the Victorian epoch was the anxiety of the Queen
herself to secure moderate men as bishops, deans, and
canons, and even in the ordinary ranks of the beneficed
clergy, for the Crown has about nine hundred and seventy
benefices in its gift ; the Prime Minister recommends for
those over £20 in value *temp.* Henry VIII, and takes the
sovereign's pleasure.

Queen Victoria [1] claimed as in her gift the deanery
and canonships of Windsor, and Mr. Gladstone readily
accepted her recommendations, without conceding the
exclusion of his right to recommend. It was through
Dean Wellesley up to 1882, and then through Randall

[1] Keith, *The King and the Imperial Crown*, pp. 366 ff.

Davidson, who became Dean shortly after, that the Queen became sufficiently cognisant of Church affairs to be able to press her likes and dislikes. Thus the former helped her to secure Dr. Tait, despite a Liberal in sentiment, for Archbishop against the will of Mr. Disraeli,[1] and for the rest of her life she consulted Dr. Davidson [2] consistently. But even she could not persuade Lord Salisbury to give him the bishopric of Durham in 1889 or that of Winchester in 1890 ; he accepted Rochester in lieu. In 1852 she laid down to Lord Derby her dislike of Puseyites or Romanisers in the episcopal office, and even Mr. Disraeli found it hard to contend with her firm veto of those whom she suspected, while he declared he dare not appoint some of her protégés in view of the danger of disrupting his Cabinet.[3] Even the much respected Dr. Percival fell under disapproval for Hereford, because he was believed to favour disestablishment, though in truth it was only Welsh disestablishment, which Lord Rosebery, who put him forward, wished ; on Dr. Davidson's advice she yielded the point. Naturally she sought and sometimes secured preferment for her personal protégés such as Charles Kingsley, as did also the Prince of Wales.

Edward VII was not indifferent, especially in the earlier years of his reign, to ecclesiastical issues. He took the sensible view that colonial bishops should not be allowed to retain the style and dress if they took canonries, and that royal chaplains could not retain that office on becoming suffragan bishops or deans.[4] He was also partly responsible for the very interesting appointment to the see of London of Dr. Winnington Ingram, but in the latter

[1] Monypenny and Buckle, ii. 408-10.
[2] Bell, *Randall Davidson*, i. 164 ff.
[3] Cf. Monypenny and Buckle, *Disraeli*, ii. 1397 ff. (1868) ; 979 (Benson for Truro) ; 1279 (Lightfoot for Durham).
[4] Lee, *Edward VII*, ii. 52 f.

years of his reign he seems to have practised the rule, followed by George V, of considering carefully all nominations submitted by his Prime Minister with the aid of the advice of the Archbishop of Canterbury, and securing thus due appointments.[1] The general tendency of appointments since 1901 has clearly been in favour of complying with general feeling in the Church, while endeavouring to secure that in any particular diocese the bishop shall be one who will command general assent. The only case where alleged political motives may have had some slight influence is the selection of Dr. Barnes for Birmingham and Dr. Temple for York in 1924 and 1929 respectively.

The Roman Catholic influence in political matters has certainly proved of considerable importance. It has shown its strength in supporting the claims of the Church of England for the maintenance of non-provided schools, and by this system of complete control over the education of adherents of this faith it secures a certain attitude towards the State. While wholesale efforts to control adherents of the Church in political issues are not attempted, the Church feels both entitled and justified in energetic support of those candidates who adopt the views sanctioned by the Church on issues which affect moral teachings of the Church. Perhaps the most striking illustration of this attitude is the fact that Labour ministries have been unable to afford official encouragement to the propagation of doctrines of birth control, because so many Labour members are of the faith or owe their seats to Catholic votes. On the other hand, the relative weakness of the Roman and Anglo-Catholic influence in the Commons was shown by the failure to oppose successfully the wide extension of grounds of divorce in the Matrimonial Causes

---

[1] Spender, *Lord Oxford*, ii. 378 f. For Campbell-Bannerman, see Spender, ii. 359 f. ; he was against ritualists.

Act, 1937, though only a private member's Bill. The minority decision [1] on the issue of the possibility of a man after a decree *nisi* of divorce entering into a binding contract to marry is an interesting instance of the influence of religion on even the judges of the highest court, for the legal position was clearly against their position. In recent years the Roman Catholic influence has been chiefly shown in the hostility to the effort to keep faith with Ethiopia ; the exacerbation of public dislike of Germany on the ground of Herr Hitler's attacks on the Church; and the steady support of General Franco against democracy in Spain because of his claim to be a champion of the Roman Catholic faith. Whether the numerical proportion of the Roman Catholics in the population is increasing or not is impossible of decision so far as England is concerned ; in Scotland there is a steady influx, though on no large scale, from Eire, and the birth-rate among those immigrants, who unfortunately make serious demands on various forms of public assistance, is high. On the other hand, they undertake rough work which Scottish labourers do not desire.

5. *The Status of Roman Catholics, Jews, and Quakers*

To Roman Catholics full civil freedom was in essentials granted by the Roman Catholic Relief Act, 1829 ; two great offices alone were closed to them, that of Lord-Lieutenant of Ireland [2] which was opened by the Government of Ireland Act, 1920, and that of Lord Chancellor, which seems still to be closed ; the King's duty towards the Church of England would render it inexpedient to appoint a Roman Catholic, if it were so desired. In 1850, however, grave annoyance was caused in many Protestant

---

[1] *Fender* v. *Mildmay*, [1938] A.C. 1.
[2] The office disappeared in 1922.

circles by the decision of the Pope [1] to establish in England
an episcopal hierarchy to advance the cause of Catholicism
therein.   The exaggerated joy of Cardinal Wiseman and
of Dr. Newman irritated people who otherwise would have
passed the matter *sub silentio*, and the ministry felt bound
to legislate, though in 1848 [2] it had passed an Act allowing
diplomatic intercourse with the Pope.   It decided to prohibit the use by the Roman Catholic bishops of territorial
titles, though since 1829 these had been assumed harm-
lessly in Ireland.   Other proposals to invalidate any gift
made to those bishops were dropped, but, as passed in
Parliament, the brief from the Pope and all other similar
briefs were declared illegal, and the introduction of Bulls
or rescripts was made a criminal offence.[3]   The measure
was never enforced, but it may have had a salutary effect
in warning the ultramontane party that the country was
still effectively, and if challenged, ardently, Protestant.   In
1871 the Act was repealed without exciting any public
feeling.

There remained in existence certain restrictions upon
the wearing in public of vestments, and in 1908 [4] an episode
occurred which caused considerable feeling.   It was proposed to close the Eucharistic Congress of that year with
a public procession of the holy sacrament attended by
Cardinal Vannutelli and other Catholic dignitaries as " an
act of reparation for the reformation."   The Protestant
Alliance and the Church Association protested, the King
was asked to intervene, and by his initiative the Home
Secretary was moved to act ; it was stated that the procession was not in itself illegal, but that it could be prohibited if there were strong grounds for fearing a breach

[1] Papal Brief, Sept. 30, 1850 ; *Ann. Reg.* 1850, App. 405.
[2] 11 & 12 Vict. c. 108 ; 96 *Hansard*, 3 s. 169 ; 101 *ibid.* 227, 234.
[3] 14 & 15 Vict. c. 60 ; *Ann. Reg.* 1851, Ch. ii., iii.
[4] Lee, *Edward VII*, ii. 659-63 ; Spender, *Campbell-Bannerman*, i. 236 f.

of the peace. Fortunately, Cardinal Bourne was induced
by Lord Ripon to eliminate the Host and the vestments
from the procession, which passed off without interference.
Lord Ripon, however, insisted on resignation. In 1910
a procession round the newly consecrated cathedral at
Westminister was allowed to take place without interference, official or otherwise. Not until 1926, however, was
an Act passed which ended the restrictions imposed in
1829, which in fact had long been a dead letter, the entry
of Jesuits, for instance, having been allowed to pass without
notice, though no licence had been obtained for such entry.
War conditions induced the establishment of a legation at
Rome ; the coronation of Pius XII was attended by the
Duke of Norfolk to represent the King, and the appointment of an Apostolic Delegate passed without serious
notice.

The Jews suffered, curiously enough, severe disadvantages from the repeal of the Test and Corporation Acts
in 1828, which liberated Christians not of the Church of
England from the disabilities imposed on those not in
communion with that Church. They had profited with
the Christians from the annual Indemnity Acts, but on
repeal [1] the House of Lords insisted on adding to the
declaration, which replaced the sacramental test, the words
" on the true faith of a Christian ", which were fatal to the
position of the Jews. They were now not merely barred
from Parliament, as before, but also from civil, military,
or corporate office, from the profession of the law, and
from that of schoolmaster. In 1830 and subsequent years
Mr. Robert Grant's efforts to secure the removal of their
disabilities failed. The Jews were too rich, and might
obtain seats by bribery, as had the nabobs ; they were
aliens, for Palestine was their true home ; they were in

---

[1] 9 Geo. IV. c. 17 ; May, *Const. Hist.* ii. 224 ff.

any case hostile to the religion cherished by the people. In 1838, however, Lord Denman's Act [1] regarding evidence allowed men to be sworn in such manner as most bound their consciences, and thus Jews could take the oath of allegiance on the Old Testament instead of on the Evangels. In 1845 corporate office was opened,[2] and in 1847 Baron Lionel Nathan de Rothschild was elected as a member of the City of London, but could not take his seat, since the words " on the true faith of a Christian " barred him from taking the oath of abjuration still required. In 1851 the Court of Exchequer Chamber definitely ruled in the case of Mr. Salomons, member for Greenwich, that he could not sit, and only in 1858 [3] could the Lords be persuaded to allow the Commons to permit by resolution the omission of the offending terms from the oath of abjuration ; in 1860 [4] a standing order was permitted ; in 1866 [5] a new form of oath removed all difficulties.

Quakers had been much more favoured. In view of several statutes permitting them to affirm, the Commons in 1833 [6] stretched the law to permit the first Quaker elected for 140 years to sit, and in the same year allowed Quakers, Moravians, and Separatists to affirm in all cases whatever. In 1838 the permission was extended to ex-Quakers and ex-Moravians who had abandoned these sects, but still retained an objection to take an oath.

6. *Religious Liberty*

Just before the beginning of the Queen's reign a very tardy measure of justice had met an ancient grievance.

[1] 1 & 2 Vict. c. 105.
[2] 8 & 9 Vict. c. 52.
[3] 21 & 22 Vict. cc. 48, 49.
[4] 23 & 24 Vict. c. 63.
[5] 29 & 30 Vict. c. 19.
[6] Report of Select Committee, 6, 1833 ; 3 & 4 Will. IV. cc. 49, 82 ; 1 & 2 Vict. c. 77.

The law of England compelled dissenters from the Church of England to have their marriages celebrated by the rites of the English Church ; if they desired legal evidence of the births of their children, they must be baptized by a clergyman of that Church, and Christian burial had to be performed by the rites of the church wherein also registration took place. The reformed Parliament in 1836, by providing for the civil registration of births, marriages, and deaths, and by allowing dissenters to be married in their own chapels, after notice to the registrar, or by a purely civil service before the registrar, removed serious abuses.[1] There remained the question of burial, and no redress was long conceded. In populous areas dissenters might provide separate burial-grounds for their own use or have a portion of a cemetery left unconsecrated for their use ; the narrow-mindedness of the Bishop of Carlisle, who refused to consecrate a cemetery unless the unconsecrated portion were separated by a wall, led to legislation in 1857 [2] to curb episcopal intolerance. It was natural to ask that the clergy of dissenting bodies should be allowed to conduct the suitable service over their own dead, but so slight a concession was withheld until 1880.[3]

The Universities of Oxford and Cambridge were closed to dissenters ; in Oxford since 1581 matriculation was forbidden by requiring subscription to the Thirty-Nine Articles, and in Cambridge since 1616 dissenters were excluded from degrees. A Bill of 1834 was rejected by the Lords, and, though it was made possible to take degrees by Acts of 1854 and 1856,[4] much of the value of the concession disappeared, since all posts hitherto open to members of

[1] 6 & 7 Will. IV. cc. 85, 86 ; 1 Vict. c. 22.
[2] 20 & 21 Vict. c. 81, s. 11.
[3] Monypenny and Buckle, *Disraeli*, ii. 592 ff., 829, 1033 ff., 1452 show the resistance.
[4] 17 & 18 Vict. c. 81, ss. 43, 44 ; 19 & 20 Vict. c. 88, s. 45.

the Church remained closed to dissenters. In 1866 and
1869 the Lords rejected measures, and in 1870 delayed a
Bill to open to dissenters lay posts, and only in 1871 was
this conceded. In 1836 London University had started its
life without religious discrimination, and the provincial Universities, as they came into being, were free from this blot.

More generosity was displayed in the matter of religious
endowments. The decision of the House of Lords regarding
Lady Hewley's charity revealed grave dangers to nonconformist charities for religious ends. It was ruled that the
intention of the founder, though not clearly expressed,
must bind the purposes of the charitable benefaction, thus
excluding orderly progress and adaptation. In 1844 [1]
Lord Lyndhurst's Act secured the position by providing
that, in the absence of clear definition by the founder, the
usage of twenty-five years would give trustees a good title
to continue on that basis.

Much greater difficulty had to be faced on the issue of
church rates. These fell to be levied by the parishioners
assembled in vestry, and were laid upon occupiers of houses
and land within the parish according to their ability. In
1834 it was proposed to abolish rates but to give £250,000
a year from the general revenue, but this and a variant
scheme in 1837 failed. There followed a long legal contest
over the refusal of the majority of the vestry at Braintree
to levy a rate, which was finally upheld by the House of
Lords,[2] and by 1859 no rates were levied in 1525 parishes.
Repeated efforts to abolish rates in the Commons failed
against the resistance of the Lords, and in the Commons
of 1859–65 interest in the contest waned. But in 1868
Mr. Gladstone, after a two-years struggle, secured an Act
to abolish compulsion, but to allow voluntary collection,
and this the Lords allowed to pass.

[1] 7 & 8 Vict. c. 45.   [2] 4 H.L. Cas, 679.

There remained, and remains in part, the question of Chapter
XXVI. religious education. In 1870 the Liberal Government's legislation provided that grants might be made to voluntary schools which gave religious education chiefly in Anglican tenets, provided that they were open to children without regard to religious belief, and that such children should be exempt, if desired by their parents, from attendance at religious instruction. In schools provided by school boards and rate-aided there should be taught a form of religion, in which no catechism or religious formulary distinctive of any particular denomination should be taught. The measure did not meet with full approval by nonconformists, as they objected to State aid to voluntary schools, and to the omission of compulsory education or abolition of fees. In 1869 an important step was taken under which endowed schools were opened to dissenters, unless the founder had made a definite religion compulsory, and an attempt in 1874[1] by the Conservative Government to legislate to confine most of these schools to members of the Church of England failed. In 1876 and 1880 education was made compulsory, and from 1892 it was made compulsory to provide education free for those who desired not to pay. In 1897 the State aid to voluntary schools was increased by about £616,000 a year in the effort to preserve them against the competition of the better provided for board schools.

In 1902 the voluntary, non-provided schools were given rate aid, in return for the appointment by the local authority of a third of the six managers of each school, general control over instruction, and a veto on appointment of teachers, but not on religious grounds. The only obligation on the non-provided schools was to provide the buildings and keep them in repair, and from the latter

[1] Monypenny and Buckle, *Disraeli*, ii. 673, 700.

point the Lords excepted wear and tear. The nonconformists deeply resented the placing on the rates of schools privately managed, the inability of dissenting teachers to find employment in some half of the elementary schools in England, and the fact that they had to share in maintaining schools in which their children, though compelled to attend if in districts without a provided school, must either have denominational teaching they disliked, or go without any religious instruction.[1] It is not surprising that efforts were made at passive resistance which were countered by an Act of 1904.[2] The efforts of the Liberal Government of 1905–15 [3] to remedy this unfairness were destroyed by the opposition of the Church of England. Later efforts to reach a just solution have all failed through the intransigence of certain elements of that Church and of the Roman Catholics. There is not, therefore, complete religious equality in respect of education. Later suggestions of compromise have been based on the possibility of permitting denominational teaching in provided schools, but have not made serious progress, while non-provided schools have been given aid to enable them to play their part in the provision of accommodation for the extended teaching to be given to children, under the raising to fifteen of the normal school-leaving age.

[1] May, *Const. Hist.* iii. 232 ff.; Spender, *Campbell-Bannerman*, ii. 61 ff.; Halévy, *Hist. 1895–1905*, pp. 201 ff., 374 ff.

[2] Upheld in *Att.-Gen.* v. *West Riding of Yorkshire*, [1907] A.C. 29.

[3] Lee, *Edward VII*, ii. 455-65, 658 f.; Halévy, *Hist. 1905–15*, pp. 64-72.

INDEX

END OF VOL. II

Printed in Great Britain by R. & R. CLARK, LIMITED, *Edinburgh.*